Praise for PassPorter

It's the first and only book that covers Disney cruises in detail. And what splendid detail! Jennifer and Dave tell you everything you need and want to know, from embarkation to debarkation. Even if you don't currently have a Disney cruise planned, this is great armchair reading. It certainly took me back to happy thoughts of my last Disney cruise and made me want to plan the next one!

— Mary Waring
MouseSavers.com

I love it! It is clear cut, states the facts, and gives you all the detail you can't find anywhere else.

— Tracie Perez
in California

PassPorter let me know what we missed on our first Disney cruise.

— Jeff Romanowski
in New Jersey

Lots of valuable information here. I keep reading the book over and over!

— Faith Nutting
in Washington

PassPorter answered every question I had and many I hadn't thought of yet.

— Melissa Hatcher
in California

PassPorter is extremely informative. It most certainly helps our plans and takes the fear out of the whole process.

— Gerald Darmetko
in Massachusetts

I love everything! All three couples in our traveling party read it and highlighted it so much—we call it our DCL Bible! I recommend PassPorter to everyone planning a Disney vacation.

— Nate Boerman
in Illinois

W9-DEM-836

What's New in This Edition

Major Enhancements:

✓ **More than 60 brand new pages** filled with valuable information, advice, details, reviews, ratings, and photos.

✓ **More photos** than our previous edition—many of which include your authors in the picture, too!

✓ **Expanded coverage** of ports—including San Juan, Antigua, and St. Lucia—plus cruiser ratings and reviews on shore excursions.

✓ **More money-saving ideas** to get the most out of your cruise.

✓ **Sneak peek at new itineraries and possibly new ships**—our thoughts and speculations on the future of the Disney cruises.

✓ **Coverage of the recent changes** aboard the Disney Magic, including Diversions, Cove Café, The Stack, and more!

✓ **Expanded coverage** of lodging near the Disney cruise terminal, including photos and room layouts.

✓ **In-depth information** on the staterooms, including photos of every stateroom category.

✓ **More details** on Topsider's/Beach Blanket Buffet and Castaway Cay dining at Cookie's BBQ and Serenity Bay.

✓ **Enhanced listings** of possible onboard activities for kids, teens, and families.

✓ **Advice on cruising with kids, groups, and reunions**—making the most of your cruise and avoiding the common pitfalls.

✓ **More tips on staying healthy** on your cruise.

Fun New Features and Information:

✓ Thousands of small tweaks to further improve our guide.

✓ Current rates, prices, menus, and shore excursions.

✓ Enhanced index to make it easier to find things.

✓ More new reader tips, magical memories, and stories.

✓ More peer reviewers to ensure accuracy and thoroughness.

...and much, much more! Visit us at http://www.passporter.com/dcl *for a complete list of what's new and changed in this edition!*

Disney Magic/Wonder Deck Plans

Tip: Once you know your stateroom number, note it on this page and highlight the section of the ship where it is located in the profile map to the left.

Our stateroom number: _____

Profile of Ship

Forward (Fwd)

Crew pool

Stage

Wide World of Sports Deck | Overlook | Bridge

10	Vista Spa & Salon	Outlook
9	8016-8032 & 8516-8532	8000-14 & 8500-14
7	7016-7046 & 7516-7546	7000-14 & 7500-14
6	6028-6058 & 6528-6558	6000-26 & 6500-26
5	Oceaneer Lab	5000-24 & 5500-24
4	Preludes	Walt Disney Theatre
3	Shops	Beat Street/Route 66
2	2032-2058 & 2532-2558	2000-38 & 2500-28
1	1030-1053	Medical Center

Outlook Bar
Quiet Cove Adult Pool
Signals, Cove Café (Magic), Common Grounds (Wonder) & Quarter Masters Arcade

A - Crew Only
B - Crew Only

Tender Lobby

The Stack (Magic) or ESPN Skybox (Wonder)

Midship (Mid)

11		
9	Goofy's Family Pool	
8	8034-8078 & 8534-8580	
7	7048-7108 & 7548-7608	
6	6060-2120 & 5560-2620	
5	Oceaneer Club	
4	Studio Sea	
3	Lumiere's/Triton's	
2	2060-2116 & 2560-2616	Conf. Rooms
1	1054-1079	

Pinocchio's | Pluto's Kid Pool
Lobby Atrium
Promenade Lounge

Main Gangway

Aft

10	Palo	
9	Topsider's/Beach Blanket	Mickey's Kid Pool
8	8080-102 & 8582-602	
7	7110-38 & 7610-38	
6	6122-54 & 5622-54	
5	5122-50 & 5622-50	
4	Buena Vista Theatre	
3	Internet Cafe	
1	2118-53 & 2618-63	

A - Crew Only
B - Crew Only

Animator's Palate
Parrot Cay
Shutters Photo Studio
Flounder's Reef
Scoops

Tender Lobby

Deck 11 (Magic)

The Stack

Deck 11 (Wonder)

ESPN Skybox

Deck 10

Port | Starboard

Wide World of Sports Deck
Overlook

Outlook Bar

Beat Street/Route 66
Rockin' Bar D/WaveBands

Palo

Deck 9

Port | Starboard

Overlook
Fitness Room
Men's Locker | Ladies' Locker
Aerobics
Treatment Rooms | Tropical Rainforest | Vista Spa | Salon
Quiet Cove Adult Pool
Cove Café (Magic) or Common Grounds (Wonder) | Signals Bar | Arcade
Stage
Goofy's Family Pool
Pinocchio's Pizzeria
Pluto's Dog House
Mickey's Kids Pool
Beverage Station
Scoops
Topsider's/Beach Blanket Buffet

Forward (Fwd)
Midship (Mid)
Aft

Key to Deck Plans

- ☐ guest area
- ▨ crew only/inaccessible
- ⓔ elevator
- ▥ stairs
- ♿ wheelchair accessible
- 🚺 women's restroom
- 🚹 men's restroom
- smoking allowed
- ⑪ stateroom category

– 3 –

Genuine PassPorter Genuine PassPorter Genuine PassPorter Genuine PassPorter Genuine PassPorter

Decks 8, 7, 6, and 5

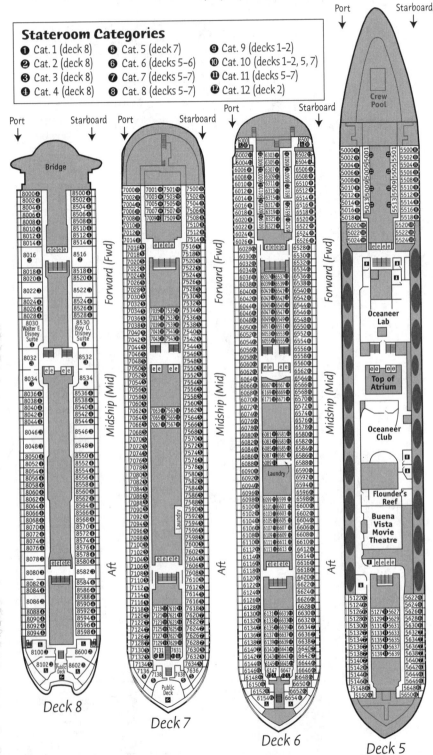

Decks 4, 3, 2, and 1

Genuine PassPorter Genuine PassPorter Genuine PassPorter Genuine PassPorter Genuine PassPorter

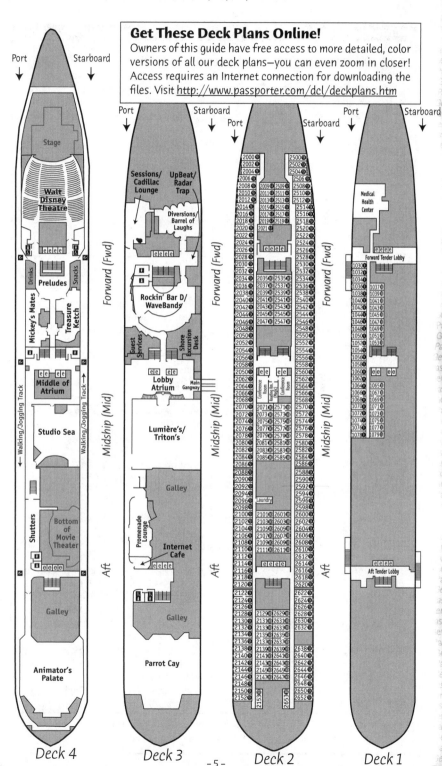

Get These Deck Plans Online!

Owners of this guide have free access to more detailed, color versions of all our deck plans—you can even zoom in closer! Access requires an Internet connection for downloading the files. Visit http://www.passporter.com/dcl/deckplans.htm

Deck 4

- Stage
- Walt Disney Theatre
- Port
- Starboard
- Mickey's Mates
- Drinks
- Preludes
- Snacks
- Treasure Ketch
- Middle of Atrium
- Studio Sea
- Shutters
- Bottom of Movie Theater
- Galley
- Animator's Palate
- Walking/Jogging Track
- Forward (Fwd)
- Midship (Mid)
- Aft

Deck 3

- Port
- Starboard
- Sessions/Cadillac Lounge
- UpBeat/Radar Trap
- Diversions/Barrel of Laughs
- Rockin' Bar D/WaveBands
- Guest Services
- Shore Excursion Desk
- Lobby Atrium
- Main Gangway
- Lumière's/Triton's
- Galley
- Promenade Lounge
- Internet Cafe
- Galley
- Parrot Cay
- Forward (Fwd)
- Midship (Mid)
- Aft

Deck 2

- Port
- Starboard
- Conference Room
- Meeting Rm. 1
- Conference Room
- Laundry
- Forward (Fwd)
- Midship (Mid)
- Aft

Deck 1

- Port
- Starboard
- Medical Health Center
- Forward Tender Lobby
- Aft Tender Lobby
- Forward (Fwd)
- Midship (Mid)
- Aft

What's Your Heading?

(M) = Disney Magic; (W) = Disney Wonder

Location	Deck	Page	Location	Deck	Page
Adult pool	9 Fwd	3	Medical Center	1 Fwd	5
Adult cafe (M)	9 Mid	3	Mickey's kids' pool	9 Aft	3
Adult district	3 Fwd	5	Mickey's Mates	4 Mid	5
Adult restaurant	10 Aft	3	Movie theater	5 Aft	4
Aerobics studio	9 Fwd	3	Nightclubs	3 Fwd	5
Animator's Palate	4 Aft	5	Nursery	5 Mid	4
Assembly stations	4	5	Oceaneer Club & Lab	5 Mid	4
Atrium (Lobby)	3-5 Mid	5,4	Outlook Bar	10 Mid	3
Arcade	9 Mid	3	Palo	10 Aft	3
Barrel of Laughs (W)	3 Fwd	5	Parrot Cay	3 Aft	5
Bars	3,4,9,10,11	5,4,3	Photo studio	4 Aft	5
Beach Blanket Buffet (W)	9 Aft	3	Piano lounge	3 Fwd	5
Beat Street (M)	3 Fwd	5	Ping-Pong tables	9	3
Beverage station	9 Aft	3	Pinocchio's Pizzeria	9 Mid	3
Bridge overlook	9 Fwd	3	Pluto's Dog House	9 Aft	3
Buena Vista Theatre	5 Aft	4	Pools	9	3
Buffet restaurant	9 Aft	3	Preludes Bar	4 Fwd	5
Cadillac Lounge (W)	3 Fwd	5	Promenade Lounge	3 Aft	5
Casual dining	9	3	Purser's office	3 Mid	5
Children's clubs	5 Mid	4	Quarter Masters arcade	9 Mid	3
Children's pool	9 Aft	3	Quiet Cove adult pool	9 Fwd	3
Common Grounds (W)	9 Mid	3	Reading room (M)	2 Mid	5
Computer cafe	3 Aft	5	Restrooms	3,4,5,9,10	5,4,3
Conference rooms	2 Mid	5	Rockin' Bar D (M)	3 Fwd	5
Cove Café (M)	9 Mid	3	Route 66 (W)	3 Fwd	5
Dance club	3 Fwd	5	Scoops	9 Aft	3
Deck parties	9 Mid	3	Sessions lounge (M)	3 Fwd	5
Diversions (M)	3 Fwd	5	Shore excursion desk	3 Mid	5
Duty-free shops	3 Fwd, 4 Mid	5	Shuffleboard	4	5
Dueling piano club	3 Fwd	5	Shutters photo studio	4 Aft	5
ESPN Skybox (W)	11 Mid	3	Shops	4 Mid	5
Family nightclub	4 Mid	5	Sickbay	1 Fwd	5
Family pool	9 Mid	3	Signals	9 Mid	3
Fantasia Reading Rm. (M)	2 Mid	5	Snack bars	9	3
Fast food	9	3	Sports deck	10 Fwd	3
Fitness center	9 Fwd	3	The Stack (M)	11 Mid	3
Flounder's Reef	5 Mid	4	Teen club	9 or 11 Mid	3
Fruit station	9 Aft	3	Tender lobbies	1 Fwd & Aft	5
Goofy's Family Pool	9 Mid	3	Theater (movies)	5 Aft	4
Guest Services	3 Mid	5	Theater (stage shows)	4 Fwd	5
Hair salon	9 Fwd	3	Topsider's Buffet (M)	9 Aft	3
Hot tubs	9	3	Treasure Ketch	4 Mid	5
Internet Cafe	3 Aft	5	Triton's (W)	3 Mid	5
Kids pool	9 Aft	3	UpBeat duty free (W)	3 Mid	5
Kids clubs	5 Mid	4	Vista Spa & Salon	9 Fwd	3
Laundry rooms	2,6,7 Mid	5,4	Walt Disney Theatre	4 Fwd	5
Liquor shop	3 Fwd	5	Waterslide	9 Aft	3
Lobby (Atrium)	3 Mid	5	Whirlpools	9	3
Lounges	3,4,9,10,11	5,3	WaveBands (W)	3 Fwd	5
Lumière's (M)	3 Mid	5	Wide World of Sports Deck	10 Fwd	1

Fwd, Mid, or Aft? These common abbreviations are for the Forward (front), Midship (middle), and Aft (rear) of the ship. Refer to the labels on our deck plans.

PassPorter's®
Field Guide
to the
Disney Cruise Line®

Second Edition

The take-along travel guide and planner

Jennifer Watson,
Dave Marx,
and Mickey Morgan

PassPorter Travel Press

An imprint of MediaMarx, Inc.
P.O. Box 3880, Ann Arbor, Michigan 48106
877-WAYFARER
http://www.passporter.com

PassPorter's® Field Guide to the Disney Cruise Line® and Its Ports of Call—Second Edition

by Jennifer Watson, Dave Marx, and Mickey Morgan

© 2004 by PassPorter Travel Press, an imprint of MediaMarx, Inc.

P.O. Box 3880, Ann Arbor, Michigan 48106
877-WAYFARER or 877-929-3273 (toll-free)
Visit us on the World Wide Web at http://www.passporter.com

PassPorter® is a registered trademark of MediaMarx, Inc.
Photographs on cover and pages 13, 18, 54, 60, 114, 118, and 242 © Disney
Photographs on page 30 © Jan Chait; page 75 © Paul McGill; and page 80 © Barb Lesniak
All other photographs © MediaMarx, Inc.
All rights reserved under International and Pan-American Copyright Conventions.

PassPorter's® Field Guide to the Disney Cruise Line® is not affiliated with, authorized or endorsed by, or in any way officially connected with, The Walt Disney Company, The Disney Cruise Line, Disney Enterprises, Inc., or any of their affiliates.

While every care has been taken to ensure the accuracy of the information in this travel guide, the passage of time will always bring changes, and consequently the publisher cannot accept responsibility for errors that may occur. All prices and operating schedules quoted herein are based on information available to us at press time. Operating hours, maps, policies, fees, and other costs may change, however, and we advise vacationers to call ahead and verify these facts and any others which are subject to change. The authors and publishers of this book shall not be held liable for any information (valid or invalid) presented here and do not represent The Walt Disney Company.

The Disney Cruise Line® is a registered trademark of The Walt Disney Company. This book makes reference to various Disney characters, trademarks, marks, and registered marks owned by The Walt Disney Company and Disney Enterprises, Inc. The use in this guide of trademarked names and images is strictly for editorial purposes, and no commercial claim to their use, or suggestion of sponsorship or endorsement, is made by the authors or publishers. Those words or terms that the authors and publishers have reason to believe are trademarks are designated as such by the use of initial capitalization, where appropriate. However, no attempt has been made to identify or designate all words or terms to which trademark or other proprietary rights may exist. Nothing contained herein is intended to express a judgment on, or affect the validity of legal status of, any word or term as a trademark, service mark, or other proprietary mark.

PassPorter's® Field Guide to the Disney Cruise Line® is authored and edited by Jennifer Watson, Dave Marx, and Mickey Morgan. The information presented is for your personal vacation planning. Any stated opinions are ours alone, unless otherwise noted, and do not represent The Walt Disney Company or anyone else. Materials submitted and credited by persons other than ourselves are here with their permission and any associated rights belong to them.

Any and all written messages, suggestions, ideas, or other information shared with the authors in response to this guide shall be deemed and shall remain the property of PassPorter Travel Press.

Special Sales: PassPorter Travel Press publications are available at special discounts for bulk purchases for sales premiums or promotions. Special editions, including personalized covers and excerpts of existing guides, can be created in large quantities. For information, write to Special Sales, P.O. Box 3880, Ann Arbor, Michigan, 48106.

ISBN 1-58771-016-1

10 9 8 7 6 5 4 3 2 1

Printed in the United States of America

About the Authors

Jennifer Watson grew up in Michigan, where you can stand anywhere within the state and be less than six miles from a lake, river, or stream. Her shipboard experiences include two weeks aboard a sailboat as a crew member and nine months working aboard the sternwheeler "Michigan" on Lake Biwa, Japan. Her first Disney Cruise Line adventure was for three nights in October 1999. A four-night cruise followed in May 2001. Her most recent cruises were aboard the Disney Magic on the seven-night Eastern Caribbean cruise in May 2003 and aboard the Disney Wonder on the four-night MouseFest cruise in December 2003. Jennifer is the author of more than 20 books, including the guide that started it all: *PassPorter Walt Disney World Resort*. Jennifer makes her home in the university town of Ann Arbor, Michigan, where she lives with her partner Dave and their Alaskan Malamute, Kippi.

Name: Jennifer Watson
Date of birth: 10/09/68
Residence: Ann Arbor, MI
Signature:

Dave Marx may be considered a Renaissance Man, a jack-of-all-trades, or a dilettante, depending on how you look at things. He took a 20-year hiatus between his early journalism training and the start of his full-time writing career. Beyond co-authoring more than a dozen books with Jennifer, he's been a radio writer/producer; recording engineer; motion picture music editor; broadcast engineer supervisor; whitewater safety and rescue instructor; developer of online publishing courses; and newsletter editor and promotions chief for an online forum. He discovered the Walt Disney World Resort in March 1997 and first cruised in October 1999. He's since cruised seven more times, including his award cruise for being a Million-Point Winner at "Who Wants To Be a Millionaire—Play It!" at Walt Disney World. Dave lives in Ann Arbor, Michigan.

Name: Dave Marx
Date of birth: 04/07/55
Residence: Ann Arbor, MI
Signature:

Name: Mickey Morgan
Residence: Newark, CA
Signature:

Mickey Morgan is at home on the water. He holds a marine engineering degree and has been in Sea Scouts for 25 years. As a San Francisco Bay Area resident, he likes to get down to Disneyland whenever he can. So when he learned that Disney was building a fleet of ships, he booked his family's first cruise a full two years before the maiden voyage! Mickey has been on three Disney cruises to date and is perhaps best known for his "Magical Disney Cruise Guide," a free online guide at http://www.allearsnet.com/cruise/dcruise.shtml. Whenever you see this "Midship with Mickey" icon in this field guide, you can look forward to great information and advice from Mickey! He also reviewed the entire book for accuracy.

Midship with Mickey

PassPorter Team

What's behind our smiling faces on the previous page? An incredible team of people who help us make PassPorter the best it can be!

Our Expert Peer Reviewers—We recruited a group of very knowledgeable Disney and travel experts. Each painstakingly checked our guide to ensure our accuracy, readability, and thoroughness. Thank you from the bottom of our hearts!

 Joanne and Tim Ernest are message board guides at PassPorter, where they enjoy discussing the magic of Disney with readers. They have two boys, David and Andrew, and are veterans of more than a dozen trips to Disney.

Debbie Hendrickson and her husband, Lee, took their first Disney cruise in September 2003, which they now call the "best vacation ever!" Debbie is a PassPorter message board guide and enjoys helping others plan their trips.

 Christina Holland-Radvon is a travel consultant with MouseEarVacations.com and a PassPorter.com message board guide. She and her husband, Walt, have one son, Donovan, who will meet Mickey for the first time at MouseFest 2004.

Dave Huiner devoured all of the cruise information he could find prior to his family's first cruise in May 2001. To return the favor, he created and maintains his own Disney Cruise Line tribute site: http://www.dcltribute.com.

 Barb Lesniak and her husband, Tony, have taken more than 40 Disney cruises since 1998. They share their vast knowledge at http://www.castawayclub.com, publish a CD planner, and frequently contribute to online discussions.

Bruce Metcalf works at a major Central Florida theme park, so cruising is his preferred form of vacation. He enjoys "messing about in boats" of all sizes, which is fortunate, as he's working on a book-length treatment of "The Disney Navy."

 Ann Smith is a PassPorter message board guide and resides in Pennsylvania with her husband, Jim, and three kids. They share a great love of anything Disney and especially love Walt Disney World and the Disney Cruise Line.

Sara Varney is a PassPorter message board guide for the Disney Cruise forums. She and her husband, Shawn, can't wait to take their son, Ryan, on his first Disney cruise! She has cruised to the Bahamas and the Caribbean.

 Brant Wigginton is a writer and Disney trivia buff. He has sailed with three different cruise lines, including Disney in 2003. You can also find him hosting weekly chats at PassPorter.com, where he is a board guide.

Sandy Zilka is a proofreader for a Big Four accounting firm. She's taken more than 20 Disney trips, including a recent four-night Disney cruise. She loves to travel and share her experiences as a PassPorter message board guide.

Printer: Malloy Lithography in Ann Arbor, Michigan
Visibility Specialists: Kate and Doug Bandos, KSB Promotions
Sorcerers' Apprentices: Kim and Chad Larner, Carolyn Tody, and Tom Anderson
Special thank yous to Margaret Adamic, Angie Bliss, Christie Erwin, Mark Jaronski, Ernie Sabella, Phil Adelman, Jeff Howell, Fred Marx, Paul McGill, John Stewart, and the crews of the Disney Magic and the Disney Wonder.

Acknowledgments

Oceans of thanks to our readers, who've contributed loads of tips and stories since the debut of the first PassPorter in 1999. A special thanks to those who allowed us to include their contributions in this field guide: Mary Waring, Tracie Perez, Jeff Romanowski, Melissa Hatcher, Faith Nutting, Gerald Darmetko, and Nate Boerman (page 1); Jan Chait and Debbie Mason (page 30); Amanda Poole and Karen Koonce (page 66); Angie James, Sandy Fiedler, and Rae Ann Reichert (page 90); Sharon King, Jesse Tindall, Mary Snow, and Amy Donenko (page 112); Angie James, Robin McConnell, Daniel Bates, and Mary Walsh (page 140); Bruce Dana, Marcie LaCava, and Tracy Brockway (page 232); and Kim Havick and Denise Fillo (page 250). May you each receive a new memory for every reader your words touch.

PassPorter would not be where it is today without the help and support of the many members of the Internet travel community. Our thanks to the friendly folks below and to all those we didn't have room to include!
- Adults at Walt Disney World (http://www.adultsatwdw.com). Thanks, Rose!
- All Ears Net (http://www.allearsnet.com). Thanks, Deb!
- Badger's Disney Countdown (http://nhed.com/countdown). Thanks, Ed!
- CruiseCritic.com (http://cruisecritic.com). Thanks, Laura!
- CruiseDirections.com (http://www.cruisedirections.com). Thanks, Gordon!
- Dave's DCL Tribute (http://www.dcltribute.com). Thanks, Dave!
- Disney Vacation Planning (http://www.solarius.com/dvp). Thank you, Paul!
- Disney World: The Unofficial Online Guide (http://wdisneyw.co.uk). Thanks, Joanne!
- Hidden Mickeys of Disney (http://www.hiddenmickeys.org). Thanks, Tom!
- Intercot (http://www.intercot.com). Thank you, John!
- LaughingPlace.com (http://www.laughingplace.com). Thanks, Doobie and Rebekah!
- Magictrips.com (http://www.magictrips.com). Thank you, Ada!
- Magical Disney Cruise Guide (http://www.allearsnet.com/cruise/dcruise.shtml).
- MouseEarVacations.com (http://www.mouseearvacations.com).
- The Mouse For Less (http://www.themouseforless.com). Thanks, Binnie!
- MousePlanet (http://www.mouseplanet.com).
- MouseSavers.com (http://www.mousesavers.com). Thanks, Mary!
- The Platinum Castaway Club (http://www.castawayclub.com). Thanks, Barb & Tony!
- Priority Seating Calculator (http://pscalculator.net). Thanks, Scott!
- Spencer Family's Disney Page (http://home.hiwaay.net/~jlspence). Thanks, Jeff!
- Unofficial Disney Information Station (http://www.wdwinfo.com). Thanks, Pete!

A special thank you to the Guides (moderators) of our own message board community: Maureen Austin, Kelley Baker, Michelle Clark, Joanne and Tim Ernest, Douglas Famy, Kristin Grey, LauraBelle Hime, Debbie Hendrickson, Christina Holland-Radvon, Robin Krening-Capra, Susan Kulick, Marcie LaCava, Tara McCusker, Michelle Nash, Allison Palmer-Gleicher, Cheryl Pendry, Tina Peterson, Susan Rannestad, Ann Smith, Donna Sonmor, Nate Stokes, Suzanne Torrey, Sara Varney, Margo Verikas, Suzi Waters, Dave Walsh, Brant Wigginton, Debbie Wright, Sandy Zilka, and the thousands of readers in our amazing community at http://www.passporterboards.com.

A heartfelt thank you to our family and friends for their patience while we were away on research trips or cloistered at our computers, and for their support of our dream: Allison Cerel Marx; Carolyn Tody; Tom Anderson; Fred and Adele Marx; Kim, Chad, Megan, and Natalie Larner; Dan, Jeannie, Kayleigh, Melanie, and Nina Marx; Gale Cerel-Marx; Jeanne and David Beroza; George Louie; Tracy DeGarmo; Ben Foxworth; Gordon Watson; and Marta Metcalf.

Last but not least, we thank Walter Elias Disney for his dream.

Contents

Jennifer poses by a porthole

© MediaMarx, Inc.

List of
Maps, Worksheets, and Charts

Dave anticipates a fine meal at Palo

Playing and Relaxing Onboard .. 113

Goofing around at the Mickey Pool

Putting Into Port 141

Contents
(continued)

Bonus Features...

Bookplate for personalization
.... inside front cover

2004/2005 Planning Calendars
........................inside back cover

Important Phone Numbers
.......................inside back cover

Photos, including many original shots by your authors
...... pages 9, 10, 12, 13, 14, 18, 19, 54, 56, 57, 58, 59, 60, 61, 71, 72, 73, 74, 75, 76, 77, 78, 79, 80, 81, 82, 83, 95, 97, 99, 101, 103, 104, 105, 106, 109, 116, 118, 120, 123, 124, 127, 128, 130, 132, 134, 137, 138, 145, 146, 148, 151, 159, 165, 170, 171, 172, 180, 199, 203, 204, 205, 207, 213, 215, 220, 223, 226, 227, 228, 235, 236, 237, 238, 239, 240, 242, 246, and 248

A little extra magic
.... sprinkled throughout

A view of the Disney Wonder from Castaway Cay

Bon Voyage!

You're about to embark on a marvelous voyage aboard one of the most beautiful and celebrated cruise lines in the world. You couldn't have made a better choice—the Disney Cruise Line will surprise and delight you with its stunning architecture, legendary service, and fun-for-the-whole-family activities. Boy, we wish we could go with you!

Our original travel guide, *PassPorter Walt Disney World Resort*, contains the essential information for the Disney Cruise Line. Even so, our readers sent in many requests to add more details on the cruises. Our answer is this field guide, which is chock-a-block with information on virtually every aspect of cruising the Disney Cruise Line. We designed it to stand alone or work in tandem with our PassPorter Walt Disney World guidebook and/or the PassPorter travel planning system. Everything you need to know to plan and enjoy a magical Disney cruise is within these pages!

You're holding the second edition of the first guidebook dedicated to the Disney Cruise Line! Based on reader feedback, we added more than 60 new pages to this edition and entirely updated the existing sections. Nonetheless, the Disney Cruise Line is constantly evolving, which makes this travel guide a work in progress. Please tell us what you like and where we've missed the boat so we can make the next edition that much better!

This field guide is the embodiment of not just our knowledge and experience, but that of our fellow cruisers and PassPorter readers as well. In essence, this is a cruise guide by cruisers, for cruisers. We share what we like and don't like, and you may find some differing opinions just within the pages of this guide. Speaking of which, we were fortunate enough to get Mickey as a contributing author! No, we don't mean the Big Cheese but rather the author of the "Magical Disney Cruise Guide" online. Mickey Morgan's experiences, opinions, and information enrich this guide, and we're delighted to work with him to make it the best it can be!

Use this field guide for planning before you embark, and then keep it handy onboard during your voyage. We hope you find this field guide a useful companion on your adventure!

Jennifer and *Dave*

We'd love to hear from you! Visit us on the Internet (http://www.passporter.com) or drop us a postcard from Castaway Cay!

P.S. This edition was last revised in March 2004. To check for new revisions or view our online update list, please visit us on the Internet at this address: http://www.passporter.com/dcl

Preparing to Cast Off

Cruising doesn't just refer to the time you're onboard—it's a state of mind. To help you get into the spirit of the adventure that awaits, try out our favorite ways to build excitement for a Disney cruise. You may discover they help you "cruise" through the planning process without a hitch!

Check Out the Literature

A trip to your local travel agent will reward you with the free Disney Cruise Line Vacations booklet—it's in full color and crammed with photos. You can also request one at 888-325-2500 or at http://www.disneycruise.com. The Disney web site is also a great source for photos, excursions, etc.

Watch the Video or DVD

Request your free Disney Cruise Line video or DVD by calling 888-325-2500 or on the web at http://www.disneycruise.com. It arrives in about 3-4 weeks. Both the video and DVD offer a fun peek at the ship and ports.

Network With Other Cruisers

Fans of Disney cruises are scattered far and wide—chances are you know someone who has been on a Disney cruise. If not, come join us on the Internet, where many Disney cruisers congregate to share tips. See page 28 for links to popular gathering places, including PassPorter.com.

Tune In to TV

Watch the Travel Channel and the Discovery Channel for specials about cruises and the Caribbean. Or have fun with reruns of "The Love Boat."

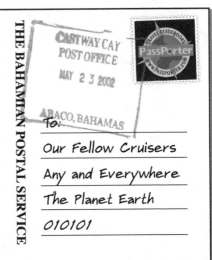

FROM CASTAWAY CAY

Being on Castaway Cay and hearing all this great music reminds us that there's nothing like steel drums to conjure up visions of cruising through the Caribbean. Find some Caribbean-style music and play it as you plan. We guarantee it'll get you in the mood. We also make suggestions on page 129 for music you're likely to hear on the cruise. If you're on AOL, try the Surf or Reggae channel at AOL keyword: Radio.

Your field guide authors

THE BAHAMIAN POSTAL SERVICE

CASTAWAY CAY POST OFFICE MAY 2 3 2002

ABACO, BAHAMAS

To:
Our Fellow Cruisers
Any and Everywhere
The Planet Earth
010101

Getting Your Feet Wet

So, you've decided to take a Disney cruise! The Disney cruise attracts many first-time cruisers. If you're among them, welcome to the world of cruising! If you're a cruise veteran, welcome back!

Now that you've decided to cruise, you're likely to have one of two reactions. You may feel overwhelmed by the complexity that looms ahead. Or you may be lulled into a sense of complacency, sure that all the details will be taken care of. We understand—before our early cruises, we wavered between these two reactions ourselves. It wasn't until we learned more about the Disney cruise that we received a welcome splash of cold water. Thanks to a boatload of knowledge and the experience of other cruisers, we were able to dispel that feeling of drifting into uncharted waters.

We figure you don't want a splash of cold water in your face, so instead we offer this chapter as a friendly introduction to the world of cruising with Disney. We filled the chapter with highlights and histories, as well as facts and figures. You can read the chapter straight through or jump to the sections that interest you. We've included articles on the Disney Cruise Line, cruising in general, hints for first-time cruisers, comparisons with other cruise lines and Walt Disney World, fleet facts, the differences between the two ships, budgeting, money-saving ideas, and the best places to find more information. We wrap up the chapter with tips and memories.

Before you delve deeper, we want to share a secret. Yes, it's true that you could plunk down your money and just show up. But you wouldn't be getting your money's worth—not by a long shot. Planning is the secret to any successful vacation. Not only do you learn the tips and tricks, but you get to start your cruise early through anticipation. By the end of this guide, you'll know more than the vast majority of your shipmates. You'll know the way to get those coveted reservations. You'll know the way to pack and what to bring. You'll even know your way around the ship before you board it. In short, you'll be cruising your way ... straight out of those uncharted waters and into the true "magic" and "wonder" of a cruise.

The Disney Cruise Line

The Disney Cruise Line is more than just another cruise. Disney designed its ships to be **innovative**, offering unique facilities and programs, each with Disney's hallmark, first-class service.

The **history** of the Disney Cruise Line actually began in November 1985, when Premier Cruise Lines signed a deal with Disney to become the official cruise line of Walt Disney World Resort. Premier's "Big Red Boat" offered Disney characters and packages that included stays at the Walt Disney World Resort. When the ten-year contract with Premier was up, Disney set off on its own with an ambitious goal: To become the best cruise line in the world. Disney commissioned the Fincanteri Shipyard (in Venice, Italy) to build a 350-million-dollar liner reminiscent of the grand, trans-Atlantic liners of the early 20th century. A private island was developed into the delightful Castaway Cay, a stop on each cruise itinerary. On July 30, 1998, the Disney Magic set sail on her maiden voyage. The magnificent new ship boasted a classic, streamlined silhouette, twin funnels, and well-appointed interiors. The Disney Magic sailed from her dedicated, art deco-inspired cruise terminal in Port Canaveral, FL on three- and four-night cruises to the Caribbean. Disney's second ship—the Disney Wonder—set sail on August 15, 1999. Seven-night itineraries to the Eastern Caribbean on the Disney Magic were added in 2000. In May 2002, seven-night Western Caribbean cruises on the Disney Magic were added. In summer 2004, new seasonal Caribbean itineraries were added for the Disney Magic. What lies ahead? See page 29 for a discussion on the future of the Disney Cruise Line, including scuttlebutt and our own personal theories.

The **Disney Magic** and the **Disney Wonder** are almost identical vessels, with only a few minor differences (see page 23). The ships' hulls are painted in dark blue (almost black), white, yellow, and red (Mickey's colors) with elegant gold scrollwork that cleverly reveals the silhouettes of several classic Disney characters. As you board, you are greeted by friendly crew members in the three-story lobby atrium, distinguished by a sweeping staircase and a bronze statue (Mickey on the Magic, Ariel on the Wonder). Warm woods, polished metal railings, and nautical touches embrace passengers in elegance. Subtle Disney touches are abundant, from character silhouettes along the staircase to valuable Disney prints and artwork on the walls. Every area of the ship is decorated and themed. Both ships are a delight to the senses.

The Disney Magic and the Disney Wonder

Why Cruise?

Cruising is something very special. Imagine yourself on a big—really big—beautiful ship. A low hum of excitement fills the air. The ship's whistle sounds smartly (Where have you heard that tune before?) and the ship begins to glide out of her berth. The ship is yours—deck upon deck of dining rooms, lounges, theaters, and staterooms.

People cruise with Disney for many reasons. Some love everything Disney, some want to be pampered, others enjoy the onboard activities, and still others want to visit foreign ports. Some families love the together-time they can have onboard, while other families appreciate the many activities for different ages. Adults love the peace of the adults-only pool, the gourmet tastes at Palo, and the evening fun at Beat Street/Route 66. Teens love having their own hangout and meeting fellow teens. Kids love the Oceaneer Club/Lab and the pools. What about us? Our first Disney cruise was to experience Disney's "next new thing." What brought us back again and again? Pure relaxation! A vacation to Disney World is wonderful, but very intense. On the cruise, we take a deep breath and slow down. We disembark refreshed and renewed, ready to tackle anything.

© MediaMarx, Inc.

Dave enjoys a tropical drink during a deck party

Cruising Myths

Here are some oft-quoted reasons why some people don't cruise—each is a common myth that we're happy to dispel. *Myth #1: It's too expensive.* Actually, cruising costs the same as a land-based vacation—a Disney Cruise is equivalent to a comparable stay at the Walt Disney World Resort. *Myth #2: I'll be bored.* If anything, there's too much to do! You'll find it hard to choose between activities, and you'll probably disembark with a list of things you wish you'd had time to do. *Myth #3: I'll get seasick.* Most people don't, but there's a chance you could be one of the unlucky few. But if you follow our tips on page 243, you should be just fine. *Myth #4: Cruises are too formal.* Hey, this is a Disney cruise! Yes, the cruise is luxurious, but you won't feel out of place. Casual clothing is the norm onboard (most of the time). *Myth #5: The Disney Cruise is for kids (or people with kids).* Kids love the Disney Cruise, but so do adults (we usually cruise sans kids). There are plenty of adult activities and areas. *Myth #6: I'll feel claustrophobic or unsteady on my feet.* Disney ships' staterooms are 25% larger than most other lines, and the ships have stabilizers to minimize rolling.

Introduction · Reservations · Staterooms · Dining · Activities · Ports of Call · Magic · Index

First-Time Cruisers

Are you going on your first cruise and wondering what to expect?

You're not alone—many of your fellow cruisers will also be on their first cruise. We remember our first cruise well—we had only "The Love Boat" reruns and stories from friends and family to rely upon. We fretted over getting seasick, which wasn't a problem at all. We worried there wouldn't be enough to do, but in fact there was too much (and we wished we had more than three days to cruise). We were even concerned we'd feel like "poor relations" beside what we figured must be wealthy cruisers, but we fit right in with everyone else.

Life aboard a Disney cruise ship is unlike most land-based vacations, unless perhaps you live the lifestyle of the rich and famous. Even if you're staying in budget lodgings, you'll receive the same level of luxurious, personal service as the deluxe guests. Your stateroom attendant will keep your room ship-shape (cleaning twice a day), see to your special needs, and turn down the bed every night with a cute animal made from towels. You'll form a personal relationship with your dining room team, who'll learn your tastes and attend you at every shipboard dinner.

And you'll eat! **Nearly all food onboard is included** in your Disney cruise—meals, snacks, room service, more snacks—so order anything you want, even if it's "seconds" or two different entrées.

The **ship hums with activity**, from sunup to the wee hours. Parties, live shows, children's programs, recreational activities, first-run movies, seminars, and guest lectures ... nearly everything is included in the price of your cruise, as is the right to do "none of the above."

Some say that modern cruise ships are "floating hotels," but "mobile resort" is a better description. Each day brings new vistas and often a new port. No matter how distracted you may be by onboard activities, the subtle vibration and motion of the ship whispers that your **luxurious little world** is going somewhere. Unlike long road trips or jet flights, your life doesn't go into an uncomfortable state of suspended animation while en route to your destination. Getting there can be far more than half the fun!

Our **advice to first-time cruisers** is two-fold: learn as much as you can about cruising, and then leave your expectations at home. Keep an open mind and be willing to try new things. You can rest assured that Disney has taken the needs of first-time cruisers into mind and considered your needs even before you realize you have them.

What's Included in a Disney Cruise?

Shipboard Accommodations: Up to 25% larger rooms than other ships—from 184 sq. ft. to 304 sq. ft. for non-suite staterooms.

Shipboard Meals: Three full-service dining room meals daily (breakfast, lunch, and dinner). Alternatives for breakfast, lunch, and dinner, such as buffets, quick-service, or room service, are also included. And let's not forget the snacks (ice cream, fruit, hot dogs, pizza), afternoon cookies, evening hors d'oeurves, and at least one midnight dessert buffet. The seven-night cruises add more midnight buffets. Soft drinks at full-service meals are included, as are juice, coffee, tea, and water at buffet meals. Milk, coffee, tea (hot and iced), cocoa, lemonade, fruit punch, water, and ice are always free at the Beverage Station (deck 9). Castaway Cay lunch is also included.

Shipboard Entertainment and Activities: Disney offers a wide variety of entertainment, including a different live stage show most evenings, first-run movies, deck parties, live bands, dancing, nightclubs, karaoke, trivia games, Disney character meet and greets, seminars, tours, social gatherings, and a reading room (Magic only).

Sports and Recreation: Three swimming pools, four whirlpool tubs, fitness center, aerobics studio (and most classes), walking/jogging track, Ping-Pong, shuffleboard, basketball, and the Wide World of Sports deck.

Kids Activities: Participation in the kids programs is included for ages 3-17, with activities and areas for varying age groups. Kids' shore excursions (other than Castaway Cay programming) are not included, however.

Ports of Call: Stops at all ports on the itinerary are included, as is transportation to the shore by tender (small boat) if necessary. Port charges are included in the price, unlike most non-Disney cruises.

What Isn't Included?

Your airfare may or may not be included in your cruise package—check when making your reservation. This goes for insurance and ground transfers from the airport to the ship (and back) as well. Accommodations, meals, and park passes for any time you spend at Walt Disney World are not included, unless you book a land/sea package that specifically includes these. Other extras: alcoholic beverages, specialty beverages (i.e., smoothies), soft drinks (outside of lunch and dinner at a full-service dining room), refillable mugs, Internet Cafe, bingo games, spa and beauty treatments, Palo meals ($10/adult), childcare for kids under 3, arcade, onboard or off-ship shopping, formalwear rental, shore excursions, meals off-ship (except Castaway Cay), medical treatment, laundry services (including the self-service washers and dryers, though you can use the iron and ironing board freely), and gratuities.

Introduction

Reservations

Staterooms

Dining

Activities

Ports of Call

Magic

Index

Introduction

Reservations

Staterooms

Dining

Activities

Ports of Call

Magic

Index

How Do They Measure Up?

Compared to **other cruise ships**, the Disney Magic and the Disney Wonder are among the most spacious ships afloat. Staterooms are 25% larger on average than those found on other ships. Other unique aspects of the Disney Cruise Line include split bathrooms (in stateroom categories 10 and up), rotational dining (different dining rooms, same servers), half a deck designed just for kids (with programs for specific age groups), areas reserved just for adults (pool, restaurant, spa, beach, and entertainment district), a visit to Castaway Cay (Disney's private island), Disney's famous characters, and that Disney magic!

Experienced cruisers may miss having a casino or a decent library aboard. The sentiment seems to be that the Disney Cruise Line offers the best family cruise afloat, but that it lacks enough activities for adults without children. We disagree (especially after the latest changes on the Magic)—we usually sail without kids and never lack adult activities. The generous adults-only areas deliver welcome isolation and surpass other "family" cruise lines. Some cruisers have also reported that the Disney Cruise Line is too, well, "Disney." Let's face it: if you don't like Disney, you may not like this cruise either. But these aren't theme parks. The quality service and elegant surroundings could easily outweigh any negative associations you have with Mickey Mouse.

Safety and **cleanliness** is a big deal on cruise ships, and all international ships are inspected by the U.S. Centers for Disease Control (CDC) on a regular basis. The Disney Magic was most recently inspected on December 6, 2003, and the Disney Wonder on January 15, 2004. Both passed their inspections—they each received 94 out of 100 points. To view the inspection results, visit: http://www2.cdc.gov/nceh/vsp/vspmain.asp.

If you've been to the Walt Disney World Resort and wonder how a Disney cruise compares to a **resort vacation**, it is really quite different. The cruise feels more laid-back yet formal at the same time. The excitement of dashing from attraction to attraction is gone, and you may feel like you're missing "something" that you can't identify. On the upside, everything is within walking distance, the food is "free," and rain isn't the same party-pooper it is at the theme parks. You'll take things a bit slower on the cruise, all the while feeling pampered by the gorgeous setting and excellent service. The Walt Disney World Resort and the Disney Cruise do share many perks, however: single key-card access for rooms and purchases, Disney character greetings, and that "red carpet" guest service. Don't expect to find "Walt Disney World on water." You'll discover the Disney Cruise Line has its own unique charm.

Fleet Facts

Home Port: Port Canaveral, Florida, USA
Country of Registry: The Bahamas
Radio Call Signs: C6PT7-Magic and C6QM8-Wonder
Captains: Captain Tom Forberg, Captain Henry Andersson, Captain John Barwis, Captain Gus Verhulst, and Captain Thord Haugen
Crews: 950 crew members, multinational
Guests: 2400 (1750 at double occupancy)—maximum is near 3000
Space ratio: 48.3 (The ratio of passengers to space, namely 4830 cubic feet per passenger. A ratio this high means a roomy, uncrowded ship.)
Tonnage: 83,000 (measured by volume, not weight—for an explanation of tonnage, see http://www.stutt.com/cruising/f-tonnage.html)
Length: 964 ft./294 m. (longer than the *Titanic* at 882 ft./268 m.)
Beam: 106 ft./32.25 m. (the width of the ships at their widest)
Draft: 25.3 ft./7.7 m. (the depth below the waterline when full)
Speed: 21.5 knots, or 25 mph/40 kph (max. is 24 knots/28 mph/44 kph)
Systems: Five 16-cylinder diesel engines, two 19-megawatt GE propulsion motors, three bow thrusters, two stern thrusters, and 1 pair fin stabilizers
Passenger Decks: 11 (see front of book for our detailed deck plans)
Lifeboats: 20, with each seating 150 passengers (plus 50 life rafts)
Staterooms: 877 (252 inside, 625 outside)—see chap. 3
Theatres: 2 (977 seats and 268 seats)—see page 131
Restaurants: 4 (138 seats in Palo, 442 seats in the others)—see chap. 4
Buffets and Snack Bars: 4 (294 seats inside, 332 seats outside)
Lounges: 5 (or 8 if you count the three nightclubs)
Shops: 5   **Pools**: 4 (one is for crew)   **Hot Tubs**: 4   **Spa**: 1

Differences Between the Magic and the Wonder

Feature	Disney Magic	Disney Wonder
Year built	1998	1999
Itineraries	7-night cruises	3- and 4-night cruises
Decor:	Art Deco	Art Nouveau
Bow decoration:	Sorcerer Mickey	Steamboat Willie (Mickey)
Stern adornment:	Boatswain Goofy	Donald and Huey
Atrium statue:	Helmsman Mickey	Ariel, The Little Mermaid
Grand dining room:	Lumière's	Triton's
Casual dining room:	Topsider's Buffet	Beach Blanket Buffet
Adults-only district:	Beat Street + Cove Café	Route 66
Dance club:	Rockin' Bar D	WaveBands
Pub or Dueling piano bar:	Diversions (pub)	Barrel of Laughs (pianos)
Jazz piano bar:	Sessions	Cadillac Lounge
Specialty coffee cafe:	Cove Café	n/a
Teen club:	The Stack	Common Grounds
Navigator's Verandah:	Round porthole	Larger oblong porthole

Introduction | Reservations | Staterooms | Dining | Activities | Ports of Call | Magic | Index

Introduction
Reservations
Staterooms
Dining
Activities
Ports of Call
Magic
Index

Can I Afford It?

Cruises were once reserved for wealthy globetrotters. These days, cruises are **more affordable**, though we would hesitate to say "inexpensive." A seven-night Disney cruise is just about the same price as a seven-night land vacation at the Walt Disney World Resort. To determine what you can afford, make a budget as you work through this field guide. Budgeting ahead of time not only keeps you from spending too much, it encourages you to seek out ways to save money. With a little research, you can often get **more for less**. To get an idea of what an actual cruise costs, check out our December 2003 cruise expenses at the bottom of the page.

A **cruise package** may include ground transportation, airfare, insurance, lodging at Walt Disney World, theme park admission, and other extras. This may seem convenient, but planning each aspect of your cruise yourself saves you more money. Learn about cruise packages on pages 40-41.

Your **cruise expenses** fall into six categories: planning, transportation, lodging, cruise passage, port activities, and extras. How you budget for each depends upon the total amount you have available to spend and your priorities. Planning, transportation, lodging, and cruise passage are the easiest to factor ahead of time as costs are fixed. The final two—port activities and extras—are harder to control, but we provide sample costs throughout this field guide to help you estimate.

Begin your cruise budgeting with the **worksheet** on the following page. Enter the minimum you prefer to spend and the maximum you can afford in the topmost columns. Establish as many of these ranges as possible before you delve into the other chapters of this book. Your excitement may grow as you read more, but it is doubtful your bank account will.

As you uncover costs and ways to save money, return to your worksheet and **update it**. Your budget is a work in progress—try to be flexible within your minimums and maximums. As plans crystallize, write the amount you expect (and can afford) in the Goals column. If you are using PassPockets (see the Deluxe Edition on page 263), **transfer the amounts** from the Goals column to the back of each PassPocket when you are satisfied with your budget.

> **Our Dec. 2003 Expenses**
> *(four-night cruise, two adults)*
>
> Round-trip airfare: *$380*
> Round-trip shuttle: *$160*
> 4-night cruise (cat. 11): *$960*
> Port activities: *$120*
> Souvenirs: *$100*
> Beverages/Palo: *$100*
> Phone/Internet: *$40*
> Gratuities: *$90*
>
> TOTAL: *$1950*

Budget Worksheet

As you work through this field guide, use this worksheet to identify your resources, record estimated costs, and create a budget. We provide prices and estimates throughout the book.

	Minimum	Maximum	Goals
Total Projected Expenses	$	$	$
Planning:			
📋 Phone calls/faxes:			
📋 Guides/magazines:			
Transportation: *(to/from)*			
📋 Travel/airline tickets:			
📋 Rental car:			
📋 Fuel/maintenance:			
📋 Ground transfer/shuttle:			
📋 Town car/taxi:			
📋 Wheelchair/ECV:			
📋 Parking:			
Lodging: *(Pre-/Post-Cruise)*			
📋 Resort/hotel/motel:			
📋 Meals/extras:			
Cruise Passage:			
📋 Ship accommodations:			
📋 Protection plan/insurance:			

Port Activities:	Per Port	Total	Per Port	Total	Per Port	Total
📋 Excursions:						
📋 Meals:						
📋 Attractions:						
📋 Rentals:						
📋 Transportation/taxis:						

	Minimum	Maximum	Goals
Extras:			
📋 Souvenirs/photos:			
📋 Beverages:			
📋 Resortwear/accessories:			
📋 Palo/formal wear:			
📋 Spa treatments:			
📋 Childcare (nursery):			
📋 Phone/Internet/stamps:			
📋 Gratuities/duties:			
📋 Other:			
Total Budgeted Expenses	$	$	$

Introduction

Reservations

Staterooms

Dining

Activities

Ports of Call

Magic

Index

Money-Saving Ideas and Programs

The Disney Cruise Line enjoys great popularity, so discounts can be scarce. Here are the ways we've found to save money on your cruise:

Reserve Early to Get Early Booking Savings

Reserve early enough and you could save approximately $100–$890 per stateroom (7-night cruises) or $30–650 per stateroom (3- and 4-night cruises). Staterooms at this discount are limited, however. To get the best early booking savings, reserve your cruise as soon as dates are announced (generally up to 18 months in advance).

Go à la Carte

Disney emphasizes the 7-night Land and Sea package combining 3 or 4 nights at the Walt Disney World Resort with a cruise. This is appealing to many vacationers, but it is pricier than making your own arrangements as you can usually find better deals on hotel rooms at Walt Disney World.

Find Promotions and Discounts

Historically, Disney has offered seasonal discounts with some of the best cruise deals. These off-season specials (February-May and September-December) have had discounts up to 40% in the past. Disney claims to have switched their strategy away from these promotions to encourage early bookings: the earlier you reserve, the better your rate. That said, deals and specials are available, including the last-minute Magical Rates deals on select cruises within the upcoming three months. To learn more, visit http://www.disneycruise.com. Be sure to also visit MouseSavers.com (http://www.mousesavers.com), which summarizes the currently available discounts and codes, and http://www.themouseforless.com.

Use a Travel Agent

Larger travel agents, such as MouseEarVacations.com, are able to pre-book blocks of staterooms, locking in discounts for you to snag later on. Always check with travel agents before booking on your own (see page 44 for a list). Travel agents are also very good at finding the best prices, too! MouseEarVacations.com (http://www.mouseearvacations.com, see page 265) has saved us considerable money on our more recent cruises!

Watch for Onboard Credits

Wouldn't it be nice to have an extra $50 or $100 sitting in your onboard account? Keep an eye out for onboard credit specials. At the time of writing, cruises paid with the Disney Visa card can get a $50 onboard credit—be sure to mention booking code DDC at the time of reservation. Onboard credits may also be available when you book onboard (see next page) and through special deals offered by travel agents.

Move to Florida

We're not serious about moving, but if you're already a Florida resident you may get discounts up to 50% off select cruises (limited staterooms). Call Disney at 888-325-2500 to inquire about Florida resident discounts, or check http://www.mousesavers.com for a list of available cruises. Note that proof of Florida residency is required at embarkation.

Book Your Next Cruise Onboard

On your next Disney cruise, check the *Personal Navigator* for onboard booking specials. Not only does booking onboard offer great prices, but sometimes even onboard credits as well. Two catches: the best rates are for the cruises offered at the exact same time next year, and you must book your cruise before you disembark. Tip: You can change or cancel your cruise date later if necessary; just call Disney at 888-325-2500.

Stay Off-Site Before Your Cruise

If you're like us and prefer to arrive at least a day ahead of your cruise, look for an inexpensive hotel or motel. In-airport hotels can be pricey—to save money, see page 58. See pages 56–58 for Port Canaveral lodging. It can sometimes be less expensive to fly in a day early, so always investigate.

Compare Local Transportation Costs

Depending on your party size, it can be less expensive to rent a car to drive from the airport to the port and back again. On the other hand, transportation companies such as Tiffany Town Car may offer the best deal plus convenience. Explore your options on page 52.

Special Tips for Special People

✔ **Infants and kids** 12 and under are less expensive than adults, but only if there are two adults along as well (the first two stateroom guests always pay full adult fare). The third and fourth adults in a stateroom can also cruise at great prices. See page 42.

✔ **AAA and Costco** members can get rates and make reservations through these companies and often get excellent deals. AAA members: Ask about your local AAA chapter's "Disney Month" for extra savings and goodies, and be sure to inquire about getting a free refillable soda mug with your AAA Disney package.

✔ **Disney Vacation Club** members and **Annual Passholders** may be eligible for exclusive cruises at good rates. Check with those programs or the Disney Cruise Line for details.

✔ **Canadian residents** may get special rates on select cruises. Contact the Disney Cruise Line or a travel agent.

✔ **Military personnel** may be eligible for some last-minute rates, similar to those offered to Florida residents. Call the Disney Cruise Line or a travel agent for more details.

✔ **Repeat cruisers** are automatically members of the Castaway Club and can use a toll-free number (800-449-3380). If you book your next cruise while you're still onboard, you may qualify for an onboard credit! For details and rates, call Disney Cruise Line, or visit http://www.disneycruise.com and click Castaway Club.

Note: The Disney Club program and its benefits were discontinued on 12/31/2003.

Porthole to More Cruising Information

While this field guide could serve as your single source, we recommend you gather as much information as possible. Each of the sources described below offers its own unique porthole into the world of Disney cruising.

Official Disney Information—Definitely get the free booklet and video/DVD we mention on page 16, and visit the web site (http://www.disneycruise.com). Any other brochures you can get from your travel agent will be helpful, too. Disney also sends cruise documentation (more about this on page 46) which contains some basic information.

Books—While virtually all Walt Disney World Resort guidebooks mention the Disney Cruise Line, most only give it a few pages. The two with the most information are "Walt Disney World with Kids" by Kim Wright Wiley (Fodor's) and "The Unofficial Guide to Walt Disney World" by Bob Sehlinger (Wiley). Both have about 10 pages on the topic.

Magical Disney Cruise Guide—This excellent, free online guide offers a detailed overview of Disney cruising, including reviews. http://www.allearsnet.com/cruise/Dcruise.shtml

CD Planner—Expert peer reviewer Barb Lesniak and her husband, Tony, are finalizing a new CD that offers even more planning help! The "Platinum Disney Cruise Planner" is a CD with information in both Microsoft Word and HTML format and includes planning worksheets. The CD is $23, which includes shipping and handling. For more information and to order, visit http://www.castawayclub.com.

Web Sites—Some of the best sources of information are the official and unofficial sites for the Disney Cruise Line. Here are our picks:

Disney Cruise Line Official Site—http://www.disneycruise.com
PassPorter.com (that's us!)—http://www.passporter.com/dcl
Magical Disney Cruise Guide—http://www.allearsnet.com/cruise/dcruise.shtml
Platinum Castaway Club—http://www.castawayclub.com
Dave's Disney Cruise Line Tribute—http://www.dcltribute.com
DIS—http://www.wdwinfo.com/wdwinfo/cruise and http://www.disboards.com
Disney Echo—http://disneyecho.emuck.com
CruiseDirections—http://www.cruisedirections.com/disney
The Magical Mouse—http://www.themagicalmouse.com/dcl
All Ears Net—http://www.allearsnet.com/cruise/cruise.shtml
MagicTrips—http://www.magictrips.com/cruise
ThemeParks.com—http://www.themeparks.com/cruise/default.htm
Kolb Family—http://www.kolbfamily.com/2000cruise/disney_cruise.htm
Disney World Online Guide—http://www.wdisneyw.co.uk/cruise.html
Vicky's Cruise Line Page—http://www.vicky-web.com/dmc
Pettits' Page—http://www.richpettit.com/vacations/ourvacations.htm
Minniescruises—http://www.minniecruises.com
epinions.com (http://www.epinions.com) and search on the ship names.

These are excellent sites on general cruising:
CruiseCritic—http://www.cruisecritic.com
About.com—http://cruises.about.com

CruiseMates—http://cruisemates.com
AvidCruiser—http://avidcruiser.com
Cruise2.com—http://www.cruise2.com

The Future of the Disney Cruise Line

Fans of the Disney Cruise Line, like fans of Disney's parks and resorts, are always looking forward to the next great thing. So what's next? Here are our thoughts, theories, and the most recent rumors.

For several years, folks have been hoping for **additional ships**. Some time ago, Disney CEO Michael Eisner suggested the Disney fleet could grow to nine or more ships, serving destinations worldwide. Certainly, that's the approach of most major cruise lines—ships on the Atlantic/Caribbean routes, America's West Coast, Europe and the Mediterranean, and East Asia. Disney has theme parks in all these areas, so the tie-in and potential for Land/Sea vacations is easy to imagine.

Well, Disney Cruise Line fans are getting impatient. Disney executives have told the press that **a new ship (or ships) has been designed**, and that shipyards have placed bids on the project. Walt Disney World President Al Weiss even stated that the only thing delaying the construction contract is the unattractive exchange rate between the U.S. dollar and other currencies (the shipyard will almost certainly be European). It typically takes more than a year to build a cruise ship, so the earliest we could expect to see a third ship would be late 2005 or 2006, with a possible fourth ship coming a year later. If exchange rates continue to rule this decision, we may be in for a long wait. We think the dollar's value will continue on its current course through the 2004 U.S. Presidential election.

We have long expected that the Disney Cruise Line will be a part of the upcoming 50th anniversary of the Disneyland Resort in 2005. (In fact, Disney Cruise Line's previous president, Matt Ouimet, recently moved to California to be President of Disneyland Resort.) We suspect the start of that (probably) 15-month party will be in April or May of 2005, roughly three months before the actual July 17th anniversary date. All indications are that Disney plans to offer **California-based cruises** as part of that celebration. Currently, it looks like the Disney Magic will be reassigned to California-based itineraries starting in mid-May of 2005 and will return to the Caribbean in September. Logically, the Magic will sail 3-, 4-, or 7-night itineraries to Mexican ports, tied in with stays at the Disneyland Resort. We don't expect to see Alaskan cruises, which run only in the summer and typically require 7-night sailings, until after the Disney Cruise Line has at least three ships in service. Meantime, the Disney Cruise Line calendar shows the Wonder plying Florida/Bahamas routes on 3- and 4-night itineraries throughout 2005.

What about the **seven-night Caribbean sailings** offered by the Disney Magic? They'll resume on September 3, 2005 and continue at least through year-end. By then, either a new ship can enter service, or the California-based cruises will be promoted as a special "taste" of the Disney Cruise Line for the Disneyland Resort's 50th Anniversary Celebration to whet appetites for the new ship(s) to come.

For now, Disney will probably be **quite cautious** about offering cruises elsewhere in the world, as international travel by Americans is still ailing. However, if the Disney Cruise Line's market researchers can prove there's sufficient local demand (European cruises by Europeans, Pacific cruises by Asians) things may move faster than we think.

When **news finally breaks** on new ships and/or new itineraries, we'll post all the detail you need at our site (http://www.passporter.com/dcl).

Cruise Reviews You Can Use

Cruiser reviews and reports are one of the absolute best ways to evaluate and get acquainted with the Disney Cruise Line before you embark. With that in mind, we've collected several tips and memories from our own experiences and those of our readers. Enjoy!

If you have access to the **Internet**, make it a point to get online and explore the web sites listed throughout this field guide. In particular, we recommend you visit MousePlanet's Trip Reports web site, which offers a nice collection of Disney Cruise Line trip reports (fun reading!) as well as room to include your own. The site is located at http://www.mouseplanet.com/dtp/trip.rpt.

"There's a lot to see and a lot to do on your Disney cruise! While you can't possibly do everything, knowing more about what's going on definitely improves your too-short cruise experience. For this, I recommend not only this guidebook but also the Magical Disney Cruise Guide which I've been offering free since the Disney Cruise Line began sailing. Read it at http://www.allearsnet.com/cruise/dcruise.shtml."
— by contributing author Mickey Morgan

Midship with Mickey

Magical Memories

"When we started planning our cruise, my kids (and we) were ecstatic that we were going on our first cruise to see Mickey. We ordered the PassPorter Field Guide Cruise Edition which was loaded with GREAT information and the fun/planning began! The kids started saving all their Disney Dollars they'd earned so they could have their own onboard spending account. We also made a huge paper chain and the kids removed a link each night so they could see how close we were to vacation. The planning/anticipation of a vacation is half the fun!"

...as told by Disney cruiser Debbie Mason

"I was a little hesitant to let the children (ages 9 and 11 at the time) use their Key to the World card as a charge card. I voiced my thoughts to the children and they came up with a solution: I would give them a 'budget' and they would keep track of their expenditures by writing each down on a pad of paper and subtracting from the previous total. It worked! They didn't go over budget and, for this year, I've increased their ship allowance. I believe it was because I allowed them to come up with a solution themselves. And, of course, because they each had a PassHolder Pouch to store their pad and pencil!"

...as told by Disney cruiser Jan Chait

© Jan Chait

The Chait grandchildren

Plotting Your Course

By now, we're certain you're hooked on the idea of a Disney cruise vacation. The time has come, the Walrus said, to turn those Disney dreams into a voyage filled with "wonder" and "magic."

Every journey starts with the first step, and this vacation is no exception. That step, of course, is planning. Planning is the keel upon which the rest of your cruise is built. This chapter is filled with the principal planning steps you'll need to take, plus a cargo of savvy advice and a chartroom filled with maps, charts, and worksheets to help keep you on course.

Some of you may be embarking on a cruise and/or leaving the United States for the very first time. While you will be visiting the cozy, nearby Caribbean, you'll encounter some subtle and not-so-subtle differences between cruise preparations and land journeys. Start your planning as far ahead as possible. Not only can you save some money, but you may need that head start to obtain the proper identity documents.

So just how do you plot the course that takes you from your front door to the gangway of your Disney cruise ship? In this chapter we'll chart the many steps in the journey, from selecting your cruise itinerary and sail dates to steering your way around tropical storms. You'll be able to pick your way through the turbulent waters of cruise rates and packages and safely reserve your snug stateroom.

Your ship's captain will ably plot your course on the high seas, but you'll need your own map and compass to get to Port Canaveral. We cover all the highways and byways that form your journey-before-the-journey, including fair lodgings at the port itself.

Finally, it's Embarkation Day! We make sure you aren't waylaid enroute to the Disney Cruise Line Terminal, that your important identity papers are all in order, and that your trunks and sea bags are packed with everything you need for a comfortable voyage.

Choosing Your Itinerary

The Disney Cruise Line currently offers **several different itineraries**: one 3-night cruise, one 4-night cruise, two 7-night land/sea combinations, two regular 7-night cruises, two special 7-night cruises, and one special 10-night cruise. Your choice of itineraries may be solely based on price or length, particularly if you combine your cruise with a stay at Walt Disney World (see page 40). If you can't decide which itinerary works best for you, read our descriptions and comments below for insight:

3-Night Cruise Itinerary: The shortest and least expensive cruise, with three nights at sea aboard the Disney Wonder and two ports of call: Nassau and Castaway Cay. Actual time spent afloat: about 68 hours (almost three days). This cruise whizzes by, and you may feel like it's over before it's barely

3-Night Itinerary:
Thursday: Set sail
Friday: Nassau
Saturday: Castaway Cay
Sunday: Return to port

begun. On the flip side, this is a great cruise on which to get your feet wet if you're new to cruising. If you plan to stay at the Walt Disney World Resort before your cruise, the 3-night cruise works best for this as it falls at the end of the week. Also, this cruise departs on Thursdays, which also happens to be the day that most space shuttles depart from Cape Canaveral (see pages 146–147 for more details on shuttle launches).

4-Night Cruise Itinerary: More sailing time with four nights at sea on the Disney Wonder. Like the 3-night, the 4-night stops at Nassau and Castaway Cay. The extra day is spent at sea—there used to be an alternate itinerary that stopped in Freeport instead of a day at sea, but this ceased in 2004. Actual time spent afloat: about 92 hours (almost four days). If cruising is your focus, you'll be happier with a 4-night cruise than a 3-night—the extra night

4-Night Itinerary:
Sunday: Set sail
Monday: Nassau
Tuesday: Castaway Cay
Wednesday: At sea
Thursday: Return to port

is more relaxing and it gives you a greater chance of dining at Palo without missing one of the other three restaurants. A benefit: If the Captain has to bypass Castaway Cay due to weather, he has the option to try again the next day. Note: It's possible that the Freeport stop could return in the future.

How Many Days to Cruise?

Should you do three days at Walt Disney World and four days at sea, or vice versa? I don't think you can possibly see everything at Walt Disney World in three or even four days, so take three nights at Walt Disney World, get a taste of it for a future return trip, and spend most of your time at sea. You can always book extra days at Disney after your cruise when you're rested.

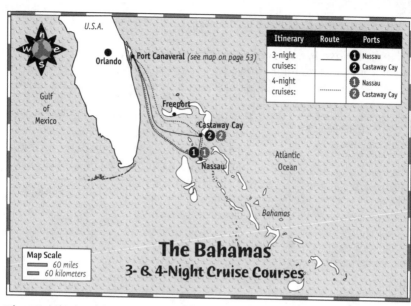

Itinerary	Route	Ports
3-night cruises:	———	❶ Nassau ❷ Castaway Cay
4-night cruises:	·········	❶ Nassau ❷ Castaway Cay

U.S.A.

Orlando   Port Canaveral *(see map on page 53)*

Gulf of Mexico

Freeport

Castaway Cay ❷ ❷

❶ ❶
Nassau

Atlantic Ocean

Bahamas

Map Scale
60 miles
60 kilometers

The Bahamas
3- & 4-Night Cruise Courses

The 7-night land/sea combination itineraries are really just Walt Disney World resort vacations combined with the 3-night and 4-night cruises.

4 Nights on Land/3 Nights at Sea Itinerary: Of the two land/sea itineraries, this is the one we recommend. If you're a fan of Walt Disney World, you may find anything less than four days at Walt Disney World is just too short. With four major parks, you need at least a day to visit each. The cruise portion of this itinerary is identical to the 3-night cruise. The cruise is short, yes, but after four days at Walt Disney World, that may feel just right. Another advantage to this itinerary is how neatly it falls within the space of one week—you leave on Sunday and return on Sunday. If you're new to Walt Disney World and cruising, we think you'll like this itinerary best—it gives you a reasonable amount of time in the parks and a taste of the cruise. Of course, you can book a 3-night cruise-only and arrange your accommodations on your own—this is our preference. See page 40 for details.

3 Nights on Land/4 Nights at Sea Itinerary: We think three days at Walt Disney World is too short. And this itinerary does start and stop on Thursday, which makes for a lopsided week. There are some advantages, however. First, you get four nights on the cruise, which also means four days of meals. If you'd spent that extra day at Walt Disney World, you'd have to feed yourselves for that day, so you get more bang for your buck. And the 4-night cruise has some added perks that you don't get on the 3-night cruise, such as an at-sea day, a variety show, and a special dinner menu. (See the chart on page 37 for a comparison). If your focus is on cruising and you want to save some money on your vacation, then this may be the itinerary for you!

Choosing Your Itinerary *(continued)*

7-Night Cruise Itineraries: Almost an entire week onboard the Disney Magic with two regular itineraries (Eastern Caribbean and Western Caribbean) and two special itineraries (both to the Eastern Caribbean).

7-Nt. E. Caribbean #1:
Saturday: Set sail
Sunday: At sea
Monday: At sea
Tuesday: St. Maarten
Wednesday: St. Thomas
Thursday: At sea
Friday: Castaway Cay
Saturday: Return to port

The first and original **Eastern Caribbean cruise** has three ports of call (St. Maarten, St. Thomas, and Castaway Cay) and three days at sea. In 2004, two new special Eastern Caribbean itineraries were introduced: the first goes to St. Thomas, San Juan, and Castaway Cay; the second goes to Antigua, St. Thomas, and Castaway Cay (see itinerary boxes for full schedules). At the time of writing, these two special Eastern Caribbean itineraries are held only during summer 2004: the St. Thomas/San Juan itinerary departs on August 7, August 21, and September 4, 2004; the Antigua/St. Thomas itinerary departs on September 18 and October 2, 2004. We don't believe the special Eastern Caribbean itineraries will be offered in 2005, but check with Disney. The **Western Caribbean cruise** offers four ports of call (Key West, Grand Cayman, Cozumel, and Castaway Cay) plus two days at sea. Note that the Disney Magic normally alternates between an Eastern Caribbean itinerary and a Western Caribbean itinerary. Actual time spent afloat: 164 hours (almost seven days). The 7-night cruise is a great choice for experienced cruisers or those who really want to relax. Cruisers on 7-night itineraries also enjoy formal and semi-formal evenings, theme nights, and a wider variety of onboard activities. Night for night, the 7-nights are no more costly than shorter cruises. There are no land/sea packages offered with these.

7-Nt. E. Caribbean #2:
Saturday: Set sail
Sunday: At sea
Monday: At sea
Tuesday: St. Thomas
Wednesday: San Juan
Thursday: At sea
Friday: Castaway Cay
Saturday: Return to port

7-Nt. E. Caribbean #3:
Saturday: Set sail
Sunday: At sea
Monday: At sea
Tuesday: Antigua
Wednesday: St. Thomas
Thursday: At sea
Friday: Castaway Cay
Saturday: Return to port

7-Night W. Caribbean:
Saturday: Set sail
Sunday: Key West
Monday: At sea
Tuesday: Grand Cayman
Wednesday: Cozumel
Thursday: At sea
Friday: Castaway Cay
Saturday: Return to port

Can I Do a 7-Night in Summer 2005?

At the time of writing, no 7-night cruises appear on Disney's schedule for summer 2005. What's up with this? See pages 29 and 36 for our thoughts on what's happening in summer 2005.

Itinerary	Route	Ports
7-night E. Caribbean #1 cruises	——	① St. Maarten ② St. Thomas ③ Castaway Cay
7-night E. Caribbean #2 cruises	··········	① St. Thomas ② San Juan ③ Castaway Cay
7-night E.Caribbean #3 cruises	- - - -	① Antigua ② St. Thomas ③ Castaway Cay
7-night W. Caribbean cruises	- · - · -	① Key West ② Grand Cayman ③ Cozumel ④ Castaway Cay

The Caribbean 7-Night Cruise Courses

10-Night Caribbean:
Saturday: Set sail
Sunday: Key West
Monday: At sea
Tuesday: At sea
Wednesday: St. Maarten
Thursday: St. Lucia
Friday: Antigua
Saturday: St. Thomas
Sunday: At sea
Monday: Castaway Cay
Tuesday: Return to port

10-Night Cruise Itinerary: As of this writing, this special itinerary is being offered just once, setting sail on December 18, 2004. This itinerary goes to Key West, St. Maarten, St. Lucia, Antigua, St. Thomas, and Castaway Cay, with three days at sea. If you've always wanted a longer Disney cruise, this is your opportunity. Actual time spent afloat: 236 hours (almost ten days). As you can imagine, this itinerary is pricey, but it does promise to be a grand time! We can't say what sort of special events are likely to take place on this itinerary, but as it falls over Christmas, there are sure to be some special festivities. Like the 7-night itineraries, this special itinerary is aboard the Disney Magic.

Do Itineraries Ever Change?

Yes, as you can see by the mention of the special 2004 cruises, itineraries can and do change. For the most part, however, you will know if your itinerary has been officially changed before you book it. For example, the announcement of these new itineraries came 12 to 18 months before the cruises themselves are set to sail. With that said, occasionally itineraries are modified immediately before or during your cruise, but it is rare. Most last-minute itinerary changes are due to bad weather, and usually other ports are substituted. Castaway Cay is more often bypassed due to weather, but even that is an uncommon occurrence (it seems to happen most in January and February). If you have plans at a port that cannot be modified (e.g., a wedding), you shouldn't count on a cruise to get you there—you're best off flying in and leaving the cruise for another time.

Choosing Your Itinerary (continued)

Future West Coast Itineraries: While we don't have a crystal ball, we are reasonably confident that the Disney Cruise Line has some West Coast itineraries in its future. Our next edition will certainly detail these, as well as any other new itineraries that may pop up. Let's get a head start now with a map of the popular West Coast ports, along with some thoughts.

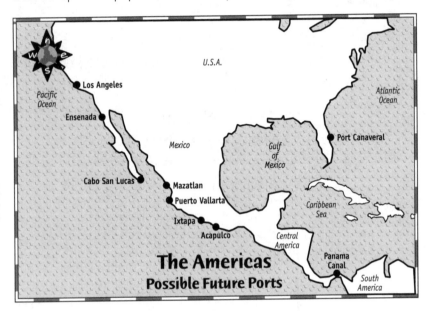

If the Disney Cruise Line does offer West Coast-based cruises, it will likely offer a couple of "repositioning" itineraries between Port Canaveral and Los Angeles via the Panama Canal, in May and September 2005. This repositioning itinerary would likely be a 10- to 12-night cruise and offer stops in various ports along the way. If Disney does base a ship on the West Coast, it's likely to choose the recently renovated Port of Los Angeles in San Pedro, California (http://www.portoflosangeles.org), a mere 22 miles from Disneyland. From there, we expect it would offer 3-, 4- and/or 7-night Mexican Riviera cruises, stopping at venerable ports like Cabo San Lucas, Mazatlan, Puerto Vallarta, and Acapulco (think "Love Boat"). And it seems likely that Disney would also offer land/sea packages with stays at the Disneyland Resort (http://www.disneyland.com) to coincide with Disneyland's 50th Anniversary Celebration. Prices for the Mexican Riviera cruises would likely be comparable to existing Bahamas and Caribbean cruises offered by Disney. What about other destinations? Some rumors have floated about Alaskan cruises, which are also a possibility, though less likely. We are expecting an announcement about new ports in late spring 2004—visit http://www.passporter.com/dcl to get the latest news.

Itinerary Comparison Chart

Wondering about the specific differences between the various cruise itineraries? Below is a chart of the **differences only**. As you read through the book, you can assume that any feature mentioned applies to all four cruise itineraries unless we specifically state otherwise.

Feature	3-Night	4-Night	7-Night E. Caribbean	7-Night W. Caribbean
Ports of call	2	2	3	4
Sea days	0	1	3	2
Embarkation day	Thursday	Sunday	Saturday	Saturday
Debarkation day	Sunday	Thursday	Saturday	Saturday
Hours afloat	68	92	164	164
Special dinner menus	0	1	4	4
Character breakfast			✔	✔
Champagne brunch			✔	✔
High tea			✔	✔
Tea with Wendy			✔	✔
Dessert buffets	1	1	2	2
Semi-formal nights			1	1
Formal nights			1	1
Stage shows	3	3	4	4
Variety shows	0	1	2	2
Adult seminars		✔	✔	✔
Adult coffeehouse			✔	✔
Reading room			✔	✔

As you might imagine, the 7-night cruise offers more activities than the 3- or 4-night cruises—there are more days to fill, after all! Activities differ from cruise to cruise, but here's a list of some of the extra activities that have been offered on the 7-night cruises in the past:

- ✔ Intro to Internet session
- ✔ Dance lessons
- ✔ Family & Adult Talent Show
- ✔ Team Trivia
- ✔ Family Mini Olympics
- ✔ Mr. Toad's Wild Race
- ✔ Mickey 200 Race
- ✔ Ping-Pong tournament
- ✔ NHL Skills Challenge
- ✔ Mixology demonstrations
- ✔ Ice carving demonstrations
- ✔ Artist-led workshops

See chapter 5, "Playing and Relaxing Onboard," starting on pages 118–119 for many more details on the various activities aboard.

Introduction · Reservations · Staterooms · Dining · Activities · Ports of Call · Magic · Index

Selecting Your Sail Dates

Once you've selected an itinerary, it's time to choose a sail date. The Disney Cruise Line operates year-round, so you have many choices. Deciding when to go is based on many factors: your schedules, your plans, price, itinerary availability, and weather. Let's go over each of these in detail:

Your Schedules—It's better to book as far ahead as possible, so check now with your employer/school for available vacation dates.

Your Plans—Do you want to go to Walt Disney World? If so, do you want to go before and/or after your cruise? If you do plan a visit to Orlando, you'll want to select a sail date that works in tandem with your Walt Disney World plans—see the "To Go To the Walt Disney World Resort or Not?" topic on page 40 for tips. Are you hoping to visit relatives or spend some time at Kennedy Space Center in Cape Canaveral? If so, you will want to go when you can add extra time before and/or after your cruise.

Price—The Disney Cruise Line has rate trends that correspond to demand (check out our rate trends chart on page 43). In general, cruising is more affordable in January and September through early December (excluding Thanksgiving). Spring, summer, and major holidays are the most expensive times to cruise. See pages 42–43 for more pricing details.

Itinerary Availability—The various cruise itineraries depart and return on particular days of the week (see chart below), which may be important to your vacation schedule. Additionally, the 7-night cruise alternates between the Eastern Caribbean and Western Caribbean every other week. For specific dates of future cruises, visit http://www.disneycruise.com, or check your Disney Cruise Line booklet.

Cruise	Depart	Return
3-Night	Thurs.	Sun.
4-Night	Sun.	Thurs.
7-Night	Sat.	Sat.

When do we like to sail? We're fond of May—great weather, great rates!

Are Any Dates Unavailable?

Typically, yes. Ships do fill up near certain dates—such as Christmas and New Year's Eve. And some dates are reserved for members of a certain group only. Also, the ships go into drydock for maintenance once every couple of years. The Disney Wonder is scheduled to be in drydock from 10/4 to 10/16 in 2004. A quick call to the Disney Cruise Line can tell you if your preferred dates are available.

Weather

The Caribbean and the Bahamas generally enjoy **delightful weather** year-round. Even so, it can get cool in the winter and a little warm in the summer. The summer also brings more rain than usual. See our weather chart below for details. The most important weather condition to consider is hurricane season, which runs from late May through November (see tropical storm levels in the chart below). The worst months for hurricane activity are August and September. Cruising during hurricane season means you're more likely to have a port change or two and have a rocky ride on rough seas. Even so, cruising during hurricane conditions isn't very dangerous, as ships can sail faster than hurricanes and captains have plenty of time to navigate around the storms.

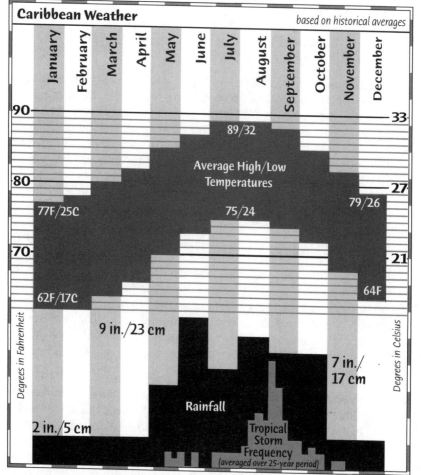

Caribbean Weather — based on historical averages

Months: January, February, March, April, May, June, July, August, September, October, November, December

Average High/Low Temperatures
- 89/32
- 77F/25C
- 75/24
- 79/26
- 62F/17C
- 64F
- Degrees in Fahrenheit (90, 80, 70)
- Degrees in Celsius (33, 27, 21)

Rainfall
- 9 in./23 cm
- 7 in./17 cm
- 2 in./5 cm

Tropical Storm Frequency (averaged over 25-year period)

Sidebar tabs: Introduction, Reservations, Staterooms, Dining, Activities, Ports of Call, Magic, Index

Genuine PassPorter Genuine PassPorter Genuine PassPorter Genuine PassPorter Genuine PassPorter

Introduction | Reservations | Staterooms | Dining | Activities | Ports of Call | Magic | Index

To Go to the Walt Disney World Resort or Not?

Perhaps you're tempted by Disney's land/sea vacation package, or you just can't resist the urge to visit The Mouse while you're in Florida. Whatever your reason for visiting the Walt Disney World Resort, you're not alone—the majority of your fellow cruisers will also visit the parks on their trip. If you're just not quite sure yet, let's weigh the pros and cons:

Reasons to Visit the Mouse House:
- ✔ You love Walt Disney World and can't go to Florida without a visit.
- ✔ You've never been, and this is a great opportunity.
- ✔ You're not sure you'll feel the "Disney magic" if you skip the parks.
- ✔ You have the time and money.

Reasons to Just Cruise:
- ✔ You want a laid-back, really relaxing vacation.
- ✔ You've been there, done that, and don't need to go back yet.
- ✔ You don't have the time or money.

If you do **decide to go** to Walt Disney World, you'll need to choose between a land/sea vacation package and arranging it yourself. We always make our own arrangements for Walt Disney World—we save money and enjoy greater flexibility. The land/sea package offers a limited choice of Disney resorts, based on your choice of stateroom (though you can upgrade to a different resort if you pay the difference). Further, you can't get full value out of the Ultimate Park Hopper Passes that come with the package as the last day of your pass (which you could normally use at a park) is spent in transit to and on the Disney cruise. Would you like to stretch your dollars at a value resort or book a bare-minimum stateroom and stay at Animal Kingdom Lodge? Not on the land/sea! You also can't grab hotel discounts that are often available. We prefer a minimum of a four-night cruise and at least a four-night stay at Walt Disney World. That's not in the package, either. But you can't beat the land/sea for convenience—you'll be ushered everywhere with a minimum of fuss. No matter what, we refer you to our PassPorter Walt Disney World guidebook for loads of details, tips, strategies, maps, and plans. You can pick up our guidebook at most bookstores, online at http://www.passporter.com, and at 877-929-3273.

Should you visit Walt Disney World **before or after** you cruise? The Disney land/sea vacation package places the Walt Disney World leg before the cruise leg by default, though you can request it be switched. If you're new to Walt Disney World, visit the parks first—Walt Disney World is an intense vacation experience, and the cruise will be a relaxing break. Walt Disney World fans may prefer visiting the parks after the cruise. As much as we like the cruise, the parks are our first love and we save the best for last.

Cruise Add-Ons

If you decide to let Disney make the arrangements for your visit to Walt Disney World, there are a number of packages and add-ons designed to help you get the most out of it. Below are the basic packages offered at press time. Please call the Disney Cruise Line for specific packages and prices. Prices quotes below are good through 12/31/2004.

Romance Plan—Guests on a 7-night land/sea package can add a horse-drawn carriage ride, one dinner at a select table-service restaurant, one "romantic choice" (spa treatment, a round of golf, or Cirque du Soleil admission), two Disney lanyards with pins, a romantic gift onboard, one couples massage in the Vista Spa, romance turndown service (one night), champagne breakfast in bed (one morning), and priority seating at Palo for one evening. $599 per couple.

Romantic Escape at Sea—Guests on a 3-, 4-, or 7-night cruise can add a romantic gift basket, romance turndown service (one night), champagne breakfast in bed (one morning), priority seating at Palo one evening, and one couples massage in the Vista Spa. $299 per couple.

Family Reunion—Guests on a 3-, 4-, or 7-night cruise or 7-night land/sea package can add a personalized Disney Cruise Line family reunion shirt (one per person), a leather photo portfolio with a complimentary photo (one per stateroom), and a commemorative family reunion certificate (one per person). Families booking eight or more staterooms can also choose one of the following: an hour-long reception with open bar and snacks, a Bon Voyage Memory Box (one per stateroom), or a bottle of wine (one per stateroom). Costs $29 per person for the first and second guests in the stateroom, $19 per person for additional guests in the same room. Package must be purchased for all guests (regardless of age) in the party.

Walt Disney World Packages

If you book your stay at Walt Disney World separately from your cruise, you can take advantage of a number of other packages. The Fairytale Vacation Package offers three or more nights' accommodations, Ultimate Park Hopper tickets, and special framed character art—rates vary by season, hotel, and age of guests. The Dream Maker packages add in yet more options and start at $359/adult or $188/child for three nights. There's even a special add-on Dream Maker package for your "prince" or "princess," offering such kid-friendly perks as a character breakfast, luggage tags, 50 Disney Dollars per kid, and special seating at select shows, all for $23/adult or $64/child (yep, kids cost more). To learn more about the available packages for Walt Disney World vacations, call the Walt Disney Travel Company at 800-828-0228, ask your travel agent, or visit http://www.waltdisneyworld.com.

Introduction
Reservations
Staterooms
Dining
Activities
Ports of Call
Magic
Index

Cruise Rates

While we can't give you exact prices, we can give you rate ranges for various itineraries and stateroom categories. The rates below are based on our own research of 2004 rates—we feel these are realistic numbers, but we can virtually guarantee that you'll get different rates when you do your own research. Use these as **guidelines only**. Actual rates are based on demand and fluctuate during the year. To get actual rate quotes, call the Disney Cruise Line, visit http://www.disneycruise.com, or talk to your travel agent. Note that the rates below are for **two adult fares** with early booking savings, but do not include air, insurance, or ground transfers.

Typical Cruise Rate Ranges (for two adults in one stateroom)

Category	3-Night Cruise Low to High	4-Night Cruise Low to High	7-Night Cruise Low to High	7-Night Land/Sea Low to High
1	$4898–5498	$5698–6298	$7798–9998	$7798–9998
2	$4298–4898	$4898–5498	$7198–9398	$7198–9398
3	$3698–4298	$4098–4698	$5998–7998	$5998–7998
4	$2078–3698	$2278–3898	$3498–6398	$3498–6398
5	$1678–3198	$1878–3398	$2898–5398	$2898–5398
6	$1578–2998	$1778–3198	$2698–5198	$2698–5198
7	$1478–2798	$1678–2998	$2498–4998	$2498–4998
8	$1378–2498	$1578–2698	$2298–4398	$2298–4398
9	$1178–2298	$1378–2498	$2098–4198	$2098–4198
10	$1078–1998	$1278–2198	$1898–3798	$1898–3798
11	$818–1798	$1018–1998	$1798–3598	$1798–3598
12	$818–1798	$1018–1998	$1658–3398	$1658–3398
3rd & 4th Guest: Kids Under 3	$99	$99	$139	$139
3rd & 4th Guest: Kids 3-12	$229–799	$329–899	$399–1399	$399–1399
3rd & 4th Guest: Ages 13 & up	$279–799	$379–899	$599–1699	$599–1699

✔ Each stateroom booked must include at least one adult, and no more than 3–5 total guests may occupy a stateroom, depending upon occupancy limits. If your party size is greater than five, you'll need to book a suite (categories 1-2) or more than one stateroom.

✔ Staterooms with just one adult and one child are charged the price of two adults.

✔ Guests cruising alone (one adult in a room) are charged roughly 80% of the above rates.

✔ Guests booking a land/sea package can choose to stay at the Grand Floridian Resort with categories 1-3; a deluxe resort (Beach Club, Polynesian, Animal Kingdom Lodge, Swan, or Dolphin) with categories 4-7; or a moderate resort (Port Orleans-French Quarter, Port Orleans-Riverside, or Caribbean Beach) with categories 8-12. No other resorts are options.

✔ Note: Women who are past their 24th week of pregnancy and infants under 12 weeks cannot sail with the Disney Cruise Line.

Confused by all those rate ranges? We feel the same way. Before we went to press, **we researched every 2004 cruise** and its rates (at early booking discounts). We then graphed the minimum rates (for two adults in a category 12 stateroom) into the chart below. This chart gives you a very useful overview of the general trends for specific times in 2004 (and 2005 will likely be very similar). Rates for higher categories follow the same basic trends as category 12, so you can use this chart to pinpoint seasons for the best rates. Keep in mind, however, that these rates can change at any time. Don't take the numbers in this chart at face value—concentrate on the trends instead. Also note that this chart does not take into account seasonal discounts which may be offered, thereby reducing the rates for a specific period. You may want to compare this to the chart on page 39 to pick the best compromise between great cruise rates and great weather (we're partial to May ourselves).

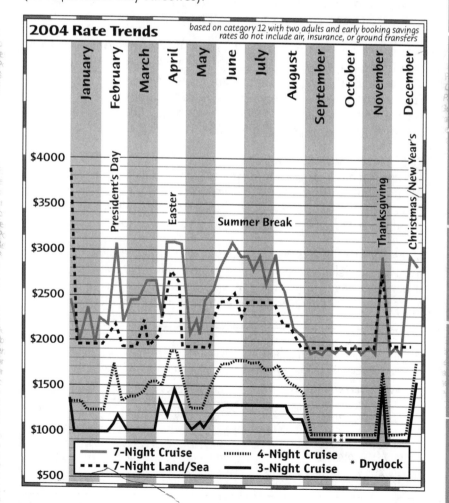

2004 Rate Trends — based on category 12 with two adults and early booking savings, rates do not include air, insurance, or ground transfers

Legend:
— 7-Night Cruise
········ 4-Night Cruise
- - - 7-Night Land/Sea
— 3-Night Cruise
* Drydock

Introduction

Reservations

Staterooms

Dining

Activities

Ports of Call

Magic

Index

Reserving Your Cruise

Once you know when, how, and where you want to cruise, it's time to **make reservations**. You can call the Disney Cruise Line directly or use a travel agent (see sidebar at bottom). There are pros and cons to both. Calling directly may give you more control over stateroom selection, while travel agents (such as MouseEarVacations.com—see page 265) may get better deals. Disney Vacation Club (DVC) members who want to cruise on points (see sidebar on next page) should contact DVC directly.

Before you make your reservations, **use the worksheet** on page 47 to jot down your preferred sailing dates along with alternates. Even a small change in your travel dates can open the door to a great deal. Be familiar with all stateroom categories (see chapter 3) in your price range, too.

Reservations can be made by calling **888-325-2500**, 9:00 am to 10:00 pm ET (weekdays) and 9:00 am to 8:00 pm (weekends). From outside the U.S., call +1-407-566-6921. Representatives offer assistance in English, Spanish, Japanese, French, Portuguese, and German. Castaway Club members have a special phone number (see page 249). You can get quotes at http://www.disneycruise.com and at cruise-related sites—see below.

Call Disney Cruise Reservations as far in advance as possible. Ask for any **special deals or packages** for your dates—Disney generally doesn't volunteer this information. If you have a Walt Disney World Annual Pass or Disney Visa, or are a Disney Vacation Club member or Florida resident, ask about those discounts. If your dates aren't available, check alternates.

Make any **special requests**, such as a handicap-accessible room or the need for special meals, at the time of reservation. If you have a particular stateroom or deck in mind (we make several suggestions in chapter 3), make sure to tell the reservations agent at the time of booking.

Shopping Around

You can also make reservations through various travel reservation sites or travel agents specializing in Disney Cruise reservations (in alphabetical order):

Travel Reservation Sites	Travel Agents
http://www.cruise.com	http://www.aaa.com
http://www.cruise411.com	http://www.costco.com
http://www.cruise-locator.com	http://www.cruisedirections.com/disney
http://www.expedia.com	http://www.dreamscruise.com
http://www.orbitz.com	http://www.kingdommagictravel.com
http://www.travelocity.com	http://www.mouseearvacations.com
http://www.vacationstogo.com	http://www.yourmagicaljourneys.com

You will be asked if you want the **Vacation Protection Plan**, and the cruise line agents automatically include it in their quote. This insurance plan covers trip cancellations, travel delays, emergency medical/dental, emergency medical transportation/assistance, and baggage delay, loss, theft, or damage. The plan price is based on the length of your cruise vacation—$49 (3 nights), $59 (4 nights), and $99 (7 and 10 nights) per person for the first and second individuals in your stateroom (additional guests are $39, $49, and $59, respectively). If your flight could be affected by weather, seriously consider insurance. Note that your airfare and your air travel-related delays will not be covered unless you're also using the Disney Air Program. Also note that the Protection Plan does not cover some preexisting medical conditions. If you don't want this insurance, ask to have it removed from your quote.

You may save money on **vacation insurance** by booking it yourself—visit http://www.insuremytrip.com or call your insurance agent. But don't delay—most companies will waive preexisting medical conditions only if you buy insurance within 7–14 days after making your trip deposit. Trip interruption/cancellation coverage is great for circumstances beyond your control, but it doesn't help if you simply change your mind. If the cruise is only part of your vacation, make sure your policy covers the entire trip. Policies vary, so shop carefully. You may already have life, medical, theft, and car rental protection in your regular policies (be sure you're covered overseas). Credit cards, AAA, and/or other memberships may also include useful coverage. Airlines already cover lost baggage—make sure your policy exceeds their limits. Seniors and travelers with preexisting conditions should seriously consider insurance—the costs of evacuation, overseas medical care, and travel/lodging for a companion while you're under treatment are very high.

You may also be asked if you want **airfare**. In general, we've found it is less expensive to book our own airfare, but you may prefer to leave the flight details up to Disney. The biggest drawback to using the Disney Air Program is that they decide which flight you'll take, and you may arrive later than you prefer or have tight flight transfers. If you do use Disney Air, ground transfers are automatically included in your package (see next page).

Disney Vacation Club Members

Members of Disney's innovative time-share program, the Disney Vacation Club (DVC), have the option to use their points for cruises. Contact Disney Vacation Club directly at 800-800-9100 or visit http://www.disneyvacationclub.com to get point charts and details on reserving cruises. Note that you can use a combination of points and cash (or credit) for a cruise. Reservations with points can be made up to 11 months in advance. We've heard mixed reports from guests who use DVC points to cruise—some feel it works out well for them, while others feel the cruise requires too many points. Disney Vacation Club members booking cruises without points may also be entitled to an onboard credit—inquire when making reservations.

Reserving Your Cruise *(continued)*

Another option is **ground transfers**, available to those using the Disney Air Program and those arranging their own flights. Ground transfers are available to/from the Walt Disney World Resort, Port Canaveral, and Orlando International Airport. Price is $46/guest (for 3-, 4-, 7-, and 10-night cruises) and $63/guest (for 7-night land/sea packages). The ground transfers include pickup at the airport, round-trip ground transportation, and baggage handling. As long as you are flying in on the day of your cruise and you affix the Disney-supplied luggage tags prior to checking your bags with your airline, your bags go directly from the plane to your resort/ship—no stopping at baggage claim! One-way transfers to or from the airport are also available for $25/guest. See page 54.

A **deposit** of $200/guest (3-/4-night) or $250/guest (7-/10-night) is required to confirm your reservation. Reservations are held for seven days without confirmation, and then they are deleted if no deposit is received. Pay your deposit by 8:00 pm ET on the seventh day—you can do it over the phone with Visa, MasterCard, Discover, JCB, Diner's Club, American Express, or The Disney Credit Card. Record deposits on the worksheet on page 47.

Once your cruise is confirmed, Disney mails a **confirmation** of your reservation. If you need to cancel, most reservations can be cancelled for full credit up to 60 days prior to your vacation. If you cancel 30–59 days prior to your cruise/package, you lose your deposit. If you cancel 8–29 days prior, you lose 50% per person. And there is no refund if you cancel 7 days or less prior to your cruise/package. There is a $50/person fee if you change your sail dates 0-59 days prior to your cruise. Insurance may help with these penalties. Also note that there is a $35/person fee for document reissue and name/air changes within 30 days of your vacation.

Your **cruise documents** are mailed to you within 28 days of sailing, though most cruisers get them about two weeks ahead. Read everything in your cruise document package and fill out the embarkation form, immigration form, cruise contract, and payment authorization before you leave home. Luggage tags are included in each cruise booklet and should be placed on your bags before you arrive (see page 62 for details). Other items in your cruise document package include a guide to the document package, shore excursion booklet and advance reservation form, onboard gift brochure, Disney's Vacation Plan (insurance) brochure/policy, and the Passport to Disney Magic/Wonder booklet (a brief guide to the cruise).

Get Your Passports and/or Birth Certificates Together Now

Your cruise takes you to foreign ports, so you must have proper I.D. We recommend passports but photo I.D.s along with certified birth certificates with raised seals work for U.S. residents, too. You also need passports/birth certificates for kids. It can take months to obtain these if you haven't already, so get started now! See pages 60–61.

Cruise Reservation Worksheet

Use this worksheet to jot down preferences, scribble information during phone calls, and keep all your discoveries together. Don't worry about being neat—just be thorough! 🖋 Circle the cruise you finally select to avoid any confusion.

Cruise length: 3 nights   4 nights   7 nights   7 nights land/sea   10 nights

Departure date: _____   Alternate: _____

Return date: _____   Alternate: _____

We prefer to stay in category: _____   Alternates: _____

Discounts: Disney Visa   Disney Vacation Club   Castaway Club
AAA   Seasonal   Florida Resident   Canadian Resident   Other: _____

Dates	Itinerary	Category	Rates	Insurance	Total

Reservation Number: _____

Confirm reservation by this date: _____

Deposit due by: _____   Deposit paid on: _____

Balance due by: _____   Balance paid on: _____

Do we need to order passports/birth certificates? _____

Introduction

Reservations

Staterooms

Dining

Activities

Ports of Call

Magic

Index

Getting to Florida

By Car, Van, Truck, or Motorcycle

Most vacationers still arrive in Florida in their own vehicle. It's hard to beat the **slowly rising sense of excitement** as you draw closer or the freedom of having your own wheels once you arrive (helpful when you're combining your cruise with a land vacation). Driving may also eliminate any concerns you or family members may have with air travel. And driving can be less expensive than air travel, especially with large families. On the downside, you may spend long hours or even days on the road, which cuts deeply into your time with Mickey. And you'll need to park your car while you're cruising, which is pricey (see page 59).

If you opt to drive, carefully **map your course** ahead of time. You can do this with a AAA TripTik—a strip map that guides you to your destination. You must be a AAA member (see page 27) to get a TripTik, but you can easily join for $40-$55/year. If you're driving I-75, we recommend "Along Interstate-75" (Mile Oak Publishing, http://www.i75online.com) by Dave Hunter. I-95 drivers will benefit from the "Drive I-95" guide by Stan and Sandra Posner (Travelsmart, http://www.drivei95.com) or a visit to http://www.usastar.com/i95/homepage.htm. Or try a trip-routing service such as AutoPilot at http://www.freetrip.com. **Tip**: Florida's Interstate exit numbers changed in 2002/2003, and we use the new exit numbers here. See http://www.dot.state.fl.us for details.

If you live more than 500 miles away, **spread out your drive** over more than one day, allotting one day for every 500 miles. If your journey spans more than a day, decide in advance where to stop each night and make reservations. If possible, arrive a day ahead of your cruise departure day for a more relaxing start to the cruise (see pages 56–58 for lodging in Cape Canaveral). Compare the price of driving versus flying, too.

By Train

The train is a uniquely relaxing way to travel to Central Florida. **Amtrak** serves the Orlando area daily with both **passenger trains** and an Auto Train, which carries your family and your car. The **Auto Train** runs between suburban Washington D.C. and suburban Orlando (Sanford, FL). Prices vary depending upon the season, the direction, and how far in advance you make your reservation. The Auto Train is also available one-way, and in many seasons, one direction is less expensive than the other. Late arrivals are the norm, so allow extra time. Keep in mind that you may need to take a taxi or town car from the train station, or you can rent a car from the nearby Hertz office. For Amtrak's rates, schedules, reservations, and more information, call 800-USA-RAIL or visit them at http://www.amtrak.com.

By Bus

Greyhound serves Cocoa, Orlando, and Kissimmee. Buses take longer to reach a destination than do cars driving the same route. Fares are lowest if you live within ten hours of Central Florida. For fares and tickets, call Greyhound at 800-231-2222 or visit them at http://www.greyhound.com.

By Airplane

Air travel is the fastest way for many vacationers. Air travel may be less expensive than you think, too. You have two choices: use the Disney Air Program and let them include your airfare in your package—inquire about pricing when you book your cruise—or book your own flight. It'll be less expensive and more flexible if you book your own flight—Disney Air Program arrival and departure times aren't always optimal. To find an **affordable flight**, be flexible on the day and time of departure and return—fares can differ greatly depending on when you fly and how long you stay. Second, take advantage of the many "fare sales" available—to learn about sales, visit airlines' web sites or travel sites such as Travelocity (http://www.travelocity.com), Expedia (http://www.expedia.com), or Orbitz (http://www.orbitz.com). Third, try alternate airports and airlines (including low-fare airlines like Song and jetBlue). Fourth, be persistent. Ask for their lowest fare and work from there. When you find a good deal, put it on hold immediately (if possible), note your reservation on page 51, and cancel later if necessary. Finally, don't stop shopping. If your airline offers a cheaper fare later, you may be able to rebook at the lower rate. Consider researching fares on your **airline's web site**—you can experiment with different flights and may get a deal for booking online. Priceline.com (http://www.priceline.com) is another option—you can name your own price. But only use it if you are flying out a day or more ahead of time and a day or more later. To arrange **ground transportation**, see page 52.

Our Top 10 Tips, Reminders, and Warnings

1. Call your airline/airport for any new or changed requirements, and check the status of your flight before departing for the airport.
2. Pack (or pick up) a meal for the flight.
3. Leave potentially dangerous items at home—they aren't allowed on the plane or the ship. This includes pocket knives, hand tools, and many kinds of sporting gear. If you must bring needles or syringes, also bring a note from your doctor. Nail clippers, tweezers, and eyeglass repair kits can be packed in your carry-on. Call the Disney Cruise Line to confirm any questionable objects.
4. Carry undeveloped film in your carry-on as the checked luggage screening devices may damage undeveloped film. Film at 800 speed and up should be hand-checked.
5. Limit your carry-ons to one bag and one personal item (purse, briefcase, etc.) and assume they will be searched.
6. Plan to arrive at the airport two hours prior to departure.
7. A boarding pass will probably be required for you to pass through security.
8. Before passing through security, put all metal items in the provided tray.
9. E-Ticket holders should bring a confirmation and/or boarding pass.
10. Be patient with long lines and polite with travel personnel.

Getting Around the Orlando Airport

Most cruise-bound passengers will arrive in the Orlando International Airport, which is a large, sprawling hub and one of the better (and cleaner) airports we've flown into. When you arrive, your plane docks at one of the **satellite terminals** (see map below). Just follow the signs to the automated **shuttle** that takes you to the main terminal—there you'll find **baggage claim** and ground transportation. Once you reach the main terminal (Level 3), either look for Disney Cruise Line representatives (if you've purchased Disney's ground transfers) or follow signs down to baggage claim (Level 2). Shuttles, town cars, taxis, and rental cars are found on Level 1 (take the elevators opposite the baggage carousels). Each transportation company has its own ticket booth, so keep your eyes open. If you get lost, look for signs that can get you back on track.

As your authors used to live in entirely different parts of the country, we became quite good at **meeting up at the airport**. It's best to meet your party at their baggage claim area as you won't be allowed past security without a valid boarding pass. The trick here is knowing which airline and baggage claim area. Use the map and airline list below, or call the airport directly at 407-825-2001. Be careful when differentiating between the side A and side B baggage claim. Also note that gates 1-29 and 100-129 use side A, while gates 30-99 use side B. Check the arrival/departure boards in the main terminal for flight status, too!

Another meeting option is an **airport restaurant**, especially for long waits. Call 407-825-2001 or visit http://www.orlandoairports.net for details on the airport's eateries. Travelers can be paged at 407-825-2000.

American Airlines, America West, ATA, Continental, SunWorld, Thomas Cook, and TWA use gates 1-29; Air Canada, ANA, Northwest, United, and U.S. Air use gates 30-59; Delta, British Airways, Midwest, Song, Sun Country, and Virgin use gates 60-99; and AirTran, jetBlue, Southwest, and Spirit use gates 100-129.

Travel Worksheet

Use this worksheet to jot down preferences, scribble information during phone calls, and keep all your discoveries together. Don't worry about being neat—just be thorough! ✎ Circle the names and numbers once you decide to go with them to avoid confusion.

Arrival date: _____ Alternate: _____

Return date: _____ Alternate: _____

We plan to travel by: ☐ Car ☐ Plane ☐ Train ☐ Bus ☐ Tour
☐ Other: _____

For Drivers:

Miles to get to Orlando: _____ ÷ 500 = _____ # days on the road

We need to stay at a motel on: _____

Tune-up scheduled for: _____

Rental car info: _____

_____

For Riders:

Train/Bus phone numbers: _____

Ride preferences: _____

Ride availabilities: _____

Reserved ride times and numbers: _____

Routes: _____ Gate: _____

For Flyers:

Airline phone numbers: _____

Flight preferences: _____

Flight availabilities: _____

_____

Reserved flight times and numbers: _____

_____

Introduction
Reservations
Staterooms
Dining
Activities
Ports of Call
Magic
Index

Getting to Port Canaveral

Port Canaveral, Florida is Disney's home port. Situated in the city of Cape Canaveral, it's easily accessible from anywhere in Central Florida.

From the Orlando International Airport

Port Canaveral is about one hour (45 mi./72 km.) east of the airport. You have five options: transfer, shuttle, town car/limo, taxi, or rental car.

Disney Cruise Line Ground Transfer—If you're sailing the day you arrive at the airport and you've booked ground transfers, a Disney Cruise Line representative meets you at the airport and directs you to a motorcoach. Check your cruise documents for transfer details. If you're not on a package, you can purchase these transfers for $46 to $63/person—inquire at 800-395-9374, extension 1. For more details on the Disney Cruise Line motorcoaches, see page 54.

Shuttle—You can take a shuttle, which you share with other passengers bound for Port Canaveral, in two ways. You can use the Transfer Coupon (in your cruise documents) at the designated counter on the first floor of the airport, and the charges will appear on your shipboard account. Or, if you prefer, you can arrange your own transportation through Mears (800-759-5219). Cost is about $30 per person, round-trip.

Town Car/Limo—A luxurious alternative is a town car or limo, through a company like Tiffany Town Car (888-838-2161). The driver meets you in baggage claim, helps you with your luggage, and drives you to the port. Cost is $160–180 for a round-trip town car and $170–195 for a round-trip van that holds 12. For more details, see http://www.tiffanytowncar.com.

Taxi—This is an option, but at approximately $90 one-way for up to nine people, it's a pricey one. You can get taxis at the airport on level 1.

Rental Car—This option works well if you'll be spending time elsewhere before you cruise and need the wheels, and it can also be less expensive than any of the above options. All the major car rental companies are located at the airport, but we recommend Budget (800-527-7000) or Avis (800-831-2847) because they are convenient, affordable, and offer a complimentary shuttle to the cruise terminal. Hertz (800-654-3131) also offers a complimentary shuttle, but National does not. All four rental car companies have offices near the cruise terminal for drop-off/pick-up.

Driving directions from the Orlando airport: Follow airport signs to the "North Exit" and take the Bee Line Expressway (528) east 43 mi. (69 km.) to Cape Canaveral. You'll need $1.25 in small bills/coins for tolls.

Getting to Port Canaveral

(continued)

From Orlando and Walt Disney World—You have four options: shuttle, town car/limo, rental car, and your own car. Mears offers shuttles and Tiffany Town Car offers town cars/limos/vans to Port Canaveral (see previous page). If you're driving, take I-4 to exit 72 and then take the Bee Line Expressway (528) east 53 miles (85 km.) to Cape Canaveral. Allow at least one hour and $2.50 for tolls. See directions below to the terminal.

From I-75—Take I-75 south to Florida's Turnpike. Take the turnpike south to exit 254 and take the Bee Line Expressway (528) east 50 miles (80 km.) to Cape Canaveral. Expect $5.75 in tolls. See directions below to terminal.

From I-95—Take I-95 to exit 205 East and take the Bee Line Expressway (528) east 12 miles (19 km.) to Cape Canaveral.

From Cape Canaveral to the Disney Cruise Line Terminal—As you drive east on the Bee Line Expressway (528), you'll cross two bridges (see if you can spot your ship when you're atop these bridges). After the second bridge, take the Route 401 exit to the "A" cruise terminals and follow the signs to the Disney Cruise Line Terminal (detailed on page 59).

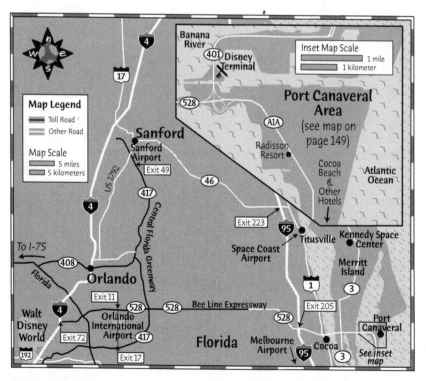

Port Canaveral Area (see map on page 149)

Disney Cruise Line Motorcoach (Ground Transfers)

Passengers on a Disney land/sea vacation package and those who've booked ground transfers separately (see page 52) may get to ride in a comfortable Disney Cruise Line motorcoach. These **deluxe buses** are painted to look like classic motorcoaches. On board, the comfy seats recline and there's even a restroom in the back. On the way to Port Canaveral, you're treated to a delightful video that heightens your anticipation. On the way back, you may watch a Disney movie on the overhead monitors.

Disney Cruise Line Motorcoach

There are some **downsides** to the ground transfers. There's no guarantee you'll get a Disney Cruise Line motorcoach just because you purchased the transfers. When we used the transfers in fall of 1999, we rode in the motorcoach on the way to Port Canaveral, but on the way back to the Walt Disney World Resort, we were squeezed into a drab shuttle van instead. This is more likely to happen if you're going to the Walt Disney World Resort after your cruise. Another downside is that you usually need to wait to board the bus. This could mean you miss the opportunity to get reservations for Palo and the spa or feel rushed when you arrive at the airport. And check-in goes slower, since you're in the midst of a large group of people who've arrived with you. You'll need to decide which is more important: convenience (take the bus) or speed (use another method). If you opt for the transfer, sit as near to the front as you can to be among the first off.

Boarding at the airport: Passengers with ground transfers who arrive between 9:00 am and 1:30 pm will be met in the terminal (just past security) by a Disney representative and told where to board the motorcoach. Your luggage (if properly tagged) is intercepted and transported to the ship.

Boarding at Walt Disney World Resort: If you're staying at one of the Disney hotels affiliated with the Disney Cruise Line (Grand Floridian, Beach Club, Polynesian, Disney's Animal Kingdom Lodge, Swan, Dolphin, Port Orleans, and Caribbean Beach), you'll be instructed to set your luggage by the door for pick-up on the morning of your cruise. Around 10:00 am to 11:00 am, you meet in a central location in the resort and then proceed to the motorcoach, which generally leaves between 11:00 am and 11:45 am. You may have the option to depart from Disney's Animal Kingdom theme park the morning of your cruise, giving you an extra half-day in the park—inquire at the cruise desk at your resort (generally open from 8:00 am to noon daily).

Ground Transportation Worksheet

Use this worksheet to research, record, and plan your transportation to and from Port Canaveral.

Method	Price	Details	Reservation #
Disney Cruise Line Transfers: 800-395-9374			
Shuttle: Mears: 800-759-5219			
Town Car/Limo/ Van: Tiffany Town Car: 888-838-2161			
Rental Car: Avis: 800-230-4898 Budget: 800-404-8033 Hertz: 800-654-3131	(don't forget tolls)		

Scheduling Pick-Up and Departure Times

Allow 90 minutes to get to Port Canaveral from either Orlando Airport or Walt Disney World. Thus, if you hope to board the ship as soon as possible, a pick-up/departure time of 9:30 am or 10:00 am is good. If necessary, you could depart as late as 1:00 pm or 1:30 pm to reach Port Canaveral by 3:00 pm at the latest. For your return trip, the earliest you can expect to disembark the ship is 7:45 am to 8:30 am (and yes, you can still do the sit-down breakfast). It takes about 15 to 20 minutes to collect your bags and go through customs. Thus your pick-up/departure time could be set between 8:00 am and 9:15 am. We do not recommend you book a flight with a departure time before 11:30 am—a 1:00 pm or later flight would give you more breathing room.

Introduction

Reservations

Staterooms

Dining

Activities

Ports of Call

Magic

Index

Lodging Near Port Canaveral

You may want to take advantage of the visit to the "Space Coast" to squeeze in a trip to Kennedy Space Center or a day at the beach. Or perhaps you want to arrive in advance to avoid stress on the morning of your cruise. While there are many motels and hotels in the area, we've stayed at three (Radisson, Quality Suites, and Motel 6), all of which we recommend. We also detail three other hotels. To see the location of each, check the map on page 149.

▣ Radisson Resort at the Port $115+   2.7 mi/4.3 km to port

This 284-room luxury resort is the closest lodging to the Disney Cruise Line terminal and quite popular with cruisers. While it is not an oceanfront hotel, it does feature a themed pool (see photo at bottom), wading pool, hot tub, tennis, fitness center, room service, and 1- and 2-bedroom suites in addition to its standard, Caribbean-themed rooms (see photo at left). All

rooms have ceiling fans, TVs, coffeemakers, hair dryers, voice mail, and dataports. Suites add another TV and phone line, whirlpool tub, microwave, refrigerator, and walk-in showers. An on-site restaurant, Flamingos, is open from 6:30 am to 10:00 pm daily and serves American food, with Caribbean/ Floridian cuisine on Saturday nights and a champagne brunch on Sundays. Check-in time: 3:00 pm; check-out time: 12:00 pm. One notable feature is the complimentary shuttle between the

Our standard, king bed room at the Radisson

hotel and the port (make your shuttle reservation up to two weeks in advance). Note, however, that the Avis rental car office that used to be housed in the resort has moved about a mile down the road—the closest car rental office is now Budget. Special cruise prices allow you to park in their lot while you cruise. Great promotional rates are often available on the Internet for less than $100, but pay attention to the cancellation details as you may have to pay a $25 fee to cancel. Visit http://www.radisson.com/capecanaveralfl or call 321-784-0000. Address: 8701 Astronaut Boulevard, Cape Canaveral, FL 32920

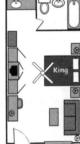

Typical floor plan

The beautiful, themed pool, complete with a waterfall and perching lioness and eagle

Quality Suites $89+ 6.1 mi/9.8 km to port

Quality Suites

Suite living room

This small, new, all-suite hotel offers 48 spacious rooms and reasonable rates. The two-room suites offer a living room with a queen sofa bed, kitchenette with sink, microwave, refrigerator, and coffeepot, TV, and phone, and in the bedroom a king bed (no double beds available), another TV, phone, and a desk. All rooms have hair dryers, iron and ironing board, and dataports. A free breakfast buffet (pastries, eggs, potatoes, bacon, cereal, and juice) is offered on the second floor. No on-site restaurant, but Taco Bell and Waffle House are next door. This hotel has no swimming

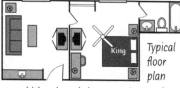

Typical floor plan

pool; it does have a large whirlpool, and the ocean is 300 feet away. Ron Jon Surf Shop is one block away. Free shuttle to the port—make a reservation at the desk the day before. Cruise parking packages are available, but you'll need to drive to and park at the Radisson. Check-in time: 3:00 pm; check-out time: 12:00 pm. For details, visit http://www.qualitysuitescocoabeach-portcanaveral.com or call 321-783-6868. 3655 N. Atlantic, Cocoa

Motel 6 Cocoa Beach $46+ 6.1 mi/9.8 km to port

The Motel 6 in Cocoa Beach has the lowest published rates in the area. The clean motel features an outdoor swimming pool, cable TV, and a laundry room. While there is no restaurant on-site, a Waffle House is within walking distance. This motel is also close to tourist attractions such as Ron Jon Surf Shop, and it's only one block from the beach. No shuttle is available to the port; expect to pay about $11 to $15 for a taxi. Check-in time: 2:00 pm; check-out time: 12:00 pm. Visit http://www.motel6.com or call 321-783-3103. Address: 3701 N. Atlantic Avenue, Cocoa Beach, FL 32931

Motel 6 room

Resort on Cocoa Beach $210+ 7.2 mi/11.6 km to port

Resort on Cocoa Beach

A gorgeous, 8-story beach resort within reasonable distance of the port. The 147-suite resort features two-bedroom "condominums" which sleep six with one king bed, two queen beds, and a sleeper sofa. Features include balconies, two bathrooms, full kitchens, two phone lines, two TVs, VCR, whirlpool tub, and washer/dryer. Resort amenities include beach access, outdoor pool with kid's water play area, sauna, hot tub, fitness center, playground, tennis and basketball courts, a 50-seat movie theater, and a drop-in childcare center. This is a true resort! An on-site restaurant, Mug's, is an ocean grill and sushi bar (open 11:00 am–10:00 pm daily). No shuttle is available to the port; expect to pay about $11-15 for a taxi. Check-in time: 4:00 pm; check-out time: 10:00 am. Visit http://www.vrivacations.com/resorts/rcb/index.html or call 800-352-4874. Address: 1600 N. Atlantic Avenue, Cocoa Beach, FL 32931

Introduction · Reservations · Staterooms · Dining · Activities · Ports of Call · Magic · Index

Lodging Near Port Canaveral (continued)

☐ Holiday Inn Express $130+   4.7 mi/7.5 km to port

Holiday Inn Express

This new hotel opened in late 2000, offering 60 guest rooms in a variety of family-friendly configurations. Beyond the standard queen bed and king bed rooms, Holiday Inn Express offers KidSuites with a separate room for the kids, Family Suites (for older kids or two couples traveling together), Romantic Suites with whirlpool tubs, and Executive Suites with workspace. All rooms have a microwave, refrigerator, coffeemaker, free high-speed Internet access, hair dryer, iron and ironing board, and free newspaper delivery. A free, continental breakfast is provided each morning. Amenities include an outdoor pool, whirlpool, and a fitness center ($3 fee), plus it is just two blocks from the beach. There is no on-site restaurant, but Durango Steakhouse and Perkins are nearby. You can take Art's Shuttle (http://www.artsshuttle.com, 800-567-5099) for $3/person to the cruise terminal. Check-in time: 3:00 pm; check-out: 11:00 am. For details ,visit http://www.hiexpress.com/es-cocoabeach or call 321-868-2525 (local) or 800-465-4329 (toll-free). Address: 5575 N. Atlantic, Cocoa Beach, FL 32931

☐ Ron Jon Cape Caribe Resort $100+   3.2 mi/5.2 km to port

January 2004 saw the opening of this new timeshare resort, which claims to be the closest oceanfront resort to Orlando (as well as to the port). You don't need to own a timeshare to stay here, however—anyone can rent one of the villas. Accommodations come in the form of studios (up to 4 people), one-bedroom (6 people), two-bedroom (8-10 people), and three-bedroom villas (12 people). All villas have a sitting or living room, whirlpool tub, refrigerator, microwave, and coffeemaker. The one-, two-, and three-bedroom villas add a balcony and full kitchen. Resort amenities include a "water park" with large heated pool, 248-ft. water slide, lazy river, and beach, plus an on-site restaurant, fitness center, children's play center, movie theater, miniature golf, and organized activities. This resort is 600 yards (about 3 blocks) from the beach, but it does provide a shuttle to the beach. At the time of writing, no shuttle is available to the port, though one may be added in the future; expect to pay about $9 to $12 for a taxi. Check-in time: 4:00 pm; check-out time: 10:00 am. Visit http://www.ronjonresort.com or call 888-933-3030. Address: 1000 Shorewood Drive, Cape Canaveral, FL 32920

Lodging in Orlando and at Walt Disney World

You may prefer to stay near the Orlando International Airport or even spend some time at Walt Disney World before or after your cruise. For Disney resorts and hotels nearby, we recommend you pick up a copy of PassPorter Walt Disney World Resort (see page 263)—it goes into great detail on Walt Disney World lodging. If you just want a hotel near the airport, a Hyatt Regency (407-825-1234) is located right inside the terminal but it is pricey ($164 and up). Instead, we recommend you shop around for an inexpensive hotel within a few miles of the airport. We've had great success with Priceline.com (http://www.priceline.com), where you can bid on hotels in particular areas. Last May, we got the Marriott Orlando Airport through Priceline.com for about $35. If you do decide to try Priceline.com, read the directions thoroughly, and keep in mind that once your bid is accepted, you can't cancel. We recommend you visit BiddingForTravel.com (http://www.biddingfortravel.com) for Priceline.com advice and tips. Another place to try for hotel deals is Hotwire.com at http://www.hotwire.com.

For more information and good rates on area lodging, visit http://www.travelocity.com. Excellent details on lodging can be found at http://www.dcltribute.com/lodging.

The Disney Cruise Line Terminal

Not content to use an existing, plain-Jane terminal for its cruise line, Disney had a **beautiful terminal** built to its exact specifications for $27 million. The Disney Cruise Line Terminal (terminal #8) is easily recognized by its 90-foot glass tower and art deco design. The terminal opens between 10:00 am and 10:30 am on cruise days for embarking passengers.

The cruise terminal

If you're driving to the terminal, a gated, fenced lot with 965 parking spaces is available across from the terminal for $10 per 24-hour period (vehicles over 20 ft. long pay $20/day). You'll need to **pay for parking up front** with cash, U.S. travelers checks, Visa, or MasterCard. The Canaveral Port Authority operates the parking and we know of no discounts. If you do not drop your luggage off curbside (see below), you can take it to one of the white tents in the parking lot. You may find it less expensive to rent a car, drive, return the car to a rental office in Port Canaveral, and catch a shuttle to the terminal than to park at the terminal. Warning: Ants are plentiful around here and may be attracted to food or crumbs in your car.

Security at the terminal is excellent. Have photo I.D.s for everyone in the car handy when you drive up. Guests and their luggage may be dropped off at the terminal curbside or the parking lot. A porter **collects all luggage** (tip $1 to $2/bag) except your carry-ons before you enter the terminal—luggage is scanned and delivered to your stateroom later, so be sure to attach those luggage tags. Security scans your carry-ons before you enter the terminal. Inside the terminal doors are escalators and an elevator that take you upstairs for check-in and embarkation. In the terminal, look down at the gorgeous, 13,000 sq. ft. terrazzo tile Bahamas map.

Plan to arrive before 1:00 pm. Ships are scheduled to leave at 5:00 pm, but they have left as early as 4:00 pm when weather dictated.

Address: 9150 Christopher Columbus Drive, Port Canaveral, FL 32920

Telephone: 321-868-1400

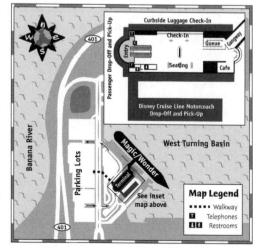

Check-In and Embarkation

If you're on a Disney land/sea vacation package, your check-in was completed when you checked in to your Walt Disney World resort hotel. Have your **Key to the World card and photo identification** out and proceed down the gangway (discussed on the next page).

If you've booked a cruise-only or made your hotel arrangements on your own, don't worry—the check-in/embarkation procedure is remarkably smooth, especially if you **fill out the cruise forms before arrival**. Check your Travel Booklet (which comes in your cruise document package—more on this on page 46) for the various forms to be completed in advance.

A total of 28 **check-in counters** are lined up along the left-hand side of the terminal as you enter. Check-in generally begins around 10:45 am or 11:00 am. If you are a member of the Castaway Club (see page 249), there's a special check-in counter at the far right end. Castaway Club members are encouraged to check in here, and the lines are sometimes a bit shorter.

Have your cruise travel booklets, photo identifications, birth certificates, naturalization certificates, and/or passports handy. If you've misplaced your immigration forms, you can get extra copies in the terminal. Be sure to bring **original or official documents**; no copies will be accepted.

Check-in takes about 10 minutes (you may spend more time in line). Once your forms are filed, you'll each get a **Key to the World card**, which is your identification/ charging card and room key for the duration of the cruise (see below). Keep this card with you at all times.

A Key to the World card

Your Key to the World Card and Money

In addition to being your stateroom key and boarding pass to the ship, your Key to the World card is also your shipboard charge card. Everything you buy on the ship will be charged to your card, even the game cards used for the arcade games in Quarter Masters—no other cards, cash, checks, or Disney Dollars can be used for purchases onboard. So go ahead and put your wallet in the stateroom safe, because you probably won't need it until you go off-ship. At check-in time, you'll be asked to put down a deposit of at least $500 with a credit card (any of those listed on page 46 work), traveler's checks, cash, or Disney Dollars. If your balance goes over the deposit amount, your credit card will be charged—if you aren't using a credit card, you'll be asked to come to Guest Services (Disney's version of a Purser's Office) on deck 3 mid to increase the deposit amount. Once you get your card, sign the back right away to use it—that bon voyage drink is calling! If you have kids cruising, you have the option of not activating their cards for charging. Guest Services can later remove charging privileges from your kids' card(s) if you'd like.

Midship with Mickey

Non-U.S. residents (including alien residents of the U.S.) have special check-in counters—look for the signs as you approach the counters. You will need to present your passport with any necessary visas at check-in to ensure that you can reenter the U.S. upon the ship's return. (Canadian citizens must also present a passport, according to Canada's Passport Office at http://www.ppt.gc.ca). If you live in a country that participates in the U.S. Visa Waiver Program (see http://travel.state.gov/vwp.html) and plan to be in the U.S. for 90 days or less, you don't need a visa, but you do need to present proof of return transport, proof of financial solvency, and a signed visa waiver arrival/departure form (I-94W form) that you get from your airline. For more information on visas, check with the U.S. consulate or embassy in your country (see http://usembassy.state.gov). Note that non-U.S. residents must surrender their passports at check-in; they will be returned upon disembarkation—see page 249. For this reason, you should bring extra forms of photo identification, which you will use when you leave and reenter the ship in your ports of call.

Embarkation usually begins between noon and 1:00 pm. A line forms in front of the 16 ft. (5 m.) high Mickey-shaped embarkation portal (see photo). Only one member of your party needs to stand in line to hold your place. While you're waiting to embark, you can relax on cushy sofas, watch Disney cartoons, and read the papers Disney gave you (usually a *Personal Navigator* or summary sheet). Around 11:00 am, Captain Mickey, Donald, or other characters may appear for photos and autographs. Be sure to visit the museum-quality, 20-foot-long model of the Disney Magic in the middle of the terminal. You'll also find a small cafe (R.E. Fresh's Gulf Steam Coffee Bar) inside the terminal if you just can't wait for your lunch buffet onboard—the cafe serves coffee ($2.25), tea ($2.25), hot cocoa ($3.50), espresso ($2.75–4.25), and pastries ($2.25). Look for more than 50 images of Mickey (both obvious and hidden) in and around the terminal! See the terminal map on page 59 to get your bearings before you arrive.

© MediaMarx, Inc.

Inside the Disney Cruise Line Terminal

When it's **your turn to board**, you'll present your Key to the World card, which is swiped through a card reader and handed back to you. If for some reason security didn't inspect your carry-ons before you entered the terminal, you'll have them checked here. That's it! You've made it! Proceed on down the gangway to the magic and wonder that await you.

Packing for Your Cruise

Some folks hear "cruise" and start packing enough clothes for an around-the-world tour. If you tend to overpack, a cruise is the best place to do it. Guests on land/sea vacations or ground transfers may only need to handle their luggage at the very start and end of their trip. But if you're combining your cruise with a stay in Florida without Disney's help, you'll appreciate having **less luggage**. The Disney Cruise Line limits each guest to two suitcases and one carry-on. Need help packing light? Visit http://www.travelite.org.

When you arrive at the terminal, luggage is collected and you won't see it again until later that day, when it's delivered to your stateroom (usually between 2:00 pm and 6:00 pm). Pack a **separate carry-on** (no larger than 22" x 14"/56 x 36 cm) with your identification, cruise documents, prescriptions, swimsuit, and a change of clothing in the event your luggage doesn't arrive by dinner. Keep this bag light as you may be carrying it around for a few hours. You'll also need this carry-on for your last night, when you place the rest of your luggage outside your stateroom by 11:00 pm for collection.

A word about your **personal documentation**: The Disney Cruise Line requires that all U.S. citizens have one of the following proofs of citizenship: valid U.S. passport, certified birth certificate (with a raised seal or multiple colors), or a certified naturalization certificate with photo I.D. Don't have your birth certificate? Order it at http://www.usbirthcertificate.net (see coupon on page 266). In addition to this, guests 17 and older should have photo identification, such as a driver's license or government photo I.D. We also recommend you bring a backup photo I.D. (such as a membership card) for emergencies.

When your cruise documentation arrives, you'll find two **luggage tags** for each individual, with your ship, name, stateroom, and departure date. Read your cruise documentation to find out if you should tag your luggage before or after you arrive at the terminal. In general, if you're not on a land/sea package or haven't booked Disney's ground transfer, don't tag your luggage until you arrive at the terminal. You wouldn't want your bags collected prematurely. Don't forget to I.D. every piece of luggage with your own tags, too (use http://www.passporter.com/wdw/luggagelog.htm).

Deciding what **clothing** to pack depends a bit on what time of year you're cruising and your itinerary. Cruises in the cooler months require a few more jackets and sweaters, while you'll want to be ready with raingear in the summer. Pack dress clothing for dinner (see page 93) regardless of your itinerary. Guests on the 7-night itineraries will want to add more dress clothing for the formal and semi-formal evenings (see page 238) as well as festive garb for the Tropicali-/Mexicalifragilistic evening. Guests on shorter cruises can get by with just one nice outfit.

Packing Tips

Our **packing list** on the next two pages is complete, but for an exhaustive list visit: http://www.geocities.com/Calgon1/Ultimate_Packing_List.html.

The air-conditioned public rooms on the ships can be **chilly**, as are the winds up on deck. Bring sweaters or jackets.

Pack comfortable **shoes** with non-slip rubber soles for walking around on deck and on shore. You'll also appreciate sandals and water shoes.

While room service is free, delivery is not immediate. If you need snacks on hand, bring packaged **snacks** like crackers or granola bars. You could also bring your own bottled water (it's pricey onboard), but the drinking water tastes fine to most. Note that Disney prohibits personal coolers onboard unless they are for medications, baby foods, or dietary needs. Ice buckets are provided in the staterooms, as are small refrigerators.

The health-conscious may want to consider a well-stocked **medicine kit**, as trips to the onboard infirmary cost you. Beyond the usual items, consider anti-nausea aids (see page 243), anti-diarrheal aids, sunblock, sunburn gel, and "Safe Sea," a sunblock that helps protect against the stinging of most jellyfish, sea lice, coral, and sea anemone (see http://www.nidaria.com).

Two-way radios can be handy for keeping in touch onboard—use the ones with extra subchannels. The radios won't work everywhere due to all the metal in the ship—they only seem to work up to a few decks away.

You can bring your own **stroller** or just borrow one free-of-charge at Guest Services onboard and/or at Castaway Cay (first come, first served). Wheelchairs can also be borrowed free-of-charge.

Unlike many other cruises, you can bring your own **alcohol** onboard to save money on drinks. Beer and wine are the best items to bring; you can usually buy hard liquor for great prices on the islands. Note that you won't be able to bring opened bottles home with you at the end of the cruise.

Worried about **lost or delayed luggage**? Don't pack all your items in one bag. Instead, split items between bags. Couples can pack half their things in their suitcases and half in their partner's suitcases to be safe.

Knives, pocket tools, and other **potential weapons** are prohibited onboard. All luggage is inspected prior to boarding, and confiscated items will be held until you return to port. This can seriously delay the arrival of your luggage to your room.

Introduction   Reservations   Staterooms   Dining   Activities   Ports of Call   Magic   Index

Packing List

Packing for a cruise is fun when you feel confident you're packing the right things. Over the years, we've compiled a packing list for a great Disney cruise vacation. Just note the quantity you plan to bring and check them off as you pack. Consider packing items in **bold** in your carry-on.

The Essentials

☐ Casual, nice clothing for daytime and late-night wear
___ Shorts ___ Long pants ___ Shirts ___ Skirts/dresses
___ Underwear (lots!) ___ Socks ___ Pajamas ___ Robes

☐ Jacket and/or sweater (light ones for the warmer months)
___ **Jackets** ___ Sweatshirts ___ Sweaters ___ Vests

☐ Formal and semi-formal clothing for special evenings
___ Suits and ties ___ Dresses ___ Jewelry ___ Tropical dress

☐ Comfortable, well-broken-in shoes, sandals, and dress shoes
___ Walking shoes ___ Sandals ___ Dress shoes ___ _____

☐ Swim wear and gear (regular towels are provided)
___ **Suits/trunks** ___ **Cover-ups** ___ Water shoes ___ Goggles

☐ Sun protection (the Caribbean sun can be brutal) ☞
___ **Sunblock** ___ **Lip balm** ___ **Sunburn relief** ___ **Sunglasses**
___ **Hats w/brims** ___ **Caps** ___ **Visors** ___ _____

☐ Rain gear 🐌 (for your port excursions)
___ Raincoat ___ Poncho ___ Umbrella ___ _____

☐ Comfortable bags with padded straps to carry items in port
___ Backpacks ___ Waist packs ___ Shoulder bags ___ **Camera bag**

☐ Toiletries ✂ (in a bag or bathroom kit to keep them organized)
___ **Brush/comb** ___ **Toothbrush** ___ **Toothpaste** ___ Dental floss
___ Favorite soap, shampoo, & conditioner ___ Deodorant ___ Baby wipes
___ **Anti-nausea aids** and **pain relievers** ___ **Band aids** ___ **First aid kit**
___ **Prescriptions** (in original containers) ___ Vitamins ___ Fem. hygiene
___ Makeup ___ Hairspray ___ Cotton swabs ___ Curling iron
___ Razors ___ Shaving cream ___ Nail clippers ___ Spare glasses
___ Lens solution ___ Safety pins ___ Bug repellent ___ Insect sting kit
___ Mending kit ___ Small scissors ___ Ear plugs ___ _____

☐ Camera/camcorder and more film 🖊 than you think you need
___ **Cameras** ___ **Camcorder** ___ **Film/batteries** ___ **Memory cards**

☐ Money in various forms and various places
___ **Charge cards** ___ **Travelers checks** ___ **Bank cards** ___ **Cash**

☐ Personal identification, passes, and membership cards
___ **Documents** ___ **Birth certificates** ___ **Drivers' licenses** ___ **Passports**
___ **AAA card** ___ **Travel perks cards** ___ Discount cards ___ Air miles card
___ **Other I.D.s** ___ **Insurance cards** ___ **Calling cards** ___ SCUBA cert.

Tip: Label everything with your name, phone, and stateroom to help reunite you with your stuff if lost. Every bag should have this info on a tag as well as on a slip of paper inside it. Use our Luggage Tag Maker at http://www.passporter.com/wdw/luggagelog.htm.

For Your Carry-On

❑ **PassPorter, cruise documentation, ground/air confirmations, multiple photo I.D.s (driver's licenses, passports), birth certificates,** and a **pen/pencil!** ✏
Remember not to pack any sharp or potentially dangerous items in your carry-on.
❑ **Camera** and/or **camcorder,** along with **film** and **batteries**
❑ Any **prescription medicines, important toiletries, sunblock, sunglasses, hats**
❑ **Change of clothes,** including **swimwear** and **dress clothes** for dinner
❑ **Snacks,** ✿ **water bottle, juice boxes, gum, books, toys, games**
❑ **PassHolder Pouch** for passports, I.D.s, cash, etc. (see page 262)

For Families

❑ **Snacks** and **juice boxes**
❑ **Books, toys,** 🎲 and **games**
❑ **Familiar items from home** 🧸
❑ **Stroller** and accessories
❑ **Autograph books** and **fat pens**

For Couples

❑ **Champagne** for your send-off
❑ Wine and favorite adult beverages
❑ Portable CD player, speakers, and CDs
❑ Good beach novels
❑ Massage oil

For Connected Travelers

❑ **Handheld/Palm organizer**
❑ Laptop, cables, extension cord
❑ Chargers
❑ GPS system or compass
❑ Security cable with lock
❑ **Cell phones** and/or **two-way radios**

For Heat-Sensitive Travelers

❑ **Personal fan/water misters**
❑ **Water bottles**
❑ Loose, breezy clothing
❑ **Hats** with wide brims
❑ **Elastics** to keep long hair off neck
❑ Sweatbands

Everyone Should Consider

❑ **Penlight** or flashlight (for reading/writing in dark places)
❑ Battery-operated alarm with illuminated face and nightlight (or just open the closet)
❑ Earplugs, sound machine, or white-noise generator (for noisy staterooms)
❑ **Water bottles** and personal **fans/water misters**
❑ Plastic storage bags that seal (large and small) and plastic cutlery for snacks ✂
❑ Address book, envelopes, and stamps (with numeric denominations) ✉
❑ Laundry detergent/tablets, bleach, dryer sheets, stain stick, and wrinkle remover
❑ **Binoculars** and a **soft-sided, insulated tote** for going ashore
❑ Currency exchange calculator or card (if you'll be doing a lot of shopping)
❑ Collapsible bag or suitcase inside another suitcase to hold souvenirs on your return
❑ **Small bills** and **coins** for tipping and quarters for laundry
❑ Photo mailers or large envelope with cardboard inserts (for safeguarding photos)
❑ **Highlighters** (multiple colors for each person to mark activities in your *Personal Navigator*)
❑ Closet organizer (the kind used to hold shoes) to store small items and avoid clutter
❑ **Sticky notes** (to leave your fellow cabinmates messages)
❑ Plenty of **batteries** (and don't forget the charger if you're using rechargeables)
❑ An electrical power strip if you'll need extra outlets for lots of chargers
❑ Something to carry your small items, such as a **PassHolder Pouch** or evening bag

Our Personal Packing List

❑ _____   ❑ _____
❑ _____   ❑ _____
❑ _____   ❑ _____

Adventuring!

Here are our tried-and-true cruise traveling tips:

- In light of our security-conscious culture, we recommend you bring **more than one photo I.D.** in the event you lose one. Membership cards (such as Sam's Club) with your photo work fine as a backup. Leave your backup I.D. in your in-room safe.

- "Travel delays can happen to anyone. A cancelled flight, bad weather, or mechanical problems can cause a cruiser to panic. You can avoid the worry if you arrive in central Florida **the day before** your ship sails. There are numerous hotels surrounding the Orlando International Airport, and good deals may be found by checking the hotel web sites or by making an offer at http://www.priceline.com. If you arrive early enough, you can travel to Port Canaveral or Cocoa Beach where some of the hotels offer free parking and shuttles to the Disney terminal. Enjoy an evening on the beach then head over to the ship to begin your cruise. What could be better?"– by contributing author Mickey Morgan

- "If you want to use a soft-sided cooler at one of your ports, make it useful. For boarding/embarkation day, pack it with clothes/swimsuits for immediate use (so you don't have to wait on your suitcases). Then when it's time to leave, pack it with all your new purchases so you have no wasted space." – contributed by Disney cruiser Amanda Poole

- "If you're driving, look for the Ron Jon Surf Shop billboards along the Florida highways—they countdown the mileage remaining to their store, which isn't far from the terminal." – contributed by Dave Huiner

Magical Memories

- "My family of six (2 adults, 4 children) stayed at the Radisson at the Port before our December 2003 cruise. Their king whirlpool suite was the greatest! It was so nice to have room to rest and relax before the trip, and the two king-size beds (plus a sleeper sofa in the living room) made sleeping arrangements the best we've ever had in one accommodation. We could easily picture staying there for a longer stay."
  ...as told by Disney cruiser Karen Koonce

- "For our MouseFest 2003 cruise, my family (mother, sister, brother-in-law, sister-in-law, and two nieces) decided to join Dave and me. We met at our house around 5:00 am to take a taxi to the airport. I surprised my family by reserving a stretch limousine instead! When it showed up in our driveway that morning, everyone was so shocked! We snacked on doughnuts and felt like stars. It was the perfect way to begin our trip!"
  ...as told by Jennifer Watson

Staying in Style in a Stateroom

Style is, indeed, the operative word for Disney Cruise Line staterooms. Every stateroom, regardless of its price, category, or location onboard, is resplendent in warm, natural woods, luxurious fabrics, imported tile, nautical touches, and dramatic lighting. Robert Tillberg, esteemed naval architect, worked with Disney to design the stateroom interiors with more storage space and the innovative split bathrooms available in categories 10 and up. Unlike many other ships, 73% of the staterooms have an ocean view, while 44% of all rooms have private verandahs. Better yet, staterooms on Disney ships have the "luxury of space"—they are substantially larger (up to 25%) than those on many other ships. Many cruise industry insiders consider Disney Cruise Line staterooms to be among the best afloat. You'll actually enjoy being in your stateroom!

Every stateroom has a generous queen-size bed that can be converted to two twin beds, ample closet space, shower/tub combination (or roll-in showers in the handicap-accessible rooms), hair dryer, desk/vanity, phone with voice mail, safe, color TV with remote, small refrigerator, individual climate controls, and room service. Most staterooms also have a sitting area with a sofa that converts into a twin bed, and many also have a pull-down single berth. A curtain separates the sleeping area from the sitting area. Staterooms sleep 2–7 guests, though most sleep 3–4. Staterooms are located on decks 1-2 and 5-8, all of which are above the waterline. Crew quarters are on decks A and B, which are off-limits to guests.

Choosing your stateroom is one of the first things you'll do after you decide to cruise, so we put this chapter before dining and playing. We recommend you read this chapter in conjunction with chapter 2 before you make your cruise reservations. This will ensure you make the best possible choice in staterooms. Different stateroom categories offer different amenities, and there are some special rooms and decks that have an added benefit or two. The ship will be your home away from home for several days. Stateroom changes and upgrades are rarely available once you board, as the ships often sail completely full.

Selecting Your Stateroom

The Disney Cruise Line offers 12 different categories of staterooms on both the Disney Magic and the Disney Wonder. You'll need to specify a category when you make your cruise line reservation, so it is important to know as much as possible about each one in advance.

The most obvious difference between categories is **price**. Category 1 is the priciest, while category 12 is the least expensive. Price may be your only determining factor, and if so, we encourage you to check the current cruise category rates at http://www.disneycruise.com or in your Disney Cruise Line booklet. You can find typical rates on page 42.

Beyond price, we can combine the stateroom **categories** into four groups: outside stateroom suites with verandahs (1-3), outside staterooms with verandahs (4-7), outside staterooms with portholes (8-9), and inside staterooms (10-12). We devote one overview page to each of these four groups, plus one page of delightful detail for each category.

The Disney Cruise Line may offer different "categories," but old-fashioned "classes" are a relic of the past. If you choose a category 12 stateroom, you won't be made to feel like you're in a lower class than any other passenger. You will have **access to all facilities** on your ship and dine in the same style, regardless of your category. We booked our first cruise in a category 12 and never once felt funny about it. (We were later upgraded to category 9, which we loved. For more on upgrades, see page 87.) Guests on a land/sea package stay at different hotels based on their category, however (see chart on the next page). If you want to stay in a nicer hotel, you may be able to upgrade for an additional charge—inquire when reserving.

Another deciding factor may simply be **availability**. This is particularly true of the higher and lower category staterooms, which are in shorter supply. You can find out what categories are available before you make a decision by calling Disney at 888-325-2500. To learn how to check specific stateroom availability, see page 74. Note that you may get a "guaranteed category" rather than a specific stateroom. This tends to happen when all of the staterooms in a certain category are booked. A guaranteed category means you're guaranteed a room in that category or higher. Guaranteed category guests do occasionally get upgraded.

Each class of stateroom offers its own **charms and drawbacks**. Check our chart of stateroom pros and cons on the next page for an overview of the staterooms, and then turn the page for a more in-depth look.

Staterooms Side-by-Side

Charms and Delights	Cons and Drawbacks
Outside Stateroom Suites With Verandahs (categories 1-3)	
Huge staterooms, two with room for up to 7 people. Total separation of sleeping and sitting areas. VCRs, CD players, walk-in closets, wet bars, and some whirlpool tubs. Extra-long verandahs. Concierge and expanded room service. Guests with land/sea packages stay at the Grand Floridian Resort & Spa.	Very expensive and deals are almost never offered on the suites (although per-guest cost is good if you fill the suite to capacity). Very popular and are usually booked long in advance. There are only 22 suites on the entire ship (all on deck 8). Most category 3 staterooms have the pull-down bed in the master bedroom.
Outside Staterooms With Verandahs (categories 4-7)	
Verandahs! It's like having a private deck to watch waves or gaze at passing islands. And the wall-to-wall glass adds light and a sense of extra space. Located on decks 5-8, which are the most convenient. One category (4) sleeps 4-5; the others sleep 3-4. Staterooms are 268-304 sq. ft. Guests with land/sea packages stay at Disney's deluxe resorts, such as the Beach Club.	Still on the pricey side, and may be out-of-range for many vacationers. Sitting and sleeping areas are in same room. Category 5-7 layouts and square area are identical to those in categories 8-9. Verandahs on deck 5 are slightly more shallow than on decks 6-8. Wind and/or bad weather can make the verandah unusable. Category 7 sleeps only three.
Outside Staterooms With Portholes (categories 8-9)	
Portholes! Some natural sunlight and the ability to see where you are (i.e., already docked in port!) are real blessings. These staterooms are also more affordable. Some rooms sleep up to four guests. Category 8 and 9 staterooms feature split bathrooms (unlike category 11 and 12 staterooms). Provides the same access to the ship as higher categories. Portholes on decks 2 and up are picture-window sized.	No verandahs. Category 9 rooms are on decks 1 and 2, which aren't as convenient as the higher decks. And while category 8 staterooms are on decks 5-7, they aren't in the most desirable of spots, being all located forward in the ship. Sitting and sleeping areas are in the same room, and rooms are smaller at 214 sq. ft. Guests with land/sea packages stay at Disney's moderate resorts, along with category 10-12 guests.
Inside Staterooms (categories 10-12)	
The least expensive staterooms available. Some rooms sleep up to 4. Category 10 has the same square footage as categories 8-9. Some category 10-11 staterooms are on decks 5-7. Six staterooms in category 10 actually have an obstructed porthole (bonus!). Same access to the ship as higher categories. Guests with land/sea packages stay at Disney's moderate resorts, such as Port Orleans or Caribbean Beach Resort.	No windows, making your stateroom seem small, slightly claustrophobic, and dark. Smaller room size (184 sq. ft.) for categories 11-12. Category 12 rooms sleep no more than three guests. All staterooms in category 12 are on deck 2, and there are only 13 staterooms in this category (making them hard to get). Categories 11 and 12 don't have split bathrooms (see explanation on page 80).

Introduction

Reservations

Staterooms

Dining

Activities

Ports of Call

Magic

Index

Outside Stateroom Suites
(categories 1, 2, and 3)

The most luxurious of the ship's staterooms, these suites (all located on deck 8) offer virtually every convenience. All feature extra-large verandahs, VCRs, CD players, dining areas, wet bars, walk-in closets, bathrobes and slippers, marble bathrooms, plus concierge and expanded room service.

AMENITIES

Suite guests may get **perks** like priority boarding, a separate waiting area in the terminal, a special planning meeting once you're aboard, a private party with the Captain, personalized stationary, and some special surprise gifts. You can also request water and soda for your stateroom at no extra cost. All suites come with **concierge service**. You'll have help making arrangements for Palo, childcare, and Vista Spa, and they'll help with other special requests. You can borrow from a library of videos, CDs, and games (board and electronic)—check the concierge book in your stateroom for a list. And the crew often adds goodies, such as a fruit basket or cookies. Suite guests also get **expanded room service**, meaning you can order a full breakfast in the mornings (same menu as Lumiere's/Triton's breakfast menu—see page 96) and order a full dinner from one of the restaurants at dinner—menus are available from your concierge, or check our menus in chapter 4. Suite guests can also book massages in their staterooms or on their verandahs.

TIPS & NOTES

The suites are extremely popular; if you do not book one far in advance, expect to be put on a waiting list.

Guests with land/sea packages have **first pick of suites**; any suites available 30 days before sailing can be booked by all. No restrictions are placed on the 7-night cruise suites.

The meeting with the concierge staff on your first afternoon is important, as it gives you **priority booking service** for shore excursions, spa treatments, Palo reservations, children's programming, and babysitting. Plan to have at least one member of your party attend.

Suite guests may request a regular **hand-held blow dryer**.

While some lucky guests in the suites may be **invited to dine** with the Captain, this isn't a given.

Did you know? Suite guests have **gold Key to the World cards**, not blue/purple like others.

Category 1 Staterooms

(Walter E. and Roy O. Disney Suites—sleep 7 guests)

The two **category 1 suites**, known as the Walter E. Disney Suite and the Roy O. Disney Suite, are the height of cruising. The 1,029 sq. ft. (95 sq. m.) suites luxuriate with warm, exotic woods, two bedrooms, 2 ½ bathrooms, whirlpool tub, a media library with a pull-down bed, a baby grand piano (Walter suite only), and a quadruple-wide verandah. Sleep up to seven.

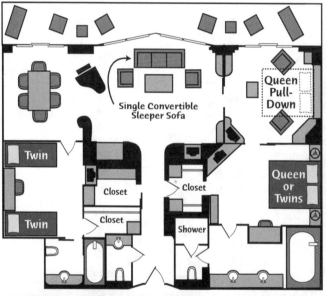

Single Convertible Sleeper Sofa

Queen Pull-Down

Twin

Closet

Closet

Twin

Closet

Shower

Queen or Twins

Entryway

The baby grand in the Walter E. Disney suite

A view from the media library into the bedroom in the Walter E. Disney suite

Jennifer enjoys the quadruple-wide verandah of a category 1 suite

Introduction · Reservations · Staterooms · Dining · Activities · Ports of Call · Magic · Index

Category 2 Staterooms
(Two-Bedroom Suite—sleeps 7 guests)

The **category 2** suites (at 945 sq. ft./88 sq. m.) have two bedrooms, 2½ baths, a whirlpool tub, and a triple-wide verandah. There are just two of these suites onboard, and both sleep up to seven.

Note: Categories 1 and 2 can sleep up to seven guests, but the sixth and seventh guests will require booking an additional resort hotel room at an extra cost (for those on land/sea packages).

Tip: Connecting rooms are great for larger groups. Many of the category 3 suites have connecting doors to a category 3 or 4, which holds four to five more guests. Alas, the category 1 and 2 suites do not have connecting staterooms.

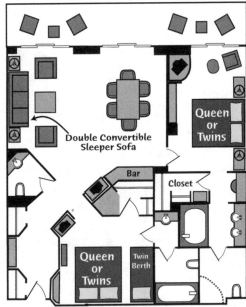

Double Convertible Sleeper Sofa

Queen or Twins

Bar

Closet

Queen or Twins

Twin Berth

The triple-wide verandah of a category 2 suite

A category 2 bedroom

The entertainment center

© MediaMarx, Inc.

Category 3 Staterooms
(One Bedroom Suite—sleeps 4-5 guests)

The 18 stateroom suites in **category 3** (614 sq. ft./57 sq. m.) offer a bedroom separate from the living room and dining room, two baths, a double-size convertible sofa in the living room, and a double-wide verandah. Most category 3 suites have a pull-down twin bed in the bedroom (as shown on the layout). Four suites (#8032, #8034, #8532, and #8534) have a slightly

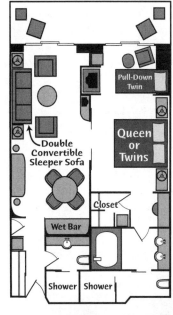

different layout with a bit more floor space and feature the pull-down twin bed in the living room, which guests find more convenient—these four suites are under the Goofy Pool, however, and are noisier. Suites #8100, #8102, #8600, and #8602 are handicap-accessible and have deeper verandahs. Category 3 suites sleep four to five guests (see chart on pages 88–89 to see which suites sleep only four).

A category 3 bedroom

© MediaMarx, Inc.

© MediaMarx, Inc.

Dave relaxes in the living room of stateroom 8034 (different layout than pictured above)

Outside Staterooms With Verandahs
(categories 4, 5, 6, and 7)

Welcome to the luxury of a private verandah at just a fraction of the cost of the higher categories! Staterooms with verandahs (categories 4-7) comprise the largest percentage of the ship's staterooms at a whopping 42%, and all have split baths (see page 80). All are located on decks 5-7.

AMENITIES

The main amenity in categories 4-7 is the verandah (balcony). Not only does the verandah offer fresh air and a gorgeous view, but it extends the space of your stateroom considerably. The option to sit outside and enjoy a sunset or read a book while someone else watches TV or sleeps inside is a huge bonus. Verandahs in categories 4-6 are open to the air, covered, and have privacy dividers. Category 7 staterooms (same size as categories 5 and 6) have either a slightly obstructed view from the verandah, or a Navigator's Verandah, which offers more privacy by hiding the verandah behind a large, glassless "porthole" (see photos on page 77). All verandahs have exterior lighting that is controlled by an on/off switch inside the stateroom. All the verandah staterooms can sleep at least three guests, and most category 4 rooms sleep up to five guests. See the chart on pages 88–89 for more specific room capacities.

Verandah with plexiglass railing

Verandah with metal railing

Most verandahs have a clear, plexiglass-covered railing (shown in the first photo). Others have a solid, metal railing (as shown in the second photo). There are fans of both styles, though we personally prefer the clear railings.

Which Staterooms Are Available for My Cruise?

Most guests let Disney or their travel agent select their stateroom. If you'd rather have a specific stateroom, find out which staterooms are available by calling Disney (888-325-2500). If you have Internet access, get online and visit Travelocity.com (http://www.travelocity.com)—follow the directions to choose your cruise, then continue through the windows to check rates and to see any availabilities. If you have your heart set on a particular stateroom, call Disney or check the Internet to find a cruise with that room available. When you make your reservations, indicate the exact stateroom you want. Confirm that the stateroom you requested is printed in your travel booklet when it arrives.

Category 4 Staterooms

(Deluxe Family With Verandah—sleeps 4–5 guests)

Category 4 is the Deluxe Family Stateroom, which sleeps up to four or five guests (304 sq. ft./28 sq. m.). The room has a pull-down twin bed for the fifth guest, along with a convertible twin sofa bed, a pull-down twin berth, and a queen-size bed that can be separated into twin beds. The 80 **category 4** family staterooms are all up on deck 8. Avoid staterooms directly below the Goofy Pool (#8036–8044 and #8536–8544) due to noise during deck parties. Note that staterooms #8092–8094 and #8596–8698 have a solid railing, rather than a plexiglass railing. Access to the verandah is limited when you have the twin bed pulled down.

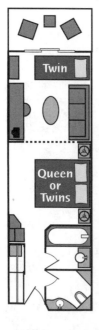

Squidgy the teddy bear naps in a category 4 stateroom (8544)

Desk/vanity area in category 4 stateroom

Another view of category 4

Category 5 & 6 Staterooms

(Deluxe Stateroom With Verandah—sleeps 3-4 guests)

Categories 5 and 6 are the Deluxe Staterooms With Verandahs. These staterooms are identical to category 4 (see previous page) except they are 268 sq. ft. (25 sq. m.), sleep three to four guests, do not have the extra pull-down twin bed, and are missing a handy bench across from the bed. The 114 **category 5** staterooms are located on deck 7, mostly midship and aft. Staterooms to the aft have quick access to a secluded public deck. Staterooms #7130–7138 and #7630–7638 have a solid, four-foot metal railing (as opposed to the plexiglass railing on other verandahs), but the verandahs may be deeper and quieter, too. Avoid #7590 as it is across from a laundry room. **Category 6** staterooms number 138 and are situated on decks 5 and 6. We recommend deck 6 for its slightly larger verandahs. Avoid #6588 as it is across from a laundry room. Staterooms #5142–5150, #5642–5650, #6144–6154, and #6644–6654 have a solid railing.

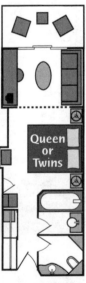

Queen or Twins

© MediaMarx, Inc.

© MediaMarx, Inc.

Verandah at sunset   *Jennifer enjoys the verandah in our category 5 stateroom (7618)*

Category 7 Staterooms
(Navigator's Verandah—sleeps 3 guests)

There are only 30 **category 7** staterooms, of which 26 are Navigator's Verandahs (enclosed verandah with open-air porthole). All are located on the quietest decks: 5, 6, and 7. We recommend deck 7 for its easy access to the public deck to the aft. Note that the verandahs on deck 5 are a bit shallower at 42" (106 cm.) than those on upper decks at about 48" (122 cm.). We noticed this on our May 2002 cruise when we compared our verandah to that of a friend's. Note that four of the category 7 staterooms (#6134, #6634, #7120, and #7620) were originally category 5 and 6 staterooms—they have plexiglass railings and partially obstructed views due to the hull design, and their verandahs aren't enclosed like the other category 7 rooms.

Disney Magic
Navigator's
Verandah

Disney Wonder
Navigator's
Verandah

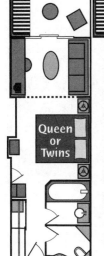

Note that the Navigator's Verandah on the Disney Wonder sports a larger porthole while the Magic's is a bit smaller. Both have a built-in, padded bench, a chair, and a small table.

Queen
or
Twins

Our category 7 stateroom was cozy and comfortable

The enclosed navigator's verandah

Dave loves the built-in bench

Introduction
Reservations
Staterooms
Dining
Activities
Ports of Call
Magic
Index

Outside Staterooms With Portholes
(categories 8 and 9)

Affordable elegance is yours if you choose a porthole over a verandah. As one of the most popular categories for cruisers, these rooms make up 27% of the staterooms onboard. They're located on decks 1, 2, 5, 6, and 7.

AMENITIES

The only real differences between these two categories are location and price—category 8 staterooms are on higher decks and cost more, while category 9 staterooms are lower in both regards. Their floor space and room layouts are identical. Both categories are considered "deluxe," which simply means they have the split bath (see page 80). Both are approximately 214 sq. ft. (20 sq. m.) and feature the sitting area in the rear of the stateroom. The natural light of the porthole is a real bonus over inside staterooms, especially for kids. We've included the layout for these staterooms on the next page.

© MediaMarx, Inc.

Our category 9 stateroom had lots of light

Note that the portholes on deck 1 differ from those on the higher decks. Photographs of the two different styles of portholes are shown below. We've stayed in rooms with both types, and we prefer the larger porthole.

© MediaMarx, Inc.

Deck 1 portholes

© MediaMarx, Inc.

Deck 2 and up porthole

Category 8 & 9 Staterooms
(sleep 2-4)

There are only 60 **category 8 staterooms**, scattered among decks 5-7 forward. This is due to the hull design of the ship, which features portholes rather than verandahs near the ship's bow. Staterooms on deck 5 are convenient to the kid's clubs. The fact that these staterooms are directly over the Walt Disney Theatre shouldn't be a problem—you aren't likely to be in your room during a show. Staterooms on decks 6 and 7 are excellent, by all accounts. Note that two category 8 rooms are handicap-accessible (#6000 and #6500). **Category 9 staterooms** are limited to decks 1 and 2. In general, we don't recommend deck 1 because it only has access to the forward and midship elevators and stairs, making it harder to get around. Additionally, staterooms #1030–1037 are fairly noisy on port days, which may be bothersome. Perhaps more importantly, the outside staterooms on deck 1 have two small portholes, rather than the one large porthole found on the other decks. We stayed in stateroom #1044 (deck 1) on our first cruise and liked it well enough, but we much prefer the staterooms we've had on deck 2. That said, there are certainly some staterooms which are better than others on deck 2. Due to fairly constant noise and vibration, we recommend you avoid these staterooms: #2000-2004, #2036-2044, #2078-2096, #2114-2129, #2140-2152, #2500-2508, #2586-2600, #2626, and #2630-2653. Unless you need connecting rooms, we recommend you avoid them (38 of the 177 category 9 staterooms are connecting) due to noise from the connecting stateroom. Our family stayed in rooms #2610-2616 on one cruise and we loved them—quiet and convenient (near the aft elevators and stairs).

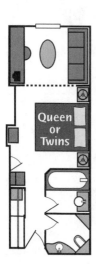

© MediaMarx, Inc.

Relaxing in our category 8 stateroom with a porthole (#7514)

Inside Staterooms
(categories 10, 11, and 12)

Resplendent with the same luxurious decor found in the other staterooms, inside staterooms are just smaller and more affordable versions of the higher-category staterooms. Inside staterooms make up 29% of the staterooms onboard and are located on decks 1, 2, 5, 6, and 7 (all above the waterline).

AMENITIES

Inside staterooms come in three price categories, but in only two layouts—categories 11 and 12 have identical layouts. Category 10 is the Deluxe Inside Stateroom and is 214 sq. ft. (20 sq. m.) with a split bath (see below). Categories 11 and 12 are the Standard Inside Staterooms at 184 sq. ft. (17 sq. m.). Beyond the size and the split bath, there's little difference. All three categories of staterooms put the sitting area before the sleeping area, presumably because without a window there's no need to have the sitting area at the farthest end of the stateroom. One notable difference between category 10 and 11/12 is the orientation of the bed (see room layout diagrams on following pages). It is also important to note that none of the staterooms in categories 11/12 have connecting rooms, while many of the category 10 staterooms are connecting. The lack of a connecting door makes for a subtle difference in room layout.

The split bathroom found in category 10 (as well as 4-9) is convenient for families.

The toilet/sink room *The shower/tub/sink room*

The one-room bathroom in categories 11 and 12 is much more compact. We show two views: a regular bathroom and a handicapped bathroom.

A category 11/12 bathroom *A cat. 11 handicapped bathroom*

Category 10 Staterooms
(Deluxe Inside Stateroom—sleeps 4 guests)

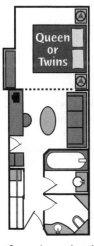

Queen or Twins

Inside staterooms are scattered over five decks of the ship. The 96 **category 10 staterooms** occupy four decks: 1, 2, 5, and 7. The staterooms on deck 1 are our least favorite because the corridor doesn't run the entire length of the deck, making it harder to reach destinations in the aft of the ship. Many of the staterooms on deck 2 are immediately below noisy places. To avoid noises from above, try for odd-numbered staterooms between #2071-2075, #2571-2575, #2101-2111, #2601-2611, #2629-2635, and #2129-2135. We also recommend the staterooms on deck 7. You should also note that almost half of the category 10 staterooms have connecting rooms, unlike the category 11 and 12 staterooms, which have none. Get a category 10 if you're traveling with a large family or friends and want connecting rooms.

If you have booked only one stateroom, however, our advice is to avoid these connecting rooms. Many cruisers have reported that the connecting doors do not dampen noise well. Try to swing a category 10 on deck 5 (#5020, #5022, #5024, #5520, #5522, or #5524) with a partially obstructed, "secret" porthole—see the next page for details. All category 10 staterooms sleep up to four guests.

© MediaMarx, Inc.

A cat. 10 inside stateroom with a round mirror on the far wall

Outside or Inside Stateroom?

Midship with Mickey

No longer does your stateroom class determine your cruise experience. Now, once guests leave their staterooms, the cruise is nearly identical to all. So, is it worth the extra expense to book the outside stateroom? That extra space in the outside stateroom would be nice to have while getting ready for the evening. And who wouldn't like to sit out on the verandah, sipping coffee first thing in the morning or enjoy a nightcap while the luminescent wake glows under the brilliant stars? But is it worth it? The outside staterooms cost more. That precious cruise money can be spent on an unforgettable excursion, on that necklace in the window in Nassau, or even on a few more Drinks of the Day. Besides, who wants to spend a lot of time in the stateroom when there's so much to do all over the ship, regardless of your stateroom class? I'm not recommending one over the other—you'll have to decide for yourself. But either way, I think you'll enjoy it!

Special Category 10 Staterooms
("Secret Porthole"–sleeps 4 guests)

Six of the category 10 staterooms (see previous page) have a different layout–and a porthole! Now before you get too excited, the porthole has an obstructed view (see photo below), but most cruisers are delighted with these "secret porthole rooms." We've included the layout for these special staterooms below as well–they were once category 9 staterooms, but were later reclassified as category 10 because of the obstructions. These six special category 10 staterooms are all located on deck 5 (#5020, #5022, #5024, #5520, #5522, or #5524), and all sleep up to four guests.

Getting one of these special category 10 staterooms can be difficult. You can simply try calling The Disney Cruise Line or your travel agent to see if one of these staterooms (use the stateroom numbers noted above) are

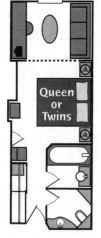

available for your cruise. If your cruise is still some time away and you haven't yet booked it, you can use the Internet to find out which staterooms are still available for your cruise–then if you find that one of these coveted secret porthole staterooms is available, book that cruise. See page 74 to learn which staterooms are still available for your cruise.

If you're considering a "secret porthole" stateroom but aren't sure how you feel about the obstructed view, we refer you to the excellent Platinum Castaway Club web site (http://www.castawayclub.com), which has photos of each of the six "secret portholes" so you can judge for yourself. Just click on the "Secret Porthole Rooms" link in the left column to get the photos and a list of pros and cons to help you make your decision.

A "secret porthole" stateroom (#5024)   Another view of this category

© MediaMarx, Inc.

Category 11 & 12 Staterooms

(Standard Inside Stateroom—sleeps 3-4 guests)

The 147 **category 11 staterooms** are located on decks 5, 6, and 7, making them convenient to many destinations within the ship. We recommend the aft staterooms due to their convenience to food and relative quiet. Families with young children may prefer a stateroom on deck 5 for quick access to the movie theater and Oceaneer Club/Lab. Aft staterooms on deck 7 are just down the hall from a secluded, public deck. Category 11 staterooms are also the only ones in this group to offer handicap-accessible rooms (#6147, #6647, #7131, and #7631—see photos below). Staterooms #6002, #6004, #6502, and #6504 are on the ship's outer side, but they have no portholes.

A handicap-accessible, category 11 inside stateroom (6647)

Another view of stateroom 6647, a handicap-accessible category 11 room

Category 12 staterooms (all 13 of them) are on deck 2 forward. While the staterooms closer to the elevators and stairs are convenient, they are also noisier (they are directly below Beat Street/Route 66). Request another stateroom for less noise.

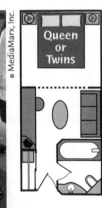

Queen or Twins

A standard category 11/12 inside stateroom

Stateroom Amenities and Services

Bathrooms—All staterooms have their own bathrooms, while categories 4-10 have innovative split bathrooms with a sink/toilet in one small room, and a sink plus tub/shower in another room—see page 80. We love the split bathrooms—it makes getting ready much easier. Note that the light switches are located outside the bathrooms—turn them on before you enter!

Beds—Every room has a comfy queen-size bed that can be unlocked and separated into two twin-size beds by your stateroom host/hostess if needed. Most staterooms also have a twin-size, convertible sofa (72"/183 cm. long). Category 3 has a double-size convertible sofa instead. Some rooms have a pull-down, twin-size berth (72"/183 cm. long with a weight limit of 220 lbs./100 kg.) with safety rails. Category 4 has an extra twin-size bed.

Closets—Every stateroom has a roomy closet with a clothes rod, a dozen or so hangers, a set of drawers, a safe, your life jackets, and an overhead light (that turns on automatically when you open the closet). If you don't have enough hangers, ask your stateroom host/hostess for more.

Cribs—Portable, "pack-n-play" cribs are available, as are bed safety rails—request when reserving. High chairs are also provided in the dining areas.

Outlets—Staterooms are outfitted with four standard U.S. 110v, three-prong electrical outlets: two near the desk/vanity and two behind the TV. Two special outlets—one in each bathroom—are marked "for shavers only" and have a standard U.S. 110v, two-prong outlet along with a European 220v outlet (20 watts/20VA max.). You can't plug your hair dryer into these outlets, but electric toothbrushes should be OK. There's no outlet near the bed, so bring an extension cord or power strip if necessary.

Hair Dryers—Attached to the wall of the bathroom in each stateroom. They aren't terribly high-powered, though, so you may want to bring your own if you are particular about drying your hair.

Laundry—Self-service laundries are available, as is valet laundry service. The three laundry rooms onboard are located across the hall from staterooms #2096, #6588, and #7590. Each laundry has several stacked washer/dryers ($1.00), two irons and boards (no charge), detergent vending machine ($1.00), change machine, and table. Estimate $3.00 for a full load of laundry. Use four quarters for the washer (38 minutes) and use eight quarters to get clothes fully dry (48 minutes for $2.00). If you plan to do laundry, pack some detergent and a mesh bag to tote your items. Plan to visit in the mornings—afternoons are very busy. You can bring your own iron or steamer to use in the laundry room, but their use is prohibited in the staterooms for safety reasons.

Lights—The staterooms are well illuminated, but it can get pitch black in your room when you turn off the lights (especially the inside staterooms without a porthole). If you need it, bring a nightlight, leave the bathroom light on, or open your closet door a crack to trigger its automatic light.

Luggage—Once you've unpacked, you can store your empty luggage in the closet, slide it under the bed (it has a 9"/23 cm. clearance—lift up the bed and put the luggage underneath if you can't slide it), or ask your stateroom host/hostess to store your luggage elsewhere until it is time to repack. You'll have plenty of drawers to unpack your belongings—we counted more than 20 drawers and shelves in our inside stateroom!

Messages—There are a variety of ways to leave and retrieve messages. First, the phone system allows you to call staterooms directly (dial 7 + the stateroom number) and leave voice mail messages. To check and retrieve your messages, just pick up the phone and press the "Messages" button. If you have messages, the light on your phone will blink until you listen to them. For a lower-tech message system, a decorative fish ornament outside your door serves as a message holder—you may find messages from crew members or fellow passengers. Third, we recommend you pack a pad of sticky notes—these are handy for messages to your cabinmates!

Phones—All staterooms have phones. For the most part, you'll use your phone to call other staterooms, room service, guest services, and other places on the ship. You can call locations off the ship for $6.95/minute at ship-to-shore rates (Disney uses the Maritime Telecommunications Network—http://www.mtnsat.com). You cannot call toll-free numbers from your stateroom phone, nor can you use calling cards. If someone needs to reach you while you're on the cruise, they can call toll-free 888-DC-ATSEA (callers from outside the U.S. can call +1-732-335-3281). Regardless of which number your caller uses, they will be prompted for a major credit card number. Your caller's card will be charged $6.95 for each minute the call is connected. Less expensive options include using your cell phone when in port and when sailing past islands with cell service (you'll need international roaming) or use a pay phone in port (bring calling cards). Castaway Cay has neither pay phones nor cellular coverage, however.

Refrigerator—While it may be best described as a beverage cooler, there is a small refrigerator in the sitting area of your stateroom. It's cool enough to chill your drinks (roughly 55°F/13°C). It is large enough (8"d x 12"w x 16.5"h, or 20.3cm x 30.5 x 50) to store several bottles of water, cans of soda/beer, and a bottle of wine or champagne. It seems to work best when it's 3/4 full. There's also an ice bucket in the room, and you may request ice for it.

Room Service—Free room service is available 24 hours for most of your cruise. For details, see page 108. When your food arrives, raise your coffee table (it adjusts like an office chair), and use it as a dining table.

Stateroom Amenities and Services (continued)

Safes—Every stateroom has its own safe—they are roughly shoebox-size (9"d x 6.5"h x 14"w, or 22.9cm x 16.5cm x 35.6cm) and located in the closet. To lock the safe, swipe your Key to the World card through the mechanism. Note that you must use the same card to unlock the safe. Tip: Use another card with a magnetic strip (any will work) to lock/unlock the safe, then hide the card in the room so anyone in your party can access the safe.

Special Needs—Handicap-accessible, barrier-free staterooms (16 total available in categories 3, 5, 6, 8, and 11) are larger—see photos on page 83. Special features include open bed frames, ramped bathroom thresholds, fold-down shower seats, rails, emergency call buttons, and lowered bars. To reserve a handicap-accessible stateroom, call Disney and request the special medical form. Guests with young kids may request bed railings, pack-and-play cribs, and high chairs from the stateroom host/hostess. Strollers are available on a first-come, first-served basis from Guest Services, as are wheelchairs for emergencies. If you need a wheelchair while onboard or in ports, bring your own or rent one through Brevard Medical Equipment with delivery and pick-up right at the ship (866-416-7383 or http://www.brevardmedicalequip.com). Beach wheelchairs are available on a first-come basis at Castaway Cay.

Stateroom Host/Hostess—This crew member attends all your stateroom needs. See page 247 for details on the customary gratuity.

Television—All staterooms have 13" televisions with remote control, and categories 1 and 2 have multiple televisions. A channel listing with movie schedules is provided in your stateroom upon arrival (see page 130 for a typical channel listing). Channels may change as you sail, especially when you're in port—expect to see some international networks show up on a channel or two. Special channels offer cruise details, such as "What's Afloat" and onboard shows. Recordings of the special talks on golf, shore excursions, shopping, and debarkation are also broadcast on your TV. Check channel 50 to trace your voyage's progress and channel 52 for bridge reports and views, including the current time, weather conditions, etc. You can use the TV as a wake-up "alarm" by setting it to turn on at a certain time—just be sure you set it to a channel that always has sound (avoid the movie channels). Here's how we set the alarm on our stateroom's television: menu → setup → alarm → use volume buttons to set time.

Temperature—Every stateroom has individual climate controls. The thermostat is normally located near the bed, high on the wall.

Toiletries—Your stateroom is stocked with basic bar soap, lotion, and a shampoo/conditioner combo. They are sufficient, but not luxurious. We recommend you bring your favorites from home instead. Tissues and toilet paper are also provided in your stateroom's bathroom. The suites offer upgraded toiletries, including bath/shower soap and a shower cap.

Verandahs—All staterooms in categories 7 and up have a private verandah. A heavy, sliding glass door opens to reveal a deck as wide as your stateroom. Dividers offer privacy from your neighbors and the deck overhead protects you from most of the elements. The sliding door has a child-proof latch that can be difficult to open at first—the trick is to grasp the handle and pull hard without turning. Turn the handle horizontally to lock the sliding door. Two plastic/fabric chairs and a small table are on the verandah, along with an ashtray and two deck lights (the light switch is inside the stateroom, somewhat concealed by the curtains). The deck can be slippery, and the railing can be sticky from salty, moist air. Most verandahs have a clear plexiglass-and-metal railing which you can see through, while some staterooms in the aft have a solid railing—see photos on page 74. If you leave your verandah door open, your room will get warm and muggy quickly. Parents should supervise children when they're on the verandah. If you are concerned about kids climbing on the deck furniture, you may ask to have it removed.

Wake-Up Calls—A clock may be provided in your stateroom, but it does not have a lighted dial or numbers. You may prefer to set wake-up calls from your stateroom phone. Try it at least once—Mickey Mouse himself calls you! Alternatives to the wake-up call service are to bring a clock, set the alarm on your television (see page 86), or preorder room service for breakfast (a crew member may give you a reminder call before delivery).

Will I Get an Upgrade?

We've worn out keyboards trying to find the answer to this question. The short answer is ... maybe. The long answer is ... possibly. Although they officially deny it, the Disney Cruise Line does from time to time upgrade some passengers to better staterooms. These passengers learn of their upgrade only when they receive their cruise documents and notice that their assigned stateroom isn't what they expected it to be. Occasionally, the guest learns about the upgrade during check-in, making for a pleasant surprise. Can you do anything to guarantee an upgrade or improve your chances of getting one? Not to our knowledge. Again, Disney is secretive of their method for choosing upgrades. We do know that cruise lines may upgrade passengers in the less expensive staterooms when those categories are selling faster than more expensive ones. This puts more fare-paying, drink-buying, souvenir-shopping passengers on the ship, which more than makes up for any loss of fares. Using years of observations, we've come up with some completely speculative, non-guaranteed ways of possibly improving your odds:

1. Book early. You can't get an upgrade if you aren't booked.
2. Book a guaranteed category rather than a specific stateroom or location. Picking guests in guaranteed categories avoids upsetting a guest who wanted a specific stateroom.
3. Book the least expensive staterooms: These are more likely to sell at the last minute.
4. Book off-season. You won't get an upgrade if the ship is full; on the other hand, they won't give upgrades if they don't need to free up staterooms.

Of course this is all speculation, but we do know of one sure-fire way of getting an upgrade. If you're still dying for an upgrade, you can pay for one when you check in if space aboard the ship allows.

Midship with Mickey

Stateroom Details

Connecting Rooms

2038 ┐	or	2120
2039		2122 ┐
2040 ┘		2124 ┘

This chart lists every stateroom, organized by room number, with each room's category and its sleeping capacity. Handicap rooms are marked "H." Connecting rooms are in bold and bracketed. Even numbers are outside rooms; odds are inside. Capacity of rooms marked "3/4" could not be confirmed and may sleep either 3 or 4. This chart has been updated from the first edition. Discrepancies exist between this and Disney's cruise brochure, but we've taken pains to make this more accurate. Due to ship capacity regulations, Disney may limit the number of guests in any room at the time of booking, regardless of the room's maximum capacity. However, if your party is booked into a particular room, you can rest assured that room will hold everyone in your party. In the event of confusion, call Disney at 888-DCL-2500.

Room #	Cat.	Sleeps	Room #	Cat.	Sleeps	Room #	Cat.	Sleeps	Room #	Cat.	Sleeps	Room #	Cat.	Sleeps	Room #	Cat.	Sleeps
Deck 1			2028	9	4	2116	9	4	2545	10	4	2638	9	4	5514	8	4
1030	9	4	2030	9	4	2118	9	4	2546	9	3/4	2639	10	4	5516	8	4
1032	9	3/4	2032	9	3/4	2120	9	3/4	2547	10	4	2640	9	4	5518	8	4
1034	9	4	2034	9	4	2122	9	3/4	2548	9	3/4	2641	10	4	5520	10	4
1036	9	4	2035	10	4	2124	9	4	2550	9	3	2642	9	4	5522	10	4
1037	10	4	2036	9	4	2126	9	4	2552	9	3	2643	10	4	5524	10	4
1038	9	4	2037	10	4	2128	9	4	2554	9	3	2644	9	4	5622	6	3
1039	10	4	2038	9	4	2129	10	4	2556	9	3	2645	10	4	5624	6	3
1040	9	4	2039	10	4	2130	9	4	2558	9	3	2646	9	4	5626	6	3
1041	10	4	2040	9	3/4	2131	10	4	2560	9	3	2647	10	4	5627	11	3
1042	9	4	2041	10	4	2132	9	4	2562	9	3	2648	9	3/4	5628	6	3
1043	10	4	2042	9	3	2133	10	4	2564	9	3	2650	9	4	5629	11	3
1044	9	4	2043	10	4	2134	9	3/4	2566	9	3	2652	9	4	5630	6	3
1045	10	4	2044	9	3/4	2135	10	4	2568	9	3	2653	10	4	5631	11	3
1046	9	4	2045	10	4	2136	9	4	2570	9	3	**Deck 5**			5632	7	3
1047	10	4	2046	9	3/4	2137	10	4	2571	10	4	5000	8	4	5633	11	3
1048	9	4	2047	10	4	2138	9	3/4	2572	9	3	5001	11	4	5634	7	3
1049	10	4	2048	9	4	2139	10	4	2573	10	4	5002	8	4	5635	11	3
1050	9	4	2050	9	4	2140	9	4	2574	9	3	5004	8	4	5636	7	3
1051	10	4	2052	9	3	2141	10	4	2575	10	4	5005	11	4	5637	11	3
1052	9	4	2054	9	3	2142	9	4	2576	9	3	5006	8	4	5638	7	3
1053	10	4	2056	9	4	2143	10	4	2577	10	4	5008	8	4	5639	11	3
1054	9	4	2058	9	3	2144	9	4	2578	9	3	5009	11	4	5640	7	3
1056	9	4	2060	9	4	2145	10	4	2579	10	4	5010	8	4	5642	6	3
1058	9	4	2062	9	3	2146	9	4	2580	9	3	5012	8	4	5644	6	3
1060	9	4	2064	9	3	2147	10	4	2581	10	4	5013	11	4	5646	6	3
1062	9	4	2066	9	4	2148	9	4	2582	9	3	5014	8	4	5648	6	3
1064	9	4	2068	9	3	2150	9	4	2583	10	4	5016	8	4	5650	6	3
1065	10	4	2070	9	3	2152	9	4	2584	9	3	5018	8	4	**Deck 6**		
1066	9	4	2071	10	4	2153	10	4	2585	10	4	5020	10	4	6000	8	2H
1067	10	4	2072	9	3	2500	9	4	2586	9	3	5022	10	4	6002	11	4
1068	9	4	2073	10	4	2502	9	4	2588	9	3	5024	10	4	6003	11	4
1069	10	4	2074	9	3	2504	9	4	2590	9	3	5122	6	3	6004	11	4
1070	9	4	2075	10	4	2506	9	4	2592	9	3	5124	6	3	6006	8	4
1071	10	4	2076	9	3	2509	12	3	2594	9	3/4	5126	6	3	6007	11	3
1072	9	4	2077	10	4	2510	9	4	2596	9	3	5127	11	3	6008	8	4
1073	10	4	2078	9	3	2511	12	3	2598	9	3	5128	6	3	6010	8	4
1074	9	4	2079	10	4	2512	9	4	2600	9	3	5129	11	3	6011	11	3
1075	10	4	2080	9	3	2513	12	3	2601	10	4	5130	6	3	6012	8	4
1076	9	4	2081	10	4	2514	9	4	2602	9	3	5131	11	3	6014	8	4
1077	10	4	2082	9	3	2515	12	3	2603	10	4	5132	7	3	6015	11	3
1078	9	4	2083	10	4	2516	9	4	2604	9	4	5133	11	3	6016	8	4
1079	10	4	2084	9	3	2517	12	3	2605	10	4	5134	7	3	6018	8	3/4
Deck 2			2085	10	4	2518	9	4	2606	9	4	5135	11	3	6019	11	3
2000	9	4	2086	9	3	2519	12	3	2607	10	4	5136	7	3	6020	8	4
2002	9	4	2088	9	3	2520	9	3/4	2608	9	4	5137	11	3	6022	8	4
2004	9	4	2090	9	3	2521	12	3	2609	10	4	5138	7	3	6024	8	4
2006	9	4	2092	9	3	2522	9	4	2610	9	4	5139	11	3	6026	8	3/4
2008	9	4	2094	9	4	2524	9	4	2611	10	4	5140	7	3	6028	6	4
2009	12	3	2096	9	3/4	2526	9	4	2612	9	4	5142	6	3	6030	6	4
2010	9	4	2098	9	3	2528	9	4	2614	9	4	5144	6	3	6032	6	4
2011	12	3	2100	9	3	2530	9	4	2616	9	4	5146	6	3	6034	6	4
2012	9	4	2101	10	4	2532	9	4	2618	9	4	5148	6	3	6036	6	4
2013	12	3	2102	9	3/4	2534	9	4	2620	9	4	5150	6	3	6037	11	3
2014	9	4	2103	10	4	2535	10	4	2622	9	3/4	5500	8	4	6038	6	3/4
2015	12	3	2104	9	4	2536	9	3/4	2624	9	4	5501	11	4	6039	11	4
2016	9	4	2105	10	4	2537	10	4	2626	9	4	5502	8	4	6040	6	4
2017	12	3	2106	9	4	2538	9	4	2628	9	4	5504	8	4	6041	11	4
2018	9	4	2107	10	4	2539	10	4	2629	10	4	5505	11	4	6042	6	4
2019	12	3	2108	9	4	2540	9	3/4	2630	9	4	5506	8	4	6043	11	4
2020	9	4	2109	10	4	2541	10	4	2631	10	4	5508	8	4	6044	6	4
2021	12	3	2110	9	4	2542	9	3/4	2632	9	4	5509	11	3/4	6045	11	4
2022	9	4	2111	10	4	2543	10	4	2633	10	4	5510	8	4	6046	6	3/4
2024	9	4	2112	9	4	2544	9	3/4	2635	10	4	5512	8	4	6047	11	4
2026	9	4	2114	9	4				2637	10	4	5513	11	4	6048	6	4

For recent updates to this chart, visit http://www.passporter.com/dcl/stateroomdetailchart.htm

Room #	Cat.	Sleeps
Deck 6 (continued)		
6049	11	4
6050	6	4
6051	11	4
6052	**6**	**3/4**
6053	11	4
6054	**6**	**3/4**
6055	11	4
6056	6	4
6058	6	4
6060	6	4
6062	6	4
6064	**6**	**3/4**
6066	**6**	**4**
6067	11	4
6068	**6**	**3/4**
6069	11	4
6070	**6**	**3/4**
6071	11	4
6072	**6**	**3/4**
6074	**6**	**3/4**
6076	6	3
6078	6	3
6080	6	3
6081	11	4
6082	6	3
6083	11	3/4
6084	6	3
6085	11	3
6086	6	3
6087	11	3/4
6088	6	3
6089	11	3
6090	6	3
6092	6	3
6094	6	3
6096	6	3
6098	6	3
6099	11	4
6100	**6**	**3/4**
6101	11	4
6102	**6**	**3/4**
6103	11	4
6104	**6**	**3**
6105	11	4
6106	**6**	**4**
6107	11	4
6108	6	4
6109	11	4
6110	6	4
6111	11	4
6112	**6**	**3/4**
6113	11	4
6114	**6**	**4**
6116	6	4
6118	6	4
6120	**6**	**4**
6122	**6**	**4**
6124	6	3
6126	6	3
6128	6	3
6130	6	3
6131	11	3
6132	6	3
6133	11	3
6134	7	3
6135	11	3
6136	7	3
6137	11	3
6138	7	3
6139	11	3
6140	**7**	**3**
6141	11	3
6142	**7**	**3**
6143	11	3
6144	6	3
6145	11	3
6146	6	3
6147	11	3H
6148	6	3
6150	6	3
6152	6	3
6154	6	3H
6303	11	3
6305	11	3
6307	11	3
6309	11	3
6311	11	3
6313	11	3
6315	11	3
6317	11	3
6319	11	3
6321	11	3
6323	11	3
6500	8	2H
6502	11	4
6503	11	3
6504	11	3
6506	8	4
6507	11	3/4
6508	8	4
6510	8	4
6511	11	3
6512	8	4
6514	8	4
6515	11	3
6516	**8**	**4**
6518	**8**	**4**
6520	8	4
6521	11	3
6522	8	4
6524	**8**	**4**
6526	**8**	**4**
6528	**6**	**4**
6530	**6**	**4**
6532	6	4
6534	6	4
6536	**6**	**4**
6537	11	4
6538	**6**	**4**
6539	11	4
6540	6	4
6541	11	4
6542	6	4
6543	11	4
6544	**6**	**4**
6545	11	4
6546	**6**	**3/4**
6547	11	4
6548	6	4
6549	11	4
6550	6	4
6551	11	4
6552	**6**	**4**
6553	11	4
6554	**6**	**4**
6555	11	4
6556	6	4
6558	6	4
6560	6	4
6562	6	4
6564	**6**	**4**
6566	**6**	**3/4**
6567	11	4
6568	**6**	**4**
6569	11	4
6570	**6**	**3/4**
6571	11	4
6572	**6**	**3**
6574	**6**	**3**
6576	6	3
6578	6	3
6580	6	3
6581	11	4
6582	6	3
6583	11	3
6584	6	3
6585	11	3
6586	6	3
6587	11	3
6588	6	3
6590	6	3
6592	6	3
6594	6	3
6596	6	3
6598	6	3
6599	11	4
6600	**6**	**3**
6601	11	4
6602	**6**	**3/4**
6603	11	4
6604	**6**	**3/4**
6605	11	4
6606	**6**	**4**
6607	11	4
6608	6	4
6609	11	4
6610	6	4
6611	11	4
6612	**6**	**4**
6613	11	4
6614	**6**	**4**
6616	6	4
6618	6	4
6620	**6**	**4**
6622	**6**	**4**
6624	6	3
6626	6	3
6628	6	3
6630	6	3
6631	11	3
6632	6	3
6633	11	3
6634	7	3
6635	11	3
6636	7	3
6637	11	3
6638	7	3
6639	11	3
6640	**7**	**3**
6641	11	3
6642	**7**	**3**
6643	11	3
6644	6	3
6645	11	3
6646	6	3
6647	11	3H
6648	6	3
6650	6	3
6652	6	3
6654	6	3H
Deck 7		
7000	8	4
7001	10	4
7002	8	4
7003	10	4
7004	**8**	**4**
7005	**10**	**4**
7006	**8**	**3/4**
7007	**10**	**4**
7008	8	4
7009	11	3
7010	8	4
7012	8	4
7014	8	4
7016	**5**	**4**
7018	**5**	**4**
7020	5	4
7022	5	4
7024	5	4
7026	5	4
7028	**5**	**4**
7030	**5**	**3/4**
7032	5	4
7034	5	4
7035	11	4
7036	5	4
7037	11	4
7038	5	4
7039	11	4
7040	**5**	**4**
7041	11	4
7042	**5**	**4**
7043	11	4
7044	5	4
7046	5	4
7048	5	4
7050	5	4
7052	5	4
7054	5	4
7056	5	4
7058	5	4
7060	5	4
7062	5	4
7063	11	4
7064	5	4
7065	11	4
7066	5	3
7067	11	3
7068	5	3
7070	5	3
7072	5	3
7074	5	4
7076	5	4
7078	5	4
7080	**5**	**4**
7082	**5**	**3/4**
7084	5	4
7086	5	4
7088	**5**	**4**
7090	**5**	**4**
7092	5	4
7094	5	4
7096	5	4
7098	5	4
7100	**5**	**4**
7102	**5**	**4**
7104	5	4
7106	5	4
7108	**5**	**4**
7110	**5**	**4**
7112	5	3
7114	5	3
7116	5	3
7118	5	3
7119	11	3
7120	7	3
7121	11	3
7122	7	3
7123	11	3
7124	7	3
7125	11	3
7126	7	3
7127	11	3
7128	7	3
7129	11	3
7130	5	3
7131	11	3H
7132	5	3
7134	5	3
7136	5	4H
7138	5	4H
7500	8	4
7501	10	4
7502	8	4
7503	10	4
7504	**8**	**3/4**
7505	**10**	**4**
7506	**8**	**3/4**
7507	**10**	**4**
7508	8	4
7509	10	4
7510	8	4
7512	8	4
7514	8	4
7516	**5**	**4**
7518	**5**	**4**
7520	5	4
7522	5	4
7524	5	4
7526	5	4
7528	**5**	**4**
7530	**5**	**3/4**
7532	5	4
7534	5	4
7535	11	4
7536	5	4
7537	11	4
7538	5	4
7539	11	4
7540	**5**	**4**
7541	11	4
7542	**5**	**3/4**
7543	11	4
7544	5	4
7546	5	4
7548	5	4
7550	5	4
7552	5	4
7554	5	4
7556	5	4
7558	5	4
7560	5	4
7562	5	4
7563	11	3
7564	5	4
7565	11	4
7566	5	3
7567	11	3
7568	5	3
7570	5	3
7572	5	3
7574	5	4
7576	5	4
7578	5	4
7580	**5**	**4**
7582	**5**	**3/4**
7584	5	4
7586	5	4
7588	**5**	**4**
7590	**5**	**3/4**
7592	5	4
7594	5	4
7596	5	4
7598	5	4
7600	**5**	**4**
7602	**5**	**3/4**
7604	5	4
7606	5	4
7608	**5**	**4**
7610	**5**	**4**
7612	5	3
7614	5	3
7616	5	3
7618	5	3
7619	11	3
7620	7	3
7621	11	3
7622	7	3
7623	11	3
7624	7	3
7625	11	3
7626	7	3
7627	11	3
7628	7	3
7629	11	3
7630	5	3
7631	11	3H
7632	5	3
7634	5	3
7636	5	4H
7638	5	4H
Deck 8		
8000	4	5
8002	4	5
8004	**4**	**5**
8006	**4**	**4**
8008	4	5
8010	4	5
8012	4	5
8014	4	5
8016	2	7
8018	4	5
8020	4	5
8022	**3**	**5**
8024	**4**	**4**
8026	4	5
8028	4	5
8030	1	7
8032	**3**	**5**
8034	**3**	**5**
8036	4	5
8038	4	5
8040	4	5
8042	4	5
8044	4	5
8046	3	5
8048	3	5
8050	4	5
8052	4	5
8054	4	5
8056	4	5
8058	4	5
8060	4	5
8062	4	5
8064	4	5
8066	4	5
8068	**4**	**5**
8070	**4**	**5**
8072	4	5
8074	4	5
8076	4	5
8078	3	5
8080	**3**	**5**
8082	**4**	**5**
8084	4	5
8086	3	5
8088	4	5
8090	**4**	**5**
8092	**4**	**5**
8094	4	5
8100	**3**	**4H**
8102	**3**	**4H**
8500	4	5
8502	4	5
8504	**4**	**5**
8506	**4**	**5**
8508	4	5
8510	4	5
8512	4	5
8514	4	5
8516	2	7
8518	4	5
8520	4	5
8522	**3**	**5**
8524	**4**	**5**
8526	4	5
8528	4	5
8530	1	7
8532	**3**	**5**
8534	**3**	**5**
8536	4	5
8538	4	5
8540	4	5
8542	4	5
8544	4	5
8546	3	5
8548	3	5
8550	4	5
8552	4	5
8554	4	5
8556	4	5
8558	4	5
8560	4	5
8562	4	5
8564	4	5
8566	4	5
8568	**4**	**5**
8570	**4**	**5**
8572	4	5
8574	4	5
8576	4	5
8578	4	5
8580	4	5
8582	**3**	**5**
8584	**4**	**5**
8586	4	5
8588	4	5
8590	4	5
8592	4	5
8594	**4**	**5**
8596	**4**	**5**
8598	4	5
8600	**3**	**4H**
8602	**3**	**4H**

Genuine PassPorter Genuine PassPorter Genuine PassPorter Genuine PassPorter Genuine PassPorter Genuine PassPorter

Rocking to Sleep

Sleeping on a moving vessel can be a magical experience. Make more magic in your stateroom with these tips:

- Bring something from home to **personalize your stateroom**, like a photo in a frame, a bouquet of silk flowers, or a radio or CD player. How about a small Christmas tree or menorah during the holidays?

- "The refrigerators in the staterooms don't have much cooling capacity. To get your beverages cooler, try pre-cooling them in the ice bucket. Then add ice in a resealable bag to the refrigerator to give the drinks a head start." – *by contributing author Mickey Morgan*

- "Bring along a collapsible **hanging shoe organizer** to make the most of your space. These shoe organizers also help store small stuff (not just shoes!), which can clutter up your room. Hang them up on the back of your bathroom door." – *Contributed by Disney cruiser Angie James*

- "While traveling with two children (ages 12 and 14) who wanted independence, my sister left a **small pad of paper** in the stateroom and had them sign in every time they passed through the room for any reason. All she asked was that they put the time and where they were going. That way if anyone was looking for someone, they ran by the stateroom, checked the log book, and knew right where to find them. She and her husband used it as well so the kids could find them. Not only did it act as an 'attendance log,' it turned out to be a record of great notes for their trip journal and scrapbook after the cruise." – *Contributed by Disney cruiser Sandy Fiedler*

Magical Memory

- *"With all the activity and excitement of the ship, it was very hard getting our young son to sleep. After our first cruise, we decided that we would make coming back to the stateroom something special for him by having a 'treasure hunt!' Every evening I would hide a wrapped gift for my young son in our stateroom. After all the evening hygiene was complete, he was encouraged to 'search' for his surprise. It was always a Disney-related item (battery-operated toothbrush, plush Mickey, small Buzz Lightyear toy, etc.). It made getting him back to the room and his hygiene completed a whole lot easier and faster, and once he laid down with his 'treasure,' he fell asleep FAST! No more problems getting him back to his room and into his bed!"*

    ...as told by Disney cruiser Rae Ann Reichert

Dining on the High Seas

LEARN the basics of rotation dining

DECIDE how and when to dress for dinner

FIND your dining options

EXPLORE the various restaurant menus

Cruises are famous for food—buffet breakfasts, brunches, snacks, pool-side lunches, high tea, elegant dinners, dessert buffets, and room service! You won't be disappointed by the food on the Disney Cruise Line. Sure, there's plenty of it—we like to say, "If you're hungry, you're not trying hard enough." More important, in our opinion, is the quality of the food. As restaurant critics, we pay attention to food—presentation, preparation, quality, and taste. We would grade virtually every dish we tried during our cruises as a B or B+. There were some disappointments, sure, but in general we've been very happy cruisers with no rumblies in our tummies.

In all fairness, we have heard a few complaints about the food from a few other cruisers. Some feel there should be even more food offered, like on some other cruise lines. (Our poor waistlines!) Others feel the food options are a bit too exotic for their tastes (and Disney has since responded by adding some simpler choices to the menus). Yet others say the Disney Cruise Line isn't as "gourmet" as some European lines. Most cruisers, however, rave about the food onboard.

Dining options abound during your cruise. For **breakfast**, try room service (page 108), Topsider's/Beach Blanket Buffet (page 103), Lumière's/Triton's (pages 95–96), Parrot Cay (pages 99–100), or Palo's Champagne Brunch (pages 101–102). For **lunch**, try Topsider's/Beach Blanket Buffet (page 103), Pluto's Dog House (page 104), Pinocchio's Pizzeria (page 104), Lumière's/Triton's (pages 95–96), Parrot Cay (pages 99–100), or room service (page 108). For **snacks**, try Scoops and Fruit Station (page 104), Pluto's Dog House (page 104), Pinocchio's Pizzeria (page 104), or room service (page 108). For **dinner**, you may eat in Lumière's/Triton's (pages 95–96), Animator's Palate (pages 97–98), Parrot Cay (pages 99–100), and Palo (pages 101–102). Topsider's/Beach Blanket Buffet (page 103) may also be open for dinner. Dessert buffets are held on special nights (see page 96). Whew! Read on to learn about Disney's innovative dining rotations and your delicious choices.

Bon appetit!

Introduction

Reservations

Staterooms

Dining

Activities

Ports of Call

Magic

Index

Rotation Dining

Unlike other ships that stick you in one dining room throughout your cruise, the Disney ships offer **three uniquely themed dining rooms** for all. Your family rotates together through these dining rooms during your cruise, enjoying a different menu each evening. Best of all, your tablemates and servers rotate with you. You can bypass the regular rotation and choose an adults-only restaurant, one of several snack counters, or room service—a buffet restaurant may also be open. You'll find it hard to do them all!

You learn your **dining room rotation** on your first day aboard—look for a set of "tickets" in your stateroom indicating which dining rooms your party has been assigned to for dinner on which days. These tickets are not required to dine, but they do help the servers direct you to your table. To learn your dining rotation a bit earlier, check your Key to the World card for a code (i.e., "APT" or "LAPLAPL"), like the one shown on page 60. This code indicates your rotation: L or T = Lumière's/Triton's, A = Animator's Palate, and P = Parrot Cay. Your rotation assignment is generally based on the ages of guests in your party. On the first night, you'll find more kids in Animator's Palate, families in Parrot Cay, and adults in Lumière's/Triton's. Rotation dining only applies to dinner—see page 99 for breakfast and lunch.

There are **two dinner seating times**: main (first) seating is at 6:00 pm and late (second) seating is at 8:30 pm. Dinner takes from 1.5 to 2 hours to complete. Your seating time is noted in your cruise documents. Guests with main seating watch the evening show after dinner, while guests with late seating see the show first. If you have a seating preference (see page 110 for tips), have it noted on your reservation prior to cruising. Parties with kids tend to get assigned the early seating.

Your **assigned table number** is printed on your dinner tickets and your Key to the World card. Your party has the same table number at dinner in all three of the main dining rooms. Like the dining room assignment, table assignments are determined by factors like age and association (i.e., Disney Vacation Club members may be seated together); your stateroom category does not affect your table assignment. You can request to be seated with your traveling companions—call the Disney Cruise Line well ahead of your departure date and have it noted on your reservation. Table sizes range from four to twenty guests, though most tables seat eight guests. If you want to switch to another table or feel uncomfortable with your assigned tablemates, check your *Personal Navigator* for a Dining Assignment Change session (held on your first afternoon) or see your head server.

Please note: This chapter reflects the most current menus available as of March 2004. The menus do change, but usually with only minor differences during the course of a year.

Dressing for Dinner

One of the delights of cruising is its inherent excuse to turn back the clock and get dressed up for dinner. How you dress for your dinner depends on your cruise itinerary, which we describe below.

In keeping with its **guest-friendly policies**, Disney doesn't strictly enforce dress codes. They won't deny you access if you don't have a jacket, though they will ask you to put on shoes or a shirt. Disney requests that you wear shoes and shirts and refrain from wearing bathing attire in the dining rooms.

Three- and Four-Night Itineraries—In Lumière's/Triton's, Animator's Palate, and Parrot Cay in the evening, men wear casual, open-collared shirts (such as polo or camp shirts) and slacks (such as khakis or Dockers), and women wear a blouse or casual dress. In the elegant setting of Palo, jackets and ties are preferred for men, and the ladies are encouraged to don dresses or pantsuits. Disney requests that you avoid shorts, jeans, and T-shirts in the dining rooms in the evenings, and this is enforced at Palo.

Seven-Night Itineraries—The dress code for the seven-night itineraries is the same as for the three- and four-night cruises with the exception of the formal nights. There is one formal and one semi-formal night on the seven-night itineraries—see page 238 for details and tips on formal nights.

The Disney Cruise Line requests that guests dress for dinner because they are trying to set a **special atmosphere** in the evenings. The Disney Magic and the Disney Wonder are elegant ships—dressing for dinner shows respect for the occasion, the atmosphere, and your fellow guests. We understand that some guests aren't comfortable in a jacket or suit. If this sounds like you, try stateroom dining. Snacks are available on deck 9 (see Casual Dining on page 104). And on the seven-night itineraries, Topsider's Buffet (deck 9 aft) may be open for an early dinner on some evenings (never the first or last nights) for those guests who don't wish to get dressed up.

Dining Room Etiquette

Don't worry—thanks to Disney's family atmosphere, there's no finicky, starched-up rule of etiquette here. Just remember to arrive on time for dinner, greet your tablemates and servers with a smile, place your napkin in your lap, and have your meal and beverage orders ready for your servers. If the elegant table confuses you, keep in mind that your bread plate is always on the left, your glasses are always on the right, utensils are used from the outside in, and wine glasses are held by the stem for white wine and by the base for red wine. When you get up from the table before you've finished eating, place your napkin on your chair to indicate you will be returning again. At the end of your meal, place your unfolded napkin on the table.

Special Diets

Guests with **special dietary requirements** of virtually any type (i.e., kosher, low-sodium, allergies, etc.) are accommodated. When you make your reservation, let the representative know about any requirements. The representative notes the information with your reservation and may instruct you to meet with the Food/Beverage team after you board—they are usually available in Sessions/Cadillac's (deck 3 fwd) from 2:00 pm to 3:30 pm on your first day—check your *Personal Navigator*. The Food/Beverage team gets details from you and passes it on to your servers. We recommend you remind your server of your requests at your first meal. Jennifer is lactose-intolerant and requests soy milk with her meals—the attention to her request is impressive and she is always offered soy milk.

While Disney excels at these special, pre-cruise requests, we found it **more difficult to get a special dish or variant** ordered at meal time. For example, it generally isn't possible to order a dish from the menu and have sauces or dressings kept on the side. This is because the dishes are prepared *en masse* in the kitchen. However, you can order a plain salad or simple entrée (vegetarian, grilled chicken, etc.) without the highfalutin' extras—ask your server. We note the vegetarian items in the menus later in the chapter. Kosher is only available in the table-service restaurants.

Will I Gain Weight on My Cruise?

Short answer: No, you don't have to gain weight on your Disney cruise! Long answer: Cruises are renowned for their ability to add inches to your waistline. All that scrumptious, "free" food can send your diet overboard. But if you're determined to maintain your weight and healthy eating habits, it's not at all difficult to do. Jennifer successfully maintains her weight on cruises while still enjoying treats. The first key is **moderation**. Eat well—don't restrict yourself too severely and don't overeat. Not only is it okay to sample a little of everything, it's a good idea—if you deny yourself, you'll likely break down halfway through your cruise and eat everything in sight. Remember that just because the food is included with your cruise doesn't mean you have to overindulge. If the temptation seems too great, grab some of the delicious fruit available at Scoops (deck 9 aft). If you just can't resist that chocolate ice cream cone, order one, eat half, and ditch the rest. You'll also find that buffet meals may actually be easier for you—there are more food choices. The second key to maintaining your weight is **activity**. Most of you will be more active than usual on your cruise—swimming, snorkeling, biking, and walking around the ports. Take advantage of every opportunity to move your body! You can walk a mile every morning around deck 4 (it takes four laps), take the stairs instead of the elevator, and enjoy free exercise classes at the Vista Spa (deck 9 forward). Check your *Personal Navigator* for a session at the Vista Spa that shows you how to lose weight on your cruise, too.

For more tips, surf to: http://www.passporter.com/wdw/healthyeating.htm

Lumière's/Triton's

Have you ever yearned to dine elegantly in a gorgeous, grand dining room aboard a majestic ocean liner? This is your chance. On the Disney Magic, the grandest dining room is known as Lumière's; on the Disney Wonder, it's called Triton's. Both are located next to the ships' breathtaking lobby atriums on deck 3 midship and serve breakfast, lunch, and dinner. Breakfast and lunch have open seating—just show up when and where you will.

Decor—Lumière's (Magic) has a decidedly French flair, just like its namesake, the saucy candelabra in Disney's *Beauty and the Beast*. Rose-petal chandeliers, inlaid marble floors, and graceful columns set the mood for elegance and romance. Large portholes look out to the sea on one side of the restaurant. A mural depicting a waltzing Beauty and her Beast adorns the back wall. Look for the glass domes suspended from the ceiling—inside each is Beast's red rose. Triton's (Wonder) takes you "under the sea" with Ariel's father from Disney's *The Little Mermaid*. The Art Nouveau-inspired dining room is decorated in soft colors with blue glass-and-iron "lilypads" floating on the ceiling. A breathtaking Italian glass mosaic of Triton and Ariel graces the back wall. The lighting changes during the dinner, casting an "under the sea" effect.

Dinner Dress—Unless the evening is formal, semi-formal, or "tropical" (see pages 93 and 238), dress is upscale casual: jackets are appropriate (but not required) for men and dresses/pantsuits for women. No shorts or jeans.

Our Review—The elegant surroundings are the restaurants' best feature. These are the only restaurants offering full table service at breakfast and lunch. The extra attention and elegance at dinner is a treat. Breakfast here is good, but service is slow and the selection is more limited than at Parrot Cay or at Topsider's/Beach Blanket Buffet. Lunch is enjoyable, though portions may be a bit smaller than you'd expect. Dinner is very elegant and the food is finely prepared. We highly recommend this restaurant over Parrot Cay and Animator's Palate. Jennifer and Dave's rating: 8/10.

© MediaMarx, Inc.

Dave and our good friend Laura enjoy Triton's

Lumière's/Triton's Sample Menus

While we can't predict exactly what you'll be offered at Lumière's or Triton's, we can share the menus from past cruises. Below are typical breakfast, lunch, and dinner menus. We've underlined those menu items we and our fellow cruisers have enjoyed and recommend that you try.

Breakfast at Lumière's/Triton's *(menu does not change day-to-day)*
chilled juices (orange, grapefruit, cranberry, prune, V-8, apple, tomato); **fresh fruit** (grapefruit, melon, banana, fruit cocktail); **yogurt** (fruit and plain yogurt, assorted low-fat yogurt); **hot cereal** (oatmeal, <u>Cream of Wheat</u>); **cold cereal** (Corn Flakes, Raisin Bran, KO's, Rice Krispies, Frosted Flakes, low-fat granola, Froot Loops); **Mueslix** (mixture of toasted whole grain flakes, sun-dried raisins, dates, almonds, and brown sugar); <u>**lox and bagel**</u> (served with cream cheese); **pastries** (Danish pastries, muffins, <u>croissants</u>, bagels, <u>donuts</u>, English muffins, <u>toast</u>—white, wheat, or rye); **preserves** (assorted jellies, jams, marmalades); <u>**Express Breakfast**</u> (scrambled eggs, bacon, link sausage, oven-roasted potatoes); **Eggs Benedict**, **eggs to order** (scrambled, fried, poached, or boiled—with oven-roasted potatoes and your choice of breakfast meat: link sausage, grilled ham, or bacon); **omelets** (Denver, ham and cheese, plain, Egg Beaters—with oven-roasted potatoes); **hot off the griddle** (<u>buttermilk pancakes</u>, blueberry pancakes, French toast, waffles); **daily skillets** (American beef hash with fried eggs, scrambled eggs and smoked salmon, or creamed chicken with biscuit); **beverages** (coffee—regular or decaf, assorted teas, hot chocolate, milk—whole, low-fat, skim, or chocolate).

Lunch at Lumière's/Triton's *(menu changes daily)*
starters (<u>shrimp cocktail</u>, chips and salsa, roasted vegetable tart, hummus "chickpea" dip, <u>curried pumpkin soup</u>, mixed greens and arugula, or niçoise salad); **main courses** (<u>mushroom risotto</u>, classic Reuben sandwich, traditional American meatloaf; broiled filet of tilapia, roasted chicken, or traditional hamburger); **desserts** (banana cream pie, carmelized rice pudding, double chocolate cake, <u>key lime pie</u>, or chef's sugar-free dessert).

Dinner at Lumière's/Triton's *(for your first rotational visit only)*
appetizers (deep-fried camembert fritters, <u>shrimp medley</u>, <u>pearls of seasonal melon</u>, <u>baked escargot</u>); **soups and salads** (cauliflower soup, chilled vichyssoise soup, mixed garden salad, tossed field greens, <u>Boston bib lettuce</u>); **main courses** (rigatoni pasta, <u>garlic-roasted beef tenderloin</u>, <u>herb-crusted prime fillet of cod</u>, braised lamb shank, <u>roasted duck breast</u>, sirloin steak, grilled chicken breast, salmon steak, or vegetarian selections—potato and cauliflower curry and stack of vegetables); **desserts** (apple tart, cherries jubilee, <u>Grand Marnier souffle</u>, crème brûlée, white chocolate domes, ice cream sundae, or sugar-free dessert—seasonal fruits, chocolate cheesecake, or sugar-free ice cream).

Tip: No matter where you dine, you can request a simpler, off-menu item like steak, roasted or grilled chicken, or plain broiled fish.

Dessert Buffets
You've saved room for dessert, right? On select nights of your cruise (any length), a fruit and dessert spread of monumental proportions is laid out for your gastronomic pleasure. Check your *Personal Navigator* for days, times, and locations. A "midnight" dessert buffet is generally held from 11:00 pm to midnight on deck 9 on one night of most cruises. The seven-night cruises may feature a Gala Dessert Buffet in Lumière's, typically held from 11:30 pm to 12:30 am on an at-sea day. The line can get long at the dessert buffets—to avoid a long wait, arrive just as it begins. Desserts vary, but typical treats include crepes, cheesecakes, tortes, pies, cookies, and pastries.

Animator's Palate

Disney's true colors shine in this imaginative, $4.3 million restaurant. Animator's Palate—which serves dinner only—is located on deck 4 aft.

Decor—Entering the large, windowless restaurant feels a bit like walking into a black-and-white sketchpad. The tables are draped in white, the chairs are black, and the walls are covered in line drawings of classic Disney animated characters. Where's all the color? Don't worry—it's coming, along with your food. As each course is served, color is added to the walls and ceilings, and the characters come to life in full color. There's a colorful surprise at the end, but we won't give it away. This production is limited to the first, second, and third nights; on subsequent evenings, the room remains black and white (this is a good time to visit Palo—see page 101).

© MediaMarx, Inc.

Dress—Unless the evening is formal, semi-formal, or "tropical" (see page 93 and 238), dress is resort casual. Polo and camp shirts are fine, but please don't wear shorts or jeans in this dining room.

Our Review—Animator's Palate is a fun place for all ages. The "show" is breathtaking, and food is decent. Inventive dishes have an Italian flavor and offer enough choices to please most. Service is fine, though you may feel rushed or stymied as servers need to keep pace with the show. When you take your seat at the table, try to get a view of one of the video screens. Jennifer and Dave's rating: 7/10.

Jennifer's mother Carolyn gets the royal birthday treatment at Animator's Palate

---

"The Best of..." (formerly Master Chef Series)

This special menu is offered in all three of the main dining rooms on the fourth night of the four-night itineraries and on the last night of both the Eastern and Western Caribbean cruises.

appetizers (artichoke and garlic dip, California roll with caviar, <u>seafood medley</u>, or honey-mustard chicken tenderloins); **soups and salads** (<u>crawfish and lobster bisque</u>, chilled split pea soup, romaine salad, Florida citrus and baby spinach, or bib lettuce); **main courses** (<u>grilled beef tenderloin</u>, <u>Kentucky Bourbon and maple-glazed pork tenderloin</u>, roasted lamb filet, seafood pappardelle pasta, roasted red snapper, sirloin steak, grilled chicken breast, grilled salmon, or vegetarian selections—vegetable curry, risotto with black-eyed peas, or steamed vegetables); **desserts** (<u>banana crème brûlée Napoleon</u>, chocolate decadence, celebration cake, deep-dish apple-cranberry pie, baked Alaska, ice cream sundae, or sugar-free dessert).

Introduction · Reservations · Staterooms · Dining · Activities · Ports of Call · Magic · Index

Animator's Palate Sample Menu

Dinner at Animator's Palate *(for your first rotational visit only)*
appetizers (<u>lobster and shrimp wrapper</u>, <u>duck and goat cheese flatbread</u>, smoked salmon, baked stuffed tomato); **soups and salads** (chilled gazpacho, <u>creamy butternut squash soup</u>, <u>confetti tomato salad</u>, Caesar salad, Boston bib lettuce) **main courses** (cheese cannelloni, <u>maple-glazed salmon</u>, <u>pan-fried veal chop</u>, roasted chicken breast, grilled sirloin, sirloin steak, grilled chicken breast, salmon steak, or vegetarian selection—vegetable curry, pasta marinara); **desserts** (<u>strawberry shortcake</u>, Boston cream pie, New York-style cheesecake, double-fudge chocolate dessert, Kahlúa trifle, or sugar-free dessert—seasonal fruits, pound cake, or sugar-free ice cream).

Supercalifragilisticexpialidocious Menus
You dine in the main dining rooms more than once during your seven-night cruise, so you'll enjoy additional menus. On the fourth night, enjoy the TROPICALIfragilisticexpialidocious menu (Eastern) or the Around the World menu (Western). On the fifth night, enjoy the Around the World menu (Eastern) or MEXICALIfragilisticexpialidocious menu (Western). On both itineraries, the sixth night is the Captain's Gala (see below), and last night is The Best of menu (see previous page).

Around the World *(all 7-night cruises)*
appetizers (<u>soft shell crab tempura</u>, quesadillas, scallop stir-fry, or tropical fresh fruit); **soups and salads** (lobster bisque, <u>chilled cucumber and mint soup</u>, crisp salad, or romaine and grapefruit salad); **main courses** (fettuccine Alfredo, fillet of salmon, prime rib, <u>Mediterranean seafood stew</u>, <u>roasted chicken</u>, roasted chicken breast, sirloin steak, salmon steak, vegetarian selection—stir-fry vegetables or large pasta shells); **desserts** (apple pie, chocolate torte, <u>bread and butter pudding</u>, tiramisu, ice cream sundae, or sugar-free dessert).

Tropicalifragilisticexpialidocious *(Eastern Caribbean cruises)*
appetizers (smokey barbecue chicken drum sticks, <u>pineapple fruit boat</u>, crab and scallop fritters, or Caribbean beef ravioli); **soups and salads** (Caribbean okra gumbo soup, <u>chilled honeydew and mango soup</u>, Caesar salad, or blackened chicken salad); **main courses** (garlic shrimp, sweet-and-sour chicken, roasted pork loin, grilled sirloin steak teriyaki, <u>pumpkin seed-encrusted tuna</u>, roasted chicken breast, sirloin steak, salmon steak, vegetarian selection—baked bell pepper or grilled eggplant); **desserts** (piña colada bread pudding, white chocolate cheesecake, triple layer chocolate cake, hazelnut macaroon cake, ice cream sundae, or sugar-free dessert).

Mexicalifragilisticexpialidocious *(Western Caribbean cruises)*
appetizers (cheese arepas, roasted chicken drumsticks, crab and lobster fritters, or <u>mango and papaya cocktail</u>); **soups and salads** (<u>corn and mussel cream soup</u>, black bean and cheddar cheese soup, Caesar salad, or taco salad); **main courses** (fruit stuffed pork loin, grilled shrimp, marinated roasted sirloin steak, poblano pepper glazed chicken, <u>pumpkin seed-encrusted tuna</u>, roasted chicken breast, sirloin steak, salmon steak or vegetarian selection—vegetarian enchiladas or Mexican vegetarian chili); **desserts** (chocolate cake, piña colada bread pudding, white chocolate cheesecake, <u>banana flambé</u>, sweet empañada sundae, or sugar-free dessert).

Captain's Gala *(all 7-night cruises, sixth night)*
appetizers (baked clams, <u>grilled shrimp</u>, grilled vegetables and beef prosciutto, or <u>fresh fruit cocktail</u>); **soups and salads** (<u>wild forest mushroom soup</u>, chilled tomato consommé, garden fresh salad, or Californian mixed salad leaves); **main courses** (<u>baked lobster tail</u>, grilled beef tenderloin, pan-fried halibut, grain-fed chicken breast, fettuccine with seared sea scallops, roasted chicken breast, sirloin steak, salmon steak, or vegetarian selection—eggplant parmigiana or blue cheese and asparagus risotto); **desserts** (amaretto cheesecake, <u>cherries jubilee</u>, <u>warm chocolate lava cake</u>, lingonberry cheese pudding, ice cream sundae, or sugar-free dessert).

Parrot Cay

This breezy, island-inspired restaurant is the most casual of the three main dining rooms. Parrot Cay (pronounced "key") is on deck 3 aft. The restaurant serves breakfast (buffet and character) and lunch, plus dinner with a grillhouse flair. The buffet breakfast and lunch have open seating.

Decor—The first thing you may notice is the sound of parrots—they're not real, but they sound like it as you walk through the breezeway and into the restaurant. Inside is a cacophony of colors and sounds, with parrot chandeliers that evoke the Enchanted Tiki Room at Disney's theme parks and lush tropical greens and oranges on the walls and floors. Large portholes line two sides of the restaurant, affording beautiful views.

Dinner Dress—Unless the evening is formal, semi-formal, or "tropical" (see page 93 and 238), dress is resort casual. No shorts or jeans at dinner.

© MediaMarx, Inc.

Our Review—The new grillhouse menu here is very good and a vast improvement over the old menu. Breakfast and lunch are buffet-style, which just doesn't afford the same elegance you get in Lumière's/Triton's. The food is great, with some stand-out items, and the food variety at the buffet is generous. Most outstanding still, there always seems to be one or two delightful surprises for adventurous diners. They do a good job of keeping the buffet fresh and appealing. A "show" by the servers livens things up at dinner. Alas, Parrot Cay is the noisiest dining room. Jennifer and Dave's rating: 7/10. (This is often the restaurant we skip for Palo.)

Jennifer enjoys the breakfast buffet at Parrot Cay

Open Seating at Breakfast and Lunch

Breakfast and lunch are usually open seating, meaning you dine where and when you please, and you don't sit at your assigned table—you are seated by a crew member, however. If you'd like your regular servers at breakfast or lunch, just ask to be seated at their table (if it's available and if they're on duty). Better yet, ask your servers at dinner where they are serving the following day and follow them to that restaurant.

Parrot Cay Sample Menus

Buffet Breakfast at Parrot Cay

You can usually find fresh fruit, cereals (hot and cold), yogurt, smoked salmon, assorted pastries, scrambled eggs, bacon, link sausage, ham, hash browns, pancakes, waffles, or French toast. A made-to-order omelet station may also be available.

Character Breakfast at Parrot Cay *(seven-night cruises only; seating at 8:00 am for main seating guests and 9:30 am for those with late seating)*

Special Goofy combination plate for children (scrambled eggs, chocolate pancake, Mickey waffle, and Canadian bacon); **chilled juices** (orange, grapefruit, and cranberry); **fresh fruit and yogurt** (sliced fruit, grapefruit, plain and fruit yogurt, and low-fat yogurt); **cereals** (Cream of Wheat, Corn Flakes, Raisin Bran, KO's, Rice Krispie, and Frosted Flakes); **lox and bagel** (served with cream cheese); **pastries** (Danish pastries, muffins, croissants, donuts, and toast—white, wheat, or rye); **express breakfast** (scrambled eggs, bacon, link sausage, and hash browns); **breakfast classics** (scrambled or fried eggs served with hash browns and your choice of bacon, link sausage, or ham); **omelets** (plain or ham and cheese—served with hash browns, Egg Beaters available); **hot off the griddle** (buttermilk pancakes or blueberry pancakes); **beverages** (coffee—regular or decaf, assorted teas, hot chocolate, milk—whole, low-fat, skim, or chocolate); **preserves** (assorted jellies, jams, and marmalades).

Lunch Buffet at Parrot Cay

The buffet on the seven-night cruises changes daily: day one—welcome aboard buffet; day two—Italian buffet; day three—Asian buffet; day four—Mexican buffet; day five—American buffet; and day six—seafood buffet. On the Disney Wonder, brunch is served until noon on day two and, on the four-night itinerary with a sea day, the Oriental buffet is served on day three. On the last day, the menu that is offered at Cookie's BBQ on Castaway Cay is also offered at Parrot Cay onboard the ship (all itineraries).

Dinner at Parrot Cay *(for your first rotational visit only)*

appetizers (quinoa and grilled vegetables, glazed chicken wings, hot crab Newburg, trio of salmon); **soups and salads** (cold cream of mango and papaya soup, cream of sweet onion soup, Boston bib lettuce, mixed greens with marinated roma tomatoes, fruit salad); **main courses** (roasted rib-eye of beef, oven baked chicken, mixed grill, potato-crusted grouper, baby back pork ribs, sirloin steak, grilled chicken breast, salmon steak, or vegetarian selections—gnocchi au gratin with spinach or vegetable strudel); **desserts** (crème brûlée cheesecake, Kentucky Bourbon pecan pie, lemon meringue pie, chocolate-espresso walnut cake, ice cream sundae, or sugar-free dessert—fresh berries in Jello, chocolate mousse, or sugar-free ice cream)

Character Breakfast

Seven-night cruisers have a special treat—an invitation to a character breakfast in Parrot Cay (see menu above). Typically Mickey, Minnie, Goofy, Pluto, Chip, and Dale show up in tropical garb. Each character makes an effort to visit each table, and it's not uncommon for one of Disney's photographers to snap your picture while Goofy gives you a hug. Expect lots of energy, napkin-waving, character dancing, and loud music. This character meal reminds us of Chef Mickey's at the Contemporary Resort in Walt Disney World. Character breakfasts are offered at two seatings (guests with earlier seating at dinner will have the earlier seating at breakfast). If your dining rotation starts in Animator's Palate, your character breakfast will be Sunday morning (Lumière's=Monday morning and Parrot Cay=Thursday morning). Your server usually presents your tickets on the evening before, or they may be left in your stateroom. Your character breakfast's date and time are noted on the tickets.

Palo

Palo is the adults-only restaurant offering Northern Italian cuisine, an intimate setting, phenomenal service, and a 270° view. Unlike the three main dining rooms, adults must secure reservations to dine here and there is a nominal, per-person service charge ($10 for dinner or brunch, no charge for high tea). Palo has its own servers, so be prepared to part with your regular servers for the meal. Palo is on deck 10 aft and serves dinner nightly from 6:00 pm to 9:00 or 10:00 pm. A wine tasting seminar may also offered here (see page 136), and the seven-night cruises bring a champagne brunch and a high tea (see page 102).

Reservations—Reservations for all meals are made on your first afternoon aboard—check the *Personal Navigator* for the time and place. We recommend you send just one person from your party and arrive early—Palo reservations are extremely popular and they go quickly. Know the day(s) you prefer to dine at Palo before arriving (use our worksheet on page 111)—you may need to know which line to stand in without wasting any time. Only one reservation per stateroom is allowed for each meal (brunch, tea, and dinner), but you may dine with guests from another stateroom or go on the wait list for additional meals. Cancel at least six hours before your meal to avoid the charge. If you can't get reservations, get on the wait list and check for cancellations. Guests in suites (cat. 1-3) can ask their concierge to make reservations for them.

Decor—The most striking feature of Palo is its sweeping ocean views—we have fond memories of a meal served just as the sun set. Warm wood paneling, Venetian glass, and smaller tables (yes, you can get a table for two here!) make this the most romantic spot onboard. An exhibition kitchen and wine displays set the stage for a special dining experience. The restaurant also has a private room tucked in the corner for groups.

Dress—Men should wear jackets and ties; women should wear dresses or pantsuits. Formal attire is also welcome. No jeans (this rule is enforced).

Our Review—We simply adore Palo! The servers are friendly, engaging, and incredibly attentive. The restaurant itself is quiet and mellow. The best part of dining at Palo, however, is the food—it's simply outstanding, as items are made or finished to order. We also recommend brunch and high tea—both are well-done, though we can't say they outshine dinner. While the service charge is intended to replace the gratuity, an extra tip may be justified. Jennifer and Dave's rating: 9/10.

Jennifer and Dave
dress up for Palo

Introduction
Reservations
Staterooms
Dining
Activities
Ports of Call
Magic
Index

Palo Sample Menus

Dinner at Palo *($10/person service charge; menu doesn't change on repeat visits but the chefs do try to offer different "specials" each evening).*

pizzas (pizza prosciutto, pizza margherita, pizza lucana, pizza del lavante, or chef's specialty pizza of the day); **starters and salads** (grilled eggplant, buffalo mozzarella and plum tomatoes, warm shrimp salad, grilled portobello mushroom and polenta, lightly-fried calamari, or fresh mixed salad; **soup** (minestrone or traditional fish and seafood soup); **main courses** (grilled salmon, pan-fried tuna, rack of lamb, chicken breast, grilled filet mignon, tortelloni stuffed with crabmeat, penne arrabbiata, spaghetti capone, linguini carbonara, gnocchi fiorentina, seafood risotto, or wild mushroom risotto); **desserts** (tiramisu, chocolate and hazelnut soufflé with vanilla bean sauce, panna cotta, pistachio torte, sweet pizza, cappuccino cheesecake, or assorted gelato).

Special Meals at Palo

In addition to the nightly dinners, Palo hosts two special, adults-only events, primarily on the seven-night cruises. These popular events are by reservation-only (see details on making reservations on previous page) and are generally held only on days at sea.

Champagne Brunch *($10/person charge)* — also available on the 4-night cruise
Buffet of assorted traditional breakfast and lunch items: **breakfast items** (cereals, breakfast breads, Danish pastries, specialty eggs, and pancakes); **lunch items** (shrimp, grilled marinated vegetables, Alaskan King Crab legs, smoked salmon & mixed greens, selection of cheeses and meats, pizzas, and garlic roasted tenderloin); and **desserts** (fresh fruit and berries, tiramisu, lemon meringue pie, and cappuccino mousse). One glass of champagne is complimentary, as is fresh-squeezed orange juice. (Tip: If you don't drink, ask for sparkling juice.) Champagne specialty drinks are available for $5.25.

High Tea *(no charge)*
traditional teas (Darjeeling, Yunnan Top Grade, Ceylon and Yalta, Lapsaung Souchong); **flavored teas** (California Fields and Black Currant); **herbal & caffeine free** (Chamomile Citrus, Rainforest Mint, African Nectar); **finger sandwiches** (cream cheese and cucumber, smoked salmon and sour cream, chicken and curry, and egg salad); **scones** (available with apricot jam, raspberry jam, or Devonshire cream); **desserts** (English trifle or chocolate eclairs). Specialty coffees, full bar, and extensive wine list also available.

Beverages at Dinner *(all restaurants)*

Don't be surprised if your server learns your drink preferences. We were impressed when our server remembered what we liked after our first dinner. Complimentary beverages include soda (fountain drinks), iced tea, juice, coffee, tea, and tap water. Sparkling water (Perrier or San Pellegrino) is $3.50 for a large bottle. A full bar and wine list is available. If you need suggestions, each menu has a selection of specialty drinks/apéritifs ($4.75) and featured wines ($5.25–8.25/glass). Each menu also features a themed drink, such as Lumière's French Flag (grenadine, crème de cacao, and blue curaçao), Animator's Palate's Black and White (Kahlúa and layered cream), and Parrot Cay's Island Kiss (Amaretto, Bailey's, and crème de cacao). Specialty drinks are also available without alcohol—just ask your server.

Tip: Learn more about the special "Tea with Wendy" event on page 246.

Topsider's/Beach Blanket Buffet

This casual buffet restaurant (deck 9 aft) is a pleasing alternative to the formal dining rooms. Choices are plentiful and varied, with themes such as seafood, Italian, Mexican, and Asian. The welcome aboard buffet (first afternoon) offers peel-and-eat shrimp, a popular offering with cruisers. Salad and dessert buffets are expansive, and kid-friendly food is always offered. Breakfast offerings are excellent, with hot and cold selections, omelet bar, and a cereal bar. It's usually open for breakfast (7:30 am to 11:00 am) and lunch (noon to 2:00 pm). Occasionally early-morning pastries, dinner (7:00 pm to 9:00 pm), and a late-night buffet are offered. Seating indoors and outdoors. Drinks limited to water, fruit punch, iced tea, coffee, milk, and juice—no soda is available during breakfast and lunch (but you can bring it with you).

Decor—Topsider's (Magic) is nautically themed, with bright, nautical flags, teakwood tables, and glass etchings of maritime scenes. Beach Blanket Buffet (Wonder) has a surf's-up feel, with colorful surfboards, beach towels, and beach balls decorating the floors, walls, and ceilings. Both offer indoor and outdoor seating (with and without shade).

Dress—Casual resort wear. You can wear shorts and tank tops for any meal, and dressier clothes are welcome, too. For the sake of other guests, however, do cover up that swimsuit.

Dinner—Dinner works slightly differently than breakfast and lunch— you go to the buffet for your appetizers, but your drinks and main courses are brought to your table by servers. In fact, your main course entrees will probably be the same as those offered in one of the regular restuarants that evening. And your sodas are complimentary at dinner.

© MediaMarx, Inc.

Our Review—An excellent place for a fast yet satisfying breakfast. We generally prefer the other restaurants for lunch and dinner (better food, better service, and alcohol can be purchased), but when we've stopped by for a casual meal we've always been pleased. As to whether it's best to eat lunch here or at Parrot Cay on embarkation day, we really prefer Parrot Cay for its service and slightly less crowded atmosphere. Jennifer and Dave's rating: 6/10.

Dave enjoys lunch at Beach Blanket Buffet

Casual Dining

Need to grab a bite on your way to a movie? Want to avoid the dining room at dinner? Casual dining is your ticket. Disney offers several quick-service options throughout the ship at various times during the day. All times noted below are based on previous cruises—check your *Personal Navigator* for specific hours. The soda icon (🥤) indicates that you can purchase sodas/alcoholic drinks and refill your soda mug at this location.

▪ Topsider's Buffet/Beach Blanket Buffet — Deck 9 Aft

See previous page for a full description and photo.

▪ Pluto's Dog House — Deck 9 Aft 🥤

Your basic burger stand. The menu includes hamburgers, hot dogs, veggie burgers, chicken sandwiches, tacos, bratwurst, chicken tenders, and fish burgers. All are served with fries. A toppings bar offers standard bun veggies (lettuce, tomatoes, onions, pickles) and condiments. Pluto's may also offer an express breakfast or treats like cheese fries and nachos on select days. Patio tables nearby. Hours vary—usually open from lunch until 8:00 pm or midnight.

▪ Scoops and Fruit Station — Deck 9 Aft

Vanilla and chocolate frozen yogurt (soft serve) with a variety of toppings and sprinkles. You can get your frozen yogurt in a cone or a cup. Open daily from 11:00 am to 8:00 pm. Wraps (chicken, veggie, or seafood) may also be served here on select days. Fruit (bananas, apples, mangoes, papaya, etc.) from 12:00 pm to 6:00 pm (Wonder) or 12:00 pm to 8:00 pm (Magic) daily.

▪ Pinocchio's Pizzeria — Deck 9 Mid 🥤

Pizza, pizza, pizza! Get your slice in traditional cheese or pepperoni. Special pizzas like veggie and Hawaiian may also be served at times. Beverages also available here. Generally open from 11:00 am to 6:00 pm, then again from 10:00 pm to midnight. Seating is at patio tables. (Tip: You can order more pizza types from room service—see page 108).

© MediaMarx, Inc.

Pinocchio's Pizzeria ☛

▪ Outlook Bar — Deck 10 Fwd 🥤

Chicken wings and panini sandwiches are offered here around lunchtime on select days. Check your Personal Navigator or stop up for a visit.

▪ Beverage Station — Deck 9 Aft

Breakfast pastries available early morning (6:30 am to 7:30 am). Cookies may also be served on select days. Beverages available 24 hours/day—for more details, see page 107.

Snacks and desserts are liberally sprinkled in other places, too. You'll find snacks in the Cove Café (Magic), ESPN Skybox (Wonder), and in the Promenade Lounge and Beat Street/Route 66 from 11:00 pm to midnight. Dessert buffets are available (see page 96).

Castaway Cay Dining

Two more dining opportunities bear mention, even though they are located off-ship. All itineraries visit Disney's private island, Castaway Cay, and you'll be happy to learn your food is included in the price of your cruise! The main place to eat is **Cookie's BBQ**, located directly across from the family beach (see island map on page 225). Cookie's typically serves from 11:30 am to 2:00 pm and offers the best selection with burgers, BBQ ribs,

Jennifer's nieces Megan and Natalie discuss the nutritional merits of hot dogs vs. burgers at Cookie's BBQ on Castaway Cay

grilled chicken sandwiches, lobster burgers, hot dogs, potato salad, fruit, frozen yogurt, and big chocolate chip cookies. Food is served buffet-style. Plenty of covered seating is nearby (see photo above). Basic beverages are also provided, or you can buy (or refill) a soda or alcoholic beverage across the way at the Conched Out Bar.

Adults 18 and over can eat at the **Castaway Cay Air Bar-B-Q** (see photo below) located at Serenity Bay, the adults-only beach, from about 11:00 am to 1:30 pm. Offerings include burgers, salmon, grilled chicken, steak sandwiches, lobster burgers, potato salad, fresh fruit, and fat-free yogurt. Water and juice is provided, or you can purchase sodas and alcoholic beverages at the bar nearby. A half-dozen umbrella-shaded tables are

located to the left of the food hut, or take your tray down to the beach.

In addition to the two bars already mentioned, there's a third—the Heads Up Bar—at the far end of the family beach. All bars close around 3:30 pm.

Relax at the Castaway Cay Air Bar-B-Q at Serenity Bay

Tip: If you choose not to visit Castaway Cay, a buffet is served in Parrot Cay, usually from 8:00 am to 1:30 pm.

Kids' Dining

We don't know about your kids, but Jennifer's nieces Megan and Natalie won't touch pepper-seared grouper or seafood Creole with a ten-foot pole. Megan, Natalie, and many other kids prefer the kids' menus available at each table-service restaurant (and adults can order from these menus, too!). The **menus vary slightly** and are kid-friendly. Here is a typical menu:

appetizers (chicken noodle soup or fruit cocktail); **main courses** (hot dog, macaroni and cheese, cheese pizza, chicken strips, grilled cheese, or chef's entrée of the day); **desserts** (Mickey ice cream bar, chocolate pudding, assorted ice cream, or chef's dessert of the day); **drinks** (milk—whole, low-fat, skim, or chocolate; soda, juice, water). Smoothies are $3.50 each.

© MediaMarx, Inc.

And, yes, the menus come with **kid-pleasin' activities**, like word searches and connect-the-dots. Crayons are also provided with meals (see photo).

If you are the lucky parent of children who will try anything, rest assured that your **kids can choose from the regular menu** if they wish.

Kid-friendly items are **offered elsewhere** outside of the restaurants, too. Pluto's and Pinocchio's are favorites, naturally, and Topsider's/Beach Blanket Buffet has plenty of kids' food.

If your child is checked into **Oceaneer's Club or Lab** at dinnertime, crew members take kids up to Topsider's/Beach Blanket Buffet before or at the start of the first

Megan discovers that kids are pampered on Disney cruises, too

dinner seating. The eatery reserves one buffet line just for kids. If you're hoping for a quiet dinner alone, you may be able to take your kid(s) up to Topsider's/Beach Blanket Buffet before it opens at 7:00 pm.

While lunch and dinner are provided for kids checked into the Oceaneer's Club and Lab at mealtimes, **no snacks** are made available. You can check them out and take them to get a snack, of course.

Younger children may find it **hard to sit through a meal** in a table-service restaurant. If you ask your server, you can have your child's meal served at the same time as your appetizers to curb their impatience. And the servers are typically great at entertaining the kids. Of course, you may prefer to do casual dining or room service on some nights.

Babies in **Flounder's Reef** are given apple juice and saltine crackers, as appropriate for their ages. No other food is fed to them, nor can you bring other foods for them.

Formula for infants (Similac and Isomil) is available for purchase in Treasure Ketch (deck 4 mid). Disposable bottles are also sold.

Beverages

Your food onboard is included your fare, but **most drinks are not free**. Sure, you can get tap water, coffee, tea, milk, and juice with your meals and at select locations onboard. Sodas (fountain drinks) are also available for free during meals at table-service restaurants. But soda at any other time, bottled water, specialty drinks, smoothies, and alcohol come at a price.

✔ Sodas are **priced** at about $1.50 each—selection is limited to Coke, Diet Coke, Sprite, and ginger ale. Beers range from about $3.25 to $4.00 and include tap beers (Bud, Miller Lite, Heineken), canned beers (Bud, Bud Lite, Coors Light, Icehouse, Miller Draft, Miller Lite, Beck's, Guinness, Heineken), and bottled beers (Amstell Light, Bass, Corona). Mixed drinks are $3.00 to $6.00 each, wine is $4.25 and up, and smoothies are $3.50.

✔ A 15% **gratuity is automatically added** to all beverage purchases. There's no need to give another tip, even though there is a space provided for it on your receipt.

✔ **Bring Your Own**—Many guests opt to "BYOB." Pick up some soda, bottled water, beer, wine, and/or liquor and stow it in your luggage. (If you're on a 4-night cruise, remember that you depart on Sunday and alcohol isn't sold before noon.) If you run out, pick up more at a port. Unlike other cruise lines, there are no restrictions on bringing beverages aboard, but you can only take home one liter duty-free per person and it must be unopened. (Warning: Don't expect to restock at the onboard liquor shop—you won't get your booze until the night before you disembark.) The stateroom "refrigerators" keep your beverages chilled (see page 85). If you bring your own wine to the dinner table, expect to pay $17.25 per bottle ($15 corkage fee + 15% gratuity)—ouch!

✔ **Unlimited Soda Package**—If you expect to have more than 2 to 3 sodas per day, this is a great deal. Price: $5 per day of your cruise (i.e., $35 for a 7-night cruise), plus an extra $5 to keep the mug. Buy it on your first day. How does it work? Disney places a sticker on your Key to the World card that indicates you get unlimited sodas, and if you pay the extra $5, you get a refillable soda mug to keep. Refills are available on Castaway Cay, too. If you purchase a mug, it cannot be reused on future cruises.

✔ **Beer Mug**—Check the lounges for a 22 oz. refillable, glass beer mug. Cost $15 for the mug. Get 22 oz. refills at the 16 oz. price. Note: You'd need 10 to 12 refills to break even.

✔ **Beverage Station**—Visit the beverage station on deck 9 aft for complimentary water, coffee, hot tea, iced tea, hot cocoa, whole milk, fruit punch, and lemonade—available 24 hours a day. Orange juice may also be available in the mornings.

✔ **Topsider's Buffet/Beach Blanket Buffet**—Fruit punch and iced tea are complimentary when the restaurant is open for lunch or dinner. If you want lemonade, milk, hot tea, or coffee, the Beverage Station is nearby.

✔ **Wine Package**—Commit to a bottle of wine for each night of your cruise and save more than 25% off the list prices. You can choose your wine from a list at each meal. The seven-night cruise's classic wine package is $145 and the premium package is $265. Unopened bottles may be taken home, but they count towards your customs allowance.

✔ **Fairy Tale Cuvée**—This champagne—available for purchase in the dining rooms—was created just for Disney by Iron Horse Vineyard (the White House's purveyor).

✔ **Drinks Come to You**—Servers on Castaway Cay and at the Walt Disney Theatre bring specialty drinks around on trays for purchase so you don't have to get up for them.

Stateroom Dining
(Room Service)

Midship with Mickey

So you just couldn't drag yourself out of the sapphire blue water to get back to the ship in time for dinner and now you're too pooped to go up to Pinocchio's for a slice of pizza? You'd order room service, but who can afford it? Good news—room service food is included in your cruise!

The ship's galley is open 24 hours/day (though it's closed the morning of disembarkation). Service is quick and punctual—food usually arrives in 15 to 30 minutes or less. You'll find room service menus in your stateroom, and we've included sample menus at the bottom of this page—please note that menu items and beverage prices may change. Food and basic drinks (coffee, tea, milk, juice) are free, but all other beverages carry an extra charge, just like out on deck.

To place an order for room service, simply press the dining button on your stateroom phone and relay the items you want. You can also specify a time for delivery if you are ordering in advance. Coffee drinkers may find it convenient to order a pot of coffee before going to bed—have it delivered immediately (it stays warm in its thermal carafe) or request it for a particular time in the morning (its arrival works as a wake-up call). Don't forget to tip your room service steward on delivery. They don't get automatic tips for the food, just the drinks. $1-2 dollars/person is fine.

Tip: Guests going on all-day excursions have been known to order a couple of sandwiches, have them delivered before departing, keep them cool in the refrigerator, and pack them in resealable bags for a midday snack. Be aware that the Disney Cruise Line does not encourage this.

Breakfast Menu (7:00 am to 10:00 am) Note: Guests in suites may order full breakfasts (see page 70). *Juices* (orange, apple, grapefruit); *Cold Cereal*, served with whole or skim milk (Corn Flakes, Raisin Bran, Rice Krispies, Froot Loops, KO's, Frosted Flakes, low-fat granola); **Breads and Pastries** (Danish pastries, fruit and bran muffins, croissants, doughnuts, toast, English muffins, bagel); **Condiments** (selection of jams and honey, butter, margarine); **Beverages** (whole milk, skim milk, chocolate milk, 100% Colombian Coffee, 100% Colombian Decaffeinated Coffee, selection of teas); and **Cocktails** - $4.25 (Mimosa, Screwdriver, Bloody Mary)

All-Day Menu Note: Guests in suites may order from the main dining room menus (see page 70). **Appetizers** (Port of Salad—iceberg lettuce, tomato, red onion, roasted corn, bacon, turkey, blue cheese, herb croutons, and pesto vinaigrette; Ship's Kettle—creamy tomato soup with oregano and croutons; Chili Tricolore—spicy chili con carne with shredded lettuce, tomato, cheddar cheese, and sour cream; and <u>All Hands on Deck</u>—a special selection of international cheeses served with crackers); **Sandwiches**, served with coleslaw and potato chips (tuna sandwich, roasted turkey sandwich, or grilled ham and cheese sandwich); **All-American Fare** (cheeseburger with fries and cole slaw, hot dog with fries, and macaroni & cheese); **Chef's Specialities** (triple cheese pizza, Mexican fiesta pizza, vegetarian delight pizza, and manicotti al forno); **Desserts** (daily cake selection or an extra large chocolate chip cookie); **Kid's Meals** (Captain Hook's chicken tenders with potato chips or Catch a Wave PB&J with potato chips). **Beverage Packages** (6 domestic beers for $19.50, 6 imported beers for $22.50, 3 imported and 3 domestic beers for $21, 6 Coca Cola or other sodas for $7.50, or 6 bottled waters for $7.50).

Our Recommendations

Your first hours on board can be very chaotic, and it's tough to arrange a proper family meal. We suggest you split up and **grab quick bites** whenever you can—the buffets close before the ship sets sail.

Are you still uncomfortable about wearing a jacket or a suit? Other than formal nights, **a nice shirt and slacks will be fine** at Triton's/Lumière's.

Presuming you love **Disney music** (a fair guess, we think), the soundtrack at Animator's Palate and Lumière's/Triton's takes your meal to a high "sea." You don't get a 16-piece, live, be-tuxed orchestra, but the prerecorded score is a feast for the ears. This is especially true at Animator's Palate, where the visual extravaganza is choreographed to the music.

You can't keep Dave away from **smoked salmon**, even under "lox and cay." Alas, Disney's smoked salmon is not quite the stuff of dream cruises. It's fine on a bagel with cream cheese, but it's not that firm-but-buttery/velvety, smoky-sweet stuff of his dreams. The salmon at Palo is a bit better (as is their fresh-squeezed OJ!).

We love **seafood** (especially Dave), and you'll notice that many of our choices in this chapter (all those dishes we've underlined) are seafood-based. We know there are many of you who don't share our love for it, so please rest assured that virtually all the dishes are good—it's just that we've tried the seafood the most often.

The **seating and traffic flow** for Topsider's/Beach Blanket Buffet is the most chaotic on board. It's far better, though, when you enter the buffet using the right-hand doors (port). The indoor seating on that side is also more spacious and relaxing. When the weather's right, we prefer the outdoor tables aft—they're a glorious relief from the indoor chaos.

Eating outdoors on deck 9 aft.

Get to Know Your Dining Room Servers

If you've never had the chance to bond with a good server, try it! Great servers resemble stage actors—they come alive for a good audience. Be generous with your attention and thanks throughout the cruise—don't save it all for the tip. From the start, help them understand your tastes and interests. Listen attentively when they describe dishes, ask for their recommendations (they know what's good), and ask questions while ordering—you may save them several trips to the kitchen. If something disappoints you, break the news gently—but don't suffer in silence, either. Your server likes happy guests, and you'll be even happier with a happy server. You have three crew members on your dinner service staff, all of whom should be tipped at cruise end (see page 247). Your Head Server oversees many tables, supervises your special needs (and celebrations), and should visit your table once per meal. Your Server guides you through your meal, takes your orders, serves wine, and (hopefully) pampers you beyond belief. Your quiet Assistant Server helps keep your food coming, refills drinks, and clears the table.

A Melting Pot of Notes

If you're thinking of **bringing any food onboard**, please note that it is against U.S. Public Health regulations to bring aboard any food that is cooked or partially cooked or packaged food that has already been opened. Unopened, commercially packaged foods are fine.

It's a good idea to **pack a change of clothes** for your first night's dinner in your carry-on. While it doesn't happen often, checked luggage may arrive in your stateroom too late to allow a change for dinner.

Note that the **dining rotation seating times may change**. In the past, Disney has experimented with different seating times based on guest feedback. As your cruise nears, call the Disney Cruise Line to find out your dining rotation times.

Trying to decide between the **earlier or later seating?** The earlier seating (usually 6:00 pm) is most popular with families and young children. The earlier seating is also preferred by those who like to get to sleep earlier. Early seating takes about $1\frac{1}{2}$ hours to complete your meal, while late seating can take as long as 2 hours. As you might have guessed, the later seating (usually 8:30 pm) is comprised of mostly adults and some older children. The later seating gives you more time on your port days, as you don't need to rush back for an early dinner. Keep in mind that guests with late seating see the show before dinner, so you may need a snack before the show. We prefer the late seating ourselves.

Just can't **finish your meal**? Ask your server if you can take it back to your stateroom. Most servers are happy to accommodate you.

If you are **seated with other guests**, which is likely if you aren't traveling in a large group, enjoy their company and swap tales of your adventures! Most cruisers find it more enjoyable to share a table!

On the **fourth night** of the four-night cruises, guests return to the restaurant where they dined on the first night of their cruise. Regardless of what restaurant you're in, you will enjoy "The Best Of..." menu (see page 97) on this evening. This could be a good night for Palo.

If you want to try **Palo on more than one evening** and you have friends onboard, ask them to include your party in their reservation for one evening while you do the same for them on the other evening.

Breakfast on disembarkation day is in the same restaurant you were assigned to the evening before. Note that you return to the assigned restaurant even if you chose alternate dining such as Palo on your last evening aboard. A special "Welcome Home" menu is served—it's virtually identical to the Character Breakfast menu (page 100).

Shows in Palo? This only has a bit to do with dining, but it's such a good story, we wanted to share it. On deck 10, way aft, there are a few deck chairs about, because it's a good, fairly secluded place to sunbathe. One sunny morning, there was a very attractive woman sunbathing on that deck. Some time later she got up and, seeing a big mirror nearby, stood in front of it adjusting her little yellow bikini top and bottom, turning and admiring Mother Nature's (or her surgeon's) handiwork. She kept this up for a couple of minutes then packed her bag and left. How do I know this? Well, that big mirror was the window next to my table in Palo. When it's bright outside and dark inside, those big windows reflect very well. The woman was totally oblivious to this but most of the guests in Palo were obviously amused. So beware of big mirrors on the sides of walls—they could be reflective windows!

Midship with Mickey

Dining Worksheet

Due to the nature of dining on a cruise, it isn't necessary to plan each meal as you might while vacationing at Walt Disney World. Part of the fun is deciding where to eat as the mood strikes you. If you are hoping to eat at Palo during your cruise, however, a little preplanning goes a long way. Use this worksheet to note your dining preferences and be sure to keep it with you on your first day aboard.

We have the **main seating** / **late seating** (circle the appropriate choice—if you're not sure of your seating, call the Disney Cruise Line and inquire)

Our Anticipated Dining Rotation: If the occupants of your stateroom include:
All adults—day 1: **Lumière's/Triton's**, day 2: Animator's Palate, day 3: Parrot Cay, etc.
Young kids—day 1: **Animator's Palate**, day 2: Parrot Cay, day 3: Lumière's/Triton's, etc.
Older kids—day 1: **Parrot Cay**, day 2: Lumière's/Triton's, day 3: Animator's Palate, etc.

Now write in the restaurants you anticipate being assigned to on each day:

Nights	1	2	3	4	5	6	7
Special Menus							
4-Night Eastern				"The Best Of..." Tropicali	Around World	Cap'n's Gala	"The Best of.."
Western				Around World	Mexicali	Cap'n's Gala	"The Best of.."

Notes: Guests on the **three- and four-night cruises** should cross out days that don't apply to your cruise. Guests on **seven-night cruises**, please observe that we noted the special menus for days 4 to 7. Seven-night cruisers may also want to indicate which evenings you expect to be designated as formal and semi-formal. On the Eastern Caribbean cruise, the semi-formal evening is usually day 2 and the formal evening is day 6. On the Western Caribbean cruise, the semi-formal evening is generally day 3 and the formal evening is day 6. Palo brunch is held on day 2, day 3, and day 6 on the 7-night cruise itineraries (both Eastern and Western). High Tea at Palo is held on day 3 and day 6 of both 7-night itineraries in addition to day 2 on the 7-night Eastern Caribbean itinerary. The character breakfast is on Sunday if your dining rotation starts with Animator's Palate, Monday if you start with Lumière's/Triton's, and Thursday if you start with Parrot Cay.

Now pencil in your first and second preferences for a dinner at Palo, keeping in mind which restaurants/meals you really want to try and which you are less interested in. Guests on the seven-night cruise: add in your preferences for the champagne brunch and/or high tea, if those interest you. Also note your preferences below for easy reference:

My first Palo preference is for _____ at _____ pm
My second Palo preference is for _____ at _____ pm

My Palo brunch preference is for _____
My Palo high tea preference is for _____

You can fill in this worksheet before you leave for your cruise or once you're aboard and are confident about your dining rotation—just be sure to bring this worksheet with you!

A Recipe for Fun

Make the most of your dining experience with these delicious tips:

◉ Can't decide between the lamb and the cod? Tell your server you'd like to **try both dishes**! You can also order multiple appetizers and desserts if you wish. But take our advice and don't say you want "nothing" for dessert—that's just what you may get (see below)!

◉ "Doing the three-night cruise? Try the **Disney-Double-Dip**! To experience all four restaurants during your three-night cruise, make a reservation for as late as possible at Palo, then go there for a late snack and dessert after the show. Or reserve a late meal at Palo, and precede that with a light meal (appetizers only) at your regular rotation restaurant earlier in the evening."— *by contributing author Mickey Morgan*

Midship with Mickey

◉ "I brought along my own **bottles of wine** and uncorked them myself in my stateroom prior to going to dinner. At dinner, my servers took the bottle, chilled it, and served it. No corkage fee!!" – *contributed by Disney cruiser Sharon King*

◉ "Definitely get a drink in one of the **Disney souvenir glasses**— they're plastic and easy to transport home in your suitcase. Then whether you're planning another trip and want to build excitement or simply want to relive a bit of your time on board, make yourself a drink in your souvenir glass. It may sound hokey, but it gave me a little fix of the Disney Cruise while waiting what seems like forever to my next one!" – *contributed by Disney cruiser Amy Donenko*

Magical Memories

◉ *"The first night we went to dinner, we were amazed to find that our waiters greeted us by our names. They were all so nice! One night my little brother was asked what he wanted for dessert and he said, 'Nothing.' And that's just what he got ... the word 'Nothing' written in chocolate on a plate."*

...as told by Disney cruiser Jesse Tindall

◉ *"My husband and I took our second Disney Wonder cruise to celebrate our anniversary. Late in the afternoon of our anniversary, we called room service to order the 'All Hands on Deck' (a cheese and fruit plate) and a pair of champagne glasses. We had stopped by a liquor store on the drive to the port for a bottle of bubbly. We took our cheese plate and drinks to those comfy lounge chairs on deck 4, where we spent some quality time toasting our marriage and watching the sea go by and the sun go down."*

...as told by Disney cruiser Mary Snow

Playing and Relaxing Onboard

Cruise ships are often called floating hotels, but "mobile resort" is much closer to the truth. Like the legendary "Borscht Belt" hotels of New York's Catskill Mountains, the Disney cruise offers a bewildering array of entertainment, recreation, and enrichment opportunities, from sun-up way into the wee hours.

The Disney Cruise Line has become legendary for its pacesetting children's and teens' programs, and it may seem like an ocean-going summer camp. With the kids programs open all day and well into the night, even Mom and Dad get a vacation.

Despite its emphasis on family travel, the Disney cruises are a summer camp for all ages, boasting a full range of adult-oriented activities. The single most obvious omission is the lack of a gambling casino—you'll have to be satisfied with onboard bingo and in-port casinos.

Leave time for relaxation as well as playing. On a cruise it's just as easy to over-play as it is to overeat. You'll be tempted to fill every available hour with shipboard fun, but you'll have a far more enjoyable cruise by picking only the most tempting morsels. If you shop 'til you drop in port and play 'til you plotz (collapse) onboard, you'll be one very weary vacationer.

We start this chapter with an introduction to the *Personal Navigator*, your cruise's four-page daily gazette. Then it's time to prep you for your first day onboard. There's a lot to do, and it's particularly hectic for first-time cruisers. From there, we move on to describe shipboard activities for families, teens, kids, and adults—this is where you learn about the famous kids program and adult entertainment offerings. Next, in-depth details are in order—the swimming pools, deck parties, films, stateroom TV, live entertainment, surfing (the World Wide Web), the spa, and lounges all get their moment in the limelight. Finally, now that you're completely exhausted, we help you kick back and relax, and share some insider tips. Shuffleboard, anyone?

Your *Personal Navigator*

We hope this field guide has become your "first mate." If so, we predict the *Personal Navigator* will seem like your very own "cruise director." The *Personal Navigator* is a folded, **4-page sheet** that lists the day's activities. A new *Personal Navigator* is placed in your stateroom daily, and there are special versions for kids and teens, too. While we don't have room to print the full text of *Personal Navigators* here, you can get a peek at previous edition *Personal Navigators* by visiting http://www.castawayclub.com or http://www.dcltribute.com—both of these sites maintain collections from previous cruisers and they'll give you an excellent idea of what to expect.

The first time you see a *Personal Navigator*, you may feel overwhelmed. They pack in a lot of details! Here's a **capsule review** of what you'll find:

Page 1—Date, day's destination, suggested dress, sunrise/sunset times, day's highlights
Page 2—Morning/afternoon activities, character appearances, movies, family activities
Page 3—Afternoon/evening activities, adult activities, tips, notes
Page 4—Meal times/hours, lounge hours, important numbers, policies, specials, etc.

Pay attention to the **small symbols** in the margins—these indicate which activities feature Disney character appearances, are for guests 18 and older, families, etc. You'll find the symbol key at the bottom of page 4.

We highly recommend you keep **highlighters** handy to mark those activities that appeal to you. Finding them in your *Personal Navigator* later can be tricky—on some days there are more than 80 activities listed! Obviously you can't do everything, and that's where this chapter comes in—we introduce many of the activities here, so you'll be better informed when it comes to deciding between all of your choices.

We find that life is much easier when we each have a copy of the *Personal Navigator* with us at all times. Only one copy is left in your stateroom, so stop at Guest Services (deck 3 mid) and **pick up more copies**. (The kids versions are in Oceaneer Club/Lab and the teen version is in The Stack/Common Grounds.) How do you keep it with you if you don't have pockets? We fold it and tuck it into a PassHolder Pouch, which also holds our Key to the World card and other small items. See page 262 for details.

In addition to the *Personal Navigator*, you may receive a highlights sheet covering the entire cruise, a listing of movie showtimes and TV channels, and a daily on-board shopping flyer. **Port and shopping guides** are distributed when you visit a port—they contain historical overviews, maps, shopping and dining ideas, basic information, and hours.

Your First Day Aboard

At last! Are you excited? Many cruisers report feeling overwhelmed and even a little nervous on their first afternoon. It's easy to forget to make those Palo reservations or to grab a bite to eat. To give you an idea of what to expect and help you prepare, we've made up a **sample "touring plan"** for your first day. Ok, so it's more like an Embarkation Triathalon! But keep in mind that you probably won't want to do everything in our plan, and times/ locations may differ. Modify it to fit your needs and use the worksheet on page 117 to record your own plans for your first day aboard!

As soon as you can—Board the ship and smile for the camera in the Lobby Atrium. Go to Topsider's/Beach Blanket Buffet (deck 9 aft) or Parrot Cay (deck 3 aft) for a seafood buffet. Relax and enjoy—it may get a bit hectic over the next few hours.

12:45 pm—Send one adult from your party for Palo reservations, if desired (check your *Personal Navigator* for exact time and place).

1:15 pm—Send one adult to get Vista Spa reservations (including massages on Castaway Cay), if desired. Send another person to your stateroom, which should be ready now.

Tip: If you've got kids, they may be getting antsy by now. Let them explore your stateroom, or, if they're old enough, introduce them to the pools and meet up with them later.

1:30 pm—Parents of kids under 3 go to Flounder's Reef (deck 5 aft) for reservations.

1:30 pm—If you haven't reserved your shore excursions in advance, which we highly recommend, send one person to the Shore Excursions Desk (deck 3 midship) to fill out and drop off order forms. We suggest you decide which excursions you'd like in advance.

Lunch—Take a deep breath and slow down. If you haven't eaten or visited your stateroom yet, do so now. The buffet typically closes at 3:30 pm, so don't miss it!

2:30 pm—Make dining assignment changes or special dietary requests, if needed.

2:45 pm—Register kids ages 3-12 for Oceaneer Club/Lab (deck 5 midship).

3:15 pm—Return to your stateroom and get acquainted with it. If you're in need of anything (extra pillows, bed safety rail), request it from your stateroom host/hostess. If your luggage has arrived, this is a good time to unpack.

3:45 pm—Make sure everyone meets back in the room for the mandatory assembly drill.

4:00 pm—Don your life jackets and walk to your assembly station (see next page).

4:30 pm—After returning your life jackets to your room, go up to deck 9 midship and have fun at the sailaway deck party, and/or explore the ship until it is time to get ready for dinner or the evening's show.

6:00 pm or 6:30 pm—Enjoy dinner at 6:00 pm (main seating guests) or the stage show at 6:30 pm (late seating guests).

7:00 pm—The Stack/Common Grounds (teens) and Oceaneer Club/Lab (kids 3-12) are now officially open. If you haven't yet registered your children, do this now.

8:30 pm—Enjoy the show (main seating guests) or dinner (late seating guests)

Whew! What a day! Rest assured that it all gets much, much easier from this point forward.

First Day Tips

Having a plan is the key to staying on course and feeling good. Here are a few helpful tips for your first day:

Check and double-check your **Personal Navigator** as soon as you get it (either at check-in or when you visit your stateroom). Places and times often change, and new activities and opportunities may be available.

Don't forget to eat! It can be hard to sit down together to one big family meal on your first afternoon. It's okay to split up and/or get **nibbles and bites** here and there. It's one of the advantages of cruising.

Of course, you can always **kick back and do nothing** on your first day but eat, drink, be merry, and attend the boat drill. If you prefer this tactic, you can try to get those Palo and spa reservations later, and you may get lucky with cancellations. If you've got someone in your family who just wants to relax once they're onboard, arrange to go your separate ways on this first afternoon—you'll all be much happier.

Lucky guests with **concierge service** only need to attend one meeting to make the various reservations. You'll be told when and where to meet.

Be **flexible**. Make a plan, but then be willing to change it when needed.

Mandatory Boat Drills

It's inevitable that just as you're settling in or about to leave your stateroom for an exploration of the ship, a disembodied voice from the bridge announces the mandatory boat drill. But thanks to this guide, you now know that the drill happens at 4:00 pm on departure day, and all ship services are suspended from 3:30 to 4:30 pm. You'll find bright-orange life jackets on the top shelf of your stateroom closet (if you need a different size, ask your stateroom host/hostess). The jackets have a water-activated light and a whistle—please remind your kids not to blow the whistles. Your Assembly Station location is mapped on the back of your stateroom door. Assembly stations are all on deck 4, but may be outside on deck or inside. If you forget your assembly station designation, it's printed on your life jacket (see the "E" on Dave's jacket in the photo). When you hear the loud emergency signal, put on your life jackets and walk to the assembly station—your attendance is mandatory. Be sure to bring your Key to the World card(s) with you, but leave cameras and other things behind. The life jackets are uncomfortable, but now is the time for everyone (including young kids) to get used to them. Crew members in the hallways will direct you to your assembly station. Once there, a crew member takes attendance and displays the correct way to wear and use the life jacket. If you miss the drill, you'll receive a sternly-worded letter indicating where and when to meet to go over the assembly procedures—don't miss it! When the drill is over, the captain releases everyone back to their staterooms. The drill lasts from 15 to 30 minutes. Keep your life jacket on until you return to your stateroom.

Don't worry, Dave—everyone looks funny!

© MediaMarx, Inc.

First Things First Worksheet

Use this worksheet to plan those crucial activities that occur during your first day aboard. The chart below includes times (spanning the time period with the most important activities) and two columns each for activities and decks/locations. You may wish to list activities for other members of your party in the second column to coordinate and organize your day, or use the second column for notes or alternate activities.

Time	Activity	Deck	Activity	Deck
10:00 am				
10:15 am				
10:30 am				
10:45 am				
11:00 am				
11:15 am				
11:30 am				
11:45 am				
12:00 pm				
12:15 pm				
12:30 pm				
12:45 pm				
1:00 pm				
1:15 pm				
1:30 pm				
1:45 pm				
2:00 pm				
2:15 pm				
2:30 pm				
2:45 pm				
3:00 pm				
3:15 pm				
3:30 pm				
3:45 pm				
4:00 pm	Mandatory Boat Drill ↓	Deck 4	Mandatory Boat Drill ↓	Deck 4
4:15 pm				
4:30 pm				
4:45 pm				
5:00 pm				
5:15 pm				
5:30 pm				
5:45 pm				
6:00 pm				
6:15 pm				
6:30 pm				
6:45 pm				
7:00 pm				
7:15 pm				
7:30 pm				
7:45 pm				
8:00 pm				
8:30 pm				

Introduction
Reservations
Staterooms
Dining
Activities
Ports of Call
Magic
Index

Activities for Families

When Walt Disney was asked why he created Disneyland, he replied, "I felt that there should be something built where the parents and the children could have fun together." And that's exactly what Disney does for cruising. Family activities outnumber all other activities onboard, helping families have a great time when they're together. By "family" we mean groups of all ages, including all-adult families! Here's a list of what you can expect:

Deck Parties—Celebrate with music and dancing on deck 9 midship (see page 129).

Stage Shows—Disney puts on a different stage show each night of your cruise, and all shows are designed to please both adults and kids. The "Island Magic" stage show in the Buena Vista Theatre is a particular treat for families (though it may be going away—check your *Personal Navigator*). See page 131 for more information on the stage shows.

Movies—Most of the movies playing in the Buena Vista Theater are rated G or PG (with only an occasional a PG-13 or R), making them ideal for families. Special matinees are sometimes held in the huge Walt Disney Theatre, too! See page 130 for details on movies.

© Disney

Studio Sea—This "family nightclub" (deck 4 midship) is a working TV studio. The club hosts family dance parties, family karaoke, theme parties, Tea with Wendy (see page 246), and game shows like Mickey Mania (Disney trivia) and Sailors' Tales (guess the fibber). Game shows are oriented towards families with young children, and generally contestant teams include both a parent and a child (see photo to right). Note that in the late evening Studio Sea may be reserved for teens only.

Walk the Plank game show at StudioSea

Dueling Pianos (Wonder)—Family sing-alongs may be scheduled for early evening on the Disney Wonder (see page 127).

Cabaret Shows—Shows for all ages may be held in Rockin' Bar D/WaveBands in the early evening. See page 131 for details.

Promenade Lounge—We think of this as the "family lounge"—it's non-smoking and families can relax together here in the afternoon and early evening. Watch for many family-friendly events, hosted in the Promenade Lounge. Located on deck 3 aft.

Oceaneer Club/Lab—At special times families can explore these areas together.

Swimming— Families can swim together in the Goofy Pool (deck 9 midship), where pool games are also occasionally held. See page 128 for more information on the pools.

Games—Board games, shuffleboard, Ping-Pong, and basketball. A special Family Mini Olympics may also be held on deck 10 forward.

Pin Trading—Trading cloisonne pins is a very popular activity for kids and adults alike! Trade with cast members wearing pin lanyards, attend one of the trading sessions in the Atrium Lobby, or trade casually with other cruisers. See page 139 for more details.

Character Meet & Greets—Plenty of opportunities for kids (or kids-at-heart) to get autographs and for parents to get photos. See page 246 for more information.

Shore Excursions—Most of Disney's shore excursions are great for families with kids ages 12 and up, and a good number of these work for families with kids ages six and up. Quite a few are open to all ages, as well. See chapter 6 for all the details.

Special Events—Try your hand at drawing Disney characters, or compete in a Talent Show or the "Mickey 200" veggie race—check your *Personal Navigator*.

Tip: Check your *Personal Navigator* for a special section titled "Family Activities," which lists the family-oriented highlights for the day. Also, there's usually some family-oriented entertainment between dinner and the show, such as the cabaret shows and game shows. Here is a sample of activities taken from recent *Personal Navigators* (keep in mind that not all these activities may be available on your cruise):

- ✔ Fun in the Sun Pool Party
- ✔ Pictionary—test your skills against the crew members'
- ✔ Family Line Dancing in Studio Sea
- ✔ Disney and Family Team Trivia
- ✔ Talent Show—show off time!
- ✔ Mr. Toad's Wild Race (limited to 16 teams)
- ✔ Family SPY Party—fun for all "secret agents"
- ✔ Arcade Tournament
- ✔ Family Rock 'n' Roll Sock Hop
- ✔ Father and Daughter Dance
- ✔ Family Golf Putting Contest
- ✔ The Best Disney Legs Contest
- ✔ Walk the Plank Game Show

Families That Play Together Don't Always Have to Stay Together

One of the wonderful benefits of a cruise is that each member of your family can do entirely different things all while staying within the general vicinity of one another—a cruise ship is not a big place like Walt Disney World. With all the activities on your cruise, you're going to want to go in different directions at times... and you should feel free to do it! It only makes the time you spend together that much more valuable. When the two of us sail alone, we often split up—one goes to a movie, the other to the spa—and agree on a time and place to meet again. With larger families, including extended families, you can do your own thing in small groups while still feeling like you're "together." The key to making this work is to communicate with one another and set meeting places/times for the next group get-together. Some families bring along two-way radios, which do work to keep one another in touch—keep in mind, however, that the metal bulkheads of the ship can interfere with reception. A much less-expensive, low-tech way to stay in touch is by leaving one another notes in your stateroom—or if you're staying in multiple staterooms, leaving them on one another's doors or voice mail. One reader has an excellent tip on how to keep tabs on one another—use a logbook (see the tip on page 90). On our last group cruise (MouseFest 2003—see page 241 for details), we made up our own versions of *Personal Navigators* and left them on each other's stateroom doors. During the cruise folks added new events/times/places to the list by noting them on the "master Navigator" on our stateroom door. Sometimes it's as simple as picking up a phone somewhere on the ship (they're everywhere) and letting a family member know where you are (live or via voice mail). So feel free to go your separate ways—just be sure to save some special time to spend together as a family, too!

Activities for Teens

Teens are perhaps the hardest to please onboard, given their widely varying interests and levels of maturity. Some are perfectly happy to swim all day or play in the arcade. Others prefer to hang out with the adults. Still others want to socialize with other teens and party. If your teen prefers more family-oriented activities, we refer you to the previous page. Read on for Disney's teen-oriented places and events:

Note: Disney defines a teen as a 13 to 17 year old. Older teens (18 and 19) are considered adults (although drinking age is still 21 and up).

Personal Navigators—Teens can pick up their own version of the daily schedule in the teen club (see below). The teen version lists teen activities for the day and what's coming up.

Teens-Only Club—A teens-only (ages 13 to 17) hangout is located on both ships, but with some physical differences. On the Magic, it's called The Stack (formerly ESPN Skybox) and is located on deck 11 midship. On the Wonder, it's called Common Grounds, and is located at deck 9 midship. It's very likely that the Wonder will see the teens-only club shift from Common Grounds to The Stack when it's in drydock in October 2004, but this hasn't been finalized. Both clubs schedule parties, games, trivia, and karaoke during the cruise. The teen-only clubs also serve as an assembly spot for teen activities elsewhere on the ship. Here are descriptions of both clubs:

The Stack on the Disney Magic is a hip, trendy club way up on deck 11 inside one of the ship's stacks—in fact, it's the only thing on deck 11 (which used to house the ESPN Skybox). Huge windows dominate the large dance floor, flanked by chairs, tables, and a bar serving smoothies and non-alcoholic drinks. Tucked in the corner are three Internet terminals (same rates apply—see pages 132-133). Flat-panel screens are scattered throughout the club, offering a playlist of music videos which are shown on the six, state-

The Stack on the Disney Magic

of-the-art TVs (including one giant-screen TV). In the back behind glass doors is an intimate little area with more comfy chairs, video screens, and a great view.

Commons Grounds on the Disney Wonder is an intimate, clubby room with comfy chairs, a long bar (also serving smoothies and non-alcoholic drinks), listening stations, a jukebox, foosball, game tables, video games, and three Internet terminals (same rates apply—see pages 132-133). The light-level is low in here, and it has the feel of a secret hideaway. It's located on deck 9, between the Family Pool and the Adult Pool.

Arcade—QuarterMasters is a favorite teen hangout located on deck 9 midship, near Common Grounds (Wonder) or Cove Café (Magic). See page 122.

Wide World of Sports Deck—Shoot some hoops alone or with friends on deck 10 forward.

Internet Cafe—Sure, there are Internet terminals in The Stack/Common Grounds, but sometimes it's just more convenient to come down to deck 3. See pages 132-133.

Vista Spa—Normally off-limits to anyone under 18, teens may be able to sign up for facials/manicures on port days. $69/hour treatment. See pages 134-135.

Buena Vista Theatre—Teens love free movies! See page 130 for details.

Teen Parties—On special evenings teens get dance parties, held either in The Stack (Magic) or in Studio Sea or the ESPN Skybox (Wonder).

Teen "Deck"—Deck 10 (port side) next to the Outlook Bar is designated as a teens only deck. Hangout with friends or just worship the sun.

Teen Shore Excursions—Special teen-only excursions are available at certain ports, such as the "Wild Side" on Castaway Cay. See chapter 6 for details.

Teen Beach—On Castaway Cay, teens get their own beach with activities.

Other Teen Activities—Here is a sample of activities taken from recent teen *Personal Navigators* (keep in mind that not all these activities may be available on your cruise):

- ✔ Teen Tribal Challenge—Earn points for your "tribe"
- ✔ Wide World of Sports Trivia
- ✔ Hidden Mickey Challenge
- ✔ Pump It Up—weight training in the Vista Spa
- ✔ Gotcha!—A day-long game of elimination
- ✔ Teen Karaoke
- ✔ Power Lunch in Parrot Cay
- ✔ Go Fetch—Race against each other to get all your stuff
- ✔ Animation—Learn to draw your favorite Disney characters
- ✔ Gender Wars—Girls vs. Boys
- ✔ Disney Cruise Line Ship Trivia
- ✔ PS2 Challenge
- ✔ H20 Splashdown in the Goofy Pool
- ✔ PJ Party
- ✔ Make a Mousepad
- ✔ Amazing Race—Race from location to location, following clues
- ✔ Invade the Lab—Find out what's cool in Oceaneer Lab
- ✔ Dodgeball Challenge

Tip: Even if you're not sure about all these activities, we highly recommend teens visit the club on the first evening to meet other teens and see what it's all about. This first evening is when many onboard friendships are formed.

Note to Parents of Teens

Teens have virtually the run of the ship, and aside from the times they're with you, in The Stack/Common Grounds, or at a structured teen activity, they're not chaperoned. Teens may make friends with others from around the country and the world—their new friends' values may be incompatible with your own standards. It's a good idea to know where they are and who they're spending their time with, and agree on what time they should return to the stateroom (some teen activities go late into the night). Talk before you go and remind them that being on vacation is not an excuse to throw out rules about drinking, drugs, or dating. U.S. Customs does not take drug possession lightly and penalties can be severe in other countries, too. Note also that any underage person caught with alcohol on the ship is fined $250 and could get up to three days of "stateroom arrest."

Introduction · Reservations · Staterooms · Dining · Activities · Ports of Call · Magic · Index

Introduction

Reservations

Staterooms

Dining

Activities

Ports of Call

Magic

Index

Activities for Kids

A whopping 15,000 sq. ft. (1394 sq. m.) are devoted to activities just for kids. And there are a lot of kid-oriented activities on these ships. What else would you expect from Disney?

Oceaneer Club/Lab—A fantastic program for kids ages 3 to 12 with activities available daily from 9:00 am to midnight or 1:00 am. We highly recommend you encourage your kids to give these programs a try on the first day aboard. See the next page for more information.

Discover the Magic Farewell Show—Kids registered for the Oceaneer Club/Lab have the opportunity to participate in a special show on the last day of the cruise. All participants get to sing on stage with Mickey and receive a T-shirt! Held in the Walt Disney Theatre.

Swimming—We dare you to keep them out of the water! See page 128 for details.

Trading Cards—We've heard a rumor that the trading cards are being phased out, but just in case they stick around or come back at some point, here's how they work: kids can collect free trading cards at various activities onboard. There are about 15 to 25 available on any one cruise. Four cards are exclusive to the Disney Magic, and four are exclusive to the Disney Wonder. To see the cards, visit http://www.castawayclub.com. The trick to collecting all the cards is to ask every crew member you meet if they have any trading cards, rather than just wait for someone to hand them out. Also try asking at Shutters on deck 4 midship.

Arcade—Located on deck 9 midship, Quarter Masters is a small arcade offering about 20 video games, plus air hockey and a prize "claw" game. These are straight games, though—no award tickets and no prize redemption. Most games are 50 cents to $1 each and you must use an arcade card to play. An "arcade debit card teller" machine dispenses $10 arcade cards—just use your Key to the World card to purchase. You can also purchase arcade cards at Guest Services. (Note: Keep your arcade card separate from your Key to the World card as they'll de-magnetize if they come into contact.) If you're worried about your kids racking up huge charges for arcade cards, disable the charging privileges on their cards at Guest Services and purchase arcade cards for them. Hours: 8:00 am to midnight (last game at 11:50 pm).

Games—In addition to the arcade, there are often pool games and Ping-Pong on deck 9, board games in the Oceaneer Club/Lab and Fantasia Reading Room (Magic) on deck 2 midship, basketball on deck 10, and shuffleboard on deck 4. There is no charge for these games.

Movies and Shows—Most of the movies playing are kid-friendly! The Island Magic stage show in the Buena Vista Theater is also kid-oriented. And the stage shows in the Walt Disney Theatre are well-liked by kids, especially "Disney Dreams." See page 131 for more information.

Deck Parties—The deck parties are very popular with kids! See page 129 for details.

Snacks—The opportunity to eat ice cream and hot dogs without forking over money is a real treat for kids! We don't think it's a coincidence that Scoops, Pluto's Dog House, and Pinocchio's Pizzeria are right next to the kids pools! See page 104 for details.

Character Meet & Greets—Disney friends come out for autographs and photos many times during your cruise. For details, see page 246.

Wondering about letting your **kids roam free** onboard? It depends on their age and maturity. A general guideline is kids 8-9 may be given some onboard freedom, while kids 10 and up can move about independently. If you let them loose, set down ground rules, such as no playing in elevators, keeping in touch, and set meeting times for meals, shows, and family activities.

Playing at Oceaneer Club/Lab

Oceaneer Club and Oceaneer Lab are special areas on deck 5 midship **designed just for kids**. The Oceaneer Club is for potty-trained kids ages 3 to 4 and 5 to 7, while the Oceaneer Lab is for older kids ages 8 to 9 and 10 to 12. The four age groups primarily play independently. Kids may participate in an older age group if they are within one month of the minimum age for that group, but older kids cannot join younger groups. Participation in the Club and Lab is included in your cruise fare.

The Club and Lab provides fun, **age-appropriate activities** throughout the day and into the evening. Some kids spend virtually their entire cruise in these areas, while others drop in now and then. Some prefer to spend their time with their families or just playing with other kids elsewhere. Typically, the kids that visit the Club or Lab on their first evening (when friendships are being formed) are more likely to enjoy the experience.

Parents, drop by the club/lab on your first afternoon to take a look around and register your kid(s)—you'll need to fill out a **participation form** indicating name(s), birthday(s), age(s), special considerations (such as allergies or fears), and give your authorization for first aid if necessary. Parents of kids 3 to 7 must sign them in and out, and may do so as often as needed. Parents of kids 8 to 9 can indicate whether their kids can sign themselves in and out of the Club (kids ages 10 to 12 can sign themselves in and out regardless). Each family is given one pager for the duration of the cruise. Each child gets a wristband and a nametag—they should keep the wristband on and bring the nametag with them when they go to the Club/Lab. Parents are welcome to drop in and observe.

© MediaMarx, Inc.

The **Oceaneer Club** (see photo to left) looks like a big, fanciful playroom with a pirate ship to climb on and slide down, and computer stations to play games on—it's also equipped with tables and chairs for activities, a dress-up room, and a stage. Floors and furniture are kid-friendly. It's a big hit with the 3 to 7 crowd—Jennifer's nieces fell in love at first glance and had to be pried away to do other things.

The **Oceaneer Lab** (see photo on next page) looks just like it sounds—a kids' lab! It has lots of tables and cupboards, along with computer game stations, activity stations, and board games. Allie's visit here (at age 9) is one of her best memories of the cruise—she loved making "Flubber"!

Trained **counselors** keep kids active and safe while checked in. The counselor-to-kid ratio is 1:15 (ages 3 to 4) and 1:25 (ages 5 to 12). Counselors are mostly female, college grads, and from English-speaking countries.

Megan and Natalie demonstrate the push-button sound effects on the pirate ship cannon at Oceaneer Club

Oceaneer Club and Lab (continued)

Pick up a **Personal Navigator** at the Club or Lab for the appropriate age group(s)—you'll find a great number of group activities planned, including games, crafts, movies, dancing, and theme parties (see sample activities below). The first activity typically starts at 7:00 pm on your first night aboard. Here is a sample of activities taken from recent kids' *Personal Navigators* (keep in mind that not all these activities may be available on your cruise):

Sample Activities for Ages 3-4
- ✔ Stormin' the Club—arts & crafts and playtime with new friends
- ✔ Nemo's Coral Reef Adventures—join Nemo for a magical puppet show!
- ✔ Do-Si-Do with Snow White—learn the "Dance of the Seven Little Dwarves"

Sample Activities for Ages 5-7
- ✔ Professor Goo's Magical Experiments—make your own Flubber!
- ✔ So You Want To Be a Pirate?—learn how to play pirate with Captain Hook!
- ✔ Animation Antics—learn how to draw Mickey Mouse

Sample Activities for Ages 8-9
- ✔ Bridge Tour—get a tour of the ship's control center
- ✔ Disney Game Show—test your Disney knowledge
- ✔ Goofy Files—enter the invisible world of forensics and crack a case

Sample Activities for Ages 10-12
- ✔ Animation Hour—write and create your very own commercial
- ✔ Mysterious Islands—share scary stories of lost ships and vanishing islands
- ✔ Cranium Crunchers—test your knowledge and bring your team to victory

Tips and Notes

If your kids are checked in during **mealtimes**, they'll be taken up as a group to Topsider's/Beach Blanket Buffet for a trip through a special kid-friendly buffet. Other than that, no food or drink (other than a water fountain) is provided here.

If your child is very **recently potty-trained**, have a special talk with them before leaving them alone at the Club. All that first-day excitement may give them upset tummies, and they may not know what to do without you there to help. Show them where the toilet is, and remind them that they can ask a counselor to contact you if they have a problem. If a child has an accident, you will be paged and they may be asked not to re-visit the Club for 24 to 48 hours in the event their accident was the result of an illness.

Kids may stay in the Club or Lab while you go **play in port**. Just be sure to let the counselors know where you are, and be aware that your pager won't work if you go too far afield. Also check that the Club/Lab opens early enough for your shore excursion meeting time.

When Allie cruised at age 9, her 10-year-old cousin Nina was also along. Alas, the 8 to 9 group and the 10 to 12 group have different activities. Allie and Nina found it frustrating that they couldn't stay together. Allie asked us to remind you that if you have siblings or cousins in these **different age groups**, let them know in advance that they may be separated so it's not such a huge disappointment.

The computer game stations at the Oceaneer Lab

Activities for Adults

Kids, keep out—this page is just for grown-ups! Disney may be family-focused, but rest assured Disney hasn't forgotten your adult needs. There are **plenty of adult-oriented and adult-only activities** onboard, including an entire entertainment district (see next page). If you're worried you'll be bored, it's unlikely—we never have enough time to do what we want, with or without kids. Here's a list of specifically adult-oriented activities:

Bingo—If you're not a bingo person you may want to pass this one up, but it is surprisingly popular and fun! Bingo is the only gambling onboard and attracts mostly adults. (Kids may attend, but you must be 18 or older to play.) Bingo is held once a day in Rockin' Bar D/WaveBands (and occasionally in the Promenade Lounge) and a special "Snowball" jackpot rolls over each day until won. Cards are $10 for a single pack (5 cards, one per game) or $20 for a value pack (15 cards, three per game). Your odds of winning are higher earlier in the cruise, when fewer people are playing. Prizes (cash and gifts) are awarded daily at each of the five games.

Dance Lessons—Learn the basics of ballroom dancing—check your *Personal Navigator*.

Wine Tastings—Learn how to better enjoy wine! The seminar is about $12 and only adults can participate. Make reservations at Guest Services.

Captain's Receptions—Meet the captain at various functions, including receptions and Disney Navigator Series seminars (see page 136).

Sports—Shoot hoops or play volleyball on the Wide World of Sports deck (deck 10 forward), play shuffleboard or run laps on deck 4, or try your hand at Ping-Pong (deck 9 mid). And don't forget the exercise classes in the Vista Spa (see pages 134–135).

Pin Trading—Bring along your pins and trade with crew members or other guests. Special pin trading sessions are generally held in the Atrium Lobby—check your *Personal Navigator*.

Games—Play bridge or other card games in the Fantasia Reading Room (Magic), chess or backgammon in Diversions (Magic), or start up a Scrabble game in Sessions/Cadillac Lounge. There may be pool games at the Quiet Cove pool. Check your *Personal Navigator*.

Music Trivia—So you think you know your music? Check the *Personal Navigator* for times.

Cocktail Hours—Held in the Atrium (deck 3 midship) or in Sessions/Cadillac Lounge (deck 3 forward) on certain days. Alas, the beverages—alcoholic or not—aren't complimentary, with the possible exception of the Captain's Reception.

Seminars and Tours—Get the low-down on shopping, shore excursions, and debarkation procedures with talks held in the Buena Vista Theater (note that these talks are broadcast on your stateroom TV if you can't make it). And on the 7-night cruises, adults can learn the art of entertaining, get behind-the-scenes peeks, and more. See page 136.

In addition to the above, you'll also enjoy these **adult-only places**: Palo restaurant (see pages 101–102), Vista Spa (see pages 134–135), the Quiet Cove pool (see page 128), the Cove Café (Magic only—see page 127), Signals bar (deck 9 forward), the adult entertainment district (see next page), and Serenity Bay Beach on Castaway Cay (see page 226). Other **adult-oriented places** include the ESPN Skybox (Wonder only—see page 137) and the Buena Vista movie theater in the late evenings (see page 130).

Tip: Check your *Personal Navigator* for a special section titled "Adult Activities."

Adult Entertainment District (Beat Street/Route 66)

After all those adults-only activities, you may want an adults-only place to wind down the day, too. Beat Street (on the Disney Magic) and Route 66 (on the Disney Wonder), both on deck 3 forward, are exclusively for adults 18 and older after 9:00 pm. The names and decor differ on the two ships, and a recent renovation on the Magic has introduced some functional differences, too. On both ships you can expect to find a dance club, a relaxing, adult lounge, and the ship's duty-free liquor shop. The Disney Magic also has a sports pub, while the Disney Wonder offers a dueling piano club. Here is a description of each club:

Dance Club—Rockin' Bar D (Magic) and WaveBands (Wonder) are the ships' largest clubs, offering Top 40 and Golden Oldies dance music, DJs, karaoke hours, and cabaret acts featuring entertainers from the stage shows. Typically, a special event is held each evening around 10:30 pm or 11:00 pm, such as the Match Your Mate game show, Rock and Roll Night, 60s Night, 70s Disco Night, and 80s Night. Many cruisers report a preference for the 70s night, and would pass up the 80s night. Guests are selected from the dance floor to participate in some shows—if you want to be picked, get up and be wild! The Match Your Mate game show works like the Newlywed Game. They choose three couples who've been married for various durations as contestants. Unmarried couples will enjoy watching it, but only married couples can participate. A DJ or live band generally precedes and follows these events. Hours are usually from 7:30 pm to 2:00 am. Smoking is allowed in the rear, but poor ventilation can make the entire club smoky.

Adult Lounge—This lounge is always adults-only. On the Disney Magic it's called Sessions and it has a jazzy feel. On the Disney Wonder it's called Cadillac Lounge and has a vintage auto theme. Relax in low, comfy chairs, listen to the pianist or recorded music, and get mellow. Music listening stations are available along the wall with the large portholes if you want to listen to something different. This is a dim, mellow lounge—perfect for pre-dinner or pre-show drinks and romantic interludes. It's not uncommon to find fruit and cheese platters in here between 7:30 pm and 8:30 pm. Hours are usually from 4:30 pm to midnight or 1:00 am. Smoking is permitted at the bar and in the rear of the lounge only.

Smoking Onboard

Unlike most other cruise ships, Disney restricts smoking to certain areas on the ship, and enforces their rules. Smoking is allowed in the dance club, part of the adults-only lounge, Diversions (Magic), ESPN Skybox (Wonder), and open-air guest areas such as decks 9 and 10 and stateroom verandahs. The Mickey Pool area is an exception, as it is all non-smoking. No smoking is allowed in any of the staterooms. We've had no problems with smoke on our cruises. And smokers report that the accessibility of smoking areas meets their needs, though it is sometimes tough to find an ashtray (try deck 10). You can purchase cigarettes ($16/carton) in the liquor shop on deck 3 forward. For those interested in Cuban cigars, you can purchase them in virtually all of the ports except Key West. At the time of writing, cigar smoking was allowed only in ESPN Skybox (Wonder) and the usual open-air guest areas (decks 9, 10, and stateroom verandahs). Keep in mind that you cannot bring Cuban cigars back into the U.S., so smoke 'em while you can.

Pub (Disney Magic)—Formerly the Off Beat dueling piano club, renovations in September 2003 opened the space up into Diversions, an all-purpose pub and sports bar. The lounge now has huge portholes, spilling light into a clubby room filled with comfy chairs. Warm wood tones create a relaxing atmosphere, as do large chess/backgammon tables in the center of the room. Classic board games decorate the walls. The lounge still has a piano off to the side, as well as a long bar in the back of the room. A small selection of books and magazines are available for those who want a quiet respite during the day. What can you do here besides drink and relax? Check your *Personal Navigator* for sporting event broadcasts (shown on the numerous televisions in the back), beer tastings and trivia, and a British Pub Night. Smoking is allowed at the bar only.

Dave at Diversions

Dueling Pianos Club (Disney Wonder)—Known as Barrel of Laughs, this club was originally an improv comedy club. Now it sports two skillful piano players who play popular songs, and take requests from the audience. If you've been to Jellyrolls at Walt Disney World's BoardWalk, this is very similar. Family shows are offered in the early evening. After 9:00 pm, the music gets a bit more adult-oriented. Don't be surprised if you hear risqué renditions of popular songs in the late evening! Expect to sing along and even join in a little audience participation. We really enjoy this club! Hours are usually from 6:45 pm to 1:00 am on most nights. No smoking is allowed. Do note that Barrel of Laughs may be converted into a Diversions-style pub when the Wonder goes into dry dock in October 2004.

Beverages of all kinds are served at all clubs. See page 107 for details on availability and prices. Snacks may be available out in the hallway from 11:00 pm–midnight. There's a duty-free liquor shop (see page 237), but purchases cannot be consumed onboard.

Cove Café on the Disney Magic

A new adults-only area appeared on the Disney Magic after its September 2003 drydock renovations: Cove Café on deck 9, beside the adults-only pool. It took the place of the Common Grounds teen club, which moved up to The Stack (deck 11) at the same time. Cove Café is a cozy coffeehouse, lined with books and magazines and filled with light from huge, new portholes and sliding glass doors. Four Internet terminals are here (see pages 132–133 for rates), as are several music listening stations. An extensive specialty coffee menu is available—expect to pay $2.00 for espresso, $2.50 for cappuccino and café mocha, and $4.75 for coffee drinks laced with liquors. Teas ($3.75) are also available, as is champagne, wine, port, martinis, and a full bar. Light snacks such as pastries and sandwiches may be available, too. Open until midnight. This is an delightful expansion of the Magic's adults-only territory.

Cove Café

Introduction
Reservations
Staterooms
Dining
Activities
Ports of Call
Magic
Index

Swimming in the Pools

Midship with Mickey

One thing you aren't likely to hear while onboard: "Wow, that's the biggest pool I've ever seen." The Disney Magic and the Disney Wonder each have three pools on deck 9, though the pools are small (typical for cruise ships). The pools are each filled with fresh water, which tends to slosh a bit when sailing. Nonetheless, the pools are very popular—especially with kids!

Quiet Cove Adult Pool—the largest pool onboard—is on deck 9 forward. This is one of the five areas on the cruise that adults can go to for child-free relaxation. Pool depth is 48" (122 cm). No jumping or diving is permitted. Adjacent are two whirlpools (caution: the water can be hot!), Vista Spa, Cove Café (Magic only), an open shower, and the Signals pool bar.

Amidships is **Goofy's Family Pool** featuring an image of Goofy snorkeling at the bottom of the pool. Alongside Goofy's pool are two whirlpools, an open shower, and Pinocchio's Pizzeria (see page 104). Pool depth is 48" (122 cm). No jumping or diving is permitted. At the other end of the pool is a stage where the crew and Disney characters join the guests for the deck parties (see next page). The stage features extending deck sections that completely cover the pool, making it safer and providing more dance area.

The sight to see on deck 9 is **Mickey's Kid's Pool** (see photo below). True to Disney style, a regular wading pool and slide is transformed into Mickey Mouse. His face is the main part of the pool with a depth of 18" (46 cm). Mickey's ears (with a depth of 11"/28 cm) are for the very little ones. This is a very busy place on sea days. The centerpiece of Mickey's Kid's Pool is the water slide supported by Mickey's gloved hand. To use the slide, the kids must be between ages 4 to 14 and between 32" and 64" tall (81 to 162 cm). The slide is staffed by crew members, but there are no life guards. Health regulations require that kids be potty-trained—swim diapers are not allowed in the pools. Infants with swim diapers are allowed in the starboard "ear," which is a fountain play area. Pluto's Dog House as well as Scoops (see page 104) are nearby.

© MediaMarx, Inc.

A quiet, lazy day at the Mickey Pool

Typical **pool hours** are from 6:00 am to 10:00 pm for Mickey's Pool and 6:00 am to midnight for the other two pools. Goofy's pool closes during deck parties and other events that use the extending stage. Mickey's slide is only open when the pool is busy (usually 9:00 am to 6:30 pm).

Tip: When is a good time to use the pools? With a lot of guests and small pools, they can get very crowded. This is especially true on hot afternoons at sea. The trick is to think differently—go when your fellow guests are busy elsewhere, like in port or during meals. Immediately after you embark is a good time but be ready to make it to your assembly station by 4:00 pm. Other good times are in the evenings and early in the morning, as the pools open at 6:00 am.

Living It Up at Deck Parties

Every Disney cruise, regardless of its length, has at least one of Disney's famous deck parties. These high-energy parties are held on and around the family Goofy Pool on deck 9 midship. No, you don't have to dance on water—the pool is covered by a large, retractable dance floor during the parties. You can expect to be entertained by some or all of the following: a live band, DJ, dancers, fireworks, a dessert buffet, and "party animals" (Disney characters). Here are descriptions of the deck parties:

Bon Voyage Sailaway Celebration—Every cruise enjoys this celebration, held as your ship pulls away from the dock. This is probably the first time you'll meet your cruise director, who is joined by Disney characters and either a live band or a DJ. As the ship gets underway, the ship's whistle plays the first seven notes of "When You Wish Upon a Star." We highly recommend this party—it really gets you in the mood (see the photo on page 19). Tip: Celebrate your sailaway by bringing bubbles to blow or a small flag to wave! (Party typically starts at 4:30 pm or 4:45 pm and lasts for about 30 minutes.)

Tropical Deck Party—Guests aboard the 3- and 4-night cruises party under the stars on the evening of their Nassau visit. In addition to appearances from crew members and Disney characters, you may be treated to a fruit and dessert buffet around 11:00 pm. Tropical dress is encouraged! (Party starts at 9:30 pm or 10:00 pm and lasts 'til midnight.)

TROPICALI or MEXICALIfragilisticexpialidocious Deck Party—(We dare you to say that three times fast!) The 7-night cruises enjoy this deck party on the fourth night (Eastern Caribbean) or fifth night (Western Caribbean). Expect this party to be similar to the Tropical Deck Party described above. Eastern Caribbean cruisers enjoy the TROPICALI party, while Western Caribbean cruisers get the MEXICALI. Tropical (or Mexican) dress is also encouraged all evening. (Party typically starts at 10:00 pm and lasts until midnight.)

The **music** at the deck parties is quite loud and is geared towards older kids, teens, and young adults. The music CD "La Vida Mickey" (ISBN 0-7634-0666-X, available at music stores and http://www.amazon.com) gives a great preview of the kind of music played during deck parties. If you don't want to be in the thick of things, you may enjoy watching from deck 10 midship. We recommend you visit deck 10 during the sailaway party—it's the best place to enjoy the party while watching the ship pull away (see sidebar below).

To find out exactly what deck parties are offered, check the **Personal Navigator** upon arrival. Note: In inclement weather, the deck parties are held in the atrium (deck 3 mid).

Sailing Away

One of the most exciting experiences of your cruise is when your ship pulls away from the pier and makes its way down the channel, heading for the ocean. You don't want to miss it. Make time to go up to deck 10 around 5:00 pm and watch the scenery slide by as you leave port. Look for the crew members at the terminal—they don huge Mickey gloves and wave the ship off. One of the best places to watch your ship's progress is from deck 10 forward, near the Wide World of Sports courts. Mickey prefers deck 9 forward to watch the bridge crew on the wing. Look for the escort of security boats as your ship moves through the channel, too!

Watching Movies and TV

The Buena Vista Theatre on deck 5 aft is not your typical, boxy movie theater. This is a **gorgeous, sumptuous theater** with 268 stadium-style seats, a large, two-story screen, and a state-of-the-art sound system. The only thing missing are drink holders on the armrests of the seats.

You can expect to see recent Disney animated classics and first-run movies from Disney's motion picture divisions. You may also see some popular, non-Disney movies a few months after they've been released—we were treated to "Harry Potter" on our May 2002 cruise. Films are rated G and PG (with some PG-13 and R) and are shown in that order throughout the day. Movies are free, there's no need to reserve seats, and they start as early as 9:30 am—the last show usually starts between 10:00 pm and 11:00 pm. Check your *Personal Navigator* or the theater for a **list of movies** during your cruise. Matinees on at-sea days are popular—arrive early for a good seat. Wondering what will be playing on your cruise? About a week before you cruise, you can call 888-325-2500, choose the "reservations" option, then ask the representative what movies will be showing. Tip: If you like to snack during your movies, a stand outside the theater sells packaged snacks, bagged popcorn,

and beverages. If you want to save money, order room service and bring it with you or take a detour up to deck 9's snack counters.

© MediaMarx, Inc.

The Buena Vista Theatre also hosts some seminars and a 35-minute, live stage show, **Island Magic**, which relates the adventures of Minnie, Goofy, Pluto, Chip, Dale, and the dread Captain Hook on Castaway Cay. Island Magic appeals most to kids. This show may be going away—check your *Navigator*.

Anticipating the next show in Buena Vista Theater

Your **stateroom TV** has plenty to watch, too! Below is a recent channel guide (channels and stations may vary). Mickey likes to use the TV for Disney background music while he's in the stateroom, and Jennifer and Dave enjoy watching movies on it at the end of the day. Check your stateroom for a movie list. Anticipate about 12-15 distinct movies to be showing on TV—movies repeat frequently. The "all movies, all the time" channel (42) starts a new movie every two hours, beginning at midnight. The Disney Classics channel (40) also starts a Disney animated movie every two hours, beginning at 1:00 am. Both movie channels go around the clock. Tip: You may now be able to watch taped performances of *Hercules*, *Golden Mickeys*, and *Disney Dreams* on your stateroom TV—look between 6:30 pm and 10:30 pm on show nights.

16	What's Afloat	26	CNN Headline News	36	Disney Channel	46	Shopping, Etc.
18	Disney on Land	28	CNN	38	Toon Disney	48	Voyage Info
20	ABC	30	Golf/Shore Excursions	40	Disney Classics		(or DVC Info)
22	Entertainment	32	ESPN	42	24-Hour Movies	50	Ship Information
24	Channel Guide	34	ESPN2	44	CBS	52	Bridge Report

Enjoying the Shows

Look up "entertainment" in the dictionary and it says "see Disney," so naturally the Disney Cruise Line pulled out the stops to make their live shows the **best at sea**. The live shows are presented in the Walt Disney Theatre on deck 3 forward. Onboard a ship where every square foot is precious, Disney dedicated an enormous amount of space to this 975-seat theater. It fills the ship from deck 3 to 7. They added state of the art sound and lighting systems (there are 370 lighting instruments in the theater alone) and a very talented and professional cast to present the best stage shows afloat.

On all of the cruise itineraries, you can expect to see three shows: *Hercules, the Muse-ical,* the new *Golden Mickeys,* and *Disney Dreams.* The 4-night cruise add a Variety Show. On the 7-night cruises, they add the *Welcome Aboard Variety Show, Who Wants to be a Mouseketeer?,* a first-release film, and the *Farewell Variety Show.* Shows are held **twice nightly** at roughly the same times as the dinner seatings (see page 92), so if you have the early seating, you'll see the "late" show (and vice versa). Shows are 50 to 55 minutes long.

Hercules the Muse-ical—A whimsical show based on the Disney animated film Hercules. It follows the adventures of Hercules as he goes from zero to hero with lots of puns, singing, dancing, physical gags, and even Hades doing some stand-up comedy.

Golden Mickeys—This delightful, Hollywood-style award show debuted in late 2003 on both ships. A large cast of performers is on stage and in the aisles to perform favorite musical scenes from Disney films, just as you might see at the Oscars or Tonys. Flanking the stage are two movie screens that show a wide range of documentary film clips, presentations by celebrities like Roy Disney and Angela Lansbury, and excerpts from the animated films.

Disney Dreams—The must-see show for Disney fans! Anne-Marie is visited in her dreams by characters from her favorite Disney stories. It's wonderfully sentimental and the special effects at the end are not to be missed. Every Disney fan will be at least a little misty-eyed by the end of this "bedtime story." Being the most popular show aboard, Disney Dreams is often crowded. Check your *Personal Navigator* for an extra performance in the afternoon.

Who Wants to be a Mouseketeer?—Based on the popular show "Who Wants to be a Millionaire?" Contestants are selected at random from the audience by seat number and the phone a friend panel is also selected from the guests. Prizes are stateroom credits up to $750, much smaller than the one million dollars offered on television. The top prize is a seven-night cruise for two. Tip: When they select participants, they do it by seat number. If the seat is unoccupied, they move either left or right down the row to the next person. To increase your chances of being chosen, you could sit in a row with plenty of empty seats.

Variety and Cabaret Shows—Featuring guest performers who do a short sampling of the shows they'll perform later in the Rockin' Bar D/WaveBands club. Because Disney switches guest entertainers mid-cruise on the 7-night itinerary, the Farewell Variety Show features different performers than the Welcome Aboard Variety Show.

Notes: Arrive about 15 to 30 minutes before showtime to get a good seat. Disney doesn't allow videotaping, flash photography, or the saving of seats in the theatre. Preludes lounge (located just in front of the theatre) sells beverages and snacks (such as candy bars), or you can bring your own. Smoothies and beverages are sold in the theatre before the show.

Introduction · Reservations · Staterooms · Dining · Activities · Ports of Call · Magic · Index

Surfing the Internet

While it isn't as fun as a message in a bottle, the Internet is an easy, quick way to keep in touch with family, friends, and clients while you're cruising. The Internet Cafe is available 24 hours a day on the Disney Magic and Disney Wonder—it is located at the aft end of the Promenade Lounge on deck 3 midship. The cafe boasts about 8 terminals (flat panel screens, keyboards, mice, and video cameras) with comfy chairs. Typically at least one, if not several, terminals are available at any given time. Note that the Internet Cafe closes the evening before you disembark the ship.

Pricing—Alas, Internet usage is not free. Expect to pay about 75 cents a minute or $45 per hour (yikes!). If you expect to surf for more than an hour total, look for an unlimited-use package at $39.99 (3- and 4-night cruises) or $89.99 (7-night cruises). Everyone in your stateroom can use the unlimited package, but only one person can be online at a time. Look for a free access period on your first night and again on the last day (typically five free minutes), but the cafe will be very crowded during this time. Also note that you are "on the meter" from the moment you login until you logoff, and you cannot use the terminal without being logged in. You can send special "CruisEmail" ($3.95 each) or "Video Email" ($4.95 each), but note that the basic Internet usage fees are tacked on top of these rates. "CruisEmail" is an unnecessary expense—save money by using a free e-mail service such as Hotmail (http://www.hotmail.com) or Yahoo! Mail (http://mail.yahoo.com). All Internet usage fees are automatically billed to your onboard account. Parents who don't want their kids to use the Internet can contact Guest Services to disable their Internet accounts.

Applications—The terminals are installed with Web browsers and America Online. Your e-mail provider may offer a Web-based interface to check your e-mail—inquire about this before you leave home and bring any necessary web site addresses, login names, and passwords with you (see worksheet on the next page). Note that if you can access your e-mail through America Online (AOL) or the web, you avoid the CruisEmail rates noted earlier—just be sure not to send e-mail through the "E-Mail" option on the terminal and use AOL or the web instead. AOL Instant Messenger users can use the AOL application to access their buddy list and send Instant Messages. Note that if you login to any e-mail, message boards, or other sites that require a login name and password during your time on the cruise, be sure to logoff before you leave the terminal. If you do not, the next person who uses those same sites could find themselves able to access your account or post under your user name on a message board (oooooooops!). Digital Seas (http://www.digitalseas.com) provides reliable Internet access. If you have questions once you are onboard, you can check with one of the Internet Cafe managers, who are on duty during the day and early evening. There may be a printer available, though it may also incur an additional, per-page fee—inquire with the manager on duty.

One of Jennifer's hangouts, the Internet Cafe

Logging In—Expect to enter a login name—it's typically the first initial and last name of the person under whose name the cruise reservation was made, plus the stateroom number (i.e. jwatson2612). Passwords are also required, and may initially be the birthdate of person who made the cruise reservation.

Access—Only one member of your family/group can be online at the same time. Adults can use the terminals in the Cove Café (see page 127) and teens can surf in The Stack/ Common Grounds, but the same prices apply. Note that if another family member is online somewhere else, you won't be able to get online until they log off. While there are computers in the Oceaneer Club and Lab, the kids can not surf the Internet from them.

Laptops—There's no way to get your laptop on the Internet other than (possibly) connecting a laptop modem to your stateroom phone at $6.95/minute. (We haven't tried it.) You may be able to access a floppy with your data on it at the Internet Cafe, however—ask the Internet Cafe manager if this is possible. See "Doing Business Onboard" on page 245.

Off-Board Internet Access—There are Internet Cafes offering lower rates in various ports of call. In Nassau, "Tikal Tees & Tokens" has Internet access at 10 cents/min. In St. Maarten, there's an Internet Cafe at the end of the pier for 20 cents a minute. In St. Thomas, "Soapy's Station" in front of the Havensight Mall offers access at 10 cents/ min. In Key West, check out the "Internet Isle Cafe" on 118 Duval Street for 25 cents/min. In Cozumel, the "C@fe Internet" near Ave. 10 and Calle 1 has access at 10 cents/min. You can usually find Internet Cafes very near the pier—just browse or ask around.

Helpful Web Site Addresses—Use these sites while onboard to access your e-mail and other services through a Web browser. Tip: E-mail your favorite web site addresses to yourself before you cruise!

PassPorter Porthole—http://www.passporter.com/dcl/porthole.htm (offers links to all of the sites below, as well as links to PassPorter and other Disney cruise-related sites)
AOL E-Mail: http://aolmail.aol.com
AOL Instant Messenger: http://www.aim.com (click "AIM Express")
Yahoo Mail: http://mail.yahoo.com
Hotmail: http://www.hotmail.com
Comcast: http://www.comcast.net (click the "Mail" tab)
Earthlink Web Mail: http://webmail.earthlink.net
NetZero: http://www.netzero.net
uReach: http://www.ureach.com (access e-mail, faxes, and voice mail)
Mail2Web: http://www.mail2web.com (send your e-mail to the Web)
My E-Mail: _____

Account	Login Name	Password	Notes

Tip: Use some system to disguise your passwords here, just in case your PassPorter is seen by someone else.

Introduction · Reservations · Staterooms · Dining · Activities · Ports of Call · Magic · Index

Rejuvenating at the Spa

The Vista Spa & Salon on deck 9 forward offers world-class spa treatments, a hair salon, an aerobics studio, and a fitness room. The 8,500 sq. ft. (2590 sq. m.) spa is exclusively for **adults only** (with the exception of some special teen days—see your *Personal Navigator*). Like most ship spas, the facility is operated by Steiner (http://www.steinerleisure.com) and the spa staff tends to be female and young. The spa is open from 8:00 am to 10:00 pm.

If the spa interests you, we recommend you visit during the **open house** on your first afternoon (check your *Personal Navigator*). This is also the best time to make reservations for spa treatments, which can go very quickly. Read this section well so you have a good idea of what spa treatments you may want to reserve (see next page). Note that reservations must be cancelled at least 24 hours in advance to avoid a 50% cancellation fee.

The **hair salon** offers a variety of services—reservations are necessary and they fill up quickly for formal and semi-formal evenings. The hair stylists specialize in European styles and all the basics. Prices: woman's hair cuts with wash, cut, and style—$47 to $63 (depends on hair length); women's shampoo-and-style or "up-style"—$27 to $41; man's cut and style—$26; semi-permanent wave—$44 to $53; permanent wave ($62 to $89); highlights ($71 to $89); permanent color (roots)—$58 to $71; and permanent color (full head)—$76 to $94. You can also get nail services: A 45-minute manicure is $36 and a 60-minute pedicure is $50.

The **aerobics studio** is where many of the fitness classes and seminars are offered. Activities are listed in the *Personal Navigator* as well as on a schedule available in the Vista Spa. You can expect complimentary hair consultations, metabolism seminars, fatburner aerobics, detoxification seminars, skin care clinics, introduction to Pilates, de-stress techniques, Step Magic, and cardio kickbox. You are encouraged to sign up in advance for the free classes and seminars, which last about 30 to 45 minutes each. Group personal training may be offered on your cruise for $45/60 minutes. You can also get a Body Composition Analysis which measures your body's metabolic rate, water, fat, and lean tissue—price is $27 and includes analysis and recommendations from a fitness instructor. Pre-registration is required for the personal training sessions and body composition analysis.

The **fitness room** has a panoramic view and overlooks the bridge—in fact, it's the only place on the ship where you can peek into the bridge. You can use free weights, Cybex weight machines, treadmills, stair-steppers, ab-rollers, and stationary bikes. No fees or reservations are needed to use the fitness room, though there may be a waitlist for a treadmill during peak times. The fitness room is more crowded on at-sea days. Open from 7:00 am to 8:00 pm.

Tip: Walk (or jog) all around the perimeter of deck 4—the "promenade" deck. Four laps equals one mile (1.6 km). Want to walk with others? Check your *Personal Navigator* for instructor-led "Walk a Mile" morning sessions.

Relaxing in the Tropical Rainforest

Spa treatments are given in one of twelve private treatment rooms. Separate men's and women's locker rooms are available with restrooms, delightful showers, saunas, steamrooms, and lockers. Some people prefer the showers at the spa to the showers in their staterooms—there's more room and the water pressure's better. Present your Key to the World card at the check-in desk to get a robe and locker key at no charge.

Spa Treatments—A variety of treatments are available at prices ranging from $26–$288. A menu of treatments is available in the spa, but here's a sneak peek: <u>Spa Taster</u> (massage and facial for $89/50 min. total or $178 for <u>couples massage</u>); Aromaspa Ocean Wrap with Well Being Back Massage ($144/80 min.); Ionithermie Algae Super-Detox ($108/55 min.); Elemis Absolute Face and Body Treatment ($144/150 min. or $288 for a couples massage); LT Oxygen Lifting Facial ($89/55 min.); Total Glow Sunless Tan Application with Exfoliation ($89/50 min.); <u>Well Being Massage</u> ($89/50 min. total or $178 for couples massage); Chakra Balancing Capsule ($41/25 min., $99/course of 3, or $68/50 min.); <u>Tropical Rainforest</u> (see below) and the <u>Surial Ritual Chamber</u> (see below). We've underlined the spa treatments we've tried and would do again!

Tropical Rainforest—An innovative, relaxing "thermal suite" with a dry sauna, a chamomile-essence sauna, an eucalyptus steam room, and special showers that spray water overhead and on the sides. The main room has four heated, tiled loungers (see photo on previous page)—loll about on one then cool off in a fog shower. Jennifer loves this! The Tropical Rainforest is open from 8:00 am to 10:00 pm. It's very popular and can have upwards of two dozen people—men and women—at any one time. Swimsuits are required. Cost is $15 for an all-day pass, $30 for a 3-day pass, $50 for a week pass, or just $8 if you're having a spa treatment.

Surial Ritual Chamber—Pronounced "sir-eye-all," this unique treatment is inspired by the Rasul cleansing rituals performed in the Sultan's harems during the Ottomon Empire. You are escorted to the tile-lined ritual chamber, which is a suite with a sitting area, steam room, and shower. Exfoliating mud is in a small bowl—smear the mud on yourself or on each other (if you're with a friend) and relax in the steam room to absorb the minerals and trace elements from the mud. Afterwards, shower off and apply complimentary lotions and scrubs. This is very popular with couples. We loved it ourselves! Be warned that it does get very hot. Bring some bottled water—you'll probably get quite thirsty—and extra towels. Cost is $68 for 1 to 3 people for 50 minutes.

Special Treatments—Check your *Personal Navigator* or visit the spa to learn about special treatments offered during your cruise. We've seen Teen Days for hair and nails, Ladies Nights, and a Mid-Cruise Booster Package. The Ladies Night package is a massage, foot massage, and facial in a private room, plus a trip to the Tropical Rainforest where you can enjoy champagne and chocolates in the company of other women—it appears to be available on the 3- or 4-night cruises only due to popularity. Cost is $150 for 120 minutes.

Cabana Massages—Get a private or couples massage in one of the delightful cabanas on Castaway Cay. Note that the treatments in the cabanas are a bit more expensive than the same ones on the ship. Reserve early as they book up quickly. We recommend you avoid the first or second appointment of the day, just in case the ship docks late. See page 228.

Spa Products—The spa personnel push their spa products during treatments, which is uncomfortable for some guests. The products are from Elemis (http://www.elemis.com) and good, but pricey. If you don't want to buy a product, just say "no thank you" and be firm. You could also indicate on your health form that you aren't interested in purchasing products.

Tipping—It's customary to tip 15%, though really good service may deserve 20%. 10% is fine for treatments like the Surial Ritual Chamber. Just write in the amount you wish to tip on your bill and it will be charged to your onboard account.

Introduction

Reservations

Staterooms

Dining

Activities

Ports of Call

Magic

Index

Learning Through Seminars

Need help whiling away the hours at sea on the 7-night cruise? The Disney Magic offers three multi-part programs open to all guests 18 and over. There are no sign-ups, no fees, and no requirements to attend. You just show up for the program sessions that interest you.

Disney's Art of Entertaining—These presentations showcase a senior chef who prepares a dish, of course allowing you to sample it. They also include tips on place setting, decorating, and napkin folding. Some have wine sampling. Programs include Great Expectations: The Appetizer, Dazzling Desserts, and Signature Entrée. Also check your *Personal Navigator* for a Galley Tour. You get a guided tour of the main galley between Lumière's and Parrot Cay, complete with fresh-baked chocolate chip cookies at the end of the tour. Attend the last presentation in this series to get tickets for the galley tour, or check your *Personal Navigator*.

Tip: Disney Wonder has a **"Culinary Demonstration"**—check your *Personal Navigator*.

Disney Behind the Scenes—Presentations by a Disney historian, actor, or artist (either a special guest or regular crew member), usually presented in the Buena Vista Theater. These presentations vary in length and by topic but they are all entertaining and well worth the time. Programs include a Stage Works Tour (meet the stage production crew members—they demonstrate some of the stage effects, answer questions, and allow you to go up on the stage and take a look around at the set and props); Costuming Tour (see and even wear some of the costumes used in the show); and a Q&A session with the Walt Disney Theater cast (hear stories and get answers to questions).

Disney's Navigator Series—Programs include "The Making of the Disney Magic" (the captain presents a video showing the history of the Disney Magic from concept to construction to maiden voyage, and then answers questions) and Captain's Corner (a Q&A session with the senior staff covering just about everything involving the cruise and the ship—it's very impressive, informative, and fun).

Wine Tasting Seminar—This is a good place to mention the "Stem to Stern" Wine Tasting Seminar held on all cruises in either Palo or one of the lounges. For $12/adult (21 and up only), the Cellar Master introduces you to wine types, gives you tips on identifying wines, and shows you how to properly taste a wine. Seminar includes tastings of four to six wines. You may also receive a commemorative pin for attending the seminar. (Pin traders take note!) Reservations are required—stop by Guest Services to make reservations. Typically held on Sundays and Mondays (Eastern) or Mondays and Tuesdays (Western).

Beer Tasting—Check your *Personal Navigator* for a beer tasting session held in Diversions (deck 3 forward) on the Magic only.

Art of Disney Magic Self-Guided Tour—The Walt Disney Company was founded by an artist, so it's natural that its beautiful ships are full of art—original as well as reproductions. The Art of the Disney Magic tour is a self-guided tour of the art found everywhere on the Magic (sorry, the tour is not available on the Wonder). Pick up a tour booklet at Guest Services—it leads you around the ship, describing and explaining the artwork. Get the booklet early in the cruise so that you can read about the art in the restaurants as you dine in each. If you'd like to see photos of the stops on the tour, visit http://www.castawayclub.com/dmtour.htm.

Sporting Around at the ESPN Skybox and Other Lounges

Tucked up in the forward smokestack of the Disney Wonder is the ESPN Skybox. (The Skybox on the Magic made way for The Stack in September 2003—visit Diversions for sports action—see page 127.) The only way to reach the ESPN Skybox is via the midship elevators/stairs—it's on deck 11, the highest point on the ship. This **floating sports bar** is a bit on the small side, but it uses the space well. The brightly-lit main room has tables and bar stools, six state-of-the-art TV screens (including one big-screen TV), a bar along one side of the room, and a couple video games. Off to the side is a nifty stadium seating area (see photo) with yet another big-screen TV. There are 13 TVs in all. The ESPN Skybox is open to all ages, and smoking is allowed (including pipe and cigar smoking). It usually opens at 3:00 pm and closes at midnight. Note: After the Wonder's October 2004 drydock renovation, its ESPN Skybox may be converted to a teen club like The Stack on the Magic.

Unlike the ESPN Club at Disney's BoardWalk in Walt Disney World Resort, the ESPN Skybox does not serve meals. They have **plenty of drinks** plus light snacks. ESPN Skybox offers a 22 oz. refillable, glass beer mug for $15. You can get refills at the 16 oz. price ($3.25 to $4.00)—see page 107. You may be able to buy cigarettes and cigars here—ask a crew member.

Staying true to their "sports now, all the time" motto, the ESPN Skybox's TVs have satellite links, and you can also get radio broadcasts. Up to four **live sporting events** may be shown at any one time. Programming is from the domestic and international operations of ESPN, ESPN2, and ABC. If the place isn't busy and you'd like a different channel, try asking the crew member behind the bar if the station can be changed.

© MediaMarx, Inc.

While the Skybox is **small**, it isn't usually crowded—it can seat up to 70 people at one time. But the smoke can get a bit thick and conversation is difficult with the noise.

Special events may be held in the ESPN Skybox. On the 7-night cruise look for an ESPN Sports Trivia Challenge. Teens take over the ESPN Skybox one evening, too. And on New Year's Day in the past, ESPN Skybox has hosted a Tailgate Party for college football games.

Dave cheers in the ESPN Skybox

Beyond the ESPN Skybox are several **more lounges**. Besides the ones we described on pages 126–127, you'll find Preludes (deck 4 forward), open from 6:00 pm to 9:30 pm for pre-show and afterglow drinks—all ages welcome; Signals (deck 9 forward) is next to the adult pool so it's limited to ages 18 & up—it's typically open until 7:00 pm; Outlook Bar (deck 10 forward) overlooks the adult pool and seems a bit removed from the hustle of the lower decks—all ages welcome; and the Promenade Lounge (deck 4 midship) offers games in the day and live entertainment in the evenings for all ages—it's usually open to midnight.

Kicking Back and Relaxing

This chapter would not be complete without a few words on how to get the most out of your "down time" on the cruise. You know—relax, bum around, sunbathe, or whatever. This is one of the benefits of cruising, after all!

Relaxing on Deck—Looking for the best place to loll about in a deck chair? Deck 9 is great if you want to be near the pools or people-watch, but it gets very crowded. Try the deck aft of Topsider's/Beach Blanket Buffet after dinner—almost no one goes there. Deck 10 has lots of sun. Deck 7 Aft has a secluded and quiet deck. Deck 4 has very comfy, padded deck loungers and lots of shade (see photo below). The lounge chairs on decks 7-10 are made of plastic and metal and recline in several positions, including completely flat. Disney requests that you not reserve the lounge chairs, so don't drape a towel over a chair to use later. If you see loungers being saved with towels, don't be shy about using them. There are also tables and chairs on deck 9 which are mostly in the shade and protected by windows, but decks 4 and 10 can get very windy. Alas, only the larger verandahs at the very aft of the ship are large enough for lounge chairs, but regular deck chairs are on each verandah.

Sunbathing—Sunworshippers typically prefer deck 10. Deck 7 aft works well, too. Decks 4 and 9 are typically too shady. Don't forget sunscreen—the Caribbean sun is harsh.

Reading—With all the things to do onboard, you might not think to bring a book. But if you enjoy reading, you'll absolutely adore reading in a deck chair on your verandah, on deck 4 (our personal favorite), or deck 7 aft.

Strolling—Haven't you always dreamed of perambulating about a deck? Deck 4, also called the Promenade Deck, allows you to walk all around the perimeter of the ship (4 laps = 1 mile). Decks 9 and 10 are also options, though they can get crowded during the day. Deck 10 gets very windy and wet in the evenings, but if you can handle that it makes for fun walks.

Napping—There's nothing like a good nap, especially while cruising. It's something about the lulling effect of the waves. Your stateroom is a great place for a nap, but you may also catch some zzz's in a quiet spot like deck 7 aft.

People-Watching—It's hard to find a spot where you can't people-watch on a ship with this many people! Deck 9 and deck 4 overlooking the atrium are particularly good spots, though.

Spa—The Tropical Rainforest in the Vista Spa (see pages 134-135) is a relaxing spot to spend time.

Shopping—Why not? See page 237.

Relaxing on deck 4

Lost & Found
Did you leave your half-finished book on your lounge chair and forget about it? Report it to Guest Services on deck 3 midship. If you discover you left something behind after disembarking, check with Lost & Found in the terminal or call Disney Cruise Line after returning home. Don't forget to I.D. all your important items—just in case!

Overlooked Attractions Aboard

Disney is renowned for its attention to detail, and the Disney Cruise Line is no exception. There are any number of smaller, overlooked attractions and activities that may interest you. Here's a list of our favorites:

Hidden Mickey Hunt—How many Mickeys can you find onboard? The internationally-recognized Mickey Mouse head (one big circle and two smaller circles for the ears) has been hidden in murals, railings, foot stools—you name it! We know of over 25 on the ships, including one in the dinner plate at Palo. Ask at Guest Services for the Hidden Mickey Challenge—it's a fun activity geared towards kids, but still fun for adults. To see the photos of the hidden Mickeys, visit http://www.castawayclub.com/hmick.htm.

Listening Stations—Listen to your favorite tunes in the adults-only lounge (Sessions/Cadillac Lounge), the Cove Café (Magic), and Common Grounds (Wonder). Just check the playlist for the music, punch in the code on the pad, and put on the headphones.

Pin Trading—This popular activity that started at the parks has migrated to the cruises! You can buy all sorts of enamel, cloisonné-style pins on the cruise (there are about 50 unique cruise pins) to trade with crew members and guests. Or bring pins from the parks or from home. (Make sure "© Disney" is printed on the back if you hope to trade with crew members.) Check your *Personal Navigator* for trading sessions. The shopping supplement distributed daily highlights the featured pin for the day (see page 237 for shopping). There's even a PassPorter enamel pin, though you can't trade it for Disney pins—see page 262.

Silent Auction—Starting at about 6:00 pm on your first day, several collectible items from the Disney ships are displayed in Preludes (deck 4 fwd). High-priced auction items include artwork and artifacts. Here's how it works: Browse the items. If you see something you like, note the lot number and minimum bid. When you're ready to bid, write your bid on the bid sheet. The auction typically ends at 8:30 pm on the last night of your cruise—check the rules posted in Preludes for more details. If you have the highest bid when the auction ends, you win! Payment is due right away (you may charge it), after which you can claim your item.

Fantasia Reading Room—This small room on the Disney Magic is located on deck 2 between the midship elevators. There aren't many books here, but there are some board games. This is a quiet place to play cards or do homework (though kids must be with an adult). Open 8:00 am to midnight. The room exists on the Disney Wonder, but it may not be open to the public.

Off-The-Beaten-Path—A thorough exploration reveals several little nooks and crannies. Explore hallways, elevator lobbies, and staircases for Disney art. The secluded deck on deck 7 aft (open from 7:00 am to 11:00 pm) is great for sunbathing. Check out deck 6 behind the midship elevators—you can walk through and take a good look at the mural. Deck 8 aft also has a small deck that is sometimes open. And Mickey's favorite overlooked attraction is the bridge view from the fitness center—not the treadmills in front of the glass, just the view.

Religious Services

Seven-night cruisers can attend an interdenominational service in Off Beat (deck 3 forward) on Sunday at 9:00 am. Erev Shabbat (Jewish Sabbath Eve) services are held in Off Beat on Friday at 5:30 pm. Or attend services in Cape Canaveral on Sunday—see http://www.marinersguide.com/regions/florida/capecanaveral/churches.html. Western Caribbean cruisers can attend afternoon services on Sunday in Key West—see http://www.marinersguide.com/regions/florida/keywest/churches.html.

Introduction
Reservations
Staterooms
Dining
Activities
Ports of Call
Magic
Index

Playing Your Way

If you've read this chapter, you know just how much there is to do aboard a Disney ship. Here are some tips to help you make the most of it all:

- To help you **navigate the ship**, remember this general rule: we had <u>Fun</u> in the <u>Forward</u> (front of ship) and we <u>Ate</u> in the <u>Aft</u> (back).

- "Make sure all the adults/teens in your party **wear watches**—you won't want to be without them when scheduling times to meet up!" — contributed by Disney Cruiser Angie James

- "To get the **best spa reservations**, skip the tour of the Vista Spa on your first day. By the time the tour finishes, all the good appointment times might be taken. Do your research here, know what you want before you board, and make your reservations as soon as the Vista Spa opens around 1:30 pm on your first day." — by contributing author Mickey Morgan

  Midship with Mickey

- "If you lose something on the ship, don't forget to try **lost and found**! My husband's watch fell off in the ocean at Castaway Cay. He used a snorkel mask to look for it but by the time we got on the ship, he was sure it was gone for good. During dinner he checked at lost and found and there it was! A good samaritan had turned it in. There was a large box full of cameras, watches, hats, etc. Later in Ohio my oldest daughter realized she had left a sweatshirt from her swim team either in the theatre or the Oceaneer Lab—a call to lost and found later and it was shipped to our home!" — contributed by Disney cruiser Robin McConnell

- "An often overlooked activity onboard is the **'Til We Meet Again'** show on the last night of the cruise. Most of the characters from the nightly stage show meet in the lobby atrium along the grand staircase for pictures (very organized!) and a song. Very cute and a nice addition!" — contributed by Disney cruiser Daniel Bates

Magical Memory

- *"As a mother, the highlight of the cruise had to be seeing my little boys up on stage that last night during the Discover the Magic show. My son Tommy, who is usually very shy, was such a ham, singing along with his new friends from the Oceaneer Club. Then, to see the look on their faces when Captain Mickey joined them on stage—it was pure joy! Every parent in that theater was just as proud as can be to see their little one performing on that Magical stage."*

  ...as told by Disney cruiser Mary Walsh

Putting Into Port

LEARN the basics of having fun in port

GET where you want to go easily

DECIDE what ports to visit and which excursions to do

DISCOVER the ports and attractions of the Caribbean

Land, ahoy! For many passengers, the promise of visiting new places is the big appeal of cruising. The Caribbean is a world away from what most of us are familiar with, and the lure of exotic lands is great. If this describes you, then this chapter was written with your needs in mind. We hope to help you determine which ports you'd most like to visit (and hence which cruise itinerary to choose) and what you can do while you're in each port.

Each and every port on the various Disney cruise itineraries, including their home port of Port Canaveral and their private island, Castaway Cay, is represented by a "port guide." Each port guide is eight pages long (Port Canaveral is just six pages as it has no Disney shore excursions) and includes general information (time zone, currency, climate, etc.), ambience, history, transportation, safety, walking tour, layout, attractions, sports, beaches, and shopping. In addition to all this, we add one of our own maps of the port and a detailed listing of the shore excursions offered through Disney. These port guides are by no means comprehensive. (That would require an entire book for each port.) Rather, they focus on what's possible and practical during the 8 to 12 hours you'll have in port and should give most day visitors an excellent overview.

For those of you who've "been there and done that" or simply don't want to venture off the ship, feel free to stay onboard while the ship is in port. Disney offers plenty of activities onboard during port days, and you'll enjoy the slower pace and quieter atmosphere of the ship. Do note that the onboard shops will be closed while you're in port, and some places (like Flounder's Reef) will have shorter operating hours.

On all four-night and all seven-night itineraries, you'll have a day (or two, or three—see pages 32–35) when you visit no ports at all. These are called "at-sea" days, and most passengers adore them. The crew offers more stuff to do onboard than usual, and the ship hums with activity. Plus, there's just something special about "being underway" during the day, instead of at night as is more typical on port days.

Island Daze

Feeling adventurous? There's a whole world to explore off-ship. Each of the ports, all of which are islands (even Port Canaveral, which is on a barrier island), offer fun things to do and explore. Here are the details:

If you wish, you can **get off the ship** at each port (guests under 18 will need to be with an adult or have the permission of a responsible adult to go alone) and there is no additional fee to simply visit the ports—Disney folds the port fees into your cruise price. It does cost extra to book shore excursions (see next page), and if you plan to eat ashore anywhere other than Castaway Cay, that cost is also your responsibility.

It's fun to watch as the **port slides into view**. Check your *Personal Navigator* for the arrival/departure times and observe from deck 4, deck 10, or from your verandah.

While the ship and Castaway Cay have a cashless system, you'll need to **bring cash, major credit cards, and/or travelers checks** to pay for anything at the other ports. Note that there is no ATM (cash machine) on the ship, but there are ATMs on the islands (except Castaway Cay). You will want to have small bills to tip excursion operators, too.

Some of the ports attract merchants aggressively **hawking their wares** near the dock. If this makes you uncomfortable, avoid eye contact and keep walking. Most travelers find that hawkers will respect a polite, but firm, "no thank you."

If you plan to shop on shore, pick up the **Shopping in Paradise** port guide at the gangway. It lists recommended stores at which to shop, and if you purchase from one of those stores, you'll receive a 30-day guarantee on repair or replacement (but the guarantee doesn't help if you change your mind about an item). If you have questions, a knowledgeable crew member is stationed at the gangway or at the Shore Excursion Desk on deck 3 midship.

Live presentations on shore excursions and shopping are held during the cruise (freebies may be given out to lucky attendees at the shopping presentation) and later broadcast on your stateroom TV. Check the *Personal Navigator* for times. Stop by the Shore Excursion Desk on deck 3 midship for port and shopping information and excursion brochures (see examples at http://www.dcltribute.com). Desk hours are listed in the *Personal Navigator*, too.

Some guests like to bring **drinks and snacks** with them during their time onshore (see page 108). Be aware that you can't bring open containers of food back on the ship.

Changing facilities may not always be handy for those **planning to swim** or get wet. We suggest you "underdress" your swimsuit (wear it under your clothing) before going ashore.

Some guests **never get off the ship** at the ports, preferring to stay onboard and enjoy the ship's amenities. We've done this ourselves on non-research cruises. The decision to stay onboard or explore the port is a personal one, however, and no one way is right for everyone. If this is your first visit to a port, we suggest you at least get off and look around for an hour, or book a shore excursion. If you decide you like it, you can explore more!

Disney **does not guarantee** that you'll visit all ports on an itinerary. Bad weather or rough seas can prevent docking and you may spend the day at sea or at an alternate port instead. Although you will not receive a refund of cruise fare if this happens, you will not be charged for the cancelled Disney shore excursions, either. In addition, you may have port charges for the port you missed refunded to your stateroom account. In any case, Disney will do what they can to make your extra onboard time fun.

Shore Excursions

Disney offers many different shore excursions at each port, with the exception of Port Canaveral. These activities incur an additional, per-person fee, anywhere from $6 for Castaway Cay float rentals to $345 (for the Atlantis Deep Explorer in Grand Cayman). In most cases, the excursions are not run by Disney but by outside companies. The good news is that if you book one of these excursions through Disney, virtually all details are taken care of for you. All you need to do is reserve the shore excursion, pay the fees, and show up at the designated meeting point to go ashore. Here are the details:

A **variety of shore excursions** are available, from sightseeing, walking tours, and beach visits to snorkeling, scuba diving, and kayaking. Check the last two pages of each port guide in this chapter for a list of the shore excursions offered at the time of writing. You'll also receive a shore excursion guide with your cruise documentation, and you can check http://www.disneycruise.com (click "Fun Ashore") for a list of the excursions and prices. Note that the excursion details, times, and prices given in this guidebook may change.

Once you've read this chapter carefully, choose and **reserve your excursions in advance**. Some excursions are very popular and get booked quickly. To make reservations, call 877-566-0968 within 7 to 60 days of your cruise. (Tip: You may be able to make reservations earlier once you've paid in full—inquire at 888-DCL-2500.) You can also e-mail excursion requests to dcl.shore.excursion@disneycruise.com, or fill out the form that comes with your cruise documentation and fax to 407-566-7031. You can alter your shore excursion requests any time up to two days prior to sailing. After that time, all excursion reservations are considered final and cannot be changed or refunded. If you do not pre-reserve shore excursions, you can visit the Shore Excursion Desk (deck 3 midship) to check availability and reserve excursions. Use the worksheet on page 231 to record your preferences.

When you pre-reserve your excursions, fees are billed to your onboard account and your **excursion tickets** are waiting in your stateroom upon arrival. If you book excursions onboard, you'll receive your tickets in your stateroom the night before the excursion. When you get your tickets, check the time and meeting location printed on it. With each ticket is an excursion waiver form, which you should fill out and sign ahead of time.

On the day of your excursion, bring both the ticket(s) and the signed waiver(s) to the **meeting location** at the assigned time, where they are collected. You'll receive a color-coded sticker to wear, identifying yourself as a member of the excursion group. When ready, a crew member leads the group off the ship and to the excursion.

You can usually book the same excursions offered by Disney for a little less if you **do it on your own**. The excursion operators are locally known and most have web sites. You'll need to find your own transportation to and from the excursion, but in return you'll have more flexibility and you can take side trips if you wish. Weigh these benefits against the peace of mind you'll have when booking through Disney. We offer tips to do an excursion "On Your Own" at the end of excursion descriptions in this chapter. Then why book with Disney Cruise Line? First, it's simple and easy. One call and everything is arranged. Second, Disney books blocks of excursion tickets, sometimes entire excursions—so you might have trouble getting a ticket on your own. Third, if a Disney excursion is delayed, they'll hold the ship for you—do it yourself, and the ship may sail without you.

Midship
with
Mickey

All Ashore! All Aboard!

If you decide to take a shore excursion or simply explore the port on your own, you'll need to get off the ship and on the shore. Here's how:

To find out what time you can **go ashore** at a given port, look for the "All Ashore" time in your *Personal Navigator*—we also give typical times in each of our port guides. This time is typically the earliest you can disembark in the port. (You don't have to go ashore if you prefer to stay onboard.) Ports that put more limitations on disembarking (such as Grand Cayman) may require that guests not on shore excursions meet in the Walt Disney Theatre before going ashore. If this is necessary, the details will be listed in your *Personal Navigator*.

At most ports the ship **pulls up right alongside the dock** and guests step out right onto the pier. When this isn't possible, guests must be ferried ashore in "tenders." Boarding a tender isn't difficult—you simply step off the ship and onto the tender and enjoy the ride to the shore. If the seas are rough, you are more likely to feel the effects while on the tender. At the time of writing, the only port that always requires tenders is Grand Cayman—other ports may require tenders if Disney cannot secure a berth (most typically at St. Thomas) or if rough seas inhibit docking.

Before you go ashore, pack a day bag with bottled water, sunscreen, hat, raingear, a watch, and any other necessities you may need. You may also want to "underdress" your bathing suit so you don't need to find changing facilities in the port. And make sure everyone has their Key to the World card and, for those over 18, photo I.D. (If you lose your Key to the World card, go to Guest Services on deck 3 midship.)

To go ashore, follow the signs in the passageways to locate the specific "**tender lobby**" from which you'll disembark. There are two of these, both located on deck 1 (see page 5). Remember, however, that deck 1 passageways don't extend the length of the ship, so you'll need to take the proper elevator to deck 1 to reach the correct lobby—the signs won't lead you wrong. Note that if you booked a shore excursion through Disney, you'll disembark with the other guests going on the shore excursion. See page 143 for more details.

Once you're in the tender lobby, have your **Key to the World card** (and photo I.D.) in your hand so the crew may swipe your card and allow you to disembark. Guests under 18 must have an adult accompany them to the gangway to go ashore anywhere other than Castaway Cay. Once you're cleared to go ashore, simply step out onto the dock or into the tender. Watch for a crew member handing out towels for use ashore (towels are bath-size, not beach-size). If they run out of towels at the gangway, the crew members will invite you to take towels from the pool areas on deck 9.

While you're onshore, **keep an eye on the time**—you don't want to miss the boat! The "All Aboard" time is noted in your *Personal Navigator*. If you are late, the ship won't wait for you and it is your responsibility to get to the next port to reboard the ship. The exception to this rule is for guests on one of Disney's own shore excursions—if their excursion makes you late, Disney will hold the ship's departure for you.

Reboarding is simple. Just return to the dock area, present your Key to the World card (and photo I.D.) to security personnel to enter the dock, show your I.D. again to the Disney crew to either board the ship or board the tender (which then takes you to the ship). You will need to put your belongings through a security scanner once you're onboard and have your Key to the World card scanned again (so Disney knows you're back on the ship). Don't bring restricted items onboard, such as opened food and black coral.

Port Canaveral and Cocoa Beach
(All Itineraries—Home Port)

Far more than just a place to park a cruise ship, Port Canaveral offers an exciting extension to your Disney cruise vacation. This is Florida's Space Coast, home to the Kennedy Space Center, 72 miles (116 km.) of prime Atlantic beachfront, the Merritt Island National Wildlife Refuge, ecotourism, water sports, sport fishing, etc. Do you have an extra week?

Cocoa Beach at sunrise

AMBIENCE

Thundering rockets, crashing surf, and the total peace of an empty beach come together in the Port Canaveral area. You won't find built-up beach resorts like Daytona or Fort Lauderdale here, though crowds do rise for space shuttle launches. There are just a relative handful of hotels and beachfront condos—so quiet that this is where endangered sea turtles choose to nest! Whether you unwind here prior to your cruise or wind up your vacation with a visit to the astronauts, this can easily be one of the best ports you ever visit.

GETTING AROUND

You'll either want to drive your own car or rent a car to get around (taxis are not abundant). A list of area transportation companies is at http://www.portcanaveral.org/about/transport2.htm. The Space Coast region stretches from Titusville in the north to Melbourne in the south (see map on page 149). I-95 runs north/south on the mainland, paralleled by U.S. 1 for local driving. Many attractions are on the barrier islands to the east, across the Banana and Indian Rivers, and the Intercoastal Waterway. SR A1A is the principal route for beach access. Commercial airlines serve Melbourne International Airport and Orlando International. Port Canaveral is just south of Kennedy Space Center, and Cocoa Beach is immediately south of Port Canaveral, roughly halfway between Titusville and Melbourne. See chapter 2 for full details on travel to and from Port Canaveral and the Disney Cruise Terminal.

FACTS

Size: 72 mi. long (116 km.) x 15 mi. wide (24 km.) (Brevard County, Florida)	
Temperatures: Highs: 72°F (22°C) to 91°F (33°C); lows: 50°F (10°C) to 73°F (23°C)	
Population: 476,000 (Brevard)	**Busy Season:** Mid-February to April
Language: English	**Money:** U.S. Dollar
Time Zone: Eastern (DST observed)	**Transportation:** Cars and taxis
Phones: Dial 911 for emergencies, local pay phone calls = 35 cents	

Introduction · Reservations · Staterooms · Dining · Activities · Ports of Call · Magic · Index

KENNEDY SPACE CENTER

Exploring Kennedy Space Center and the Astronaut Hall of Fame

It just wouldn't be the Space Coast without the Kennedy Space Center (KSC). The huge gantries (launch towers) and Vehicle Assembly Building dominate the horizon for miles around. Those aren't high-rise condos along the beach; they're the historic launch towers of Cape Canaveral!

A view of the KSC gantries from Playalinda Beach

You can easily **spend two days** at the KSC Visitor Complex exploring the history and future of the U.S. space program. Two IMAX theaters, live talks with veteran astronauts, hands-on exhibits, historic spacecraft, and the sobering Astronaut Memorial make the **main visitor complex** an all-day experience. The complex also has a children's play area and shops offering a wide selection of souvenirs. Seven eateries include the Orbit Cafeteria, New Frontier Café, and Mila's, a full-service restaurant. When you're done at the main complex, board a bus to tour the working Space Center (allow three more hours). The bus stops at the huge **Apollo/Saturn V interpretive center**, displaying a Saturn V rocket, an Apollo command module and Lunar Module, plus several theaters, Apollo Launch Control, a snack bar, and a shop. Visit the **Launch Complex 39** observation gantry, a four-story tower affording sweeping views of the nearby shuttle launch pads, and even more interpretive exhibits.

ASTRONAUT HALL OF FAME

View historic spacecraft and memorabilia, and experience astronaut-training simulators at the **Astronaut Hall of Fame** in nearby Titusville, which is part of the KSC Visitor Complex. Here you can learn about past NASA astronauts and take a ride in various flight simulators to find out just what it is like to be an astronaut. Mission:SPACE fans take note: The G-Force Trainer is a longer, faster cousin of the simulator ride at Epcot—and at four times the force of gravity (4 Gs), it's not for the faint of heart! Almost half of the Hall of Fame is dedicated to hands-on experiences, and all exhibits and motion simulators are included in the price of admission. The Hall of Fame is a nine-mile drive from Kennedy Space Center, but it's worth the trip and good for at least an afternoon's enjoyment.

Exploring Kennedy Space Center and the Astronaut Hall of Fame

Two-day admission (Maximum Access Badge) to KSC and the Astronaut Hall of Fame: $35/adult and $25/children 3–11. Single-day admission is $29/$19 for KSC; $16/$12 for the Astronaut Hall of Fame. **Two special tours**, NASA Up Close and Cape Canaveral: Then and Now, may be available, too. These tours go even farther, with an expert guide to bring you into restricted areas omitted from the regular tour. The tours last about three hours, each costs an extra $22/$16, and they're well worth it! Also available launch days or any day of the week is a chance to **dine with an astronaut**. These meals add $20/adult, $13/child 3–11 to the price of admission.

Another program is the **Astronaut Training Experience (ATX)** available for guests 14 and older at $225/person—it's held from 10:00 am to 4:30 pm at the Astronaut Hall of Fame. This is an in-depth, immersion program which includes motion simulators, exclusive tours, first-hand experiences with veteran NASA astronauts, gear, and lunch. Guests under 18 must be accompanied by an adult. Some simulators have height/weight restrictions. Advance reservations are required—call 321-449-4400.

The Visitor Complex also sells **tickets to Space Shuttle launches**, when KSC is closed to private vehicles. For $34 to $56 you get off-site parking, a ride to the viewing area, and Visitors Complex admission (optional). The official Kennedy Space Center launch schedule is at http://www-pao.ksc.nasa.gov/kscpao/schedule/schedule.htm.

Directions to Kennedy Space Center: From Cocoa Beach/Port Canaveral take SR 528 west to SR 3 north, and follow the signs for the Visitor Complex. From the mainland, take I-95 or US 1 to Titusville, then take SR 407 east. Visit http://www.kennedyspacecenter.com or call 321-449-4444 for **more information**. Tickets are available on-site and online. Open every day but Christmas. Normal hours: 9:00 am–5:30 pm. The last tour bus departs at 2:15 pm, so be sure to start your day early!

Directions to the Astronaut Hall of Fame: From Kennedy Space Center, take SR 405 west across the Indian River and follow signs to the Astronaut Hall of Fame. From Cocoa Beach/Port Canaveral, take SR 528 to US 1 (Titusville exit), then turn right onto Vectorspace Blvd. From the mainland, take I-95 or US 1 to Titusville, get off at SR 405, and follow signs. Normal hours: 10:00 am–6:30 pm.

ADMISSION

DIRECTIONS

PLAYING

Exploring Port Canaveral and Cocoa Beach

Some of Florida's **best beaches** line the Space Coast. Cocoa Beach offers miles of soft, white sand and rolling surf. Beach access is easy, with public access points every few blocks. There's metered parking at the public accesses, or walk from the nearby motels. Cocoa Beach Pier at 401 Meade Ave. offers a variety of on-pier restaurants. For a back-to-nature experience, Canaveral National Seashore's **Playalinda Beach** is located just north of the Kennedy Space Center boundary line. It offers a long, gorgeous beach protected by a tall sand dune and great views of the Kennedy Space Center gantries. It's closed for shuttle launches and landings and closes at 6:00 pm at all times. $5 fee per car per day. Camping on the beach is allowed November–April (permit required). Take I-95 to Titusville exit 220 then SR 406 east to the park. For additional information, call 321-867-4077 or visit http://www.nps.gov/cana.

Endangered species such as bald eagles, manatees, and sea turtles call this area home. **Merritt Island National Wildlife Refuge**, just

north of the Space Center, offers hiking trails and incredible wildlife viewing. On your way in, stop by the Wildlife Refuge Visitor Center for information and some museum-style exhibits featuring the wildlife—there's also a delightful boardwalk over a freshwater pond in the back. The seven-mile Black

© MediaMarx, Inc.

Black Point Wildlife Drive

Point Wildlife Drive offers views of many kinds of birds, alligators, river otters, bobcats, and snakes. We visited the wildlife refuge just before sunset in December 2003 and were treated to beautiful panoramas and the sight of many birds roosting for the evening. A special manatee viewing platform is located at the northeast side of Haulover Canal. Located on the road to Playalinda Beach (see above), the refuge closes for shuttle launches and landings. Call 321-861-0667 or visit http://merrittisland.fws.gov.

This is the biggest **sea turtle nesting area** in the U.S. Nesting season runs May–August. Turtle encounters are organized at Canaveral National Seashore, Melbourne, and Sebastian Inlet. Call the Sea Turtle Preservation Society at 321-676-1701. More ecotourism opportunities exist, including kayak tours, airboat rides, and guided nature encounters. For listings, visit http://www.nbbd.com/ecotourism, http://www.space-coast.com, or call 800-872-1969.

Dining in Port Canaveral and Cocoa Beach

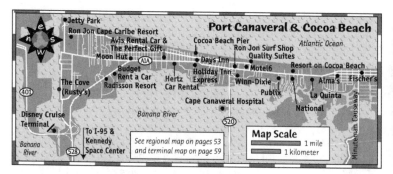

Looking for a place to eat? There are plenty of **chain restaurants**—in Port Canaveral you'll find a 24-hour McDonald's and a Subway, and down in Cocoa Beach there's a Wendy's, Taco Bell, Denny's, International House of Pancakes (IHOP), Perkins, Blimpie Subs, and a Waffle House. Over on Merritt Island, you'll also find Applebee's, Chili's, Outback Steakhouse, Olive Garden, Red Lobster, and Hooters. If you're looking for something nicer and more "local," here are the restaurants we've tried:

Alma's Seafood & Italian Trattoria—A quirky, moderately priced Italian restaurant with its own hometown charm. The food is decent and the atmosphere is a mix of checkered tablecloths and Space Coast memorabilia. Menu: http://www.dcltribute.com/spacecoast/menus/almas.htm. 306 N. Orlando Ave., Cocoa Beach • 321-783-1981

Cactus Flower Mexican Restaurant—A delightful, atmospheric cafe serving excellent Mexican cuisine. You can dine in or take out. 1891 E. Merritt Island Causeway, Merritt Island • 321-452-6606

Fischer's Seafood Bar & Grill—The moderate restaurant in the trio owned by the Fischer family (see next page). It offers decent seafood for reasonable prices. Info at http://www.geocities.com/bernardsseafood. 2 S. Atlantic Ave., Cocoa Beach • 321-783-2401

The Moon Hut—A basic diner, serving satisfying American and Greek food. http://www.dcltribute.com/spacecoast/menus/moonhut.htm. 7802 Astronaut Blvd., Cape Canaveral • 321-868-2638

Rusty's Seafood & Oyster Bar—Overlooking the port and harbor, this scenic restaurant serves quality seafood. Also owned by the Fischer family. 628 Glen Cheek Dr., Cape Canaveral • 321-783-2033

Genuine PassPorter Genuine PassPorter Genuine PassPorter Genuine PassPorter Genuine PassPorter

Playing in Port Canaveral and Cocoa Beach

Fishing (both saltwater and freshwater) is huge in this area. Charters and fishing camps are easy to find, maybe harder to choose from. Check out Coastal Angler Magazine at 888-800-9794 or visit them at http://www.camirl.com.

Lodging rates in this area are reasonable, especially in the off-season (May–December). See pages 56–58 for our lodging suggestions.

Port Canaveral Tips: For seafood, boating, and fishing charters, visit **The Cove**, a waterfront development just a stone's throw from the cruise terminals. We had a great meal and sunset views at Rusty's (321-783-2033, http://www.rustysseafood.com). To get there, exit SR 528 one exit east of the cruise terminals and follow George J. King Blvd. to the left to Glenn Cheek Drive. • **Jetty Park** is a perfect spot to watch space launches, fish, camp, or watch the cruise ships—to get there, exit SR 528 one exit east of the cruise terminals, turn right on George J. King Blvd., take Caribe Dr., then turn left onto Jetty Park Rd.

Cocoa Beach Tips: No trip is complete to the Space Coast without a visit to **Ron Jon Surf Shop** on SR A1A, souvenir T-shirt capital of Central Florida. This large, very pleasant store does sell surfboards and other serious water sports gear, but most visitors exit with items from the huge selection of swimwear, T-shirts, and other outdoor apparel. And it's open 24 hours! • Route A1A in Cocoa Beach varies between pleasant neighborhoods and somewhat seedy sections filled with cheap eats and budget motels. For the most part, though, it's very nice, and the beach is just a few blocks to the east (see photo on page 145). • The Fischer family, who also owns Rusty's in Port Canaveral, runs three fish restaurants under one roof at 2 S. Atlantic Ave. (SR A1A) in Cocoa Beach: Rusty's is cheapest and most informal, Fischer's is the mid-range choice (see previous page), and Bernard's Surf is the most upscale. • Aging sitcom fans might want to follow A1A south and look for "I Dream of Jeannie Lane," in Lori Wilson Park.

Other Space Coast Tips: Farther South, Melbourne is home to a wonderful planetarium and observatory, live theater productions, Montreal Expos Spring Training, and the Brevard County Zoo. The region also hosts a variety of space and nature events during the slow summer months. For information on all these activities and much more, contact the Space Coast Office of Tourism at 800-872-1969 or visit them online at http://www.space-coast.com.

Nassau
(3- and 4-Night Itineraries—First Port of Call)

Two-thirds of all Disney cruisers visit Nassau on New Providence Island in the Bahamas, one of the cruising world's most fabled ports. If you've heard the song Sloop John B ("'round Nassau town we did roam, drinkin' all night, got into a fight"), you might think twice about stepping ashore, but you can have an enjoyable day in this busy capital city if you do your homework.

A statue of Columbus greets visitors to Government House in Nassau

AMBIENCE

Many cruisers feel uncomfortable walking around Nassau's wharf area, where they're likely to encounter aggressive, enterprising locals intent on their piece of the tourist pie. Hair wrappers, cab drivers, street vendors, and tour hawkers swarm the seedy wharf area—hardly the squeaky-clean welcome Disney crowds prefer. But this large, attractive island boasts a long, British colonial heritage. Historic buildings, large casinos, and attractive beaches await travelers willing to take an excursion or strike out on their own.

Bahamian history starts with the first voyage of Chris Columbus. He called the area "baja mar"—low (shallow) sea—and the name stuck. The Spaniards left in search of gold and the native inhabitants were decimated by disease before the British arrived in the 1600s. Nassau, which was originally called Sayle Island, was a favorite port for fabled pirates like Blackbeard and Anne Bonney, until the islands became a Crown Colony in 1718. Governor Woodes Rogers, a former buccaneer himself, cleaned house and created a town plan which—more or less—remains in effect to this day. The islands became a haven for British loyalists fleeing the American Revolution, and for Southerners during the U.S. Civil War. Trade revived during the Prohibition era, when rum running became a major stock in trade. The islanders voted for and received independence on July 10, 1973, making the Bahamas a member of the British Commonwealth.

Size: 21 mi. long (34 km.) x 7 mi. wide (11 km.)	
Climate: Subtropical	**Temperatures:** 70°F (21°C)–90°F (32°C)
Population: 211,000	**Busy Season:** Mid-February to April
Language: English	**Money:** Bahamian Dollar (equal to U.S. $)
Time Zone: Eastern (DST observed)	**Transportation:** Walking, taxis, and ferries
Phones: Dial 1- from U.S., dial 919 for emergencies, dial 916 for information	

Sidebar labels: Introduction, Reservations, Staterooms, Dining, Activities, Ports of Call, Magic, Index

Margin labels: AMBIENCE, HISTORY, FACTS

© MediaMax, Inc.

Getting Around Nassau

GETTING THERE

Your ship berths at **Prince George Wharf** in the heart of the port. Paradise Island is across the water. A short walk puts you in the heart of town. Disembarkation starts at around 9:45 am (check your *Personal Navigator* for going ashore details), and be sure to bring photo I.D.—wharfside security is tight these days. Enjoy the view from deck 10 before going ashore to note major landmarks, including the Water Tower at the top of the hill, the towering Atlantis resort on Paradise Island, and the arching bridge to Paradise Island. Check your *Personal Navigator* for the "All Aboard" time, usually at 10:30 pm.

GETTING AROUND

Nassau is a **good port for walking**, but several popular attractions, including Paradise Island and Cable Beach, are best reached by taxi, jitney, or water taxi. The taxi stand is to the right as you leave the wharf, beyond the hair braiders stand. • As you leave the pier you'll pass through a new, pier-side welcome center, with a tourist information booth (get free tourist maps here), post office, ATM, telephone/Internet facilities, and a small, pleasant shopping mall. • As you leave the wharf, you'll find Woodes Rogers Walk, which parallels the waterfront. One block inland is the main shopping district, Bay Street. To your left you'll find the grand government buildings near Rawson Square, while a right turn on Bay Street will take you towards the Straw Market. The streets follow a rough grid, and the town is built on a slope. If you get disoriented, just walk downhill to the waterfront. • Small jitneys provide local bus service. The fare is $1 (exact change). Taxi fares are negotiable, but expect to pay $8 for a trip for two to Paradise Island, $12 to Cable Beach, and about $6 for shorter trips. The fare is good for two people, with a $3 surcharge for each extra passenger. • When crossing streets and if you rent a car or scooter, note that Nassau follows the British tradition of driving on the left-hand side of the road.

STAYING SAFE

Safety is often a state of mind, and that's especially true here. Downtown Nassau is **reasonably safe**, but it can be intimidating, with busy streets near the wharf and many locals hustling your business aggressively. The streets can be empty a few blocks beyond the wharf, so you'll feel better (and be safer) walking with a companion. You can't hide the fact that you're a tourist, so relax, look self-assured, stay alert, keep valuables out of sight, and use your big city street smarts. Panhandlers may offer their "services" as tour guides. Be firm, and don't get sucked in. Carry a few dollars in your pocket, just in case it's needed to tip a guide.

Touring Nassau

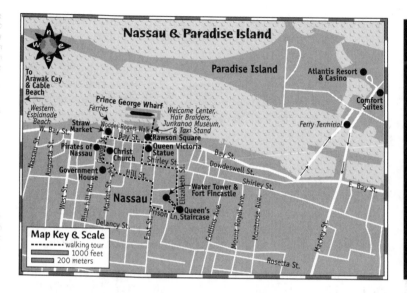

NASSAU MAP

A **self-guided walking tour** around Nassau is a break from the ordinary. Grab one of the free tourist maps distributed on the wharf, play connect-the-dots with your choice of highlighted sights, and trace a route around the perimeter of the downtown district. Allow at least two hours for a non stop walk or more if you want to spend time exploring. Finish before 5:00 pm, when the streets get empty. Here's our suggested walking tour (highlighted on map above): Leaving Prince George Wharf, turn right onto Bay St. Near the corner of Bay and George St. is the famous (or infamous) Straw Market. Turn left up George St. to continue our tour, or follow Bay St. west to the beaches of Western Esplanade and the seafood vendors of Arawak Cay. On George St., you'll soon pass Christ Church and the Pirates of Nassau attraction. Follow George St. to its end, and peer through the gates of Government House (see photo on page 151). Turn left again, cross Market St., and make your way uphill on winding Peck Slope to Hill St. for a commanding view of the port. Follow Hill St. to its end, turn right on East St. to Prison Lane, and follow the lane up to the Water Tower and Fort Fincastle. The tower can be climbed for free, or pay a fare to take the elevator. Exit via the remarkable Queens Staircase and follow Elizabeth St. down the hill. Turn left onto Shirley St., then right onto Parliament St. to view the Library (Old Jail) and the statue of Queen Victoria in Parliament Square. From there, it's a short walk back to the wharf.

WALKING TOUR

Playing in Nassau

ACTIVITIES

Bay St. is lined with **shops** offering the typical selection of upscale luxuries and downscale knickknacks, but Nassau is probably best-known for its Straw Market. There was a time when nobody could leave the port without a straw hat, basket, or handbag, but not every visitor is enchanted by the experience. The stalls and crafters of the market fill a city block between Bay St. and the waterfront—its narrow quarters are shaded by a huge, temporary awning.

The soft, white sands of Nassau are a major attraction. The nearest **public beach** to the wharf is Western Esplanade, along West Bay St. Famed Cable Beach, with its hotels, casino, and water sports, is more attractive and just a few miles farther down the road. Paradise Island has many first-class beaches, best visited as part of a shore excursion. Remote South Ocean Beach is a $33 cab fare from the wharf, or rent a car. Its quiet beauty may be worth the journey.

Casino action centers on Paradise Island's fancy Atlantis Casino and the older Crystal Palace Casino on Cable Beach. A day in either spot offers beach lounging, water sports, and similar distractions for those family members too young or disinclined to gamble. Water taxis serve both destinations from Prince George Wharf.

The **Atlantis Resort** offers aquariums and sea life exhibits to go along with the casino and recreation facilities. All-day admission is $25/adults, $19/kids 3-12, and includes a guided tour, but does not include their 14-acre water park—for that, you need to get a room at Atlantis (http://www.atlantis.com, 888-528-7155) or Comfort Suites (http://www.vacationparadiseisland.com, 800-330-8272).

Nassau offers too many scuba, snorkeling, boating, and sea life encounters to list here, but the Wonder's shore excursions (see next page) offer a good **cross-section** of these activities. Golf, tennis, fishing, and other sporting opportunities abound for those willing to do it on their own. Fortunately, you have a long day in Nassau. For details, visit the Bahamas' official site at http://www.bahamas.com.

"Goombay" and **"Junkanoo"** have become well known Bahamian catchwords. Goombay is a local musical style that gets its name from the African term for rhythm. The Bahamas famed Junkanoo parades take place when your ship is out of port, but you can view a Junkanoo exhibit right on Prince George Wharf.

Embarking on Shore Excursions in Nassau

We recommend a shore excursion if you plan to get off-ship in Nassau. As of March 2004, Disney offers 13 shore excursions to Nassau, all of which are described below and on the following pages. Note that the Regatta Racing Challenge excursion previously offered is no longer available at press time. If you'd like to try one of these activities without Disney's assistance, check the bottom of each description for details.

Blue Lagoon Beach Day [N01]   Rating: 6   ☀ 🏛 🔘

An affordable, fun day at the beach. Excursion includes a cruise to the private island of Blue Lagoon (Salt Cay)—a calypso band plays during your trip. Once there, you can swim, sunbathe, and play—water sport equipment rentals are available. Your excursion price includes lunch at the Sea Garden Grill. Typical meeting time is 9:15 am. Return ferry times are 2:00 pm and 4:00 pm. Cruiser reviews are mixed: The "nice and refreshing" ferry ride to the island was a	**Beach**
	Leisurely
	Ages 3 & up
	$38.00/adult
	$23.00/child
	4-7 hours

"highlight," but for some the ride took an "incredibly long time." The beach itself is "very relaxing" with "beautiful tropical waters," but there was a "lack of good beach areas such as are available on Castaway Cay." Lunch was "decent" but there wasn't "much variety." Some cruisers felt it was the "best time" while others "wouldn't do it again." (On Your Own: Blue Lagoon Island at http://www.bluelagoonisland.com, 242-363-3333)

Sunshine Glass Bottom Boat [N02]   Rating: 3   ☀ 🏛 🔘

Curious about what's under that aquamarine water? Take this excursion and you won't even have to get wet. The 70-foot boat has one sundeck, a covered deck, restrooms, cash bar, and (what else?) a glass bottom. You'll cruise the Nassau Harbor, then head off to the coral reefs—if the weather permits, you see a shipwreck, too. Typical meeting times are 10:30 am and 2:30 pm. Cruiser reviews are mostly negative. It is a "bit of a walk from the ship to the pier" where the glass bottom boat is moored. Once on the boat, the "scratched up" glass	**Tour**
	Leisurely
	Ages 3 & up
	$23.50/adult
	$16.50/child
	1.5-2.5 hours

bottom was "way too small" and you may have to stand to see. On the other hand, it "wasn't too expensive" and the "kids really enjoyed it." Overall, the experience was a "complete and total" waste of money for some, while others thought it was a "nice little ride."

Historical Harbor Cruise & Paradise Island Tour [N03]   Rating: 5   ☀ 🏛 🔘

Board a ferry at the Prince George Dock and enjoy a 35-minute cruise around Nassau Harbour, complete with commentary on points of interest. The ferry lets you off at Paradise Island to explore on your own. Once on the 685-acre island, you can walk up to the Atlantis Resort and have a look around. Typical meeting time is 2:00 pm. Ferries return every half-hour from 1:30 pm to 5:30 pm. Cruiser reviews are uniform: The boat ride to Paradise Island is "moderately fun." During the cruise, guide gives you a "historical tour" of the harbor, but his	**Tour**
	Leisurely
	Ages 3 & up
	$20.00/adult
	$14.50/child
	2.5 hours

or her accent is sometimes "hard to understand." During the cruise, you may get a "pretty good vantage point" to take photos of the ship. Once on Paradise Island, you are on your own to explore—if you want, you can take a "long, hot walk" up to the Atlantis Resort to shop or visit the aquarium, but otherwise there's "not much else to do" on Paradise Island. (On Your Own: Paradise Island at http://www.nassauparadiseisland.com, 888-627-7281)

See page 164 for a key to the shore excursion description charts and their icons.

Introduction · Reservations · Staterooms · Dining · Activities · Ports of Call · Magic · Index

Embarking on Shore Excursions
in Nassau (continued)

Caribbean Queen Snorkel Tour [N04]
Rating: 9

Like the Sunshine Glass Bottom Boat excursion, this trip cruises Nassau Harbour before heading off to Athol Island. Unlike the previously mentioned excursion, you WILL get wet! Snorkel equipment and instruction is provided for your open-water snorkeling adventure. Freshwater showers and cash bar available onboard the 72-foot boat. Typical meeting time is 1:30 pm. Cruiser reviews are consistently good: The "great" excursion crew offers some "sightseeing" along the way to the island. Once there, the snorkeling is "awesome" and there was a "great variety of fish." Younger children and "uptight" people may be "a little frightened at first" but the "crew is wonderful at relieving fears." Chips and beverages ("local beer" plus soda and water) are available for sale on the boat. In sum, "it was great" and cruisers would "do it again." (On Your Own: Stuart Cove's Aqua Adventures at http://www.stuartcove.com, 800-879-9832)

Sports
Very Active
Ages 8 & up
$36.00/adult
$26.00/child
2–3 hours

Discover Atlantis [N05]
Rating: 6

This excursion is identical to the Historical Harbor Cruise described on the previous page, except you get a guided tour of the Atlantis resort and aquarium on Paradise Island. We did this excursion in 2002 and we enjoyed it—be aware that you will do a lot of walking. Typical meeting times are 11:00 am or 1:00 pm. Ferries return every half-hour from 1:30 pm to 5:30 pm—don't miss it, or you'll have to pay for a taxi. Cruiser reviews are mixed: This very popular excursion begins with a "capacity-filled water taxi" ride to Paradise Island, during which the tour with "very little narrative" could not be "heard or understood over the roar of the engines." Once on the island, you are taken in "smaller groups" to the "stunning" Atlantis Resort, but the walk to it is "boring" because there is "nothing to see." Inside you may "spend a lot of time touring the retail areas," but then are led to the "breathtaking" aquarium, which was by far the highlight for most cruisers. After the aquarium, some felt you were "left somewhere in the hotel to find your own way back" while others enjoyed the "free time to explore." Expect to "spend the entire tour walking." Overall, some cruisers felt the excursion was "awesome" while others felt it "takes way too much time" and "wasn't interesting at all." (On Your Own: Atlantis Resort, http://www.atlantis.com, 888-528-7155)

Tour
Active
Ages 5 & up
$33.00/adult
$23.00/child
2–5 hours

Nassau Historic City Tour [N06]
Rating: 6

Board an air-conditioned van for a guided tour of historic points of interest in Nassau. The tour visits historic buildings and famous sites, stopping at Fort Charlotte, Fort Fincastle, the Water Tower, and the Queen's Staircase. A good overview without a lot of walking. Typical meeting time is 10:15 am. Cruiser reviews are uniform: Aboard "not very comfortable" but "air-conditioned" vans you see historic sights around Nassau. The driver may not "talk very much" or offer enough "commentary" during the tour, but you will see "much of the city" in a "short time" and stop a few times to "take some photos." Most cruisers enjoyed the climb up to the Water Tower for the "view at the top," but felt it was "more physical activity" than expected. Cruisers were dismayed at the "begging" for tips and "peddlers." Overall, most felt the excursion was a way to see "a lot of things" without a "lot of walking." (On Your Own: Bahamas Experience Tours at http://www.bahamasexperiencetours.com, 242-356-2981, or Henry's Mobile Tours at 242-356-2981)

Tour
Leisurely
Ages 3 & up
$22.00/adult
$16.00/child
2 hours

See page 164 for a key to the shore excursion description charts and their icons.

Embarking on Shore Excursions
in Nassau *(continued)*

Atlantis Beach Day [N07]   Rating: 7

Beach
Active
Ages 3 & up
$60.00/adult
$45.00/child
2-7 hours

Spend the day lolling about on the beach on Paradise Island. The excursion includes a 35-minute cruise (identical to the Historical Harbor Cruise) and a meal coupon. Upon arrival, enjoy your reserved spot on the beach, complete with chair and towel. You can explore the resort's casino and shops, but this excursion **does not include access to the Atlantis water park or aquarium**. Typical meeting time is 9:00 am. Ferries return every 30 min. from 1:30 pm to 5:30 pm. Cruiser reviews are uniform: The historical harbor tour portion was "not as detailed" as it could be, and you could "hardly hear the tour director." The highlight was the "private beach for cruisers," which is "wonderful" with "beautiful" water "so blue" and with "so many fish." On the beach you are "provided with a towel and chair," and the chair "has an umbrella." The meal coupon left a bit to be desired, as you could only get "certain items" and the food "was not that great." If you want to buy something else, it can be "difficult to pay with cash." And cruisers felt it was unfortunate that they "can't use any of the pools at Atlantis." In sum, the beach is "beautiful" but the rest is just so-so.(On Your Own: Atlantis Resort, http://www.atlantis.com, 888-528-7155)

Scuba Diving [N08]   Rating: 3

Sports
Very Active
For certified divers only
Ages 12 & up
$65.00/adult
3 hours

If you're a certified diver, this excursion offers an exciting look at the coral reefs and marine life that make their home here. Price includes basic dive equipment (regulator, tank, weight belt, buoyancy control device, mask, snorkel, and fins—wet suits are available for an extra fee). Note that guests ages 12-17 must be accompanied by parent or guardian to participate. Typical meeting time is 9:00 am. Don't forget that underwater camera. Cruiser reviews are uniform: The Disney scuba excursion is "OK" but not "great." The dive takes them "windward" and the waters can be "very rough"—rough enough that most cruisers report that they were able to do only "one of the two dives." The excursion does "provide all equipment," but you may only go "10 to 15" feet deep. The best thing about it is that you don't have to worry about "getting there or back" since it was all arranged through Disney. Overall, the dive was "disappointing" and most felt it would be best to "arrange your own scuba dive" through an outfit like Stuart Cove's. (On Your Own: Stuart Cove's Aqua Adventures at http://www.stuartcove.com, 800-879-9832 or Nassau Scuba Centre at http://www.divenassau.com, 242-362-1964)

Teen Junkanoo Jam [N10]   Rating: 7

Dance
Active
Ages 13-17
$25/teen
1-1.5 hours

For teens 13-17 only! Join your new friends and the teens-only club crew on a party boat as it cruises Nassau Harbour. Dance under the stars to the sounds of the Caribbean as well as today's top hits. Prizes awarded for lowest limbo and best dancer. Beverages and snacks available for purchase. Typical meeting time is 7:00 pm. Note that this excursion may be offered only during peak seasons. Teen cruiser comments are mixed: The party boat goes "around the harbor" while the teens "dance and party." The music is "in" and the boy/girl ratio is "about the same." Most felt that if you "were into music and dancing" you would "love it," but others weren't "too impressed." One suggestion was to "eat a little something" before the excursion because the snacks on the boat ("pretzels and punch") are "lame." Overall, most teens felt this was a "don't miss" while others gave it "mixed reviews." It probably depends a lot on the company. (On Your Own: Don't bother—this is best with people you know.)

See page 164 for a key to the shore excursion description charts and their icons.

Introduction
Reservations
Staterooms
Dining
Activities
Ports of Call
Magic
Index

Embarking on Shore Excursions
in Nassau (continued)

☐ Blue Lagoon Dolphin Encounter [N11]   Rating: 9 ☀ 🔒 📷

Sports
Active
Ages 3 & up
$113.50/adult
$88.50/child
4–7 hours

Despite the hefty price tag, this is the most popular excursion and it typically sells out quickly. Everyone wants the chance to cavort with a friendly dolphin! The excursion includes the same amenities as the Blue Lagoon Beach Day, plus a one-on-one encounter with a bottlenose dolphin in waist-high water. (If you want to actually swim with the dolphins, you'll need to book that excursion on your own—see below.) Professional photos are $8–35/each and videos are $40–60/each. Typical meeting time is 9:15 am. Cruiser ratings are positive: The excursion starts with a long, "45-minute" ferry ride some felt was "slow" and "miserable" while others found it "a lot of fun." At the dolphin encounter area, small groups of "10-12" guests stand around a "small pool" and watch a "skit" between the dolphin and "informative handlers." You get in the "cold" water for about "20 minutes" but with only about "2-3 minutes with a dolphin personally." All loved the "unbelievably intelligent animal" and the "expertise, friendliness, and humor of the trainers." Some were put off by the "expense" of the photo; others wanted them but "did not know to bring enough money." Overall, most felt it was "exactly as advertised" or "better than expected," though a few felt it "neat but not worth that much money." (On Your Own: Blue Lagoon Island at http://www.dolphinswims.com, 242-363-1003)

☐ Catamaran Sail & Reef Snorkeling [N14]   Rating: 8 ☀ 🔒 📷

Sports
Very active
Ages 5 & up
$42/adult
$30/child
3.5–4 hours

Set sail on a comfortable, 65-foot catamaran with a large sundeck and shady lounge deck. After a brief tour of Nassau Harbour, you'll sail to a coral reef for snorkeling (equipment provided). Sodas and water are served during the sail, as are snacks and alcoholic beverages after snorkeling. Typical meeting time is 9:00 am. Cruiser comments are mostly positive: The 20-minute sail is "enjoyable" and "relaxing." The snorkeling is "wonderful" though some felt it was in "pretty deep water for beginners" and you cannot "touch bottom." Most report seeing "plenty of fish." Overall, most "loved it!" (On Your Own: Flying Cloud at http://www.bahamasnet.com/flyingcloud, 242-363-4430)

☐ Stingray City & Blue Lagoon Combination Tour   Rating: n/a ☀ 🔒 📷

Sports
Very active
Ages 5 & up
$60/adult
$33/child
4–7 hours

Take a boat to Blue Lagoon Island and Stingray City Marine Park, where you'll have an opportunity to snorkel with the stingrays (equipment provided). Also includes all the features of the Blue Lagoon Beach Day described earlier. Note that kids may be scared of the stingrays. Typical meeting time is 9:15 am. This is a recently added excursion so we do not have reviews yet. (On Your Own: Nassau Cruises at http://www.bahamasgo.com/nassaucruises.htm, 242-363-1000)

☐ Ardastra Gardens and City Tour [N14]   Rating: 7 ☀ 🔒 📷

Tour
Active
All ages
$36/adult
$26/child 3–9
2.5–3 hours

First visit the jungle gardens of the Ardastra Gardens, Zoo, and Conservation Centre, famous for its marching Caribbean Flamingos. After an hour and a half at the gardens, enjoy a city tour in air-conditioned van. A fair amount of walking is required. Typical meeting time is 12:45 pm. Cruiser reviews are mostly positive: The excursion offers "variety" and a way to see a lot in a "short amount of time." Kids enjoy the "zoo" and the animals and birds are "great." The tour's worth "depends on your tour guide." Overall, most "enjoyed it" though a few felt it would have been better to "take a taxi" and do "on your own." (On Your Own: Ardastra Gardens at http://www.ardastra.com, 242-323-5806)

See page 164 for a key to the shore excursion description charts and their icons.

Freeport

Note: This port was discontinued at the end of 2003, but we're retaining the information in the event it resumes in the future.

Embracing the fine beaches and tropical climate of the Bahamas' fourth-largest island, Freeport and the adjacent resort development of Port Lucaya suggest that all any vacationer needs is a comfortable hotel, a beautiful beach, great water sports, a casino, and a large shopping area. If so, this spot has it all, and in generous amounts.

© MediaMarx, Inc.

The Disney Wonder in Freeport Harbour

AMBIENCE

Developed over the past 50 years, Freeport and Port Lucaya are unlike most Caribbean towns. They grew out of nothing, rather than from a historic old town. Large resort hotels and vacation home developments dominate the in-town areas and nearby beaches. The shopping is really grand, thanks to its tax-free status and mall-style convenience. Freeport Harbour is actually on the outskirts of town, with nothing but infamous views of industrial developments and a newly built shopping area adjacent to the pier. The island's pace is up-tempo, to compete with destinations like Miami Beach and Las Vegas. Several nature parks, remote beaches, scuba, snorkeling, and fishing provide an enticement to get out of town.

HISTORY

Uninhabited for most of the centuries following Columbus' discovery, permanent settlers didn't arrive on Grand Bahama Island until the early 1800s. Smugglers thrived during the U.S. Civil War and Prohibition, but major prosperity didn't arrive until the 1950s, when Wallace Groves set out to create an island resort from scratch, financed by his logging operations on the island. The local Bahamian culture is still strong, though, thanks to the few old-time inhabitants and Bahamians who come here in search of employment. Fishing villages to the west and east, including West End, Sea Grape, Eight Mile Rock, and McLeans Town provide the history and local flavor Freeport itself lacks.

FACTS

Size: 90 mi. long (114 km.) x 10 mi. wide (16 km.)	
Climate: Subtropical	**Temperatures:** 72°F (22°C) to 82°F (28°C)
Population: 41,000	**Busy Season:** Mid-February to April
Language: English	**Money:** Bahamian Dollar (equal to U.S. $)
Time Zone: Eastern (DST observed)	**Transportation:** Taxis and cars
Phones: Dial 1- from U.S., dial 919 for emergencies, dial 916 for information	

Introduction Reservations Staterooms Dining Activities Ports of Call Magic Index

Introduction
Reservations
Staterooms
Dining
Activities
Ports of Call
Magic
Index

Getting Around Freeport

GETTING THERE

When the Disney Wonder visited this port, it docked at the island's **Freeport Harbour cruise terminal** (see photo on previous page), which features a small, Caribbean-style retail and entertainment "village," complete with straw market. This is the only tourist-friendly area within walking distance—everything else is a taxi ride away. At the terminal you'll also find an information stand and ground transportation. Disembarkation was early, typically at 8:30 am (check your *Personal Navigator*). All aboard time: 4:30 pm.

GETTING AROUND

Grand Bahama is **not an island for walkers**. Shore excursions offer a lot of convenience, as transportation is included and you run less risk of missing the boat. If you want to go it alone, you can visit the cruise terminal's mall and return to the ship or get a ride out of the port. Avis is the only major car rental agency with an office at the cruise pier. Scooter rentals are available, and you can always take a taxi. Taxis are metered and cost $3 plus 40 cents per mile for the first two passengers. There are fixed fares to Freeport ($17) and Port Lucaya ($24). • Freeport and Port Lucaya started as separate developments but have blended together over the years. **Freeport** itself is actually several miles east of the harbor and a bit inland. **Port Lucaya** is two miles (3 km.) southeast of Freeport, on the waterfront. Both areas offer many of the same activities, but Port Lucaya has the marina, beach, and water sports that downtown Freeport lacks. You'll need a ride from Freeport to Port Lucaya if you want to visit both areas, but a visit to one is probably enough for one day. • Lucayan National Park is 25 miles (40 km.) out of town.

STAYING SAFE

Normal travel **safety rules** apply in Grand Bahama. You'll need sun protection, of course. Be wary when carrying parcels, especially as it's hard to return to the ship to drop them off. Keep your valuables secure: purses should be hung diagonally across your shoulder and under your arm on a secure strap; carry wallets in your front pocket or otherwise secured, wear waist packs with the pouch in front, kangaroo-style. Bahamians follow the English example and drive on the left-hand side of the road. Don't forget this when driving or crossing the street. Remember that the shopping may be duty-free when you pay for it, but you still have to settle up with U.S. Customs if you exceed the $800 limit. Duty-free does not mean you can bring unlimited goods back into the U.S. without paying duty. It simply means the merchant did not have to pay duty when they imported the goods to their shop.

Touring Freeport

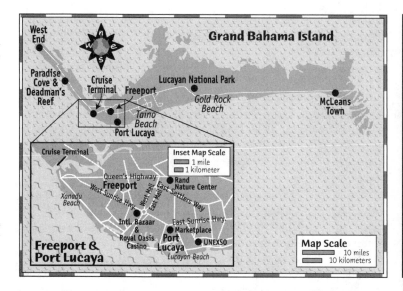

Freeport is notable for the International Bazaar shopping and dining district, the nearby straw market, and Royal Oasis Casino. The bazaar covers more than ten acres, and each "street" sports a different international theme reflected in its architecture, shops, and eateries. Dyed-in-the-wool shoppers may prefer Freeport to Port Lucaya.

Port Lucaya is by the beach, with lots of water sports opportunities. The Port Lucaya Marketplace is the other big shopping and dining destination on the island, in an attractive waterfront development. Count Basie Square in the Marketplace offers free, live music, but it may only start after you have to be back on board the ship. Port Lucaya may be the better choice for a whole-family outing.

Grand Bahama's **beaches** are known for their soft sand and gentle surf (thanks to offshore barrier reefs). Two of the best, Xanadu Beach, south of downtown Freeport, and Lucayan Beach at Port Lucaya are home to beachfront resorts, so there's a wide range of recreation offerings, dining, and other comforts. A bit east of Lucayan Beach is Taino Beach, a little less "developed" but with several seafood eateries and a children's playground. For quiet, natural surroundings, Gold Rock Beach at Lucayan National Park gets high marks (see next page). For a secluded beach, try Paradise Cove (http://www.bahamasvg.com/pcove.html).

Introduction

Reservations

Staterooms

Dining

Activities

Ports of Call

Magic

Index

FREEPORT MAP

NEIGHBORHOODS AND BEACHES

ACTIVITIES

Playing in Freeport

Golfers can be very happy here. The Our Lucaya Resort operates two courses (242-373-1066), as does the Royal Oasis (242-352-6721). Fortune Hills Golf & Country Club has a single, nine-hole course (242-373-4500). A golf excursion is listed on the next page.

If you like **ecotourism or scuba**, you'll find plenty here. Lucayan National Park has nature trails, a fine beach, and a huge network of limestone caves (most are closed to the public). A convenient shore excursion offers a kayak nature tour to this park, 25 miles east of Freeport. • The 100-acre Rand Nature Center is a short cab ride away if you're in Freeport or Port Lucaya and offers a network of attractive trails. • Garden of the Groves is a bit east of Port Lucaya, with 12 acres of tropical gardens, cascading waterfalls, wildlife, and a petting zoo. Admission $9.95 adults, $6.95 children 3-10. • The Underwater Exploration Society (UNEXSO), located at Port Lucaya, has some of the **best scuba, snorkel, and dolphin programs** available anywhere. Four different dolphin experiences ($59-$219/adults), one as a shore excursion described on the next page, a half-day no-certification-required scuba program ($99), and a variety of advanced diving options ($35-$169) are just some of the highlights. Reserve well in advance (and keep the ship's schedule in mind) at 800-992-3483 and learn more at http://www.unexso.com.

Grand Bahama is a center for traditional deep-sea **game fishing** and bone fishing, a game fish caught in shallower waters with fly fishing tackle. The Grand Bahama Island Tourism Board has a helpful listing at http://www.grand-bahama.com/fishing.htm.

Both the International Bazaar and Port Lucaya Marketplace offer a wide variety of **reasonably priced eateries** for your lunch ashore. Prices are generally higher in the resort restaurants.

The recently renovated **Royal Oasis Casino** (formerly the Bahamia and before that the Princess) serves Freeport and is adjacent to the International Bazaar. The **Our Lucaya Casino**, just across the street from the Port Lucaya Marketplace, replaced the old Lucaya Beach Casino.

For more information on **things to do** in Freeport and Port Lucaya, contact the Grand Bahama Island Tourism Board at 242-352-8044 or visit http://www.grand-bahama.com.

Embarking on Shore Excursions in Freeport

Here are the Freeport excursions offered in the past for your reference:

Snorkel Adventure [FO1]

Experienced snorkelers enjoy this visit to the coral formations at Treasure Reef, one of the prettiest reefs off Grand Bahama Island. 2.4 million dollars of treasure was found here in the remains of a Spanish galleon. Today the only treasure you'll find is its natural beauty. Instruction and snorkel equipment are provided. Typical meetings times are 9:15 am and 11:45 am. (On Your Own: Superior Watersports at http://www.superiorwatersports.com or 242-373-7863)

Sports
Very active
Ages 8 & up
$36/adult
$26/child
3 hours

Glass Bottom Boat Tour [FO2]

Freeport's waters are home to miles of coral reef and plenty of sealife, which you can catch a glimpse of from the largest glass-bottom boat in the Bahamas. Relax on the boat while you peer through a narrow window at the bottom of the boat. We hear mixed reviews on this one—some cruisers don't think you can see much out the window. Typical meeting time is noon. (On Your Own: Reef Tours at http://www.bahamasvg.com/reeftours or 242-373-5880)

Tour
Leisurely
Ages 3 & up
$23.50/adult
$16.50/child
3 hours

Lucayan Resort Beach Adventure [FO3]

Bum around at the largest resort beach in the Bahamas for a few hours on this shore excursion. The excursion price includes transportation to and from Our Lucaya Resort (formerly the Lucayan Resort), plus a reserved location, lounge chair, towel, and access to the resort's pools, water slides, and other outdoor activities. Lunch is provided. Typical meeting time is 9:00 am. (On Your Own: Our Lucaya at http://www.ourlucaya.com or 242-373-1333)

Beach
Active
Ages 3 & up
$49/adult
$39/child
3-5 hours

Sanctuary Bay Dolphin Encounter [FO4]

While this isn't a "swim with the dolphins" experience, you do get a chance to wade in waist-high water with Atlantic bottlenose dolphins—you can even touch them! You'll be taken by ferryboat to Sanctuary Bay, located on the south shore. Very popular—book early. Suitable for non-swimmers. Typical meeting times are 8:15 am, 9:30 am, and 11:00 am. See photo on page 135. (On Your Own: The Dolphin Experience at http://www.unexso.com or 561-472-1100)

Encounter
Leisurely
Ages 3 & up
$75.50/adult
$65.50/child
3 hours

Kayaking Nature Tour [FO5]

Great for all levels, this kayak tour takes you through an inland creek in a mangrove forest—expect about 90 minutes of light to moderate paddling. Then it's off for a guided nature walk through Lucayan National Park and the caves. When you're done, go for a swim or just relax at Gold Rock Beach, a private, shady beach. Lunch is provided. Typical meeting time is 8:30 am. (On Your Own: Kayak Nature Tours at http://www.thebahamian.com/kayak or 242-373-2485)

Sports
Very active
Ages 8 & up
$71.50/adult
$60.50/child
6 hours

Lucaya Golf & Country Club [FO6]

Enjoy a round of golf at a 6,824-yard course, designed by Dick Wilson and Robert Trent Jones. The course tests accuracy rather than distance, with doglegs and elevated greens. Price includes golf cart, greens fees, club rentals, and coupons for a snack at the 19th Hole. Golf balls are not included. Typical meeting time is 8:00 am. (On Your Own: Lucaya Golf & Country Club at 242-373-1066)

Sports
Very active
Ages 10 & up
$116.50/adult
5 hours

See page 164 for a key to the shore excursion description charts and their icons.

Understanding the Shore Excursion Description Charts

We describe each of Disney's shore excursions with our custom-designed, at-a-glance charts. Each chart includes a description, tips, restrictions, typical meeting times, our reviews (when available), cruiser reviews in summary form (when available), information on how to do the excursion on your own, a reader rating, and more! We've organized this array of information into a consistent format so you can find what you need quickly. Below is a key to our charts, along with notes and details.

Key to the Excursion Chart:

| Reader Rating[2] | Icons[3] |

[1] **Excursion Name** [Disney's Code Number]	Rating: # ☀ 🎒 📷
Description offering an overview of the excursion, what to expect (without giving too much away, of course), historical background, trivia and "secrets," our recommendations and review (if we've experienced it), tips on getting the most out of the excursion, height/age restrictions, typical meeting times, things you should and shouldn't bring with you, a summary of cruiser reviews we've received, and contact information if you want to do the excursion (or something similar to it) "On Your Own"—note that doing it on your own will often be with a different tour operator, however.	**Type[4]**
	Activity Level[5]
	Ages[6]
	Prices[7]
	Duration[8]

[1] Each chart has an empty **checkbox** in the upper left corner—use it to check off the excursions you want to take (before you go) or those you've taken (after you return).

[2] When available, we note a reader rating from a scale of 0 (bad) to 10 (excellent). These ratings are compiled from the shore excursion reviews we receive (see sidebar below).

[3] Icons indicate what you should (or can) bring along. The sun icon ☀ suggests plenty of sunscreen and a hat. The bag icon 🎒 means you can bring a totebag or backpack along on the excursion. And the camera icon 📷 indicates you can bring a camera or camcorder.

[4] The type of activity you can expect on the excursion, such as Sports, Beach, or Tour.

[5] The physical activity level, such as Leisurely (a mild level of activity), Active (a moderate level of activity), and Very Active (a whole lot of activity).

[6] The age requirements for the excursion. Some excursions are for All Ages, while others are for certain ages and up. A few are for teens only.

[7] Prices for adults (and kids, if available). Kids prices are for kids up to 9. Most tours that do not involve a boat transfer will allow kids under 3 to go free. Prices subject to change.

[8] The approximate duration of the excursion. If we offer a range, it's more likely that the excursion will take the maximum time noted, in our experience.

About Our Cruiser Reviews

New for this edition are excerpts from cruiser reviews, summarized at the end of each shore excursion description. These reviews are submitted by cruisers via an online form. All reviewers receive a coupon good for PassPorter guidebooks from our online store. Thanks to all who sent in a review! To submit your review, visit us at http://www.passporter.com/dcl and click the "Shore Excursion Survey" link.

St. Maarten/St. Martin
(Eastern Caribbean Itineraries—First Port of Call)

The Dutch say Sint Maarten, the French say St. Martin, but what's in a name? Where else can you visit **two countries** this easily, dine so lavishly, shop so extravagantly, and sun so beautifully? Two nations share this bit of paradise, but if we must take sides, we'll take the French. Alas, the Disney Magic docks on the Dutch side.

Dave and Allie on Pinel Island, St. Martin

With the Atlantic to the east, the Caribbean to the west and a lagoon in between, St. Maarten's 37 beaches offer **everything** from roaring surf to gentle ripples, and brisk trade winds keep the island cool. Its 37 square miles (96 sq. km.) include tall, luxuriantly green mountains, two capital cities, hundreds of appetizing restaurants, a dizzying array of shops, and a dozen casinos. Philipsburg, the bustling Dutch capital, hosts up to four cruise ships daily, and offers handy, excellent shopping. Picturesque Marigot, the French capital, offers a lot more charm and sophistication for cruisers willing to go the extra distance.

The **history** of this island begins with the Arawaks, seafaring Indians who discovered salt on the island. Later, Columbus named and claimed this island as he sailed past on the Feast of St. Martin. After harassing the Spanish for some years (here's where New Amsterdam's Peter Stuyvesant lost his leg), the Dutch and French moved in and carved it up in 1647. Relations are friendly now, but the border moved several times during the next 200 years. Sugar cane was the cash crop until slavery was abolished, and sea salt was produced in Philipsburg's Salt Pond, but this was a very quiet place until tourists came to call. And despite this long history, there's still a strong difference in culture and architecture between very French St. Martin and commerce-focused Dutch Sint Maarten.

Size: 12 mi. long (19 km.) x 8 mi. wide (13 km.)	
Climate: Subtropical	**Temperatures**: 80°F (27°C) to 85°F (29°C)
Population: 77,000	**Busy Season**: Late December to April
Language: English, French, Dutch	**Money**: Euro or Florin (U.S. dollar accepted)
Time Zone: Atlantic (no DST)	**Transportation**: Taxis and cars
Phones: Dial 011- from U.S., dial 22222 for emergencies	

Introduction

Reservations

Staterooms

Dining

Activities

Ports of Call

Magic

Index

AMBIENCE

HISTORY

FACTS

Making the Most of St. Maarten/St. Martin

GETTING THERE

Your ship docks at the **Captain Hodge Wharf** in Philipsburg in Dutch St. Maarten, at the east end of Great Bay. Taxis and tour buses leave from the wharf, and a water taxi makes two stops along Front Street ($5 buys a pass good for unlimited trips, all day long). A walkway provides direct access to the beach and the shops, casinos, and restaurants of Front Street. It's about a 10-15 minute walk to the near end of Front St., and about a mile (1.6 km) from one end of Front Street to the other. The wharf hosts a tourist information booth. Disembarkation time is typically 8:00 am with an all-aboard time around 10:00 pm.

GETTING AROUND

As with many ports, the real pleasures are found outside of town. Most destinations are within a half-hour drive of Philipsburg, and a **rental car** is the way to get there. Research and book your rental in advance, as rates skyrocket for on-site rentals. All major agencies are represented, but only five have pierside offices. • The island is really two rocky land masses. A pair of sand spits connects the roughly circular main bulk of the island with the small western portion, Terre Basses (the Lowlands). Between the sand spits is Simpson Bay Lagoon. • The French side occupies 21 sq. miles (54 sq. km.) of the northern part of the island, the Dutch 16 sq. miles (41 sq. km.) of the south. A picturesque range of mountains runs north to south, further dividing the island. From Philipsburg, nearly every point of interest including Marigot can be reached by driving around the perimeter of the island. • **Taxis** use a government-controlled rate chart. The base fare is for two persons, and each additional person costs about 1/3 the base fare. Sample fares from Philipsburg: Marigot, Orient Beach, Dawn Beach, Maho Resort, all $15; Grand Case, $20. An island tour is $50. • **Public buses** travel between Philipsburg and Marigot. The fare is around $3, U.S. funds are accepted. • Once you're in Philipsburg, Marigot, or any other community, everything will be within walking distance.

STAYING SAFE

There's nothing too unusual about staying safe on "The Friendly Island." No place is crime-free, but St. Maarten does very well. Be wary when carrying parcels, of course. Don't bring valuables to the beach. American and Canadian drivers will be happy, as the island follows U.S. driving practices (right-hand side), but beware of **speed bumps** through towns and resorts. The breeze may fool you into forgetting the sun—be sure to apply plenty of sunblock, especially if you'll be more exposed than usual (if you catch our drift).

Touring St. Maarten/ St. Martin

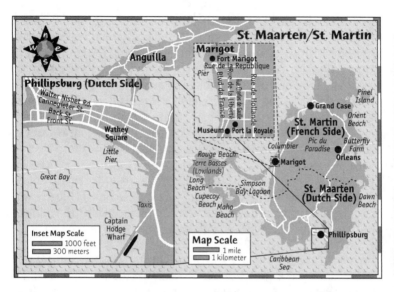

Walking Around in Philipsburg: Philipsburg is a narrow sand spit, just four streets deep and about a mile long (1.6 km.). Front Street runs the length of the town and supplies most of the town's shopping and dining. Back Street is one block over. If you take the water taxi from the wharf you'll arrive at old Little Pier, where the cruise ships' tenders used to dock. Great Bay Beach is right at hand, as are many locals, plying the tourist trade. Leave Little Pier and you'll be in Wathey Square, with its landmark Dutch courthouse. (If you walk from the ship, you'll be at the east end of Front Street, and Wathey Square will be about three blocks west.) You'll find shops, restaurants, and casinos no matter which way you turn. Just walk west until you've had your fill, then retrace your steps.

Walking Around in Marigot: The heart of Marigot is a rough rectangle, bordered on the west by the harbor. On the north, Rue de la Republique offers upscale shopping, with the local pier at its west end. From the pier, head north to climb to the ruins of Fort Marigot, or head south on restaurant-lined Boulevard de France to the Creole graveyard and small museum at the south end of town. Also on the south side, about a block inland, is Port la Royale, a marina surrounded by restaurants and shops—a perfect spot for lunch. Afterwards, head back north on shady Rue de la Liberté or shop-filled Rue Charles de Gaulle.

Playing in St. Maarten/ St. Martin

Great Bay Beach is a short walk from the ship along a new, beachfront promenade. The surf is gentle, and food and shopping are right behind you on Front Street. To the north, **Orient Beach**, with its long crescent of soft white sand and gentle surf, is called the "French Riviera of the Caribbean," but it achieved fame as the island's official nude beach. Beachfront restaurants and resorts have dressed the place up, but bathers at the south end of the beach are still very undressed (not that you have to be). **Maho Beach**, **Mullet Bay**, **Cupecoy Beach**, and **Long Beach** are way out west by the big resorts, past Juliana Airport. All are very pleasant, with Maho offering full resort amenities. Other beaches include remote Rouge Beach (one of Dave's favorites) and Grand Case Beach. Note: With the possible exception of Great Bay beach, you're likely to encounter European-style beach attire (topless women, men in thongs).

The brisk trade winds make the island very popular for **sailing**. For convenience, take one of several "shore" excursions described on the next two pages. Excursions are also available at the marinas near the wharf in Philipsburg. For **snorkeling**, Dawn Beach, several miles to the northeast of Philipsburg, is a top choice.

The island is a **diner's paradise**, with fabulous French, Creole, Indian, Vietnamese, and Indonesian restaurants (and KFC). You'll have no trouble finding a meal along Front Street in Philipsburg, but you'll do better in "France." In Marigot, head toward charming Port la Royale Marina, which is encircled by more than a half-dozen bustling bistros. Note: Many restaurants automatically include a 15% service charge (tip), so watch that bill carefully before you tip.

Twelve **casinos** dot the Dutch side. Four are within walking distance of the wharf, on Front Street in Philipsburg. The largest (and most elegant) casino is the Princess Casino at Port de Plaisance.

The **luxury goods shops** on both sides of the island present a staggering array of French perfumes and cosmetics, crystal, fine porcelain, jewelry, clothing, liquors, and wines. Philipsburg offers many of the French brands you'll find in Marigot at equal or lower prices, but somehow it feels better to shop in Marigot. The huge Little Switzerland luxury goods chain has shops in Philipsburg and Marigot. Cigar fans can find good Cubans, but be sure to smoke 'em before you arrive back home.

Embarking on Shore Excursions in St. Maarten/St. Martin

Pinel Island Snorkel Tour [SM01]   Rating: 6

Pinel Island, which is often called St. Martin's best-kept secret, is an uninhabited island in Orient Bay (French side). You'll take a bus ride, then a water taxi to reach the island. Price includes snorkeling instruction and equipment, with plenty of time to snorkel, swim, sunbathe, or shop. We visited on our own in 2003 and absolutely loved the island. Typical meeting times are 8:00 am and 12:30 pm. Cruiser reviews are mixed: Some feel the bus ride is "short," while others say it "seems like hours." All agree that the island itself is "very beautiful" with a "sandy beach" and "gradual drop-off." The snorkeling "leaves something to be desired" as it's "often windy" with "poor visibility." Some felt if you visited to "just go swimming" it would be better—others had a "great time."(On Your Own: Scuba Fun at 599-542-2333, ext. 3160)

Sports
Active
Ages 5 & up
$35/$30 (5-9)
3.5 hours

Shipwreck Cove Snorkel Tour [SM02]   Rating: 5

Experienced snorkelers may enjoy this boat trip to Shipwreck Cove to hand-feed the fish that swim among sunken ships and coral reefs. Instruction and snorkel equipment provided, but this excursion is not recommended for non-swimmers. Refreshments, Calypso music, sun decks, and restrooms onboard the boat. Cruiser reviews are mixed: Most felt the snorkeling was "lackluster" in "murky water," while a few others enjoyed "very clear water." The "shipwrecks are real," but were "relocated from somewhere else." In general, most cruisers do "not recommend it," while some "couldn't stop talking about how wonderful it was." Chances are your experience "depends on the weather," which is often windy. Typical meeting time is 1:00 pm. (On Your Own: n/a)

Sports
Active
Ages 8 & up
$39/$33 (8-9)
3.5 hours

Golden Eagle Catamaran [SM03]   Rating: 9

Enjoy a half-day jaunt to Tintamar—a real deserted island—aboard the majestic Golden Eagle. The luxurious, 76-foot catamaran sails at up to 30 knots! The excursion price includes pastries, an open bar, and complimentary use of beach floats and snorkel equipment. Typical meeting times are 7:45 am and 1:00 pm. Cruiser reviews are very positive: The ride over is "fun" and "not too fast for kids to enjoy," while the crew "friendly and courteous." The "deserted island" is a "great place to snorkel or just relax on the beach." The "beautiful" beach is "scenic" with "very clear" water. There is "music and singing" during the cruise. All cruisers report that they would "do it again," but some would be sure to "take seasickness medicine" first. (On Your Own: Eagle Tours at http://www.sailingsxm.com or 599-543 0068)

Sports
Active
Ages 5 & up
$62/$36 (5-9)
4-4.5 hours

12-Metre Regatta [SM04]   Rating: 10

Become a crew member aboard one of the famous America's Cup yachts, such as the "Stars and Stripes." You'll compete in an actual race on a shortened version of the America's Cup course. You may get to "grind a winch" or "trim a sail"—no experience is necessary. Wear soft-soled shoes. Typical meeting time is 8:15 am. Cruiser reviews are overwhelmingly positive: This excursion lets you be "as active" as you like—some cruisers were "captain" while others were "in charge of the beverage chest." The "exciting" race is "great fun" with "friendly competition." Cruisers enjoyed the option to purchase a "great photo" of their team. While the seas are "not rough," this is not for anyone "prone to motion sickness." Overall, this excursion is a "highlight of the cruise" and "a blast!" (On Your Own: America's Cup at 599-542-0045)

Sports
Very active
Ages 12 & up
$69
3 hours

See page 164 for a key to the shore excursion description charts and their icons.

Embarking on Shore Excursions in St. Maarten/St. Martin *(continued)*

Island Drive & Explorer Cruise [SM05]   Rating: n/a

Drive along the Atlantic coast of the island on a guided tour, then board the "Explorer" pleasure boat for a 30-minute cruise to Marigot (the island's French capital). Cash bars onboard. There's time for shopping and sightseeing before you return to Philipsburg. Typical meeting time is 1:00 pm. Cruiser reviews for this excursion were not submitted; it appears it is not very popular. (On Your Own: Eagle Tours at http://www.sailingsxm.com or 599-543 0068)

Tour
Leisurely
All ages
$40/$20 (3-9)
4 hours

Under Two Flags [SM06]   Rating: 7

Board an air-conditioned bus for a scenic, narrated tour of both the French and Dutch sides of the island—you'll see much of the island. The bus makes short 15-minute stops for photos, plus a 45-minute stop in Marigot (the French capital) so you can shop or explore. The tour ends back in Philipsburg. Typical meeting time is 8:45 am. Cruiser reviews are mixed: Most cruisers enjoyed the island drive in a "comfortable, clean bus" with a "friendly driver," though a few did not like to see the "ramshackle houses" along the way. There are several "photo op stops" on "both sides of the island," plus a "French market shopping stop." Most feel this is an "informative," "get acquainted tour" that is "short enough," but some felt the "shopping time is too short" and "kids will be bored out of their skulls." (On Your Own: n/a)

Tour
Leisurely
All ages
$19/$15 (3-9)
3 hours

French Riviera Beach Rendezvous [SM07]   Rating: 8

Enjoy a beach day at Orient Bay, which has been called the "French Riviera of the Caribbean." You'll receive a guided tour on your way to the beach, where you'll be welcomed with a complimentary beverage and a full-service lunch. Then it's off to your reserved beach chair for relaxation. One end of this beach is clothing-optional. Typical meeting time is 9:45 am. Cruiser reviews are mostly positive: The "20-30 minute" bus ride is informative, filled with "facts regarding the island," though some cruisers were uncomfortable with the "visible poverty" on the island. At Orient Beach, you get a "padded lounge chair" to use and a complimentary "fruit punch" with "optional rum." Lunch is "good" with "ribs, chicken, and fish." Cruisers report "topless" bathers and "full nudity," but "forgot about it" after a while. Most felt this excursion is an "adventure" and a "fun experience." (On Your Own: Just take a taxi to Orient Beach!)

Beach
Leisurely
All ages
$45/$35 (3-9)
5 hours

St. Maarten Island & Butterfly Farm Tour [SM09]   Rating: 8

Board a bus for a narrated tour through Philipsburg to the famous Butterfly Farm on the French side of the island. After the farm you'll stop at Marigot for shopping and exploration. Tip: Wear bright colors and perfume if you want the butterflies to land on you. Typical meeting time is 8:00 am. Cruiser reviews are mostly positive: The "great island tour" with "narration" from the "entertaining driver" gave insight into the "rich history" of St. Maarten. The "best part of the trip" was the Butterfly Farm, which "should not be missed" and good for "kids under 12." Most had not seen "so many butterflies so close" and were enchanted when they "landed" on them. Most felt this was a "great overall tour," but some said there are "better butterfly farms at zoos." (On Your Own: The Butterfly Farm at http://www.thebutterflyfarm.com or 599-544-3562)

Tour
Leisurely
All ages
$32/$27 (3-9)
3 hours

© MediaMarx, Inc.

The Butterfly Farm

See page 164 for a key to the shore excursion description charts and their icons.

Embarking on Shore Excursions
in St. Maarten/St. Martin *(continued)*

See & Sea Island Tour [SM10] Rating: 6

Explore the best of both worlds—land and sea—on this guided tour. First you'll take a narrated bus tour to Grand Case. Then you'll board the "Seaworld Explorer"—a semi-submarine—for an underwater glimpse of sea life. Afterwards, there's an hour for shopping and exploring in Marigot. Typical meeting times are 8:15 am and 1:15 pm. Cruiser reviews are mixed: The bus driver is "knowledgeable" and "personable," but the ride was "slow" and "harrowing" at times as the roads are very narrow. The "sea portion" aboard the "semi-sub" was "interesting" and "educational," and the "kids really loved seeing the fish." Some reports suggest that "the sea life is minimal." Overall, some cruisers liked seeing "pretty much all" of the "pretty island," while others felt there were "better ways" to see the island. (On Your Own: Seaworld Explorer at 599-542-4078)

Tour
Leisurely
All ages
$48/$35 (3-9)
3.5 hours

Lagoon Kayaking Tour [SM11] Rating: 7

Board a bus for a narrated tour to Simpson Bay Lagoon, one of the largest saltwater lagoons in the Caribbean. You'll paddle your one-person kayak through the mangroves. After a brief rest at Explorer Island, you'll make your way to a sandy beach to relax, swim, and enjoy a drink. Maximum weight is 300 lbs. Typical meeting time is 7:50 am. Cruiser reviews are limited, but those we received were positive: The "strenuous" trip is for those in "good shape" and is probably "not ideal for beginners." The beach and "rocky lagoon" is "interesting," and you can "snorkel" as well as swim and relax. Overall, most had a "great time." (On Your Own: Tri-Sport at 599-545-4384)

Sports
Very active
Ages 10 & up
$60
3.5-4 hours

St. Maarten Certified Scuba [SM13] Rating: 8

Certified scuba divers enjoy visits to some of St. Maarten's famous dive sites. Dive sites are chosen day of the dive according to weather and sea conditions. You must have your scuba certification and have completed at least one dive in the past two years to participate. Typical meeting time is 8:45 am. Cruiser reviews are limited but generally positive: The "two-tank" dive is "great," with "one divemaster per six divers." The tour operators "handled all the equipment" and "took plenty of time" at each location. Even though "St. Maarten isn't the greatest place to dive" due to "choppy waters," once you're underwater it is "beautiful." Those "prone to motion sickness" should take the "appropriate meds" before going. Overall, most felt it "couldn't have been nicer." (On Your Own: Dive Safaris at http://diveguide.com/divesafaris, 599-542-9001 or Aqua Mania at http://www.stmaarten-activities.com, 599-544-2640)

Sports
Very active
Ages 12 & up
$90
4 hours

Lotterie Farm Hidden Forest Tour Hike [SM17] Rating: n/a

Ready for a challenging hike up to Pic du Paradise, St. Martin's tallest mountain at 1400 feet (427 m.)? After an air-conditioned bus ride to the Lotterie Farm Hidden Forest, you'll begin your 1½ hour hike through a lush rainforest. After your hike you'll enjoy an open-air lunch and a brief stop in Marigot. Bring good walking shoes and water. Typical meeting time is 8:15 am. No cruiser reviews were received for this excursion. (On Your Own: n/a)

Jennifer on Pic du Paradise

Sports
Very active
Ages 8 & up
$75/$45 (8-9)
4.5-5 hours

See page 164 for a key to the shore excursion description charts and their icons.

Embarking on Shore Excursions
in St. Maarten/St. Martin *(continued)*

Mountain Bike Adventure [SM19]   Rating: n/a

Need some exercise? This excursion outfits you with a mountain bike and safety gear, then takes you for a bumpy on- and off-road bike tour. You'll ride along the coastline, through the village of Colombier, and encounter at least one steep hill. After your exertions, take 30 minutes to relax and swim at Friar's Bay Beach—includes a complimentary beverage. Typical meeting time is 7:45 am. We received no cruiser reviews for this excursion. (On Your Own: n/a)

Sports
Very active
Ages 12 & up
$65
3.5 hours

Anguilla Dolphin and Stingray Encounter [SM20]   Rating: 8

Take a 45-minute boat ride to Anguilla, where you'll get to interact and swim with the dolphins and stingrays at Dolphin Fantaseas. Afterwards, relax at Meads Bay, where you'll enjoy a Caribbean barbecue lunch. Note that underwater cameras are not allowed—professional photos are taken for you, but prices can be steep. Typical meeting time is 7:30 am. Cruiser reviews are

Sports
Active
Ages 5 & up
$180/$158
7-7.5 hours

overwhelmingly positive: Despite the "high price" for this excursion, all cruisers found it "well worth the money." After a "heck of a fun time" on the boat to Anguilla, guests get split into two groups—one group goes to the "stunningly beautiful beach" first while others get their "encounters" first. You get to spend 45 minutes with the dolphins and "swim, dance, play catch, feed, kiss, pet, and race them." When you're "not with the dolphins," you go to "the stingray tank" or "visit with the tropical birds and hermit crabs." The "really neat" stingrays are in a six-foot tank—you can "dive down to pet them and feed them." Most cruisers agreed that biggest drawback is lunch, which is "not the best" (some reported being served goat). Overall, cruisers feel the excursion is "amazing" and the "best ever!" (On Your Own: Dolphin Fantaseas at http://www.dolphinfantaseas.com or 264-497-7946)

Observer at Anguilla Dolphin & Stingray Encounter   Rating: n/a

Just want to go along for the ride with your family or friends to the Anguilla Dolphin Encounter (described above)? You can for a reduced price! You get all the same benefits except you don't interact with the animals and you don't get wet. Tip: Bring your camera so you can take photos of your loved ones playing with the dolphins! Typical meeting time is 7:30 am. (On Your Own: Dolphin Fantaseas at http://www.dolphinfantaseas.com or 264-497-7946)

Tour
Leisurely
Ages 3 & up
$125/$100
3.5 hours

Rhino Rider and Snorkeling Adventure   Rating: 9

This newly added excursion offers a chance to zoom about on your own, two-person inflatable boat (the "Rhino Rider") in Simpson Bay. After your cruise, you'll have the opportunity to snorkel (equipment provided). When your adventure is over, you can relax with a complimentary beverage. Note that each boat holds two people maximum, and only those 13 or older can drive.

Sports
Very active
Ages 10 & up
$79
3 hours

Typical meeting times are 7:45 am and 1:15 pm. Cruiser comments are positive: After a bus ride out to Simpson Bay, guests are given a "brief explanation" on how to use the "two-seater mini boats," which is a bit like a "large jet ski with an inflated rubber bottom." You then take a "30-minute" ride with "great views" to the "good" snorkeling location, where you could also "swim if you prefer." After another 30 minutes, you "take the boat back" to Simpson Bay. If the water is "choppy," you could be a "little sore" afterwards. Most cruisers agree the excursion is "worth it" and offered a "great time." (On Your Own: Atlantis Adventures at http://www.atlantisadventures.com, 599-542-4078)

St. Thomas & St. John
(Eastern Caribbean Itineraries—Second Port of Call)

Welcome to pretty St. Thomas, the **busiest cruise ship port** and duty-free shopping haven in the Caribbean! Pirates once roamed freely here, but your visit will be far tamer, thanks to its status as a U.S. Territory. Shopping not your cup of tea? The neighboring island of St. John is a prime, back-to-nature getaway.

© MediaMarx, Inc.

The Disney Magic in St. Thomas (view from Paradise Point)

St. Thomas boasts beautiful beaches like many Caribbean islands, but its **rugged mountain terrain** gives it a distinctive look. St. Thomas is shaped like an elongated hourglass and about 28 square miles (72 sq. km.) in size, making it the second largest island in the U.S. Virgin Islands (St. Croix is the largest). Shoppers throng the narrow lanes and old, stone buildings of St. Thomas' downtown Charlotte Amalie, a duty-free port since the 1700s. The neighboring island of St. John is just a ferry ride away, home to the hiking trails, wildlife, and remote beaches of 7,200 acre Virgin Islands National Park. Your day in port is brief, so a trip to St. John will take most of your day.

Adventurers from many nations visited St. Thomas, but none put down roots until Denmark colonized in the late 1600s. The Danes made the island's prime harbor a **safe haven** for pirates, cashing in on this early "tourist" trade. They also operated sugar plantations, a thriving seaport, and one of the busiest slave markets in the Americas. Charlotte Amalie's waterfront is still lined with old stone buildings from its commercial heyday. The economy crashed after slavery was abolished in the mid-1800s, so by 1917 the Danes were happy to hand the islands to the U.S. for $25 million (it's now a U.S. Territory). Then in 1956, Laurence Rockefeller donated 5,000 acres on St. John to create the Virgin Islands National Park (and not incidentally, ensure an attractive setting for his Caneel Bay resort).

Size: St. Thomas: 13 mi. (21 km.) x 4 mi. (6 km.) /St. John: 7 mi. (11 km.) x 3 mi. (5 km.)	
Climate: Subtropical	**Temperatures:** 77°F (25°C) to 85°F (29°C)
Population: 51,000 & 4,000	**Busy Season:** Late December to April
Language: English	**Money:** U.S. Dollar
Time Zone: Atlantic (no DST)	**Transportation:** Walking, taxis, cars
Phones: Dial 1- from U.S., dial 911 for emergencies	

Introduction

Reservations

Staterooms

AMBIENCE

Dining

Activities

HISTORY

Ports of Call

Magic

FACTS

Index

Making the Most of St. Thomas and St. John

GETTING THERE

Your ship docks near **Charlotte Amalie**, capital of the U.S. Virgin Islands, normally at the West India Company pier in Havensight, 1.5 miles (2.4 km.) from downtown. Occasionally, guests must be tendered ashore (if this happens, you'll arrive in Charlotte Amalie rather than Havensight). All ashore is typically at 8:15 am, with all aboard around 4:30 pm. All guests must meet with U.S. Immigration officials onboard the ship, regardless of whether you plan to go ashore (see page 248). No guests may disembark until <u>all</u> guests have met with immigration, so there's no sleeping in today (meeting times vary—refer to the letter placed in your stateroom the night before). Visitors traveling to St. John should either book a shore excursion, or take a taxi to the Red Hook ferry on the eastern end of the island—round-trip ferry fare is $6/adults, $2/kids (15-20 minute ride). There's also a ferry from downtown Charlotte Amalie for $14/adults, $6/kids, but again you'll have to take a taxi to the ferry.

GETTING AROUND

There's **plenty of shopping near the pier**, or take a cab into town or to other destinations. Havensight Mall, right next to the cruise pier, offers more than 60 shops, and several other malls are within walking distance. • The Paradise Point aerial tramway ($12/$6) is a short walk from the pier, and offers panoramic views of the island. • There's far more shopping in downtown Charlotte Amalie (1.5 miles/2.4 km). A taxi will cost about $3 (no meters, get the rate in advance). • Car rentals are available at the pier, but taxis and mini-buses are generally a better idea. • Maagens Bay, several miles from Charlotte Amalie on the island's north shore, is a beautiful and well-known beach. Nearby is Mountain Top, famed for its views and banana daiquiris. A half-mile west of Charlotte Amalie is the picturesque fishing village of Frenchtown, known for its restaurants and bars. • If you want to visit **St. John**, Disney offers shore excursions to most of St. John's most famous spots, and with the day's tight schedule, they make sense. If you want to explore on your own, Hertz and Avis both have agencies in Cruz Bay, and taxi fares to the major sights are $3–$9. Ferries arrive in Cruz Bay, and the National Park interpretive center is a short walk away. • The beach at Trunk Bay is most popular. • History buffs may enjoy the ruins of Annaberg Sugar Plantation ($4 day use fee).

SAFETY

Pickpockets and beach theft are the most notable crime problems you'll encounter, so **leave your valuables on board**, and safeguard your purse or wallet while shopping. Drinking water is collected in cisterns from rain water, so you may prefer to drink bottled water.

Touring St. Thomas and St. John

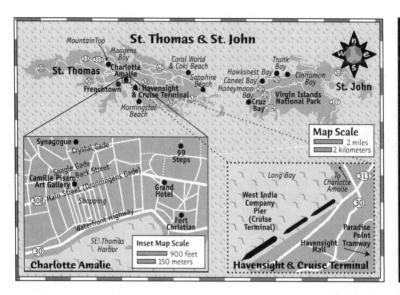

St. Thomas & St. John

Charlotte Amalie — Inset Map Scale: 900 feet / 150 meters

Havensight & Cruise Terminal

ST. THOMAS/ST. JOHN MAP

WALKING TOURS

St. Thomas: Charlotte Amalie is a nice place to stroll on steep, narrow streets with Danish names. Most sights are found on the island's many shopping streets, which are within three blocks of the waterfront. Waterfront Highway provides a harborfront promenade. One block inland is Main Street (Dronningens Gade), followed by Back Street, Snegle Gade, and Crystal Gade. More than a dozen Alleys, Gades, Passages, Plazas, and Malls run between Main Street and the waterfront, all lined with shops. Strollers will find historic Fort Christian and the Virgin Islands Museum at the southeast end of downtown. A tourist information center is located nearby, in the former Grand Hotel. One of the New World's oldest Jewish congregations in a charming, 1833 synagogue can be found three blocks inland, near the corner of Crystal Gade and Raadets Gade. Towards the west side of Main Street is the Camille Pissaro Art Gallery, named for the impressionist painter, a St. Thomas native, and featuring works by local artists. Walkers will also enjoy the many brick staircases, including the 99 Steps, that connect the steep streets in the northeast corner of downtown.

St. John's tiny port town of Cruz Bay is good for a short stroll among its cluster of shops and restaurants. The Virgin Islands National Park Visitor Center is a short walk from the dock, and several hiking trails depart from there.

ACTIVITIES

Playing in St. Thomas and St. John

There are no **beaches** within walking distance of the wharf. Morningstar Beach is the closest, and includes all the comforts of the Marriott resort. Maagens Bay ($3/day for adults) is famed for its beauty, but will be thronged with fellow cruise visitors. Sapphire Beach out on the east end offers full, resort-based recreation rentals, and nearby Coki Beach is convenient to Coral World (see below). • On **St. John**, there's a small beach right at the ferry dock in Cruz Bay, but the real attractions are elsewhere. Caneel Beach is a short ride from Cruz Bay, and part of the Caneel Bay resort (stop at the front desk on your way to the beach). Along St. John's north shore, Hawksnest Bay, Trunk Bay, and Cinnamon Bay are easily accessible, offer food, recreation, and other amenities, and are all part of the national park. Trunk Bay ($4/day) is very beautiful, most popular, and features a snorkeling trail. Cinnamon Bay has great windsurfing. • **Snorkeling** equipment can be rented at many beaches. The early departure time makes fishing excursions impractical.

Shopping is St. Thomas' biggest attraction. Shopping is duty-free, sales tax-free, and is conducted in U.S. dollars. As always, while prices can be excellent, know what you'd pay back home for the same goods. Not everything is a "deal." Some shopkeepers will bargain with you. Just ask, "Is that your final price?" With as many as eight cruise ships in port per day, it takes hundreds of shops to absorb the throngs. We suggest you head into Charlotte Amalie and start exploring. If your time is short, the malls and shops in and around the cruise wharf will be most convenient.

Visitors to St. Johns will find the **Virgin Islands National Park** web site very helpful, with a detailed map of the island, including its 22 hiking trails. Get more info at http://www.nps.gov/viis.

Coral World Marine Park and Undersea Observatory on St. Thomas' east end (adjacent to Coki Beach) offers underwater observation areas, aquariums, exhibits, stingray encounters, nature trails, and the "Sea Trekkin'" adventure where you get to walk the sea bottom ($50 extra, age 8 and up, reservations suggested). Admission is $18/adults, $9/kids, or $52 for a family of two adults and up to four kids. Visit http://www.coralworldvi.com or call 888-695-2073.

For one of the most informative and well-laid-out **web sites** for the U.S. Virgin Islands, visit http://www.vinow.com.

Embarking on Shore Excursions
on St. Thomas and St. John

☐ St. John Trunk Bay Beach & Snorkel Tour [ST01]   Rating: 6

Travel by sea and land to Trunk Bay, where you'll have 1.5 hours to swim, snorkel (equipment provided), and relax in this beautiful national park. Typical meeting time is 7:40 am. Cruiser comments are mixed: Most report that the "ferry ride" over was "long" and "boring." Once at Trunk Bay, however, cruisers found it to be "one of the most beautiful" and "breathtaking" beaches. There is a "marked snorkel trail" and some cruisers have seen a "lot of fish," "stingrays," and "sea turtles." Most felt this was the "highlight of their cruise," while some "were not impressed." (On Your Own: Take a taxi to Red Hook, a ferry to St. John, and then a taxi to Trunk Bay)

Sports
Active
Ages 5 & up
$42/$30 (5-9)
5 hours

☐ St. John Island Tour [ST02]   Rating: 9

Take a boat ride to St. John, then board an open-air safari bus for a guided tour through the unspoiled beauty of this island. Includes a stop at Annaberg Ruins. For all ages. Typical meeting time is 7:40 am. We took this excursion in May 2003 and absolutely loved it. Cruiser reviews are uniformly positive: Most enjoyed the "boat ride" to "beautiful" St. John, though it was "long." The "very good driving tour" "makes a lot of stops for pictures" and the driver is both "entertaining" and "knowledgeable." Some of the roads are "very curvy," which could bother some. Overall, the tour is a "great way" to "see a lot" of the island.

Tour
Leisurely
All ages
$39/$29 (3-9)
5 hours

☐ St. John Eco Hike [ST03]   Rating: 8

Take a ferry to Cruz Bay, where you'll embark on a 90-minute guided hike (1.2 miles). You'll stop at Lind Point Lookout and Honeymoon Beach for swimming. Typical meeting time is 8:10 am. Cruiser reviews are positive: This "wonderful way to see the island" starts with "long ferry ride" then a short walk through the city to meet your "knowledgeable guide." The "very easy" hike is "informative," with a look at "local flora and fauna" ("bring bug spray!"). At the end of the "hot" hike, you get 30 min. to "frolic" in Honeymoon Bay ("wear your swimsuit under your clothes").

Sports
Very active
Ages 6 & up
$59/$49 (6-9)
5.5 hours

☐ 5-Star St. John Snorkel & Beach Adventure [ST04]   Rating: 7

Board the 115-foot "Leylon Sneed" in St. Thomas and cruise to Trunk Bay to snorkel (equipment provided), swim, and sunbathe. Includes a complimentary beverage. Typical meeting time is 7:40 am. Cruiser reviews are mixed: Most cruisers appreciated the cruise on the "1939 Chesapeake Bay Oyster Buy Boat replica," but found the trip "long" (45 minutes) and "a little crowded." Those cruisers that made it to Trunk Bay thought it "simply beautiful" with "great snorkeling," but a significant number of reviews noted that they were "detoured to St. James" island because of "rough seas," and this was "disappointing."

Beach
Active
Ages 5 & up
$45/$32 (5-9)
4–4.5 hours

☐ St. Thomas Sapphire Beach Day [ST05]   Rating: 5

Relax on the white sands of Sapphire Beach and go swimming. Beach chairs available on a first-come, first-serve basis. Deli-style buffet lunch included. Typical meeting time is 9:15 am. Cruiser reviews are so-so: The "open-air shuttle" takes "25 minutes" to get from the pier to Sapphire Beach. The beach itself is "beautiful" with some "large rocks." Bathroom facilities are available, but "not always working." The "not very good" lunch is "horrible." Watch out for "iguanas wandering around." Most felt if they were to visit this beach again, they'd do it "on their own." (On Your Own: Just take a taxi from the pier to Sapphire Beach.)

Beach
Leisurely
All ages
$43/$32 (3-9)
4.5 hours

See page 164 for a key to the shore excursion description charts and their icons.

Embarking on Shore Excursions
on St. Thomas and St. John (continued)

Atlantis Submarine Adventure [ST06] — Rating: 5

Climb aboard the "Atlantis XV" and dive down to 90 feet (26 m.). Typical meeting times are 9:15 am, 10:15 am, and noon. Guests must be 36" tall. Cruiser reviews are mixed: This "expensive" excursion takes place in a "fairly spacious" sub which you "board in water (no dock)" "after a choppy 25-minute ride." It has portholes "running along the sides." Two people need to "share a porthole" to gaze out at the "cloudy water" with "some sea life" but "nothing spectacular." A "knowledgeable guide" points out specifics along the way. Most cruisers "enjoyed it" but probably wouldn't "do it again." (On Your Own: http://www.atlantisadventures.net or 340-776-5650)

Tour
Leisurely
Ages 4 & up
$75/$50 (4-9)
2.5 hours

Champagne Catamaran Sail & Snorkel [ST07] — Rating: 10

Take a two-hour cruise from St. Thomas to Honeymoon Bay in St. John, where you can snorkel (equipment provided), swim, or sunbathe. A champagne brunch is included. Typical meeting time is 9:00 am. Cruiser reviews are overwhelmingly positive: While this excursion is "pricey," it's also "enjoyably long" with a "two hour sail out," "two hours to play," and "two hours back." Lunch is "excellent" with a "nice spread." "Juice and soda" is served in addition to champagne. The crew is "excellent" and the catamaran is "beautiful." Every cruiser would "do it again." (On Your Own: http://www.atlantisadventures.net/stthomas or 340-776-5650)

Tour
Leisurely
Ages 5 & up
$90/$65 (5-9)
6 hours

Doubloon Sail & Snorkel [ST08] — Rating: 9

Help hoist the sails of the 65-foot "Doubloon" schooner and cruise to Turtle Cove on Buck Island. Snorkel (equipment provided) and swim. Includes snacks and drinks. For ages 5 & up. Typical meeting time is 8:15 am. Cruiser reviews are positive: This "fun" excursion with a "heavy pirate theme" is fun for "kids and adults alike." While it's not a "major sailing experience," it is "enjoyable" and the "crew is attentive." Snorkeling at Buck Island is "good," though you may not be able to walk on the beach due to "nesting birds." "Rum punch," "beer," and "soda" is served. Overall, most cruisers "recommend it."

Sports
Active
Ages 5 & up
$42/$30 (5-9)
3.5 hours

Buck Island Sail & Snorkel [ST10] — Rating: 9

Board a six-person yacht with your captain and skipper, then sail to Turtle Cove to snorkel. Snacks and an open bar included after snorkeling. Typical meeting times are 8:10 am and 12:15 pm. Cruiser reviews are positive: Unlike the Doubloon Sail, this excursion is "limited to just six people" so it's like you have a "personal tour guide" and it seems "more exclusive." The yacht tours "around the reefs" and your "guide points out flora and fauna." Most cruisers agree it is "well worth the price!"

Sports
Active
Ages 5 & up
$50/$45 (5-9)
3.5-4 hours

St. Thomas Island Tour [ST11] — Rating: n/a

Take an open-air safari bus tour to St. Peter's Great House and Mountain Top, the highest point on the island. The bus does make some stops for photo opportunities. Typical meeting times are 8:00 am and 12:15 pm. We received no cruiser reviews for this excursion, however cruisers who visited Mountain Top on their own claim it is "amazing" how you can "see so much!"

Tour
Leisurely
All ages
$33/$23 (3-9)
2.5 hours

See page 164 for a key to the shore excursion description charts and their icons.

Embarking on Shore Excursions
on St. Thomas and St. John (continued)

◻ Coral World & Island Drive [ST12] — Rating: 7 ☀ 🛍 📷

Take a guided tour to Mountain Top (highest peak) and Coral World in St. Thomas. Typical meeting times are 8:00 am and noon. Cruiser reviews are mostly positive: Coral World is a "wonderful adventure," a bit like "Sea World" but "more science-oriented." "Kids love it," and "see all kinds of sea life" and "pet a shark." The disappointments were the drive which was "not well narrated," and the length of time at Coral World ("only an hour and a half"). Cruisers did enjoy Coral World, but many suggested they'd "do it on their own" next time. (On Your Own: See page 176 to save money and see Coki Beach, too!)

Tour
Leisurely
All ages
$39/$29 (3-9)
3.5 hours

◻ Water Island Bike & Beach Adventure [ST13] — Rating: 10 ☀ 🛍 📷

Enjoy a short boat ride to Water Island where you'll explore the terrain by mountain bike. Includes all necessary equipment. Includes a beach stop. Typical meeting time is 12:15 pm. Cruiser reviews are overwhelmingly positive: Get a ride to Water Island on a "large pontoon boat" and listen to the "history" of the island. Once on the island, you get a "quick how-to" on the bikes, "fit you for your helmet," and you're off. Most of the ride is "downhill," but it does cover ground with "gravel and loose rocks." After reaching Honeymoon Bay, you can "beach it" or "keep biking" a mostly "uphill trail." Cruisers of "all shapes and sizes" enjoyed this excursion.

Sports
Very active
Ages 10 & up
$59
3.5 hours

◻ Kayak Marine Sanctuary Tour [ST14] — Rating: 9 ☀ 🛍 📷

Paddle two-person kayaks through the mangroves in a St. Thomas marine sanctuary. Along the way, snorkel or swim at Bovini Point. Bring water shoes. Typical meeting time is 8:20 am. Cruiser reviews are very positive: While "no kayak experience is necessary," this "fascinating" excursion is a "bit of a workout." The "helpful guides" explain the "mangrove habitat" you pass on your kayak "adventure." Snorkeling is "interesting" with "plenty of sea creatures," but the water is a "bit murky." "Cold water" and "bite-size candy bars" are provided after snorkeling. All cruisers agree this excursion is "great!"

Sports
Very active
Ages 10 & up
$60
3.5-4 hours

◻ Golf at Mahogany Run [ST15] — Rating: 10 ☀ 🛍 📷

Play a round of golf at this 6,022-yard course designed by George and Tom Fazio. Price includes greens fees, golf cart, and transportation. Rental clubs are additional (about $20). Typical meeting time is 8:15 am. Cruiser reviews are very positive: The excursion "includes transportation" to and from the "beautiful course" with "awesome views." Players are "matched by handicap" and play in "foursomes." Some cruisers report that the course is "challenging," but "lots of fun." Other cruisers suggest you "carry your own golf shoes" to ensure a "comfortable fit." (On Your Own: Mahogany Run Golf Course at http://www.st-thomas.com/mahogany)

Sports
Active
Ages 10 & up
$135
5-6 hours

◻ Certified Scuba in St. Thomas [ST16] — Rating: n/a ☀ 🛍 📷

Certified scuba divers can take a two-tank dive to a maximum depth of 60 feet. Equipment and transportation are provided; wet suit not included. Typical meeting time is 8:00 am. Cruiser reviews are limited: Most cruisers enjoyed this "well-organized" tour and had a "great dive." In general, most agree that St. Thomas is a "far better location for diving" than St. Maarten. (On Your Own: Coki Beach Dive Club at http://www.cokidive.com, 800-474-2654)

Sports
Very active
Ages 12 & up
$90
4 hours

See page 164 for a key to the shore excursion description charts and their icons.

Embarking on Shore Excursions on St. Thomas and St. John (continued)

St. John Barefoot Catamaran Sail & Snorkel [ST21] — Rating: 7

After a scenic drive from the port you'll board a catamaran and sail to St. John where you'll swim, snorkel, and sunbathe. Snacks, snorkel gear, and open bar included. Typical meeting time is 7:45 am. Cruiser reviews are mostly positive: This "great sailing trip" "over and back to St. John" is "excellent." The crew is "terrific" and served "drinks and snacks" both coming and going. Snorkeling at Honeymoon Bay is "very good" with "clear water, lots of fish, and even stingrays," but be aware that if you just want to lounge on the beach you'll need to "swim a short way from the catamaran to the beach." Overall, this excursion is "highly recommended" but a few would "do something else next time."

Sports
Active
Ages 5 & up
$69/$52 (5-9)
4-4.5 hours

Charlotte Amalie Historical Walking Tour [ST22] — Rating: 5

Explore the quaint town of Charlotte Amalie—along the way you'll admire a stunning vista of the town and visit Notman's Manor. Wear comfortable walking shoes. Typical meeting time is 8:30 am. Cruiser reviews are mixed: Guests board a "van" and "drive up to the highest point" on the tour. From there, you "walk downhill" and listen to your "knowledgeable tour guide" point out sites and divulge the "history of the island." This is an "interesting tour" if you are "history buff," otherwise it is a "bit dry." There are a "lot of stairs" and the tour is boring for "toddlers and young kids."

Tour
Leisurely
All ages
$29/$20 (3-9)
3.5 hours

Paradise Point Tramway [ST23] — Rating: 7

Enjoy a great view (see photo on 173) in this suspended tram. Bird shows are held twice daily. You can do this excursion anytime after 9:00 am. Jennifer tried this and found it a fun diversion with great views, but not a don't-miss. Cruiser reviews are mostly positive: The tramway is an "easy 10-15 minute walk" from the pier (but if you tender in, it's a "$3/person taxi from town"

Tour
Leisurely
All ages
$15/$7.50
(0-5 free)
1 hour

instead). The view from the tram is "just amazing" and you get a "great view of the Disney Magic." The "birds are cute" (shows are at "10:30 am and 1:30 pm") and there are some "nice shops" to browse. There is also a quarter-mile "nature walk" and a "little cafe." Most cruisers didn't bother with the excursion through Disney, but simply walked over (you can see the tramway from the pier) and purchased tickets on their own (same price). (On Your Own: http://paradisepointtramway.com)

© MediaMarx, Inc.

Boarding the tram

Captain Nautica's St. John Snorkeling Expedition [ST25] — Rating: 9

Enjoy a speedboat ride to two different snorkeling sites. Price includes snorkeling equipment, snacks, and beverages. Typical meeting times are 7:50 am and noon. Cruiser comments are very positive: The "adventurous" speedboat ride is "pretty fast" and "lots of fun." The crew is "friendly" and "helpful." The reported snorkeling sites are either "Turtle Cove off Buck Island" or "Christmas Cove," plus "Honeymoon Bay." Snorkeling is "wonderful" with "many colorful fish." The only complaint reported was with the snacks, which "weren't all that great." Overall, cruisers "loved it" and "would do it again." (On Your Own: http://home.att.net/~captainnautica)

Tour
Active
Ages 8 & up
$65/$55 (8-9)
4 hours

See page 164 for a key to the shore excursion description charts and their icons.

San Juan, Puerto Rico
(Special Eastern Caribbean Itineraries)

The Magic will be visiting San Juan three times in 2004. This large, very busy port city is one of the oldest in the New World and the one of the busiest ports in the Caribbean trade. You can easily spend your entire day within the ancient walls of Old San Juan or head out to the country for rainforest or waterfront eco-delights.

Cruise ships dock in Old San Juan, the fortified old city, which was spruced up for Columbus' 500th anniversary and is awaiting its own 500th in a few years. Located on a rocky island at the mouth of San Juan harbor, all points of interest are within walking distance. Dramatic El Morro Fortress supplies the island's best-known landmark (a World Heritage Site). As one of the few walled cities in the Americas, the spirit of the Old World and Spain's colonial heritage is all around, while east of Old San Juan rise the grand beachfront hotels and casinos of the modern city.

Discovered on Columbus' second voyage, Puerto Rico quickly became the headquarters for Spanish rule in the New World and the last stop for treasure ships bound for Spain. San Juan was founded in 1508 by Juan "Fountain of Youth" Ponce de León and was soon a fortified city that fended-off attacks by many European rivals. Unlike smaller Caribbean islands, Puerto Rico remained a Spanish colony until 1898, when it was ceded to the U.S. after the Spanish American War. Puerto Rico was a U.S. Territory until 1952, when the Commonwealth of Puerto Rico was established—a possession of the U.S. with its own constitution. As throughout the Caribbean, the native peoples didn't last long after "discovery," but hints of the native blood lines and culture survive. The culture and architecture is strongly Spanish Colonial, with African and Caribbean influences. El Yunque forest reserve is one of the New World's oldest, established by Spain in 1876. Now the Caribbean National Forest, it's both the smallest U.S. National Forest (28,000 acres) and the Forest Service's only tropical rainforest (120 in./ 305 cm. of annual rainfall).

Size: 100 miles (161 km.) long by 35 miles (56 km.) wide	
Climate: Subtropical	**Temperatures:** 70°F (22°C) to 89°F (32°C)
Population: 3.89 million	**Busy Season:** Late November to Late March
Language: English & Spanish	**Money:** U.S. Dollar
Time Zone: Atlantic (no DST)	**Transportation:** Taxis, trolleys, cars
Phones: Dial 1- from U.S., dial 911 for emergencies, local pay calls = 25	

INTRO

AMBIENCE

HISTORY

FACTS

Introduction · Reservations · Staterooms · Dining · Activities · Ports of Call · Magic · Index

Making the Most of San Juan

GETTING THERE

The Magic is scheduled to dock at **Pier 4**, one of the port's largest and most modern, towards the east end of Old San Juan. There are a few shops right at the pier, but the entire old city is close at hand. The tourism information center (La Casita) is about 1/3 mile west along the waterfront, and the ferry to Cataño (Bacardi Distillery) is next door at Pier 2. A waterfront promenade completed for the Christopher Columbus quint-centennial makes waterfront strolls very pleasant. The Magic is set to arrive at 7:00 am (expect an all-ashore of 8:00 am), and departs at 5:30 pm (expect an all-aboard time of 4:30 pm).

GETTING AROUND

Old San Juan is **made for walking**, but there's also a free trolley service across the street from the pier that wends its way throughout the old town. We don't recommend a car rental in San Juan unless you're already very familiar with the area. Considering the brief time you'll be ashore, the time spent at the rental agency will be very precious indeed. The narrow, cobblestone streets of Old San Juan are often clogged with traffic and parking is near-impossible, so why add to the frustration? To the east, the beaches and casinos of Condado Beach (3-4 miles) and Isla Verde (6-7 miles) are easy and inexpensive to reach by taxi (see below). If you're interested in the natural wonders of El Yunque or other out-of-town destinations, play it safe and take an official excursion so the ship won't sail without you. Taxi fares are regulated, but be sure to discuss the fare before you hop in. Special fixed-fares for tourism include: Pier to Old San Juan: $6.00, Pier to Condado Beach: $10, Pier to Isla Verde: $16.00. Metered fares start at $3.00 (all prices in U.S. dollars). There are no extra, per-person fees.

SAFETY

Personal safety in this metropolitan city should be approached with the **same caution** you'd show in any large urban area. Leave your flashy valuables back in the stateroom safe. Shoulder bags should be hung diagonally across your chest. If you'll be carrying purchases back to the ship, travel with a buddy and stay alert. The free trolley will take you safely from the main shopping district right back to the waterfront. If you're headed for the beach, keep a limited amount of cash and any credit cards in a small, waterproof container so you can carry it at all times. And need we say it, "Sunscreen!" Oh, and if the Pirates of the Caribbean happen to sail into port, hide behind those high, fortified city walls.

Touring San Juan

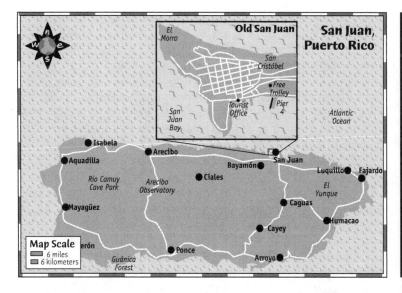

SAN JUAN MAP

The bulk of **Old San Juan** is contained in an eight-block square area to the north and west of the cruise pier, and there's far more to see than we have space to catalog. Leaving the pier, we suggest you first visit the tourist office, La Casita, for up-to-date info and maps (see location on inset map above). Afterwards, take a free trolley ride to get your bearings—start with a ride all the way to El Morro and the walk back will be downhill. There's a $3 per person per fort fee (children under 12 are free) to explore El Morro and San Cristóbal fortresses, or use your National Parks Annual Pass (for more information on the fortresses, visit http://www.nps.gov/saju). Several major points of interest are clustered near El Morro, including the Plaza del Quinto Centenario, Casa Blanca (the de León family home), the church of San José, the Museum of San Juan, and the Pablo Casals Museum. From there, head south on Cristo St. to the Cathedral of San Juan and east on San Francisco to Plaza de Armas and San Juan's City Hall. Return to Cristo St. and continue south for serious shopping, and the nearby La Fortaleza, the historic Governor's mansion—tours are available from 9:00 am to 4:00 pm, on the hour. You'll now be near the city's southern wall, which you can follow eastward back towards the cruise piers. This walking tour can take from three hours and up, depending on how much time you spend at the old fortresses and other points of interest.

WALKING TOURS

Playing in San Juan

ACTIVITIES

With the exception of walking, **recreation** of all sorts requires a journey outside this urban port. Eco-tourism is strong here, thanks to the El Yunque rainforest. We suggest booking an excursion to this distant site. Sea kayaking, snorkeling and biking are also options.

Old San Juan offers excellent **shopping opportunities**, especially for those in search of antiques and crafts. Some of the island's most unique and notable crafts are lace-making (descended from the Spanish tradition), hand-carved religious figurines called "santos," and fanciful papier-mâché festival masks. Then there are guayabara shirts, hand-rolled cigars, and rum. The island has a strong fine arts community – paintings and sculpture are also attractive possibilities. Goods purchased in Puerto Rico can be returned to the mainland U.S., duty-free—keep those receipts!

The **Bacardi Rum Distillery** (for tours and free samples) is across the harbor in Cataño. You can take an excursion that includes this stop, or grab a ferry that departs Old San Juan's Pier 2 every half-hour. It's a long walk from the dock in Cataño, or catch a bus.

There's no **beach** in Old San Juan. The Condado Beach resort area is closest to the pier and quite popular with visitors, but the somewhat-more-distant Isla Verde district is reputed to have the nicer beach. Situated between the two, the beach at Ocean Park is especially popular with wind surfers. While beachfront hotels dominate Condado and Isla Verde, the public is welcome, and those hotels offer a variety of options for recreation and refreshment.

For **gamblers**, the Wyndham Old San Juan Hotel and Casino is right on the waterfront, nearly opposite the pier. The grander casinos require a journey. Condado Beach is home to the Radisson Ambassador Plaza, Diamond Palace, San Juan Marriott, and Wyndham Condado Plaza casinos. These are good choices for beach/casino getaways. Still farther east is Isla Verde, with five more casinos: Courtyard by Marriott, Embassy Suites, InterContinental, Ritz Carlton, and the grandest of all, the Wyndham El San Juan.

For detailed information on the forts of **Old San Juan**, visit the National Park Service web site: http://www.nps.gov/saju. If you're headed to **El Yunque**, visit the Caribbean National Forest site at http://www.southernregion.fs.fed.us/caribbean.

Embarking on Shore Excursions in San Juan

As we go to press, Disney has yet to announce its round-up of shore excursions for San Juan. We provide these listings to acquaint you with the possibilities, based on typical offerings by other cruise lines and the excursions offered during the Magic's unscheduled visit (due to a hurricane) in 2002.

☐ San Juan City Bus Tours

A variety of tours are possible, focusing on various aspects of the city. A basic tour will take you for a swing past the beaches and casino hotels of Condado Beach and Isla Verde before returning to Old San Juan for a guided tour of historic spots including El Morro and San Cristóbal fortresses. Shopping stops may be included in some tours (perhaps at a mall, rather than in the old city). In 2002, Disney offered the "New and Old San Juan Tour" for $25/adult and $20/child with a tour duration of 2.5-3 hours.

Tour
Leisurely
$20-30
2-4 hours

☐ Bacardi Rum Distillery Tour

Tour the Bacardi Rum distillery, take in the gift shop, and enjoy free samples of Bacardi's wares. The 20 minute or so bus ride may also include a brief tour of Old San Juan. If you're up for a little adventure, make your own way to the distillery via the very inexpensive Cataño ferry (see page 182). In 2002, Disney offered this tour for $19/adult and $12/child with a tour duration of 2-2.5 hours.

Tour
Leisurely
$20
2.5 hours

☐ Old San Juan Walking Tour

Take a guided stroll around the historic city that's just across the street from the pier. A mini-bus ride is provided to avoid the 175-foot gain in elevation. The walking is on quaint, cobblestone streets and staircases. For the money, let's hope your tour guide provides the depth of information you may miss if you go off walking on your own.

Tour
Active
$22-33
1.5-2.5 hours

☐ El Yunque Rainforest Tour

How many chances do you get to visit a real rainforest? El Yunque is a unit of the U.S. Forest Service, about 45 miles southeast of San Juan. Most tours include a brief (~45 minute) hike, a stop at the forest's visitor center, and a chance to swim beneath a waterfall. About one million visitors come here annually. Bring insect repellent and be prepared to get damp. In 2002, Disney offered this excursion for $30/adult and $25/child with a tour duration of 4.5-5 hours, and visits to Yohaku Observation Center and La Coca Waterfall.

Tour
Very active
$30
5 hours

☐ Kayaking

The north coast of Puerto Rico offers several kayak-worthy sites. Excursions may visit the Espiritu Santo River to explore mangrove marshlands, or you may paddle out to offshore reefs. Expect a beach break, and perhaps some snorkeling (equipment provided). Refreshments included. Bring sunscreen, sunglasses, and a change of clothes. In 2002, Disney offered this excursion for $65/person with a tour duration of 4.5-5 hours.

Tour
Very active
Ages 12 & up
$65-90
5 hours

See page 164 for a key to the shore excursion description charts and their icons.

Genuine PassPorter Genuine PassPorter Genuine PassPorter Genuine PassPorter Genuine PassPorter Genuine PassPorter Genuine PassPorter

Introduction
Reservations
Staterooms
Dining
Activities
Ports of Call
Magic
Index

Embarking on Shore Excursions in San Juan *(continued)*

Ocean Trail Horseback Ride

Take a sedate 1.5-hour horseback ride at a beachfront ranch. The route may follow the beach if it's not turtle-nesting season. Otherwise, the ocean will be viewed from farther inland. Suitable for beginners— includes basic instruction. Water and refreshments are included, along with a brief beach break. Long pants, closed-toe shoes, sunscreen and insect repellent recommended. In 2002, Disney offered this excursion at Palmas del Mar for $75/person with a tour duration of 3.5–4 hours.

Sports
Very active
Ages 10 & up
$75
4 hours

Mountain Biking Piñones Reserve

Piñones Reserve, an oceanfront area of beaches and mangrove marshes on the east end of San Juan, is the site for this excursion. A tour guide, bikes, helmets, and bottled water are provided. Ride about 10 miles along an oceanfront boardwalk (minimal elevation changes). Take a brief beach break before returning to the ship. Bring sunscreen. Closed-toe shoes required. In 2002, Disney offered this excursion to Boca de Cangrejos Bridge for $59/person with a tour duration of 3–3.5 hours.

Sports
Very active
Ages 12 & up
$60
3 hours

Party Boat and Snorkel

Fajardo, a port town an hour east of San Juan noted for its coral reefs and nature preserve, is the jumping-off spot for this party cruise. Take a brief sail to an offshore islet for snorkeling and swimming. Snorkel gear, soft drinks, beer, snacks, and towels provided. Bring sunglasses and sunscreen. In 2002, Disney offered this excursion on a 46-foot boat for $75/person.

Sports
Active
Ages 10 & up
$75
5 hours

See page 164 for a key to the shore excursion description charts and their icons.

San Juan and Puerto Rico On Your Own

For those that want to get a headstart on their excursion plans, or just want to do it on their own, here is some information on tour operators in San Juan. Please note that we have not used these operators, nor is any mention here an endorsement of their services. Also note that as San Juan is a bustling home port for many cruises, it's best to let your tour operator know that you're a cruise ship passenger and the time you need to be back onboard. **Legends of Puerto Rico** offers several interesting tours, including one that visits the places "where the pirates attacked" and another that explores "exotic" trails. For more information, visit http://www.legendsofpr.com or call 787-605-9060. Or how about a self-guided walking tour of Old San Juan? **AudioGuía** offers walking tours highlighting 22 points of interest—all at your own pace. Their offices are next to the Wyndham Hotel right across from Pier 4, where the Disney Magic docks. For more information, visit http://www.audioguiapr.com or call 787-507-2905. **Rico Sun Tours** (RST) is a large tour operator offering a variety of excursions, including one to Camuy Caverns and Arecibo Observatory. For more details, visit http://www.ricosuntours.com or call 787-722-2080. If you're looking for similar tours to those we mentioned as possible Disney excursions above and on the previous page, **American Tours of Puerto Rico** offers tours to the same places. Visit http://www.puerto-rico-tourism.com/americantoursofpuertorico.htm or call 800-250-8971. Another option is to explore the San Juan excursions through ShoreTrips at http://www.shoretrips.com.

Antigua
(Special Eastern Caribbean Itineraries)

Encircled by protective reefs and blessed with sheltered anchorage, Antigua (say "an-TEE-ga") boasts 365 beaches for sunning, and fair harbors for sailing. Alas that you'll have but eight hours in port—you'll have to take in a new beach every minute to see them all (or come back and spend a year visiting a new beach every day!)

Ruined fortresses, old sugar plantations, and modern, beach-front resorts reflect a rich history and a prosperous present. With the tourist economy responsible for 75% of the island's income, you'll find pleasant shopping opportunities right at the pier, but a jaunt across the island will take you back to the glory days of Britain's Royal Navy. Whether you stay close to port in St. John's, or head for historic English Harbor (Nelson's Dockyard), you'll find first-rate beaches less than 10 minutes away by taxi. If history isn't your thing, the island offers a rich selection of water sport-based activities, from sailing and snorkeling to stingray swims.

Although named by Columbus, European settlers didn't arrive in Antigua until the mid-1600s. The first settlements were those of the Siboney (an Arawak word meaning "stone-people"), who date from about 2400 B.C. After the Siboney came the Arawaks, who were agricultural by nature. The Arawaks were displaced by the Caribs, an aggressive people. The earliest European contact came with Columbus' second Caribbean voyage in 1493, but European settlements didn't take root for another century due to the lack of fresh water and the Carib resistance. While the island was home to very prosperous sugar cane plantations, the British Navy prized the island for its easily protected, safe harbors. English Harbour was the British Navy's base of operations in this part of the Caribbean. Captain Horatio Nelson spent several unhappy years here, and many a man-o'-war was overhauled in what's now called "Nelson's Dockyard," naturally hidden from any enemy warship cruising by. With the exception of a brief occupation by the French, the island remained firmly under British rule until 1981, when it achieved full independence.

Size: 14 miles (23 km.) long by 11 miles (18 km.) wide	
Climate: Subtropical	Temperatures: 81°F (26°C) to 87°F (30°C)
Population: 68,000	Busy Season: Late December to April
Language: English	Money: E. Carib. Dollar (1 = 37 U.S. cents)
Time Zone: Atlantic (no DST)	Transportation: Walking, taxis, cars
Phones: Dial 1- from U.S., dial 911 for emergencies	

Introduction

Reservations

Staterooms

Dining

Activities

Ports of Call

Magic

Index

INTRO

AMBIENCE

HISTORY

FACTS

Introduction
Reservations
Staterooms
Dining
Activities
Ports of Call
Magic
Index

Making the Most of Antigua

GETTING THERE

Your ship docks at **Heritage Quay** (pronounced "key"), in the heart of Antigua's capital city, St. John's. This pier, and nearby Redcliffe Quay, are the town's principle tourist shopping destinations, mixtures of renovated old buildings and fresh construction. If shopping and casino gaming are your only interests, you can do it all right on Heritage Quay. You'll also find a tourist information booth on the pier, and plenty of taxis awaiting your fare. The Magic is expected to dock at 7:30 am to 8:00 am, so expect "all ashore" about an hour later. On the seven-night itinerary the expected "all aboard" time will be around 4:30 pm, pending a 5:30 pm departure. The 10-night cruise departs an hour earlier, at 4:30 pm (so expect an all-aboard time around 3:30 pm).

GETTING AROUND

The shops and restaurants at the pier, and Redcliffe Quay, are all within **walking distance** of the pier. Redcliffe Quay is about a 10 minute walk from the ship. • Taxi fares to English Harbor (Nelson's Dockyard) and many of the most worthwhile beaches will cost more than $20 for up to four passengers. Rates are set by the government, and drivers are required to carry an official rate card. Be sure to agree on the fare before you hop in. • Antigua is another island where car rentals are not advisable. Antigua's 60 miles of paved roads are in poor repair, you'll be driving British-style (on the left), and you must pay $20 for a local driving permit. If you do decide to drive, please drive with care and note that there are very few road signs—be sure to have a good map handy. • As nearly all points of interest are likely to be visited by shore excursions, excursions remain, as always, your safest bet.

SAFETY

There's **safety in numbers** on Antigua. With so many remote, unguarded beaches, beach crime is a serious concern. Bring the bare minimum with you if you set off in search of secluded sands. Leave valuables back on the ship and keep your Key to the World card, I.D., cash, and credit cards in a secure location on your person, such as a waterproof case. As always, do not carry large amounts of cash or jewelry. With most decent shopping so close to the pier, you should have no problems getting your packages safely onboard. Vendors near the pier can be pushy about selling their goods or services—a firm "no thank you" will do the trick. As mentioned above, Antiguans drive on the left-hand side of the road—don't forget this when crossing the street.

Touring Antigua

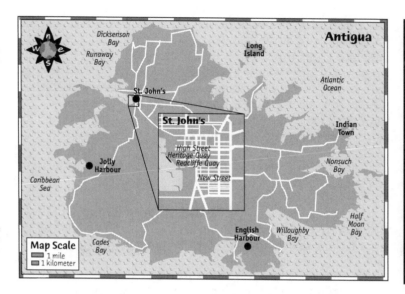

ANTIGUA MAP

St. John's is hardly the richest of port towns, if you're looking for a walking tour. There are a handful of historic sites to visit, including the Museum of Antigua and Barbuda on Long Street, just two blocks north and a few inland from Heritage Quay. In addition to worthwhile historical exhibits, the museum may offer a self-guided walking tour of the town for a nominal price. Other sights include the ornate Anglican Cathedral and the restored buildings on Redcliffe Quay. English Harbour National Park offers greater opportunities for history hounds. About 8 miles southeast of St. John's, this historical park is one of the Caribbean's foremost historical attractions. Restored buildings and anchorages abound, including Nelson's Dockyard, and no fewer than four fortresses set up to guard the mouth of the harbor and command nearby Shirley Heights. The most photographed portion of Nelson's Dockyard is a group of 12 massive columns that used to support a huge boathouse where ships could get their sails and rigging repaired. Nelson's Dockyard is also famous for its English pubs and restaurants. (For more information, visit http://www.paterson.com/nelsonsdockyard). If you'd rather, the park also offers several nature trails. Some visitors liken English Harbour to Colonial Williamsburg in Virginia. Detailed information can be found at the Visitor's Center in the Royal Artillery Barracks on Shirley Heights.

WALKING TOURS

Introduction   Reservations   Staterooms   Dining   Activities   Ports of Call   Magic   Index

ACTIVITIES

Playing in Antigua

The **closest decent beach** to Heritage Quay is Fort Bay, near the northern mouth of the harbor. Runaway Bay and Dickenson Bay are just a little farther north up the coast (about 5 to 10 minutes by taxi), and offer calm, sheltered waters and the civilized niceties that go along with the adjoining beachfront resorts. Half Moon Bay is reputed to be among the island's finest beaches, but it's all the way cross-island from St. John's. If you're visiting English Harbour, Pigeon Beach is nearby (short drive or 20 minute walk).

The only **casino**—Kings Casino—is located moments from the ship, on Heritage Quay. Visit http://www.kingscasino.com.

Golfers can play a round at the **Jolly Harbor Golf Club**, an 18-hole championship course. Visitors can play for a daily fee and club rental is available. Visit http://www.jollyharbourantigua.com/golf.html.

Scuba, snorkel, and windsurfing are all popular activities, thanks to miles of encircling reefs, and the brisk winds on the Atlantic (eastern) side of the island. Snorkeling is possible at many of Antigua's beaches. Cades Reef is part of a designated off-shore underwater park, and very popular for snorkeling and scuba-diving. The wreck of the Andes, a three-masted merchant ship that sank in 1905, is another popular spot. Sailing is also very popular here—the island hosts an annual major regatta.

Looking for a **stingray and/or dolphin experience**? Antigua has those, too. For more information on stingray and dolphin encounters, visit http://www.dolphinfantaseas.com.

Devil's Bridge at the northeastern point of the island is an amazing natural arch, created when the soft limestone was eroded away by the seawater. Devil's Bridge is located in Indian Town, one of Antigua's National Parks. Numerous blowholes spouting water surround Indian Town, making for quite a sight.

Cricket is a big sport on Antigua! If this sport interests you, matches can be found on the island at almost any time. For more information, visit http://www.antigua-barbuda.org/agcri01.htm.

For more details on Antigua, visit http://www.antigua-barbuda.org.

Embarking on Shore Excursions in Antigua

As we go to press, Disney has yet to announce its round-up of shore excursions for Antigua. We provide these listings to acquaint you with the possibilities, based on typical offerings by other cruise lines.

Antigua Historical Tour

Explore the capital city of St. John's in a bus, with stops along the way for photos and closer looks. Along the way you may visit Heritage Quay, Nelson's Dockyard, Dow's Hill Interpretation Center, Falmouth, English Harbour, Blockhouse Ruins, and Shirley Heights' Lookout (a strategic British lookout point from which enemy vessels could be clearly seen in the early days). Bring comfortable shoes as some walking will be necessary.	**Tour** Leisurely $36–42 2.5-3 hours

Island Safari Jeep Tour

Drive a four-person, 4x4 off-road vehicle and get off the beaten track! You can expect to travel dirt roads up to Buckley's Village with its gorgeous views and even drive through a rainforest. Afterwards, stop at a beach along the South Coast and cool off with a swim. This is likely to be a very bumpy ride, so pregnant women and those with bad backs are not advised to take it.	**Tour** Active $60-70 3-3.5 hours

Catamaran Snorkel Cruise

Board a large catamaran for a swift cruise along the Antigua coastline. When you reach your snorkel site, you'll be provided with instruction and equipment. Swimming may also be available on a nearby beach. Afterwards, cruise home with complimentary beverages.	**Sports** Active $50-55 3 hours

Circumnavigate Antigua (Around the Island EcoTour)

Go around the island of Antigua in a purpose-built, rigid inflatable boat. Your circumnavigation begins along the North Coast with its mangroves and sea life. Then head down the East Coast via the "Devil's Bridge," stopping along the way to snorkel and swim for about 45 minutes. Then it's back on the boat to cruise along the South Coast with its large volcanic structures and old forts.	**Tour** Active Ages 12 & up $80 4 hours

You may even have the chance to visit Nelson's Dockyard. Finally, you'll travel up along the West Coast to see the largest barrier reef in Antigua. The ride may be a bit bumpy along the way, so it's not recommended for pregnant women or those with back problems. Those prone to motion sickness may also want to skip this excursion or start taking their preventative medicine well in advance of the excursions departure.

Jolly Roger Pirate Cruise

Board an authentic wooden, two-masted schooner with billowing scarlet sails, skull-and-crossbones, and pirate wannabes. Enjoy island music and a fun-loving party as you ply the West Coast. Beverages may be included, perhaps even an open bar (we hear they make a wicked rum punch). And the	**Tour** Active $20-39 3 hours

crew may encourage guests to participate in a limbo competition or even an impromptu wedding or two. You may also anchor in one of Antigua's coves for swimming or beachcombing. The large schooner holds over 200 and has a sundeck, a shaded seating area, changing facilities, and "heads" (restrooms). (On Your Own: Jolly Roger Antigua Limited at http://www.geographia.com/antigua-barbuda/jolly-roger or 268-462-2064)

Embarking on Shore Excursions
in Antigua (continued)

Miniboat Adventure ☀ 🛍 ◉	
Take a taxi or bus ride to a marina where you'll board two-person miniboats. Cruise along the open water to a hidden lagoon where you'll have the time to swim or simply explore the area. Beverages (water and soda) are provided at the beach. Minimum age to drive a miniboat is 18; guests ages 12 to 17 must be accompanied by an adult or guardian.	Sports
	Active
	Ages 12 & up
	$75-80
	3.5 hours

Stingray Village Swim and Snorkel ☀ 🛍 ◉	
Venture out to Antigua's Stingray Village by boat for the opportunity to swim and snorkel among these gentle sea creatures. You'll visit a natural sand bar and stand in about four feet of water to meet the various stingrays. Snorkel equipment and instruction is provided. After snorkeling, complimentary beverages are provided.	Sports
	Active
	Ages 8 & up
	$65-70
	3 hours

Dolphin and Stingray Experience ☀ 🛍 ◉	
Board a boat from the pier and journey to a natural, 5.5 million gallon saltwater lagoon at Marina Bay. After a briefing, you'll have the chance to get in the water and play with the dolphins for about 25 minutes—learn how to feed them, pet them, and listen to them. Snorkel equipment will be provided during this time. After your dolphin encounter, head on over to the stingrays to touch, pet, and feed them as they swim and glide around you. (On Your Own: Dolphin Fantaseas at http://www.dolphinfantaseas.com/locations/antigua.htm, 268-562-7946)	Sports
	Active
	Ages 5 & up
	$145
	3 hours

Antigua Beach Break (Millers by the Sea) ☀ 🛍 ◉	
Take a 15-minute bus from the pier to one of Antigua's best West Coast beaches. The secluded spot at Dickenson Bay offers you your own beach chair, changing facilities, a complimentary beverage, and a BBQ lunch. The beach is home to the open-air hotspot, Millers by the Sea, which features calypso and reggae music. Bring a towel and plenty of sunscreen.	Beach
	Leisurely
	All ages
	$40-50
	5 hours

See page 164 for a key to the shore excursion description charts and their icons.

Antigua On Your Own

For those that want to get a headstart on their excursion plans, or just want to do it on their own, here is some information on tour operators in Antigua. Please note that we have not used these operators, nor is any mention here an endorsement of their services. A variety of excursions are offered through **Antigua Adventures**, and it's a popular operator with cruisers. Choose from sailing, powerboating, 4x4 adventures, helicopter rides, ecotours, hikes, and fishing excursions. For information, visit http://www.antiguaadventures.com or call 268-560-4672. If you'd like to go diving or eco-kayak touring, **Adventure Excursions** offers several morning and afternoon dives and excursions. For more information, visit http://adventure-excursions.com/antigua.htm. For unique ecotours, Antigua Paddles offers it all—kayaking, swimming, snorkeling, hiking, and boat rides, all in one four hour tour! You visit Bird Island to snorkel and hike, and Antigua's North Sound Marine Park to cruise in a boat. Minimum tour age is 7 and all guests must be able to swim. Complimentary bottled water and a snack is served while kayaking, and nutmeg rum punch is served on the return trip. For more information, visit http://www.antiguapaddles.com.

St. Lucia
(Special Eastern Caribbean Itineraries)

Towering mountains covered in lush vegetation, bubbling sulfurous hot springs, and black-sand beaches combine to make St. Lucia (pronounced "LOO-sha") a memorable stop for Caribbean vacationers. Watersport and eco-tourism opportunities abound—if only we had more time in port to hike those mountains and explore the forests!

St. Lucia is about as French as any British island can be. Most place names are French, including les Pitons, those twin mountains rising a half-mile from the sea. Les Pitons are possibly the most-photographed mountains in the Caribbean. Your entry port of Castries, alas, has little of its old architecture remaining, due to several disastrous fires. Unless your goal is to shop, head out of town to enjoy the island's many sights and activities.

St. Lucia is called "the Helen of the Caribbean." Like Homer's Greek heroine, the island's beauty is notable. Like many Caribbean islands, the Arawak Indians were settled here two thousand years ago, only to be later ousted by the aggressive Caribs in 800 A.D. The first European to set foot on the island is widely believed to be Juan de la Cosa, a prolific explorer. The first European settler was Francois Le Clerc, a.k.a. "Pegleg," who set up house on Pigeon Island and attacked passing Spanish ships. The French and British battled over "Helen" for more than 150 years—the island changed hands fourteen times during that period. The British had the final triumph in 1814 (thanks to victory in Europe over Napoleon), so cars drive on the left-hand side, but the French influence is still huge—most place names are French, and the French-based Creole patois is still widely spoken. The volcanic hot springs were developed as a military health spa under the direction of King Louis XVI, only to be destroyed several years later during the French Revolution. As with most islands in the region, St. Lucia achieved independence in the late 1970s, and is now part of the British Commonwealth. St. Lucia's tourism has grown steadily over the last 20 years.

Size: 26 miles (42 km.) long by 13 miles (21 km.) wide	
Climate: Tropical	**Temperatures**: 76°F (25°C) to 86°F (29°C)
Population: 158,000	**Busy Season**: Late December to April
Language: English, French	**Money**: E. Carib. Dollar (1 = 37 U.S. cents)
Time Zone: Atlantic (no DST)	**Transportation**: Taxis, cars
Phones: Dial 1- from U.S., dial 911 for emergencies, dial 999 for police	

Introduction
Reservations
Staterooms
Dining
Activities
Ports of Call
Magic
Index

INTRO
AMBIENCE
HISTORY
FACTS

Introduction · Reservations · Staterooms · Dining · Activities · Ports of Call · Magic · Index

Making the Most of St. Lucia

GETTING THERE

Your ship will likely dock at **Pointe Seraphine Pier** across the harbor from Castries, the capital city of St. Lucia. If that pier is busy, however, you may dock at the Elizabeth II pier. Both are located in Port Castries on the west coast of the island and are indicated on the map on the next page. The Magic is set to arrive at 9:30 am (expect an all-ashore of 10:00 am)—check your *Personal Navigator* for going ashore details—and departs at 6:15 pm (expect an all-aboard time of 5:30 pm). Taxis are available at the dock to take you into town or to another destination, or you may simply walk to the nearby shopping.

GETTING AROUND

There's **good shopping near the pier** at Pointe Seraphine, a red-roofed, harbor front shopping complex with over 20 shops, many of which offer duty-free goods. You can walk there easily. • Due to the rugged terrain of this island, shore excursions and taxis are the best way to get around. You can get a taxi right at the pier—taxis do not have meters, but rates for common routes are set by the government. A typical fare from Castries to Rodney Bay is $40 for up to four people. Confirm the fare before getting in. • If you're thinking about a rental car, we think it may be more trouble than it's worth. You are only in port for seven hours, and a temporary driver's permit is necessary (you can get these from car rental agencies for $20). Also be aware that St. Lucians drive on the left side of the road, like the British. If you have your heart set on renting a car, there are half a dozen rental agencies at the pier—prices start around $50/day. • Beaches at Pigeon Island or Choc Beach are about 20 minutes away by taxi.

SAFETY

Petty street crimes and beach theft are the most notable crime problems you'll encounter, so **leave your valuables on board**, and safeguard your purse or wallet while shopping. It's best to stay on the main roads and not wander into alleys or away from downtown Castries on your own. Lockers aren't easy to come by on the island. As always, know your prices before you shop, and agree to taxi fares in advance. Sunblock is a must. Apply it before you leave your stateroom, and dress according to your planned activities—changing rooms aren't always easy to find. Wear cover-ups while shopping or walking in town, as local customs are conservative. You should also note that it is a local offense for anyone outside of the police force to dress in **camouflage clothes**, and topless bathing is illegal.

Touring St. Lucia

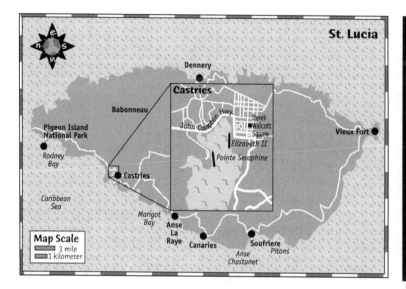

ST. LUCIA MAP

A 10-15 minute walk from Pointe Seraphine brings you into Castries proper, where you can view historical monuments, the busy harbor, and the city's farmer's market. We suggest you start your walking tour at the north end of Peynier Street where you'll find the newly-built **Central Market**, a bustling farmer's market in the mornings. In addition to the produce and spices you'd expect to find here (neither of which you can bring back into the U.S.), you'll find baskets, T-shirts, carvings, straw hats, and plenty of silly souvenirs. Across the street is Vendor's Arcade, which houses more craft stalls. Your next visit may be to **Derek Walcott Square**, located between Micoud and Brazil Streets. The square is named for the island's poet laureate, who won the Nobel Prize in 1992. In the recently refurbished square you'll see a statue in honor of the Nobel Laureate, a 400-year old Massav tree, and monuments to St. Lucian soldiers lost in the Second World War. Lining the square are historic buildings displaying both the French and English architecture of the island. The large Cathedral of the Immaculate Conception is located on one corner of the square—you can take a look inside the ornate interior unless a Mass is underway. There are plenty of other sites to see along the way, as well as the local flavor of the city. We suggest you pick up a good tourist map on your walk into town. If you feel intimidated about touring on your own, Solar Tours offers the Castries Heritage Walk—get more information at http://www.solartoursandtravel.com or call 758-452-5898.

WALKING TOUR

Playing in St. Lucia

ACTIVITIES

St. Lucia is known for its **beautiful beaches**, all of which are public (though some can only be reached by boat or by passing through private property). Closest to the pier is Vigie Beach, just a mile and a half from Castries and parallel to the nearby airport. It's a clean, pretty beach. The best beaches are a short taxi ride away. Choc Beach (sometimes known as Palm Beach) is about 20 minutes away by taxi and offers a gorgeous stretch of white sand with swaying coconut palms. This is a great family beach with calm, crystal-clear waters and plenty of amenities. The secluded beaches at Pigeon Island National Park are also a favorite among visitors, offering water sports, a restaurant, and even a small historical museum. It isn't actually an island anymore—it was connected to the mainland in '70s by a causeway. Visit http://www.slunatrust.org/pisland.htm for details. Those interested in snorkeling should visit Anse Chastanet on the southwest side of the island, about 12 miles from the pier. This is the site of a Marine Park and the Anse Chastanet Reef, which has been buoyed off specifically for snorkeling. The beautiful beach here has a volcanic black sand blanket and views of the twin Piton peaks. Be aware that a taxi trip to Anse Chastanet could take at least an hour, however, due to the steep, hilly roads and blind turns.

Shopping on St. Lucia is pretty easy. The Pointe Seraphine shopping complex (see previous page) is just steps from the pier, and the Central Market with its crafts and souvenir stalls is in downtown Castries. Note that bargaining is not customary on St. Lucia. Shopping is duty-free, sales tax-free, and is conducted in U.S. dollars. As always, while prices can be excellent, know what you'd pay back home for the same goods.

Golfers may enjoy a visit to the St. Lucia Golf & Country Club, an 18-hole golf course offering great views of both the Atlantic Ocean and Caribbean Sea. Rental clubs are available. For more information, visit http://www.stluciagolf.com or call 758-450-8522.

St. Lucia is a treasure trove of **beautiful natural resources**, including Pigeon Island National Park, the "drive-in volcano" near Soufriére (which means "smells of sulphur," by the way), and the famous Piton peaks which rise almost a half mile into the sky. These are all worth visiting if you're able!

For more information on St. Lucia, visit http://www.stlucia.org.

Embarking on Shore Excursions in St. Lucia

As we go to press, Disney has yet to announce its round-up of shore excursions for St. Lucia. We provide these listings to acquaint you with the possibilities, based on typical offerings by other cruise lines.

☐ North Coast Tour and Beach Break ☀ 🔒 📷

Board an air-conditioned bus for a tour of the Castries area with its beautiful views. Then it's on to Morne Fortune and it's impressive mountain range. After this, you'll visit Bagshaws at La Toc and see a demonstration of the 2000-year-old batik fabric making craft. Back on the bus you'll tour the countryside, visit Pigeon Island, and pass the Rodney Bay Marina. Your last stop is Reduit Beach for an hour or so of swimming and relaxing. A complimentary beverage and a reserved beach chair are waiting for you.

Tour
Leisurely
$22-36
3-4 hours

☐ Waterfall Island Bike Tour ☀ 🔒 📷

Travel down the East Coast of the island into the rainforest, where you'll meet your tour guide, get your mountain bike and safety equipment, and listen to a short orientation. Then it's off the trail to explore banana plantations, stopping along the way to sample the local fruit. You'll end up at beautiful Errard Falls, where you'll receive a complimentary beverage and have a chance to cool off with a swim at the base of the falls. This bike tour is along routes with gentle inclines, and is recommended for experienced mountain bikers and/or those in excellent physical condition.

Sports
Very active
Ages 12 & up
$65
4-4.5 hours

☐ Soufriére Cruise and Swim ☀ 🔒 📷

Board a large boat for a relaxing cruise down to Soufriére. You'll pass the Anse La Raye fishing village and the Canaries village, catching a glimpse of St. Lucia's famous Pitons, twin peaks towering 2,500 ft. above the sea. Once you reach Soufriére, you'll board mini-buses and journey to Sulphur Springs, the "world's only drive-in volcano." You may also have the chance to visit Fond Doux estate, a 250-year-old working plantation. Back on the boat you'll be treated to snacks while you take a 45-minute cruise to Anse Cochon Beach. At the beach there will be time to take a swim and enjoy a complimentary beverage.

Tour
Leisurely
$40-50
5.5 hours

☐ Pirates of the Caribbean Adventure ☀ 🔒 📷

Imagine an opportunity to board an actual ship used in Disney's film, "Pirates of the Caribbean: The Curse of the Black Pearl." The Brig Unicorn is a replica of a 138 ft., 19th century tall ship, and appears in both "Pirates of the Caribbean" (where it was named "Black Pearl") as well as "Roots." Your adventure begins in Vigie Cove, near Castries, where 16th-century pirates once docked their warships. After boarding you'll sail the same waters once dominated by genuine Caribbean pirates—you may even have the chance to swing from the ropes or walk the plank. You can expect to visit historic Pigeon Island and Fort Rodney, which was the scene of several important naval battles between the British and French. The crew even treats you to a mock pirate attack, during which you'll hear the ship's working cannons. You'll then go ashore to explore and play, with time for swimming and hiking. You may also have the chance to go on a pirate treasure hunt while ashore! Back onboard there are snacks, rum punch, and soda. (On Your Own: Sun Link Tours at http://www.sunlinktours.com, 758-452-0511)

Tour
Leisurely
$30-90
5.5 hours

See page 164 for a key to the shore excursion description charts and their icons.

Embarking on Shore Excursions in St. Lucia *(continued)*

Deep Sea Fishing

Hunt for blue marlin, wahoo, barracuda, and other big game fish off the waters of St. Lucia, home to some of the best deep sea fishing in the world. You'll fish aboard a fully-equipped fishing boat; fishing tackle, bait, and "fighting chair" are all included. Catch-and-release only. This excursion is not recommended for those who are prone to motion sickness.	**Sports**
	Active
	$130
	4 hours

St. Lucia Beach Snorkel

Take a 60-minute ferry boat ride along the St. Lucia coast to a marine preserve. After receiving your snorkel equipment and instruction, enter the waters from a special beach at the preserve. You'll have the opportunity to snorkel the Anse Chastanet Reef, voted one of the ten best snorkeling sites in the Caribbean. A complimentary beverage is served after snorkeling. (On Your Own: Scuba St. Lucia at http://www.scubastlucia.com, 758-459-7755)	**Sports**
	Active
	Ages 5 & up
	$65
	3.5 hours

Off-Road Adventure and Hike

Would you like to see areas of St. Lucia that are normally inaccessible to regular vehicles? Board an off-road, open-air, safari vehicle and drive through Castries, up Mourne Rouge, into the Cul-De-Sac Valley, over a volcanic hill, and deep into the rainforest. From here, you'll continue on foot to the upper part of the Anse La Raye valley and along a river to a waterfall. Then it's	**Sports**
	Very active
	Ages 6 & up
	$58
	3.5 hours

back in the vehicles to visit the La Sikwi Sugar mill for rest, a brief tour, and a complimentary beverage. You should be in excellent physical condition for this excursion, as there is moderate to heavy walking. You may have the chance to cool off with a swim, so we recommend you underdress your swimsuit.

Pigeon Island Sea Kayaking

Transfer to Rodney Bay for a 30-minute paddle in a two-person kayak. Safety instructions and kayaking lessons will be provided. As you paddle the calm waters, your tour guide points out local flora and fauna, as well as historical trivia. Once you reach Pigeon Island National Park, you'll have time to swim and explore the ruins of a British fortification. A complimentary beverage and light snack will be served after kayaking.	**Sports**
	Active
	Ages 6 & up
	$65
	3 hours

See page 164 for a key to the shore excursion description charts and their icons.

St. Lucia On Your Own

For those that want to get a head start on their excursion plans, or just want to do it on their own, here is some information on tour operators in St. Lucia. Please note that we have not used these operators, nor is any mention here an endorsement of their services. For land and sea adventures, try SunLink Tours—they have cruises on the Brig Unicorn "pirate" ship (see previous page), dolphin and whale-watching, deep sea fishing, island tours to Soufriére, Jeep safari tours, rainforest hikes, and biking tours. For more information, visit http://www.sunlinktours.com or call 758-452-0511. Those interested in scuba driving and snorkeling should check out Scuba St. Lucia, which is located on the southwestern shore near the Anse Chastanet Reef. A variety of diving and snorkeling excursions are offered. For more information, visit http://www.scubastlucia.com or call 758-459-7755.

Key West
(Western Caribbean Itinerary—First Port of Call)

Casually hanging out at the tip of the fabled Florida Keys, Key West is the southernmost point in the Continental U.S. Famous for Ernest Hemingway and Jimmy Buffett (and their bars); charming homes, sunsets, sport fishing; historic spots, and a way-laid-back lifestyle. You won't be in town long enough to waste away, but you sure can try.

© MediaMarx, Inc.

Key West's Mallory Square at sunset

AMBIENCE

As Florida's southernmost landfall, Americans will feel more secure wandering Key West than any other port of call. The charm of its century-old buildings and the small-town air will put you right at ease. Most attractions are a short stroll from the cruise ship piers, and streets head off in (mostly) straight lines. To visit the sights, just head there under your own power.

HISTORY & CULTURE

Spaniards called this flat, sun-drenched outpost "Cayo Hueso" (Island of Bones). The English (some buccaneers among 'em) were soon mispronouncing it "Key West." The U.S. Navy banished the pirates and has been stationed here ever since. Nearby, treacherous reefs sank countless vessels in the New Orleans trade, making salvage crews fabulously rich. A lighthouse turned that boom into a bust, and the town has been reborn again and again as a capital for spongers, cigar rollers, a President, treasure seekers, wealthy vacationers, artists and writers (James Audubon, Tennessee Williams, Robert Frost, Ernest Hemingway, and Thornton Wilder) and generations of dropouts from the rat race. Islanders declared the Conch Republic in 1982 to protest a Federal roadblock that choked access to the Florida Keys. They soon had enough media attention to restore free passage, but the Republic's flag still flies high.

FACTS

Size: 4 mi. (6.5 km.) wide x 2 mi. (3 km.) long	
Climate: Subtropical	**Temperatures:** 72°F (22°C) to 82°F (28°C)
Population: 24,832	**Busy Season:** Mid-February to April
Language: English	**Money:** U.S. Dollar
Time Zone: Eastern (DST observed)	**Transportation:** Walking, scooters
Phones: Dial 1- from U.S., dial 911 for emergencies	

Introduction   Reservations   Staterooms   Dining   Activities   Ports of Call   Magic   Index

Getting Around Key West

GETTING THERE

Your ship docks around noon right at the **Hilton Marina** (Pier B), which is an easy 5-minute walk to Mallory Square and Front Street. Tendering is not necessary, unless the ship is unable to dock (rare). You should be able to disembark by 12:30 pm or 1:00 pm (check your *Personal Navigator* for going ashore details). The marina is on the northwest corner of the island, looking out to the Gulf of Mexico. For those exploring on foot, most of the major destinations are within easy reach of the marina. Check your *Personal Navigator* for the "All Aboard" time, usually 9:30 pm to 9:45 pm.

GETTING AROUND

This is one of the **easiest ports to navigate**, thanks to its small size and pedestrian-friendly streets. Most visitors here just **walk**, and even many of the residents don't bother with cars. Almost all of Key West's streets near the docks run on a grid, making it easy to get around with a map. If you'd rather not walk, try one of Key West's famous **tram tours**. The non-stop Conch Tour Train (described on page 205) is $20/adults, $10/kids 4 to 12 (3 & under free)—board the tram near Mallory Square. If you'd prefer to get off and look around, the Old Town Trolley makes nine stops (see page 205) for $20/adults, $10/kids 4–12 (3 & under free)—board near the dock. • The Key West **bus system** is less expensive than the trams at just 75 cents/adults and 35 cents/kids and seniors (kids 5 & under are free). There are always two buses running—one goes clockwise around the island, the other goes counter-clockwise. Call 305-293-6435 for bus info. • **Taxis** are also available—the meter starts at $1.40 and adds 35 cents per quarter mile. You can get taxis near the dock—if you need to call for one, try Florida Keys Taxi (305-284-2227). • Need your own transportation? Try a **scooter** rental. Adventure Scooter (601 Front Street, 305-293-9944, http://keywest.com/scooter.html) rents scooters for about $24/day—see the coupon at their Web site.

STAYING SAFE

The "key" to **staying safe** in Key West is simple common sense. The biggest potential dangers here are overexposure to sun (bring that sunscreen and hat) and overindulgence at a local bar. Key West is very laid-back—we didn't encounter any street hawkers on our visit and we felt secure walking around on our own. If you rent a scooter, be sure to wear your helmet. If you swim, note the color-coded flags which indicate swimming conditions at the beach: blue = safe, yellow = marginal, and red = dangerous and prohibited. If you walk, wear comfortable, well broken-in walking shoes. And bring a watch so you don't lose track of time and miss the boat!

Touring Key West

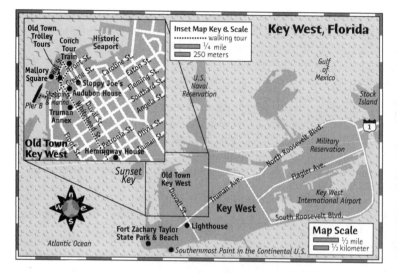

KEY WEST ISLAND MAP

WALKING TOUR

Introduction · Reservations · Staterooms · Dining · Activities · Ports of Call · Magic · Index

Key West is one of the best ports for a **casual walking tour**. Take along our map or pick one up at the Chamber of Commerce at 402 Wall Street. We've marked a walking tour on the map above. From the pier, you first reach the Truman Annex waterfront shopping area. Near the junction of Front and Greene Streets, is the brick 1891 Custom House and its Museum of Art and History. Turn left onto Front Street, passing the U.S. Customs House (and Post Office) and the Naval Coal Depot building. At the corner of Front and Whitehead is the Key West Art Center, showcasing local artists. Nearby is the Key West Shipwreck Historeum ($9/adult, $4/kids 4 to 12) with its 60-foot lookout tower, and the Key West Aquarium ($9/adult, $4.50/kids 4 to 12), Key West's oldest tourist attraction. Turning onto Wall St. you'll find the Chamber of Commerce (free maps and info), and famous Mallory Square (see next page for sunset viewing tips). Continue along Wall St., rejoining Front St., where you can board the Conch Tour Train (see previous page), or stroll another block along Front to the Historic Seaport boardwalk. Follow Front St. back towards the ship, crossing Duval St. then turn onto Whitehead for its charm and many museums. Stop where you will, but if you're in a walking mood, follow Whitehead nine blocks to the Lighthouse and Hemingway House. Whenever you've had enough, retrace your steps towards the waterfront to explore Duval and nearby side streets, or re-board the ship. For a more directed tour, try the "Key West Walking Tour" shore excursion (see page 206).

ACTIVITIES

Playing in Key West

Sloppy Joe's isn't the original Hemingway hangout, that's Captain Tony's, which used to be Sloppy Joe's. Captain Tony's gave Jimmy Buffett his first place to waste away, but now Jimmy can afford his own Margaritaville. Got all that? Regardless of your choice, these and many other atmospheric bars are a short crawl from the ship.

One of the joys of Key West is its **architecture**. Walk along Whitehead Street and turn down a few of the side streets. The old, clapboard homes, trimmed with Victorian gingerbread and surrounded by flowering foliage and white picket fences, are a delight. Household eaves are painted sky blue to ward off bugs, demons, or some such.

This isn't really a **beach zone**. The rocky bottom isn't swim-friendly. Fort Zachary Taylor State Park offers an attractive, nearby place to sun (enter via the Truman Annex gate on Thomas St.).

Your day in port is too short for an all-day **fishing or diving trip**, but a half-day may work. Plan in advance. Visit the Florida Keys & Key West Visitors Bureau at http://www.fla-keys.com or call 800-FLA-KEYS for information and lists of charter operators.

Want some authentic **Caribbean junk food**? Try hot, greasy, conch fritters for a fair price at the stand by the Aquarium entrance. For seafood and Key Lime Pie, just follow your nose.

The daily **Mallory Square sunset ritual** gathers thousands of revelers to watch the legendary sunset, and the harbor overflows with party boats. We surveyed the superb scene from deck 10. Go to http://www.mallorysquare.com and click WebCam for a preview. Sunset time is printed on the front of your *Personal Navigator*, or visit http://www.usno.navy.mil and click on "Sun Rise/Set."

Key West has too many **museums** for a brief cruise ship visit. Choose just one or two. Whitehead St. is the equivalent of Museum Mile, with nearly every attraction listed here either on the street or a block away. For glimpses inside beautiful historic homes, visit Audubon House, Harry S. Truman Little White House, Hemingway House, and/or Oldest House. All charge admission.

Key West and **T-shirts** seem to go together. Nearly every bar sells its own, Hog's Breath Saloon, Sloppy Joe's, and Margaritaville among 'em. Try the Conch Republic Store for local color. Brand luxuries can be had at U.S. prices, but you'll also find items by local designers.

Embarking on Shore Excursions in Key West

As of March 2004, Disney offers eleven shore excursions to Key West, all of which are described below and on the following pages. Note that the Key West Beach Break excursion previously offered is no longer available. We don't think you need to go on one of these shore excursions to enjoy your time in Key West, but in general they are excellent. If you want to try one of these activities on your own, we also offer information on arranging your own tours and excursions at the bottom of each description.

Sail, Kayak, & Snorkel [K01]   Rating: n/a ☀ 🛍 ⭕

This is the "smorgasbord" of shore excursions, offering three different adventures in one. You'll start with a sail in a two-masted schooner to mangrove islands. At the islands, you'll hop into kayaks and paddle about the backcountry mangrove creeks for an hour. When you're done, its time to don snorkeling equipment (provided) and explore underwater for 45-60 minutes. Top it all off with a refreshing snack of fruit, chips, salsa, and beverages back at the pier. Meeting time is typically 12:10 pm. Bring an extra pair of dry shorts for the return trip. Unfortunately, we received no reviews for this excursion, nor could we find anyone who'd experienced it. Most cruisers preferred the Back to Nature Kayak Tour or the Key West Catamaran Sail & Snorkel Tour, described later. (On Your Own: JavaCat Charters at http://www.keywestkayak.com, 305-292-3188)

Sports
Very Active
For more experienced snorkelers
Ages 10 & up
$75/person
5-5.5 hours

Catamaran Racing [K02]   Rating: 9 ☀ 🛍

You'll board your catamaran right at the pier, where your skipper assigns tasks (from navigator to timekeeper) and explains how the boat and the race works. Then you and your teammates sail out to the race course and do three timed runs. Back at the pier all sailors are treated to a victory party with a complimentary beverage, and the winning teammates get to pose for pictures with a trophy (our team won—see photo below). Don't bother with cameras or camcorders—they might get damaged. Bring sunglasses to shield your eyes from the sun and wind. Meeting time is typically 12:30 pm. We did this in May 2002 and had a blast! Even though neither of us are sailors, we never felt "out of our depth" and enjoyed the friendly competition. Cruiser reviews are positive: This "wonderful" catamaran sail is great for "adults and kids"—a "great time" is "had by all." Your "captain" teaches you "how to sail" or do whatever needs to be done, and tells you what "route" to follow. There is a "great sense of adventure" and "freedom" on this race. Be sure to "wear plenty of sunscreen" and a "hat" or you will get "burned." Overall, all cruisers who submitted reviews "loved this excursion" and would "recommend it to other cruisers." (On Your Own: Key West Cup Regatta at 305-293-8812)

Sports
Very Active
For beginners and all levels
Ages 6 & up
$64/adult
$54/child
2.5-3.5 hours

Jennifer and Dave hold the winning trophy aboard the catamaran that won the race!

© MediaMarx, Inc.

See page 164 for a key to the shore excursion description charts and their icons.

Embarking on Shore Excursions in Key West (continued)

Back to Nature Kayak Tour [K03]   Rating: 8 ☀ 🔒 ⚪

Looking for wildlife beyond Duval Street? Take a boat to the Key West Wildlife Preserve and paddle around in two-person, stable kayaks. Your tour guide leads you through the protected salt ponds and points out the many species of birds and marine life in their natural habitat. Typical meeting times are 12:15 pm and 1:50 pm. Bring an extra pair of dry shorts for the return trip—cameras and binoculars are a good idea, too. Water and soft drinks are provided. Cruiser comments are positive: You start with a 20-minute boat ride ("board at the pier") to a mangrove wash called "Archer Key." From here you board yet another boat to "receive a short lesson on using the two-person kayaks." You then kayak "beside the mangroves" and down "some passages." The "interesting guide" points out the "local birds and sea life," plus "natural history." The kayaking "is not difficult," except for those cruisers who experienced "stiff winds."

Sports
Very Active
For beginners and all levels
Ages 10 & up
$59/adult
3–3.5 hours

Sunset Sail: Western Union Schooner [K04]   Rating: 5 🔒 ⚪

The sunset sail is a quintessential Key West activity, but you must be willing to forego the early seating dinner or early show. First you explore Key West via the Conch Train Tour or Old Town Trolley (see pages 199). After your tour board the historic, 130-foot tall ship for a two-hour sunset sail. Includes live music, snacks, soda, beer, and wine. Meeting time is typically 4:15 pm. Cruiser reviews are lackluster: Some cruisers report that you "travel to the schooner" in an "air conditioned bus," "not the Conch Train or Trolley." Once aboard the "crowded" schooner, you "motor out" of the harbor then "the sails go up." There are a "lot of people" on board—"be prepared to stand." There's not "a whole lot to interest kids," and "very little sightseeing." A few cruisers "fell in love with it" and rave about the "fabulous Key West Ice Cream." The highlight is the "pretty Key West sunset." (On Your Own: http://www.schoonerwesternunion.com or 305-292-9830.) Note: You'll probably miss dinner, so order room service.

Tour
Leisurely
For beginners and all levels
All ages
$53/adult
$22/child
3–4 hours

The Western Union during a Key West sunset

© MediaMarx, Inc.

Key West Catamaran Sail & Snorkel Tour [K05]   Rating: 6 ☀ 🔒 ⚪

Set sail on a 65-foot comfortable catamaran with large sundecks, shady lounge deck, restrooms, and a fresh-water shower. The catamaran takes you about 6.5 miles (10 km.) south of the harbor to the only living coral reef in the continental U.S. Snorkeling equipment is provided for you to explore the reefs. Bring an underwater camera. Sodas and water are served, as is complimentary beer and white wine after snorkeling. Typical meeting time is 12:30 pm. Cruiser reviews are mixed: The "great crew" motors the "super clean" sailboat out of the harbor, though a few cruisers report "no sailing, just motoring." The snorkeling location "feels like the middle of the ocean" with depths of "20 feet or so." Some cruisers report that "snorkeling is great" with "plenty of coral and fish," while others note that "surge can be strong" and "kids may be afraid to snorkel" in the "bobbing water." Overall, most "enjoyed it" but "probably wouldn't do it again." (On Your Own: Fury Catamarans at http://www.furycat.com, 305-294-8899)

Sports
Active
For all levels
Ages 5 & up
$44/adult
$25/child
3–3.5 hours

See page 164 for a key to the shore excursion description charts and their icons.

Embarking on Shore Excursions in Key West *(continued)*

Conch Republic Tour & Museum Package [K08]   Rating: 4

Yes, you can do this all on your own, but if you'd prefer a more directed tour at a slightly steeper price, this is for you. First take an hour-long tour aboard the Conch Tour Train or the Old Town Trolley (see below). After the tour, you'll disembark at Mallory Square to visit the Aquarium and Shipwreck Museum on your own. Wear comfortable walking shoes and bring a camera. Typical meeting time is 12:00 pm. Cruiser reviews were uniform: The "city tour" is

Tour
Leisurely
All ages
$42/adult
$22/child
2–2.5 hours

"great," conveying a "lot of info" in a "short amount of time" (good enough that some say it "made them want to visit Key West in the future"). The downfall seemed to be the Shipwreck Historeum," for which you "have to wait outside for the group before entering" and "then listen to a guide" before you are "free to explore on your own." The Aquarium is "ok" but many have "seen better at home." In general, this excursion has "too much waiting around." (On Your Own: See pages 201–202.)

Western Union Schooner [K07]   Rating: 5

If the schooner appeals to you but you don't want to miss dinner or a show, take this midday sail on the Western Union Schooner instead. You'll start your excursion with a tour on the Conch Tour Train or Old Town Trolley (see below) and then set sail on this beautiful ship, which is registered as National Historic Landmark. You'll hear history, lore, and stories on your two-hour sail. The crew may also invite you to lend a hand. Includes snack and drink. Typical meeting time is 12:40 pm. Cruiser reviews are similar to those for the sunset sail,

Tour
Leisurely
For all levels
All ages
$43/adult
$20/child
3–4 hours

described on the previous page. The best part about this excursion compared to the other is that you don't miss dinner and "it's quite delightful on a sunny day." (On Your Own: http://www.schoonerwesternunion.com, 305-292-9830)

Old Town Trolley or Conch Train Tour [K09]   Rating: 6

A great way to get an overview of Key West and learn something on the way. The one-hour tour (either the trolley or the train) passes 100 points of interest and your tour guide offers historical and cultural commentary. We've done the Conch Tour Train and recommend it to first-time visitors as a friendly overview to Key West. Bring a camera. Young kids may get bored. Typical meeting time is 12:35 pm. Cruiser reviews are mostly positive: The "informative" tour is

Tour
All ages
$22/adult
$11/child
1–1.5 hours

The Conch Tour Train

a "lot of fun." A complete circuit of the tour route "takes about an hour," which is "good for kids who can sit still long enough." The "friendly tour guide" "driver" provides "plenty of information about the history and architecture" of "Key West." The downfall to booking this excursion through Disney is that "you cannot get on and off it" like you can when you book it yourself and want to use it as transportation as well as a tour. (On Your Own: There's not much reason to book this one with Disney—see page 200 for more information.)

See page 164 for a key to the shore excursion description charts and their icons.

Embarking on Shore Excursions in Key West (continued)

Glass Bottom Boat Tour on the Pride of Key West [K10]   Rating: 1 ☀ 🛍 📷

If you'd like to see the underwater world of Key West but don't want to get wet, this catamaran is your ticket. The catamaran boasts an air-conditioned viewing area and an upper-level sun deck. Your guide delivers a narrated eco-tour as you visit the continental U.S.'s only living coral reef about 6.5 miles (10 km.) south of Key West. Typical meeting time is 1:20 pm. Cruiser reviews were mostly negative: The boat's "bottom viewing window" is "way too small for everyone to use." And while the viewing area is air-conditioned, the sun deck is "miserably hot" with "no shade." The only refreshments were "sodas for a buck a pop." Some cruisers also report that they did not visit the reef because "the tide was too strong." Overall, most cruisers "were not impressed." (On Your Own: Key West Famous Glassbottom boats at http://www.seethereef.com, 305-289-9933)

Tour
Leisurely
All ages
$27/adult
$14/child
2-3 hours

Key West Walking Tour [K11]   Rating: n/a ☀ 🛍 📷

Here's another excursion you can do on your own at little to no cost, so you're really paying for your tour guide. This 1.5-hour walking tour visits the oldest house in South Florida (built in 1829), the Key Lime Pie Company (where you get a sample), a cigar factory (where you can watch cigars being made), and tropical gardens. Wear comfy walking shoes and bring your camera. Typical meeting time is 1:15 pm. We received no cruiser reviews for this excursion. (On Your Own: See page 201)

Tour
Active
All ages
$19/adult
$13/child
1.5-2 hours

Key West Stargazing Cruise   Rating: n/a ☀ 🛍 📷

Take the air-conditioned Bone Island Shuttle to board the Western Union Schooner for a nighttime cruise. During your cruise (under partial sail) your guides will point out Zodiac signs and other celestial figures. You'll also get a peek at how ancient mariners navigated by the stars, and get to touch a real meteorite. Complimentary Conch Chowder and beverages (beer, wine, and soft drinks) are served. Typical meeting time is 6:45 pm. As this is a recently-introduced excursion, we don't yet have cruiser reviews—see the other comments on the Western Union Schooner excursions on previous pages. (On Your Own: http://www.schoonerwesternunion.com, 305-292-9830)

Tour
Active
All ages
$59/adult
$26/child
3 hours

See page 164 for a key to the shore excursion description charts and their icons.

Key West On Your Own

Many cruisers prefer to embark on non-Disney excursions in Key West. While we don't have experience with these tour operators ourselves, here are some popular options: The **Key West Jungle Tour Mini-Speedboats** allow you to drive your own speedboat through the back country mangrove channels, with time for snorkeling and swimming. For more information, visit http://www.jungletour.com or call 305-292-3300. • For less expensive transportation, try the **Bone Island Shuttle** bus at $7/person for the entire day. It makes about 12 stops throughout both ends of the island including Mallory Square, Duval Street, and the historic waterfront. For more details, visit http://www.boneislandshuttle.com or call 305-293-8710. • Another fun option is to rent a funky-yet-fun electric car from a place like **Tropical Rent a Car** for about $60 for two hours (2-seater) or $80 (4-seater). They also rent scooters and bicycles. They are located at 1300 Duval St. For more information, visit http://www.tropicalrentacar.com or call 305-294-8136.

Grand Cayman
(Western Caribbean Itinerary—Second Port of Call)

In these days of corporate scandals, the Cayman Islands have come to symbolize shady dealings hidden by offshore banks. Cruise visitors find a different pleasure waiting offshore; some of the most spectacular coral reefs in the Caribbean. Whether you snorkel, scuba, tour by submarine, or swim with the fishes at Stingray City, Grand Cayman is the perfect island for **watery recreation**.

Dave plays with stingrays in Grand Cayman

Of all Disney's ports of call, Grand Cayman seems the **quaintest**. Visitors arrive at a small pier, adjoining a relatively modest shopping street. We find scattered, free-standing buildings and several outdoor malls, rather than the built-up waterfront of a busy port. The real action is taking place off shore, where fleets of excursion boats help visitors enjoy the island's sea life and fabled coral reefs, which offer excellent snorkeling and scuba diving.

A wayward breeze pushed the Cayman Islands onto the map in 1503, when Columbus stumbled upon these essentially flat outposts. He named them "**Tortugas**," for the plentiful local sea turtles, but soon the islands were renamed the Caimanas, after some other local reptilians (either crocodiles or Blue Iguanas, depending on who you ask). For centuries nobody bothered to settle here, but many ships visited to gather fresh turtle meat for their crews. Famed pirates visited frequently, but eventually the islands were ruled from British Jamaica. Still, with the exception of some mahogany-logging operations, there was little development here until well into the 20th century, and its famous banking industry didn't arrive until the 1950s. When Jamaica voted for independence from Great Britain in 1962, the Cayman Islanders chose to remain a British Crown Colony.

Size: 22 mi. long (35 km.) x 8 mi. (13 km.) wide	
Climate: Subtropical	**Temperatures:** 78°F (25°C) to 84°F (29°C)
Population: 37,000	**Busy Season:** Mid-February to April
Language: English	**Money:** Cayman Islands Dollar (= $1.25 US)
Time Zone: Eastern (no DST)	**Transportation:** Walking, taxis, cars
Phones: Dial 1- from U.S., dial 911 for police, or dial 555 for an ambulance	

Introduction
Reservations
Staterooms
Dining
Activities
Ports of Call
Magic
Index

AMBIENCE
HISTORY & CULTURE
FACTS

Making the Most of Grand Cayman

GETTING THERE

Currently, this is the only Disney Cruise Line destination that regularly **requires tendering**. The ship anchors a short distance offshore of George Town, Grand Cayman—capital of the Cayman Islands. Tenders ferry guests to the pier in a matter of minutes, and run continuously throughout the day. Tenders returning to the ship depart from the South Terminal pier. You'll receive a notice in your stateroom describing current tendering procedures. A taxi stand is just a few steps from the dock, and the island's duty-free shopping district is tightly clustered within several blocks of the pier. The nearest beach is Seven Mile Beach, a short drive north of George Town. Typical all ashore is 8:00 am, with all aboard around 5:15 pm.

GETTING AROUND

Grand Cayman is **shaped like a sperm whale**, with its capital of George Town where a whale's "fluke" would be (see map on next page). It's easy to get around on foot in town. • Grand Cayman hardly overflows with sights to see, so while car rentals are available, we don't suggest them. Shore excursions can take you to nearly every sight, and taxis are fine for those who want to tour on their own. Taxis use a rate chart that is posted at the taxi stand by the cruise pier. Most car rental agencies are at the airport. Reserve in advance and arrange to have the car waiting at the pier for you. • Due north of George Town are Seven Mile Beach and the settlement of West Bay, home to the Cayman Turtle Farm and a tourist trap named Hell. Just to the east, kettle-shaped North Sound takes a big bite out of the north shore. A long coral reef guards the entrance to this bay, and just south of the reef, miles from shore, is "Stingray City," where excursion boats gather and guests cavort with the gentle stingrays in warm, waist-deep water (see photo on previous page). • The resort-and-beach destination of Rum Point is at the easternmost extreme of North Sound. • A single road follows the perimeter of the island (except for a huge gap between West Bay and Rum Point) connecting the island's many scuba dive destinations. • One of the most famous is Wreck of the Ten Sails, just beyond the village of East End and as far from George Town as you can be.

SAFETY

For water-based excursions, **leave your valuables** (and change into your swimwear) on the ship. Lockers aren't easy to come by on the island. Wear cover-ups, as local customs are sedately British, and carry lots of sunscreen. As always, know your prices before you shop, and agree to taxi fares in advance (fares are posted at the pier's taxi stand).

Touring Grand Cayman

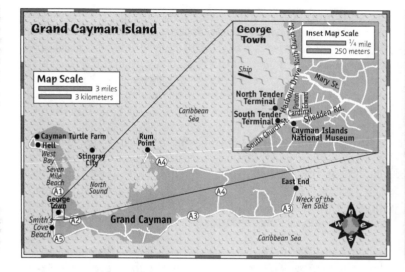

Reservations

Staterooms

Dining

Activities

Ports of Call

Magic

Index

GRAND CAYMAN ISLAND MAP

WALKING TOUR

There are **many shops** but few sights to see in George Town. After several hours of walking and shopping you'll be ready to head back to the ship. Your tender arrives at South Terminal pier, a few steps from a tourist information center, the taxi stand and tour bus loading area. North Terminal pier is just across the tiny harbor. A single road, known alternately as North Church St., Harbour Drive, and South Church St. lines the waterfront. As you face inland, North Church will be to your left, and South Church to your right. Cardinal Ave., opposite North Terminal, heads directly inland from the waterfront into the heart of the shopping district. Shops and malls line Cardinal and wrap around onto Panton St. and Edward St. You'll find the Post Office at the corner of Cardinal and Edward. The shops of Anchorage Centre can be reached from Cardinal or Harbour Drive, directly across from the docks. The worthy Cayman Islands National Museum ($5 U.S./adults, $3/children) is across from the terminal, at the corner of South Church and Shedden Rd. Follow Harbour Drive a block northward to reach Blackbeard's Rum Cake shop, and two blocks beyond, Cayman Auto Rentals and the Nautilus undersea tours. Follow South Church southward to reach Atlantis Submarines and a cluster of shops and restaurants including the local Hard Rock Cafe, Blue Mountain Cyber Cafe, and the Tortuga Rum Cake Bakery. A long walk or short cab ride along South Church brings you to small Smith's Cove Public Beach, the closest sunning spot to the pier.

Playing in Grand Cayman

The **shopping** is passable in this duty-free port, offering the usual selection of jewelry, luxury goods, and island wares. Serious shoppers report less-than-wonderful experiences, but if you know your prices and can cut a bargain, you may do fine. The principal "native" item is rum cake (yo ho, yo ho). Many visitors stock up on small sampler packages, perfect for gift giving. Turtle and coral-based items cannot be brought into the U.S., so don't buy them!

Certified scuba divers may be tempted to bring their own gear on the cruise and make their own dive arrangements. The Cayman Islands Department of Tourism at http://www.divecayman.ky has a useful online guide. Several shore excursions also exist for divers who don't want hassles. Snorkeling excursions are a good choice for those lacking scuba credentials.

While several **beaches** can be found around the perimeter of the island, we suggest you take an excursion to either Seven Mile Beach or Rum Point. Seven Mile Beach starts a short cab drive north of the port, with most of its length dominated by resorts and condos. A public beach with restrooms is found towards the beach's north end. Small Smith's Cove Beach at the south end of George Town also has restrooms, and is a long walk or short cab ride from the pier.

Unless the island's legendary coral reefs draw you elsewhere, we recommend booking an excursion that includes **Stingray City**, a submerged sand bar out in the middle of a huge bay. Guests climb from the boat right into the waist-high water for an encounter with friendly stingrays. We were instructed to "Stingray Shuffle" (shuffle our feet in the sand—the rays only sting if you step on them), and members of the crew introduced us to their aquatic protégé. While the rays are wild creatures, they've become willing partners in this enterprise—anything for a free handout (think pigeons in the park). On the ride to the sandbar one of our crew members spent his time cutting bait (frozen squid). The rays will swim right up to (or even into) a wader's arms for a snack, and the boat's crew shows us how to snuggle-up with the rays (see photo on page 207). Silky-soft rays swim among the guests, brushing past legs, sucking bait out of loosely-closed hands, and tolerating all sorts of petting zoo behavior. While the squeamish need some time to get used to the activity, eventually everyone becomes captivated by this up-close and personal encounter with these very gentle, odd creatures.

Embarking on Shore Excursions on Grand Cayman

Grand Cayman's shore excursions offer jaunts to less-than-sterling tourist sights and several attractive water-based activities.

Atlantis Deep Explorer [G01] Rating: 10

This is a very pricey trip in a real research-class submarine that dives to impressive depths of 800 feet/244 m. Your undersea voyage takes you down to explore the Cayman Wall. The sub holds only two passengers, plus the pilot, so availability is extremely limited. Note that due to the very small size of the sub, height and weight restrictions are as follows: 6'2" max. height and 230 max. pounds per person; passengers traveling as a pair must weight less than 425 lbs. combined. Typical meeting times are 7:35 am & 12:50 pm. Cruiser reviews are overwhelmingly positive: Passengers start by taking a tender "out to sea," where the sub surfaces and you board. This "once in a lifetime opportunity" goes down to depths where the "external light" may give you views of a "wreck,"a lot of marine life," and "huge limestone haystacks." Cruisers suggest you "wear something red" as there is a "cool light spectrum effect" at certain depths. All cruisers felt this excursion was "well worth the money" and "recommend doing this if you can," though it is "not good for the claustrophobic." (On Your Own: http://www.atlantisadventures.com/cayman or 345-949-7700)

Tour
Leisurely
Ages 8 & up
$345
1–1.5 hours

Two-Tank Dive Tour [G03] Rating: n/a

Certified scuba divers can take this two-tank dive. The first dive will be along the Cayman Wall, followed by a shallow dive of 50 feet (15 km.) or less. All equipment is provided. Typical meeting time is 7:45 am. We received no cruiser reviews for this excursion, but we do know it is very popular (Grand Cayman is an excellent diving spot) and has been known to fill up more than 30 days in advance. If you find this excursion is full, here are some other scuba operators used by Disney cruisers: Bob Soto's Reef Divers at http://www.bobsotosreefdivers.com, 800-262-7686 (from the U.S.) or 345-949-2022 • Abanks Scuba Diving Diving Center, http://caymanislandsdiscounts.com/AbanksDiveCenter.htm, 345-946-6444 • Don Foster's Dive Cayman at http://www.donfosters.com, 800-833-4837 (from the U.S.) or 345-949-5679. Note that Red Sail Sports (http://www.redsailcayman.com) is the exclusive dive operator for Disney Cruise Line, but you cannot book directly with them.

Sports
Very active
Ages 12 & up
$95
4 hours

SafeHaven Golf [G05] Rating: n/a

Play a round at Grand Cayman's only championship 18-hole course. Includes greens fees and golf cart. Club rental not included. Guests must wear a collared shirt. Typical meeting time is 7:35 am. We received no cruiser reviews for this excursion, nor could we find cruisers who had experienced it. (On Your Own: The Links at SafeHaven, http://www.safehaven.ky/links.htm, 345-945 4155)

Sports
Active
Ages 10 & up
$130
5 hours

Nautilus Undersea Tour and Reef Snorkel [G07] Rating: 8

Board a semi-submarine for a peek at shipwrecks and the Cheeseburger Reef, then spend some time snorkeling (equipment included). Typical meeting time is 7:30 am. Cruiser reviews are mostly positive: This excursion is "great if you have both snorkelers and non-snorkelers in your group." The "tour is short" and "you stay close to the shore." Snorkeling is "great" and the "view is phenomenal," with "fish," "plants," and a "wreck." (On Your Own: http://www.nautilus.ky)

Beach
Leisurely
Ages 5 & up
$45/$40 (5-9)
2 hours

See page 164 for a key to the shore excursion description charts and their icons.

Embarking on Shore Excursions
on Grand Cayman (continued)

☐ Stingray City Snorkel Tour [GO8]   Rating: 9

Enjoy a ride in a double-decker catamaran to snorkel with the stingrays in 3-6 feet of water along a natural sandbar (see photo on page 207). All snorkeling equipment is provided. Complimentary water and lemonade served after snorkeling. If you want to see stingrays, this is the excursion we recommend. Cruiser reviews are very positive: You start with "hot," "20-minute van ride" to a harbor, where you board the "great" catamaran. The cruise to Stingray City is "fun," with "great scenery." The stingrays are "amazing," but be aware that "some kids may be afraid at first" and the "water may be over their heads" if it's "high tide." Overall, this "unique" excursion is one "the whole family can participate in." Typical meeting times are 7:30 am and 1:00 pm. (On Your Own: Captain Marvin's—see page 214 or Native Way Water Sports at http://www.nativewaywatersports.com, 345-946-8656)

Sports
Active
Ages 6 & up
$45/$35 (6-9)
3 hours

☐ Seaworld Explorer Semi-Submarine [G10]   Rating: 9

Take a ride on this semi-submarine to discover shipwrecks and sea life. A marine expert is on board to provide narration and answer your questions. Note that this excursion is very similar to the Nautilus Undersea Tour (see below). Cruiser reviews are very positive: This "short" excursion takes you down "five feet below the water" to view "Cheese Burger Reef" and two "shipwrecks," with "coral reefs" and "many fish." The "viewing windows" are "generous" and "clear." Cruisers note that it is a bit cheaper to "book this one on your own ($32/adult)." Overall, a "fun time for the whole family!" Typical meeting times are 8:10 am and 11:15 am. (On Your Own: Atlantis Adventures at http://www.atlantisadventures.com/cayman or 345-949-7700)

Tour
Leisurely
All ages
$39/$29 (0-9)
1-1.5 hour

☐ Atlantis Submarine Expedition [G11]   Rating: 6

This submarine dives down to 90 feet (27 km.). Guests must be at least 36"/91 cm. tall. Typical meeting times are 9:10 am and 1:15 pm. Cruiser reviews are very similar to those on same excursion in St. Thomas (see page 178), but it gets a slightly higher rating thanks to the better views and visible sea life. (On Your Own: http://www.atlantisadventures.com/cayman or 345-949-7700)

Tour
Leisurely
Ages 4 & up
$75/$50 (4-9)
1.5 hours

☐ Nautilus Undersea Tour [G12]   Rating: 9

Cruise on a semi-submarine with a marine expert. The Nautilus glides like a boat and never entirely submerges. This excursion is very similar to the Seaworld Explorer described earlier, except that kids under 3 are free on the Nautilus. Typical meeting time is 9:05 am. Cruiser comments are positive: The "view is phenomenal" and cruisers loved seeing "actual wrecks," "sea creatures," and "water plants." The "friendly" crew identified the wrecks and sealife. The "comfortable" boat was "a lot of fun."(On Your Own: http://www.nautilus.ky or 345-945-1355)

Tour
Leisurely
All ages
$39/$29 (3-9)
1-1.5 hours

☐ Rum Point Beach Adventure [G13]   Rating: 6

Enjoy a relaxing half-day at a secluded beach. Includes lunch and a soft drink. Watersport rentals available for extra fee. Cruiser reviews are mixed: Take a "long journey ("first a bus then a 45-min. ferry") to reach the "nice" but "small" beach. Cruisers suggest you "try to secure beach chairs as soon as you arrive." Lunch is "good" with a "variety of food." Overall, some cruisers enjoyed "being able to relax" while others felt "herded like cattle." Typical meeting time is 8:20 am.

Beach
Leisurely
All ages
$43/$35 (3-9)
5-5.5 hours

Embarking on Shore Excursions
on Grand Cayman (continued)

☐ Rum Point Beach Adventure & Stingray City Tour [G14] Rating: 7 ☀ 🔒 ⭕

Add a visit with the stingrays to the previous excursion for $22–25 more. After playing at the beach, you'll board a glass bottom boat and cruise out to Stingray City to snorkel. Cruiser reviews were mixed but very similiar to those for Rum Point Beach Adventure and Stingray City tours on the previous page—basically the big winner is the stingrays. Typical meeting time is 8:20 am.

Sports
Active
Ages 6 & up
$65/$60 (6-9)
5.5 hours

☐ Shipwreck and Reef Snorkeling [G15] Rating: 9 ☀ 🔒 ⭕

Explore one of the Cayman's most famous shipwrecks, the "Cali," where you'll learn a history of the ship and snorkel. You'll also visit a coral reef for more snorkeling. Includes snorkel gear and soft drinks (water and lemonade). Cruiser reviews are very positive: This "great" excursion is "good for beginners." Some cruisers report snorkeling "within sight of the Disney Magic," where they explored the "way cool" "shipwreck" which rests in about "15 to 20 feet of water." Then move about a "quarter mile" down to snorkel among "protected reefs" and see "awesome" sea "critters." Overall, cruisers "loved" this "fun excursion." Typical meeting times are 7:45 am and 1:40 pm.

Sports
Active
Ages 6 & up
$35/$30 (5-9)
2-2.5 hours

☐ Stingray City Observatory and Island Tour [G18] Rating: n/a ☀ 🔒 ⭕

Take in the island's sights on an air-conditioned bus—you'll see the Governor's House, Seven Mile Beach, Cayman Turtle Farm, and Hell. Then head out to sea to board a moored, semi-submarine for an underwater peek (so you won't get wet) at the stingrays. Ends with a trip to George Town with time to shop. A variety excursion! We received no cruiser reviews for this excursion, as it appears most would prefer to actually swim with the stingrays, an option not offered by this excursion (and you can always just observe on the other stingray excursions). Cruiser reviews on the island tour portion of this excursion are given below. Typical meeting time is 7:30 am.

Tour
Leisurely
Ages 6 & up
$55/$45 (3-9)
3-3.5 hours

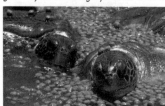
© MediaMarx, Inc.

Turtles at the Cayman Turtle Farm

☐ Grand Cayman Island Tour [G17] Rating: 7 ☀ 🔒 ⭕

Take an air-conditioned bus tour through the streets of George Town, past the Gingerbread House, on through "Hell," and to the Cayman Turtle Farm. This is very touristy—we personally didn't enjoy it much and felt like it was mostly a tour of souvenir shops, but other cruisers liked it. Cruiser reviews are mostly positive: A "nice overview" of the island in "cool" air-conditioned "buses." The tour guide is "informative" and "friendly." The turtle farm is "the best part" and "fun for the kids" (ask if you can "hold a turtle"), though some may be "appalled by the crowding of the turtles in the tanks.". Hell was "not a favorite" and "didn't impress" most cruisers, however. Highlights are the "low price" and "learning the history in a short time;" downfalls are the "short stops" and "no interaction with locals." Overall, most cruisers felt it "worth their time" even though is "isn't a sophisticated" excursion. Typical meeting times are 10:00 am and 1:25 pm.

Tour
Leisurely
All ages
$27/$21 (3-9)
2 hours

See page 164 for a key to the shore excursion description charts and their icons.

Introduction · Reservations · Staterooms · Dining · Activities · Ports of Call · Magic · Index

Embarking on Shore Excursions
on Grand Cayman (continued)

■ **Island Tour and Snorkeling with Stingrays** [G19]	Rating: 8 ☀ 🛡 🔘

Take an air-conditioned bus for a tour of several tourist highlights on Grand Cayman (see previous excursion for a more detailed description and cruiser reviews). Then board a ferry and cruise out to the Stingray City sandbar to snorkel with the rays. (See previous stingray excursion descriptions for more details on this.) This is just another set of options that may fit your schedule and interests. We did this excursion in May 2002—we loved the stingrays but didn't care for the island tour. Cruiser reviews gave this a slightly higher rating than the Island tour alone thanks to the interaction with the stingrays. Typical meeting time at 10:45 am. About 3.5 hours. (On Your Own: Captain Marvin's—see below.)	**Sports**
	Active
	Ages 6 & up
	$60/ $50 (6-9)
	3.5 hours

■ **Stingray City Reef Sail and Snorkel**	Rating: n/a ☀ 🛡 🔘

Yet another stingray excursion, this one featuring a nice, seven-mile sail in a 65-foot catamaran. For details on the stingray experience, see pages 210, 212 and 213. Includes snorkel equipment and beverages (water and lemonade). This excursion is relatively new, so we have no cruiser reviews to offer. Typical meeting time at 12:40 pm.	**Sports**
	Active
	Ages 5 & up
	$40/$30 (5-9)
	3 hours

■ **Aquaboat & Snorkel Adventure**	Rating: n/a ☀ 🛡 🔘

Another new excursion with an exciting twist—piloting (or riding) in your own, two-person inflatable motorboat. You'll cruise along Grand Cayman's shores, then explore an uninhabited island (Sandy Cove). Then it's off to Smith's Cove to swim and snorkel (equipment provided). On your way back, you'll stop at the Cali shipwreck. When it's all done, enjoy a complimentary beverage (fruit or rum punch) at Rackams Bar on the dock. Note that guests must be 13 or	**Sports**
	Active
	Ages 10 & up
	$79
	3 hours

older to pilot a boat, and must be accompanied by a parent or guardian. We have no cruiser reviews for this excursion yet as it is still new. Typical meeting time at 12:45 pm.

See page 164 for a key to the shore excursion description charts and their icons.

Grand Cayman On Your Own

Grand Cayman is another port where you find cruisers going on non-Disney excursions. Here are some popular options, though please note that we have no experience with these tour operators: **Captain Marvin's Watersports** is a very popular and well-liked outfit that offers snorkeling, island tours, and fishing charters at great prices, fewer crowds, and excellent service. For information, visit http://www.captainmarvins.com or 866-978-0022/345-945-7306. Another option is **Captain Bryan's Stingray City Sailing Charters**, which offers nicer boats with large sundecks and restrooms—better than the typical excursion boats. For more information, visit http://www.cayman.org/captainbryan or 345-949-0038. A third option, also popular, is **Native Way Water Sports**—they have excursions to Seven Mile Beach and Coral Gardens in addition to Stingray City. Get more information at http://www.nativewaywatersports.com or 345-946-8656. There are a slew of other tour operators offering a variety of excursions, including horseback riding on the beach, a scuba resort course, and driving tours. You can pick up a lot of information on the options at http://grandcaymancruiseexcursions.com.

Cozumel
(Western Caribbean Itinerary—Third Port of Call)

Welcome to **Mexico**! The island of Cozumel, just off the northeastern tip of Mexico's Yucatan peninsula and a bit south of Cancun, offers the Disney Cruise Line's primary taste of the Caribbean's Hispanic heritage. You can stay on the island, or visit the Mayan ruins on the mainland. Cozumel offers a wide range of enticing activities and Mexican handcrafted goods.

Relaxing on the beach on Cozumel

Cozumel is a **destination of contrasts**. For some, it's a crowded shopping port, intimidatingly foreign to some, exciting for others. It can be a jumping-off point for a visit to ancient ruins, or a gateway to some of the world's greatest reef diving. A unique nature park offers underwater and jungle adventure, and white, powdery beaches offer sheltered, resort/upscale experiences on the western shore, or remote, raucous rolling surf on the eastern shore.

With a history as a **religious destination** dating back into Mayan pre-history (the name Cozumel derives from the Mayan for *island of swallows*), this is one port where you can visit ruins that actually pre-date Christopher what's-his-name. The island's substantial population was destroyed after the Conquistadores brutal arrival, and its many coves and inlets served as hideouts for pirates such as Jean Lafitte and Henry Morgan. Settlers returned in the mid-1800s and cultivation of rubber here and on the mainland made this once again a trading center. The island's beautiful beaches made it part of the State of Quintana Roo's "Mexican Riviera." Undersea explorer Jacques Cousteau really put the island on the tourism map in the 1960s, thanks to the island's prime coral reefs, part of the second-largest coral reef formation in the world (after Australia's Great Barrier Reef).

Size: 30 mi. (48 km.) long x 9 mi. (16 km.) wide	
Climate: Subtropical	**Temperatures**: 75°F (24°C) to 90°F (32°C)
Population: 65,000	**Busy Season**: Mid-February to April
Language: Spanish, English	**Money**: Nuevo Peso ($10 Pesos = $1 U.S.)
Time Zone: Central (DST observed)	**Transportation**: Walking, taxis, scooters
Phones: Dial 011- from U.S., dial 060 for emergencies, dial 20092 for police	

AMBIENCE

HISTORY & CULTURE

FACTS

Introduction
Reservations
Staterooms
Dining
Activities
Ports of Call
Magic
Index

Making the Most of Cozumel

GETTING THERE

Your ship docks at the new **Punta Langosta** pier in the city of San Miguel de Cozumel, on the island's western shore. Tendering is not required. You can see Playa del Carmen on the mainland, just two miles (3 km.) across the channel. The typical all ashore time is 10:30 am, with all aboard at 10:30 pm. A tourist information office is at the end of the pier, as is the glitzy Punta Langosta shopping plaza. The plaza is reached via a pedestrian bridge over Avenida (Avenue) Rafael Melgar, and provides a convenient, secure shopping and dining destination. There is no beach within walking distance.

GETTING AROUND

You disembark the ship near the **center of town**, about five blocks south of Muelle Fiscal, the city's central plaza and ferryboat dock (ferries to the mainland). Several miles to the south are the International and Puerta Maya piers, in the resort hotel district. The waterfront road, Avenida Rafael Melgar, goes right past the pier, and leads to most of the sights in town and on the island's west shore. Just five blocks north you'll find Avenida Benito Juarez, which heads directly to the San Gervasio ruins and the beaches of the eastern shore. Drive south on Ave. Rafael Melgar to reach Chankanaab Nature Park, San Francisco Beach, Playa Del Sol, and Palancar Reef. • Car and scooter rentals are advisable for those who wish to set off on their own, but taxis ($4 for up to four passengers) are more convenient for in-town travel. Four wheel drive vehicles are especially useful if you head for the eastern beaches. Executive Car Rental (529-872-1308) is located in the Punta Langosta Mall, and several other agencies are nearby.

STAYING SAFE

Safety is always, in part, a **state of mind**. Certainly the crowds of sprawling San Miguel will put most travelers on the defensive, as may the dominant, Spanish language (though most shop owners speak some English). Take typical big-city precautions, then try to relax and enjoy. A polite, friendly attitude towards the locals will ease your way—it always helps to treat your host with respect. "Do you speak English?" is a good way to start your conversations. Drinking water and food safety are a classic concern for visits to Mexico. Be sensible. Drink bottled water and commercially-prepared beverages, and think twice about dining from street vendors. However, most restaurants will be well up to stateside health standards. As always, sunblock is a must. Apply it before you leave your stateroom, and dress according to your planned activities—changing rooms are hard to find at the beach.

Touring Cozumel

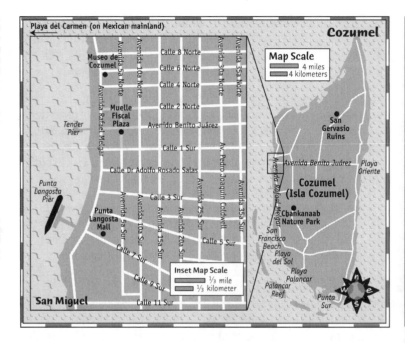

COZUMEL ISLAND MAP

WALKING TOUR

There's not much to see on a **walking tour** other than Punta Langosta Mall. Just across the street from the cruise pier, the mall is brand-new, with stylish architecture reminiscent of fashionable stateside malls (it reminds us a bit of Downtown Disney in Orlando). You'll find upscale souvenir and luxury shops, the popular bars Carlos 'n' Charlie's and Señor Frog, a Tony Roma's Steakhouse, and a Burger King. While the Punta Langosta Mall offers a secure experience, you'll get a better taste of the town by taking a short stroll or cab ride five blocks north to Muelle Fiscal, the town's central plaza. A six-block area has been converted to a pedestrian mall, featuring many restaurants, shops, and a large souvenir and crafts market. Three blocks farther north on Ave. Rafael Melgar is the island's museum ($3 admission), which features two floors filled with archaeological and ecological exhibits and a very popular rooftop restaurant (Del Museo), which is open until 1:30 pm in the afternoon. Most tourist-oriented restaurants and shops are clustered along a 10-block stretch of Avenido Rafael Melgar between Punta Langosta on the south and the museum on the north. However, if you're bargain-hunting, the shops on the side streets and a block inland may offer better deals.

ACTIVITIES

Playing in Cozumel

The best of the island's and mainland's **play spots** and attractions are featured in shore excursions on the next four pages, which we recommend for most visitors. Many are day-long experiences. Serious divers may prefer to make their own arrangements.

The island does not produce much in the way of local crafts, but you can find a wide range of silver, carved wood, and stone items and other Mexican specialties, imported from the mainland. **Shops** near the cruise pier will tend to be the most expensive. Know your prices, and be prepared to bargain. Silver items are typically sold by weight, and black coral cannot be brought back into the U.S.

White, powder-soft sands and clear, turquoise waters make the island's **beaches** very attractive. The strong undertow found on the wild beaches of the east end can be perilous for swimmers, but the big surf, dunes, stretches of rocky coastline, and small crowds are very tempting. Playa Oriente is at the far eastern end of the central, cross-island road, and others can be found by turning right and following the paved road southward. Several of these beaches offer restaurants and watersport rentals. The safe, gentle beaches on the sheltered west side of the island are generally built-up, offering a wide variety of recreational and dining opportunities. Top picks (all south of San Miguel) include San Francisco Beach, Playa del Sol, Playa Francesa, and Playa Palancar.

Palancar Reef, at the island's southwest corner, is probably at the top of most serious divers' list, but dozens more **dive sites** dot the map. Visit http://www.travelnotes.cc/cozumel/links/scuba.html for a good introduction to Cozumel diving, listings, and reviews.

Chankanaab Park offers first-rate snorkel, nature, and wildlife encounter opportunities. • On the mainland, the **Xcaret** Eco-Archeological Park offers many unusual opportunities (book an excursion for either of these). The island's archeological sites are quite minor, with the most developed at San Gervasio, near the island's center. Archeology buffs should book an excursion to Tulum Ruins, about 80 miles (128 km.) away on the mainland. Alas, famed Chitchen Itza is a bit too far for a day trip.

Your schedule allows for both **lunch and dinner** ashore. Carlos 'n Charlies is a town fixture, relocated to Punta Langosta Mall. In the center of town, Casa Denis and La Choza offer regional specialties.

Embarking on Shore Excursions on Cozumel

☐ Cozumel's Golf Excursion [CZ01]   Rating: n/a   ☀ 🔒 🔲

Play a round at the Cozumel Country Club on a course designed by the Nicklaus Group. Includes greens fees, golf cart, and golf balls. Lunch and club/shoe rentals are additional. Golf attire required. Typical meeting time is 10:10 am. We received no cruiser reviews for this excursion. (On Your Own: Cozumel Country Club, http://www.cozumelcountryclub.com.mx, 987-872-9570)	**Sports** Active Ages 10 & up $130 5-6 hours

☐ Certified Scuba Tour [CZ02]   Rating: 9   ☀ 🔒 🔲

Certified divers enjoy two dives—first to Palancar Reef (70'-80' or 21-24 m.) and then to a shallower dive (50'-60' or 15-18 m.). Includes equipment, fruit, and drinks. Typical meeting time is 11:35 am. Cruiser reviews are positive: Two "drift dives" offer the opportunity to see more "unique underwater life" than in many other ports. Palancar Reef is "phenomenal" and the reef wall is "very deep" with "lots to see." Visibility is "incredible." (On Your Own: Eagle Ray Divers, http://www.eagleraydivers.com, 987-872-5735)	**Sports** Very active Ages 12 & up $95 4-4.5 hours

☐ Dolphin Discovery Cozumel [CZ04]   Rating: 7   ☀ 🔒 🔲

This popular excursion takes you to Chankanaab National Park where you'll encounter dolphins in waist-deep water. Afterwards, stay and enjoy the park. If you want to swim with the dolphins, you will need to book that on your own—see below. Typical meeting times are 10:20 am, noon, 1:00 pm, and 2:00 pm. Cruiser comments were mixed: Listen to a "brief training session,"	**Encounter** Leisurely Ages 3 & up $105/$90 3-3.5 hours

don "bulky life jackets," then enter one of five "water areas" where you stand in the water. Several cruisers report that the "waist-high" water was in fact "chest-high" or even "chin-high" instead, and that it could be over the heads of guests under 7. Most cruisers loved being able to "touch and interact" with the "amazing" dolphins. Cruisers note that you cannot wear "water shoes." Some feel this excursion isn't really great for cruisers "under 12" due to the depth of the water. (On Your Own: Dolphin Discovery Cozumel at http://www.dolphindiscovery.com/cozumel.htm, 800-417-1736)

☐ Mayan Frontier Horseback Riding Tour [CZ05]   Rating: 6   ☀ 🔒 🔲

Giddyup! Mosey on down a Mayan trail on horseback, passing ruins on your way. Afterwards, visit a ranch. Includes complimentary soft drinks and beer after riding. Typical meeting time is 11:15 am. Cruiser reviews were mediocre: The "very friendly staff" is "helpful," but the "saddles are old and unpadded." The horses are also "over the hill" (which could be a good thing as they are more sedate than younger horses). Cruisers also note that some of the "ruins and artifacts" are "not real." Younger guests "enjoyed it," but most cruisers were "not impressed."	**Sports** Very active Ages 12 & up $82 4 hours

☐ Tulum Ruins and Beach Tour [CZ06]   Rating: 9   ☀ 🔒 🔲

An all-day adventure to the mainland for a visit to the sacred ruins. Includes a beach visit, drinks, and sandwiches. Note that there is an extra fee if you bring a camcorder. Typical meeting time is 9:40 am. Cruiser reviews are positive: The "boat to Mexico" is "large and comfortable," though a "little bouncy." The "fantastic" tour guides are "knowledgeable," making the ruins "way more interesting than you'd expect." The "beautiful" beach is "perfect," but be aware there are "no changing rooms." Overall, a "worthy" and "fun" excursion.	**Sports** Active All ages $90/adult $70 (5-9) 7-7.5 hours

See page 164 for a key to the shore excursion description charts and their icons.

Embarking on Shore Excursions
on Cozumel (continued)

☐ Sea Lion Discovery and Snorkel Tour [CZ07]   Rating: 7   ☼ ♠ ⓘ

Journey to Chankanaab National Park to enjoy the sea creatures at the Sea Lion
Show. Afterwards, snorkel for 45 minutes. Stay longer at the park if you wish.
Typical meeting time is noon. Cruiser reviews are mostly positive: This "cute"
and "entertaining" show is "a lot of fun for kids," particularly "young ones"
(under 10). Also includes a "bird show," though a common complaint is that
there are "too many people" and "not everyone gets the chance to hold a bird."
Afterwards, go snorkeling at the "pretty beach" but beware of "crowded conditions" where
you may "constantly bump into one another in the water." All agreed this is a "beautiful
park." (On Your Own: Just take a taxi to Chankanaab National Park.)

Sports
Active
Ages 6 & up
$55/$45 (6-9)
3.5-4 hours

☐ Chankanaab Sea Lion Discovery [CZ08]   Rating: 8   ☼ ♠ ⓘ

Just the Chankanaab's Sea Lion Show and the Wacky World of Birds Show
mentioned above (no snorkeling), but it still includes transportation. Stay at
the park longer if you wish and explore the botanical gardens. Typical meeting
time is 12:30 pm. Cruiser reviews are very similar to the those mentioned in the
previous description, but considered slightly better without the snorkeling.

Tour
Leisurely
All ages
$40/$30 (3-9)
3.5-4 hours

☐ Tropical Jeep Safari Tour [CZ09]   Rating: 7   ☼ ♠ ⓘ

Drive a four-person, standard-shift, 4x4 vehicle through the "tropical" scrub.
After bump-bump-bumping along the dirt roads, enjoy a yummy lunch on the
beach and explore some low-key ruins. If you're a party of two, you'll share a
vehicle with another couple and take turns driving. Cruiser reviews are mostly

Tour
Active
Ages 10 & up
$84
4.5 hours

positive: After a "long walk," you get
into your "open air" vehicle ("no air
conditioning") and "take a fun drive" through town.
Once on the dirt roads, it's "very bumpy and dusty"
but "adventuresome." Lunch at a "beautiful beach"
is "very good," though the ruins are "unimpressive."
Overall, most cruisers enjoyed the "entertaining
tour guides" and "had a good time." Typical meeting
time is 12:20 pm.

Our Jeep Safari

© MediaMarx, Inc.

☐ Xcaret Eco Archeological Park [CZ10]   Rating: 9   ☼ ♠ ⓘ

This mainland park is a favorite—it's like a natural water park. Swim, visit
an aquarium, and see ruins. Includes transportation, lunch, and entrance
fee. Bring cash. Regular sunscreen is not allowed; you will be provided with
environmentally-friendly sunscreen upon arrival. Cruiser reviews are very
positive: While the "travel time is long" (about "1.5 hours"), the "beautiful nature
park" is "well worth the journey." A favorite feature is the "unique underground
fresh water river" that you "float through" (but beware that it is "cold water"). There are
also "good spots for snorkeling" with "lots of fish." Many cruisers feel this excursion is the
"highlight of their trip." Typical meeting time is 9:45 am.

Tour
Active
All ages
$99/$79 (3-9)
6.5-7.5 hours

☐ Snorkeling at Chankanaab National Park [CZ11]   Rating: 5   ☼ ♠ ⓘ

Snorkel in a lovely nature park. Afterwards, relax or explore gardens. For ages 6 &
up. Typical meeting times are 9:45 am and noon. About 3 hours. Cruiser reviews
indicate the snorkeling is hampered by crowds and is not highly recommended.

Sports
Active
$45/35 (6-9)

Embarking on Shore Excursions
on Cozumel *(continued)*

■ Fury Catamaran Sail, Snorkel, & Beach Party [CZ12]   Rating: 10

Board a 65-foot catamaran and cruise out to snorkel in 3'–20' (1–6 m.) of water. Afterwards, party on the beach with free soft drinks, margaritas, and beer. Typical meeting time is 12:30 pm. Cruiser reviews are overwhelmingly positive: Enjoy a 35 minute sail on a "large," "unexpectedly smooth" catamaran with an "exceptional" crew. Then snorkel for 45 minutes in a "beautiful" area with "many fish and coral." Hop aboard for "short," "20 minute" sail to a "gorgeous beach" with "plenty of shady areas." The food served at the beach is "very good" (about "$8/person"). Then it's back onboard for a "30–45 minute" sail back, with "music" and "dancing." "Plenty of free drinks." "Bring cash" for food and tips. Note that you "do need to be mobile to exit and reenter the catamaran at sea." Overall, cruisers had a "great time" and would "do it again." (On Your Own: Fury Catamaran at http://furycat.com/cozumel.htm, 987-872-5145)

| **Sports** |
| Active |
| Ages 6 & up |
| $42/$25 (6–9) |
| 4 hours |

■ Fury Catamaran Teen Cruise [CZ13]   Rating: 7

Teens can take an evening cruise aboard a 65-foot catamaran—includes music, snacks, and beverages. Chaperoned by counselors from the teen-only club. The cruise is similar to the one described above, but without the snorkeling, beach, or alcoholic beverages. Teen cruiser reviews are mixed: Some thought it was "way fun" others just "so-so." Like all teen events, its success probably depends on who attends. Typical meeting time is 6:00 pm. (On Your Own: Don't bother)

| **Dance** |
| Leisurely |
| Ages 13–17 |
| $35 |
| 2.5 hours |

■ Kayaking Adventure [CZ14]   Rating: 8

Paddle through the unspoiled beauty of Parque Punta Sur ecological reserve. Weight limit of 250 lbs. Double and triple kayaks available. Includes fruit and water. Typical meeting time is noon. Cruiser reviews are limited, but positive: This "really cool" kayak trip takes you through "mangroves," ending up at a "beautiful lagoon." Snacks of "cookies, pastries, and fruit" are provided, plus "soda" and "bottled water." Beware of bugs—bring "lots of insect repellent."

| **Sports** |
| Very active |
| Ages 10 & up |
| $59 |
| 4.5 hours |

■ Cozumel Beach Break [CZ15]   Rating: 8

Bum around the Playa del Sol Beach. Price includes taxi fare to and from the beach, admission, use of pool and beach, open bar (mixed drinks, beer, soda, and juice), water toys, recreation, entertainment, and lunch buffet. Typical meeting time is 10:30 am. Cruiser comments were mostly positive: The beach has a "family party atmosphere" with "lots to do," including "water trampolines" and "a climbing iceberg" (though these are "pretty far out in the water"). Keep in mind that while the drinks may be free, they are also "watered down." Lunch is "good" by most accounts, though you have to "contend with vendors" to get to the food area. (On Your Own: Playa Sol at http://www.playasol.com.mx, or Mr. Sanchos—see next page)

| **Beach** |
| Leisurely |
| All ages |
| $49/$39 (3–9) |
| 5–5.5 hours |

■ Caverns Exploration and Beach Tour [CZ18]   Rating: n/a

Take an all-day journey via a ferry and air-conditioned bus to the Mexican mainland to explore natural caverns in Playa del Carmen. Afterwards, relax on the beach with your own beach chair. Includes a Mexican lunch and beverages. Note that there are rocky areas and rough terrain; strollers are not allowed. Typical meeting time is 9:50 am. We received no cruiser reviews for this excursion.

| **Tour** |
| Active |
| Ages 6 & up |
| $83/$63 (6–9) |
| 6.5–7 hours |

See page 164 for a key to the shore excursion description charts and their icons.

Embarking on Shore Excursions
on Cozumel *(continued)*

▪ Cozumel Ruins & Beach Tour [CZ19]　　Rating: 3

Tour the San Gervasio Ruins, then its off to Playa Sol Beach for an hour and a half of relaxation. Includes beverages. Watersports available for extra fee. Typical meeting time is noon. Cruiser reviews were mostly negative: While the "water is beautiful," there "wasn't enough time" to spend at the beach. The food at the beach "didn't seem fresh." Most of your time is spent at the "ancient sites" which are "interesting," but not "spectacular." Overall, cruisers were not impressed and "do not recommend it."	**Tour/Beach**
	Leisurely
	All ages
	$45/$32 (3–9)
	4–4.5 hours

▪ Atlantis Submarine Expedition [CZ20]　　Rating: 6

Board the "Atlantis" submarine and dive up to 110' (33 m.), viewing tropical fish and 30' (9 m.) coral heads. Includes beverages. Height restriction of 36"/91 cm. minimum. Typical meeting times are 12:35 and 2:35 pm. Cruiser reviews are very similar to those on same excursion in St. Thomas (see page 178), but it gets a slightly higher rating thanks to the better views and visible sea life. (On Your Own: http://www.atlantisadventures.com/cozumel or 987-872-5671)	**Tour**
	Leisurely
	Ages 4 & up
	$75/$50 (4–9)
	2.5 hours

▪ Reef Snorkel [CZ21]　　Rating: n/a

Take a taxi to Playa Corona, where you get to snorkel the beautiful reefs of Cozumel. Snorkel gear, instruction, and transportation provided. This is a good excursion for beginners as you enter the water from the beach. Typical meeting time is 9:55 am. We received no cruiser reviews for this excursion. (On Your Own: Bring your snorkel gear and take a taxi to Playa Corona.)	**Sports**
	Active
	Ages 6 & up
	$28/$22 (6–9)
	2.5–3 hours

▪ Ocean View Explorer Tour [CZ22]　　Rating: 5

Explore the coral of Paradise Reef in this semi-submersible. Typical meeting times are 11:00 am and 12:45 pm. Cruiser reviews on this excursion are limited, but those we received were mixed: Some felt it was a good "compromise" between the Atlantis sub and a snorkeling excursion, while others felt it was "boring" and would not do it again. Compared to the Atlantis, it is less expensive and allows kids 0-3. (On Your Own: AquaWorld at http://www.aquaworld.com.mx)	**Tour**
	Leisurely
	All ages
	$39/29 (0–9)
	1.5–2 hours

See page 164 for a key to the shore excursion description charts and their icons.

Cozumel On Your Own

Want to set out on your own? There are several popular tour operators and destinations preferred by Disney cruisers. While we haven't tried these outfits ourselves, we offer the information here for your reference: **Mr. Sancho's Cozumel Beach Club** is a nice alternative to the Cozumel Beach Break excursion—just take a taxi to Mr. Sancho's and enjoy a less expensive day at the beach with plenty of amenities should you wish to use them. For more information, visit http://www.mrsanchos.com. **Wild Tours ATV** is an adventurous excursion during which you can tool around the "jungle" in an ATV, go kayaking, then do a bit of snorkeling. For more information, visit http://gocozumel.com/wild-tours-atv or call 987-872-2244. And for those that want something more familiar, try **Cozumel Mini-Golf** with a fun, tropical course just a short distance from the pier. For more information, visit http://cozumelminigolf.com or call 987-872-6570.

Castaway Cay
(All Itineraries—Last Port of Call)

We saved our **favorite port** for last (and so has Disney). Castaway Cay is Disney's private island, exclusively for the use of Disney Cruise Line guests and crew. It's clean, safe, and well-themed, and lunch is complimentary on the island. We recommend you get up early on your Castaway Cay day—you don't want to miss a minute of the fun!

Megan and Natalie on Castaway Cay

Castaway Cay (pronounced "Castaway Key") is a **tropical retreat** with white sandy beaches, swaying palm trees, and aquamarine water. What makes it so magical is its theming—it not unlike visiting one of Disney's excellent water parks, such as Typhoon Lagoon. The island even has its own legend—they say three explorers set sail with their families to the scattered islands of the Bahamas in search of fame and fortune. Their adventures brought them to this island, where they found sunken treasures, the secret of youth, and the skeletal remains of a giant whale. The explorers and their families remained on the beautiful island for years as castaways—you can still see the original structures and artifacts left behind.

Disney may call this out-island Castaway Cay, but in its previous incarnation it was **Gorda Cay**. The island is a part of the Abaco Bahamas island archipelago. Its history is murky. It may have first been inhabited by Lucayan Indians, "discovered" by the Spanish, later used as a harbor for pirates, and was long used by the Abaconians for farming pumpkins and sweet potatoes. In the '70s and '80s, the island was a base for drug operations. Disney purchased the island and, over the next 18 months, spent $25 million to fix up 55 acres (only about 5% of the island). 50,000 truckloads of sand were dredged to make the beautiful beaches. Its extensive facilities are the best in the cruise industry. For more history, visit: http://web.outsideonline.com/magazine/0199/9901blackbeard.html

Size: 2 mi. (3.2 km.) x 1.25 mi. (2 km.)	**Distance:** 260 nautical miles from home port
Climate: Subtropical	**Temperatures:** 66°F (19°C) to 88°F (31°C)
Language: English	**Money:** U.S. Dollar/stateroom charge
Time Zone: Eastern (DST observed)	**Transportation:** Walking, bicycles

Sidebar tabs: Introduction | Reservations | Staterooms | Dining | Activities | Ports of Call | Magic | Index

Section tabs: AMBIENCE | HISTORY | FACTS

Introduction   Reservations   Staterooms   Dining   Activities   Ports of Call   Magic   Index

Making the Most of Castaway Cay

GETTING THERE

Thanks to a deep channel Disney dredged when they acquired the island, **your ship pulls right up to the dock** on Castaway Cay. Typical all ashore time is 8:30 am, and you have until about 4:30 pm (or just eight hours) to play on this delightful island. When you alight from the ship, proceed down the dock (picking up towels on your way) to the island—it's about a 3-minute walk to the tram. Be aware that when the seas are rough, the ship may be unable to dock at Castaway Cay, and therefore you'll be unable to visit. This is most likely to happen in January and February, but it can occur at anytime.

GETTING AROUND

Castaway Cay is the **easiest port to get around**, thanks to the well-marked paths and convenient trams. As you walk down the dock to the island, you'll pass the Castaway Cay post office on your right and Marge's Barge's sea charters dock on your left, after which you'll reach a tram stop—hop aboard the next tram, or simply take the 10-minute walk to the family beach. Once you're at the family beach, you can continue down the path past buildings that house the restrooms, shops, and services. At the far end of the main path is the teen beach. The adults-only beach is accessible by another tram (or a long, hot, 25-minute walk down the airstrip) near the end of the main path. All locations are marked on the map on the next page, as well as on the color map Disney provides with your *Personal Navigator*.

DINING

Unlike the other ports, the Disney Cruise Line provides lunch on Castaway Cay. For complete details on Castaway Cay dining, see page 105 (we've repeated some of the same information here for your reference). Everyone can eat at **Cookie's BBQ** across from the family beach. Cookie's typically serves from 11:30 am to 2:00 pm, and offers the best selection with burgers, BBQ ribs, chicken sandwiches, lobster patties, fruit, frozen yogurt, and cookies. Food is served buffet-style. Plenty of covered seating is nearby. Basic beverages are also provided, or you can buy a soda or alcoholic beverage across the way at the Conched Out Bar. Adults can eat at the **Castaway Cay Air Bar-B-Q** located at Serenity Bay, the adults-only beach, from about 11:00 am to 1:30 pm. Offerings include burgers, salmon, lobster patties, potato salad, fresh fruit, and fat-free yogurt. Sodas and alcoholic beverages can be purchased at the bar nearby. If you choose not to visit Castaway Cay, a buffet is served in Parrot Cay, usually from 8:00 am to 1:30 pm.

Exploring Castaway Cay

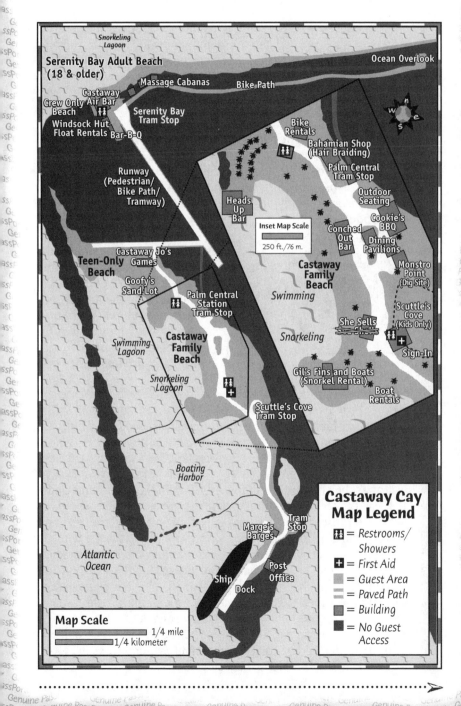

Snorkeling Lagoon

Serenity Bay Adult Beach (18 & older)

Ocean Overlook

Massage Cabanas

Bike Path

Castaway Air Bar

Crew Only Beach

Serenity Bay Tram Stop

Windsock Hut Float Rentals

Bar-B-Q

Bike Rentals

Bahamian Shop (Hair Braiding)

Palm Central Tram Stop

Runway (Pedestrian/ Bike Path/ Tramway)

Heads Up Bar

Outdoor Seating

Cookie's BBQ

Inset Map Scale
250 ft./76 m.

Conched Out Bar

Dining Pavilions

Castaway Jo's Games

Teen-Only Beach

Goofy's Sand Lot

Castaway Family Beach

Swimming

Monstro Point (Dig Site)

Palm Central Station Tram Stop

Castaway Family Beach

Swimming Lagoon

Snorkeling Lagoon

Snorkeling

She Sells Shells

Scuttle's Cove (Kids Only)

Sign-In

Gil's Fins and Boats (Snorkel Rental)

Boat Rentals

Scuttle's Cove Tram Stop

Boating Harbor

Atlantic Ocean

Marge's Barges

Tram Stop

Ship Dock

Post Office

Castaway Cay Map Legend

- 👫 = Restrooms/ Showers
- ➕ = First Aid
- = Guest Area
- = Paved Path
- = Building
- = No Guest Access

Map Scale
— 1/4 mile
— 1/4 kilometer

Introduction

Reservations

Staterooms

Dining

Activities

Ports of Call

Magic

Index

Playing in Castaway Cay

ACTIVITIES

Most **activities** on Castaway Cay require no advance booking—the exceptions are things like parasailing, Banana Boat rides, fishing excursions, and the teen Wild Side excursion (see page 230). You can reserve floats, bikes, and snorkel equipment rentals in advance, though these are usually available on a walk-up basis. Strollers and beach wheelchairs are free for use on a first-come, first-served basis.

The **beautiful beaches** are a big draw at Castaway Cay. The family beach is the largest and busiest—arrive early to get a good beach chair. Float rentals are available near Gil's Fins snorkel rentals and at the bike rental shack. The adults-only beach—Serenity Bay—is a wonderful place to spend a little grown-up time. The beach there is a little more

Midship with Mickey

The kids water play area at the family beach

barren than the family beach. Bring some water shoes as the bottom is coarser and sometimes uncomfortable. Walk farther down the beach for the most privacy. The teen beach—which is exclusively for teens—offers teen activities like volleyball and dancing.

© MediaMarx, Inc.

Snorkeling is a very popular activity on Castaway Cay, and an excellent spot for beginners to try out the sport. You can rent equipment at Gil's Fins near the family beach—prices are $25/adult and $10/kid (includes masks, fins, and vest). You can reserve your snorkel rental in advance (see page 229), though this is not necessary. The snorkeling lagoon is extensive—there's plenty of fish and sunken treasure to discover, as well as a submarine from Walt Disney World's "20,000 Leagues Under the Sea." Look for the map that shows the snorkeling course before you get in. Put sunscreen on your back—the water intensifies the sun's rays and you can get badly sunburned. Consider clipping a water bottle to your vest to rinse out your mouth—the saltwater can be bothersome. Note that there is an unofficial snorkeling lagoon at Serenity Bay (it's straight out from the first massage cabana)—rent your equipment at Gil's and tote it over. You can use your own snorkel gear in the lagoons, too. (Disney requires that all snorkelers wear a flotation device—you may need to pay a small fee of $6 for its use.) Some families like to bring their own (better) equipment, or simply purchase cheap snorkel sets for kids and then leave them behind.

Playing in Castaway Cay

Boat rentals are primarily available at the boat beach (Relay Bay). Rent paddle boats ($8 for two-seater, $10 for four-seater), <u>Aqua Trikes</u> ($15),

<u>sea kayaks</u> ($8 for one-seater, $10 for two-seater), small Aqua Fins sailboats ($15), and <u>Hobie Cat sailboats</u> ($18)—all prices are for a half-hour. (Underlined boats may also be at Serenity Bay, along with Banana Boats). No advance reservations for rentals other than Banana Boats.

Watercraft on Castaway Cay

Would you like to see a bit more of the island? You can **rent bicycles** near the family beach—prices are $6/hour for all ages. It takes about one hour to cycle down the airstrip and along the unpaved trail that borders the Serenity Bay beach. Child seats can be requested. Water is provided along the bike trail, too.

Kids have their own supervised playground at **Scuttle's Cove**. If you've registered your kids for Oceaneer Club or Lab, you can check them in here while you go play at Serenity Bay. Counselors guide kids in structured activities, but they do not take them swimming. Beside Scuttle's Cove is Monstro Point, which has a huge whale "skeleton" to dig up! Programming ends at 3:30 pm. Note that kids can check-out sand toys at Scuttle's Cove—first come, first served.

Family games are available at Castaway Jo's (also known as the Grouper Pavilion), a shaded patio with shuffleboard, billiards, foosball, Ping-Pong, basketball/football toss, horseshoes, a giant checkerboard, and a sandbox with toys. This area is often overlooked, yet can really be a lot of fun, especially when you or a family member need some time out of the sun.

Goofy's Sandlot is the **sport beach** on Castaway Cay—it's right next to Castaway Jo's. You can play volleyball and tetherball here. Watch for an organized volleyball game in the late morning. The sport beach is often very quiet and uncrowded, making it an ideal spot for families to hang together. And it's proximity to the teen beach (right next door), Castaway Jo's, and the Heads Up Bar make it very convenient, too. This is also a good spot to find a hammock if they are all occupied on other beaches.

Playing in Castaway Cay

ACTIVITIES

Adults can get **cabana massages** near Serenity Bay. If you do just one treatment, this is the one we recommend. Cabana massages are $110/person—reserve on your first day. If you are sensitive to the sun, book a massage for later in the day—the oils make your skin more likely to sunburn. You can bring your sunscreen and ask to have it applied at the end of the massage, too.

© MediaMarx, Inc.

A massage cabana on Castaway Cay

Shopping is limited to two small shops. She Sells ~~Sea Shells~~ is a Disney themed shop with unique Castaway Cay logo items. Visit this shop early, as the crowds are huge later in the day and some items and sizes get gobbled up quickly. A Bahamian-run retail shop near the end of the family beach sells arts and crafts—this is also where you can get hair braiding for $1/braid or $2/cornrow—expect to pay about $30 for the whole head (which takes about 3 hours). There is sometimes a merchandise cart at Serenity Bay, too. The shops on the ship are closed while the ship is docked at Castaway Cay.

Meet your favorite **Disney characters** on Castaway Cay. Check the back of the Disney-provided Castaway Cay map for times. Photo opportunities are available all over the island. Look for ship's photographers near the ship and at the family beach.

While it's not possible to **hike** around the island, you can take a leisurely stroll down the bike path near the adult beach. Water is provided along the trail, and there's a scenic ocean overlook at the end of the hike. If you're looking to see parts of the island that are normally off-limits, we recommend the Walking & Kayak Adventure excursion described on the next page. It's quite delightful, and it was fascinating to see the undeveloped parts of the island that are usually considered "backstage."

Let's not overlook one of our favorite activities on Castaway Cay—**relaxing**! You can do it practically anywhere, but we really like lounging about in hammocks on the family beach or adults-only beach. We've had the best luck finding empty hammocks behind Gil's Fins (the snorkel rental shack). If you find a hammock, please enjoy it, but don't try to save it by leaving your things on it.

Advance Rentals on Castaway Cay

These rentals are non-refundable unless your cruise skips Castaway Cay.

■ Snorkel Equipment [C01]

Explore Disney's 12-acre snorkeling lagoon—price includes all-day rental of mask, fins, and vest (light flotation). Beginners can take the Discover Trail, experienced snorkelers may like the longer Explorer Trail. Both trails have lots to see. Pick up your snorkel equipment at Gil's Fins. Note that children under 13 must be with an adult. (On Your Own: Bring your own equipment and use the lagoon!)	**Sports**
	Active
	All ages
	$25/adult
	$10/kids 5-9

■ Float Rentals [C03]

Enjoy the water with a lounge float or tube. (On Your Own: Purchase inflatable floats from a dollar store at home and bring along on your cruise.)	**Beach**
	$6/each

■ Bicycle Rental [C04]   Rating: 8

Dozens of bikes are available for rent. Training wheels, child seats, and helmets are available. The biking paths are on flat terrain, and there's plenty of drinking water along the way. Look for the ocean outlook at the end of the bike path! Cruiser reviews are positive: The bikes are "comfortable" and the "trail is beautiful." At the end of the trail is a "very peaceful," "secluded beach."	**Sports**
	Active
	All ages
	$6/hour

■ Castaway Cay Getaway Package [C05]   Rating: 7

This package includes a float rental, snorkel equipment rental, and a bike rental for one hour, for a savings of $5-6. Very popular—book early. But don't bother if you are planning other activities—there's not enough time for it all! Cruiser reviews are positive: Cruisers enjoyed having the rentals "secured" and felt it is "good deal," though many noted they weren't able to use all three rentals.	**Sports**
	Active
	All ages
	$32/adult
	$16/child

■ Banana Boat Rides [C06]   Rating: 8

Ride a big, yellow, inflatable water "sled" around Relay Bay and out around the ship. The banana boat holds 10 people and is pulled by a Jet Ski. You must be able to swim, as you could fall off. Departure times are every 30 minutes beginning at 8:50 am (Wonder) or 10:30 am (Magic). When we rode it, half the passengers fell off when we hit a big wave. Cruiser reviews are positive: This	**Sports**
	Very active
	Ages 8 & up
	$14/person
	20 minutes

"very bouncy," "fun" ride is "exhilarating" and "very fast." Many cruisers did get "bounced off" in the water, but "enjoyed it." Most cruisers agree that this is "great fun." We are in the minority as we didn't like this—it was much too rough and we couldn't enjoy the scenery with all the saltwater spray in our eyes. Tip: Wear swim goggles.

■ Parasailing [C08]   Rating: 9

If you've never tried parasailing, this is a great experience for beginners. You can go solo or tandem, and you'll take-off from the boat and land in it when you're done. Expect to be airborne for 5-8 minutes, with 600-feet of rope between you and the boat. Guests must be 90-350 lbs. (40-158 kg.) to parasail. Tandem parasailing is possible if you're both under the maximum weight combined. Be sure	**Sports**
	Active
	Ages 8 & up
	$70/person
	45 minutes

to take a disposable camera for some amazing photos while in the air! Cruiser reviews are very positive: "No experience is necessary" to enjoy this "amazing flight" over the water. The "views" are "stunning." It's a "real adrenaline rush" and a "genuine highlight" of the cruise. "Book early" as "spots fill up quickly." Cruisers say "go for it!"

See page 164 for a key to description charts and their icons.

Introduction
Reservations
Staterooms
Dining
Activities
Ports of Call
Magic
Index

Embarking on Shore Excursions
on Castaway Cay

☐ The Wild Side (for Teens Only) [CO7]   Rating: 9

Retrace the adventures of the first teens on the island—Molly and Seth. There's plenty of action, and you'll get to do some snorkeling, biking, and sea kayaking. Typical meeting time is very early for teens—8:20 am at The Stack/Common Grounds. Teen cruiser reviews are overwhelmingly positive: First, "wait until you see who else is going" before you book—this tour "is best when you go with people you know" (but don't wait too long—it can book up). On Castaway Cay, you "do the bike ride first," "kayak for about 20 minutes," then bike back to go "snorkeling." After lunch at Cookies, you "hook up with other teens at the teen beach." Many think this was the "highlight" of their cruise; those that disagree had issues with "other teens," not the excursion.

Sports
Very active
Ages 13–17
$35/teen
4 hours

☐ Walking & Kayak Nature Adventure   Rating: 8

Explore areas of Castaway Cay normally off-limits to guests! Start with a 40-min. nature hike to reach your kayak launch site, then enjoy an hour-long kayak trip through mangroves. Afterwards, swim at a deserted beach, then take a 20-min. walk back. Typical meeting times are 9:00 am, 9:15 am, and 12:45 pm. This is a new excursion and we received no reviews. We did this ourselves recently and really enjoyed it—we recommend it to anyone who wants to be active and explore the ecosystem. Wear appropriate footwear. It's best for those who've visited the island before.

Sports
Very active
Ages 10 & up
$60
2.5–3 hours

☐ Glass Bottom Boat Scenic Voyage   Rating: 2

Board a 46-foot trawler with a glass bottom for an hour long ecotour of the barrier reefs surrounding Castaway Cay. Typical meeting times are 9:45 am, 11:15 am, 12:45 pm, and 2:15 pm. Cruiser reviews are uniform: The "rocky," "overcrowded boat" is filled with people "pushing and shoving" to see out the "cloudy" glass bottom. "Very limited fish" are visible. There are "very few seats" meaning most have to stand the entire time. Overall, cruisers say "don't bother."

Tour
Leisurely
Ages 3 & up
$25/20 (3-9)
1.5 hours

☐ Seahorse Catamaran Snorkel Adventure   Rating: 4

If the snorkeling lagoon doesn't satisfy your itch to snorkel, this excursion puts you aboard a 63-foot catamaran to sail to a prime snorkeling area. Snorkel gear and instruction provided. Complimentary beverages and snacks are served after snorkeling. Typical meeting times are 9:15 am and 1:15 pm. Cruiser reviews are mixed: The "excellent" catamaran trip was "delightful" for most. The snorkeling proves trickier, however—some enjoyed an "abundance of sea life," while others battled with "wind and currents." All agreed the "snack" is "unimpressive" ("a couple bowls of potato chips"). Cruisers felt the "open water can be choppy" and this is "not good for those prone to motion sickness or snorkeling beginners."

Sports
Active
Ages 5 & up
$49/29 (5-9)
2–2.5 hours

☐ Castaway Cay Bottom Fishing [CO2]   Rating: 9

Up to six guests can enjoy a ride around the Abaco Islands for bottom fishing (catch and release). Tackle, bait, and beverages (soda and water) are provided. Guests 12 and under must wear life jackets. Typical meeting times are 9:00 am, 9:15 am, and 1:00 pm. Very popular—book early! Cruiser reviews are very positive: The "friendly" captain takes you out to a "beautiful setting" to fish. There are "lots of fish," and "plenty to catch." Cruisers do note that there is no "head" (restroom) on the boat. All cruisers had a "great time" and considered it a "highlight" of their cruise. This excursion may be suspended without notice depending on the season and other conditions.

Fishing
Active
Ages 6 & up
$110
3 hours

Port Activity Worksheet

Use this worksheet to keep track of the activities and shore excursions you want to do most on your cruise. List your activities in order of preference—when booking shore excursions with Disney, you'll be more likely to get an excursion if you list a second and third choice along with the first. When you're ready to book your shore excursions through Disney, call 877-566-0968 from 7–60 days in advance of your sail date. Note that you cannot make excursion reservations until Disney has received your final payment for your cruise. Check off any excursions you've booked with a notation in the "Reserved?" column. Once you know what excursions you're confirmed for, circle them and cross off the others.

My sail date: _____ less 60 days = _____ (first reservation date)

Activity/Excursion	Location	Time	Cost	Reserved?	Notes
Port: _____ Date:					
1.					
2.					
3.					
Port: _____ Date:					
1.					
2.					
3.					
Port: _____ Date:					
1.					
2.					
3.					
Port: _____ Date:					
1.					
2.					
3.					
Port: _____ Date:					
1.					
2.					
3.					

Notes:

Introduction
Reservations
Staterooms
Dining
Activities
Ports of Call
Magic
Index

Cavorting in Port

We predict that some of your favorite cruise memories will be made at your ports of call! Below are tips to help you get the most out of your jaunts, as well as port memories to get you in the mood.

"If you want to mail a **postcard home from Castaway Cay** and get the Castaway Cay postmark (see page 16), be sure to bring some cash ashore. The post office on Castaway Cay is run by the Bahamian postal service, not Disney, so you can't use your shipboard charge. They do accept U. S. currency, however—bring small bills and change, as they can't always break large bills." – *by contributing author Mickey Morgan*

Midship with Mickey

Pack a disposable **underwater camera**! You'll love it when you swim and snorkel, and you won't worry about it getting wet or stolen.

The **Caribbean sun** is brutal. Be sure to wear sunscreen on your visits to the shore—you are likely to be in the sun more often than the shade. Sunglasses also come in handy against the glare of the bright sun off sidewalks and water. And don't forget hats with wide brims to protect your face and neck, and shield your eyes. You'll find a soft fabric, crushable hat with a chin strap to keep it on your head is invaluable on shore, especially on active excursions.

"Go **snorkeling early** on Castaway Cay. As the day wears on, the crowds come and kick up a lot of sand. This severely reduces visibility. Go first thing in the morning, and if you are an adult, do a little snorkeling at the adult beach later. There is some old airplane wreckage in the adult beach area that is usually loaded with colorful fish." – *contributed by Disney cruiser Bruce Dana*

Magical Memories

"My sister and I did the 7-night land/sea package. I packed an underwater camera and it was one of the best things that I did. I got some great pictures of Castaway Cay from the water while I was swimming. I also used it on deck to finish the roll off and those are among my favorite photos. (Be sure to pack your camera in your carry-on to avoid x-ray damage.)"

...as told by Disney cruiser Marcie LaCava

"We were on the three-night cruise for my parent's 50th anniversary. While my 12-year-old son was swimming at Castaway Cay, a fish swam between his legs. That night at dinner he said that he just could not have fish to eat after his "close encounter" (and he LOVES fish) so he had cheese pizza."

...as told by Disney cruiser Tracy Brockway

Making Magic and Wonder

Is your mind still filled with nagging little questions? This chapter may just banish the last of those concerns. Among other topics, we'll discuss toddler care, special occasions, seasickness, meeting Disney characters, clearing U.S. Customs, how much to tip, and what happens when you arrive back in Port Canaveral. These are some of the little (and not so little) things that can make the difference between an ordinary vacation and a trip filled with magic and wonder.

Is your tot too small for the regular children's programs? We tour Flounder's Reef, the ship's childcare center. Children of all ages can get the lowdown on meeting Disney characters. Learn how to preserve fond memories with your own photographs and glossies from the ship's photographers. Do you have money left after shopping in port? We describe all the stores and shopping opportunities on board, too.

While modern cruises aren't the fancy dress extravaganzas they used to be, every cruise includes opportunities to dress up. In fact, the seven-night sailings include officially-designated formal and semi-formal nights (one of each). Here's where we button-down all the details on appropriate attire, tuxedo rentals, and other dress-up options. Do you want a real excuse to dress up? We describe special and celebrity cruises, and deliver tips for creating your own special celebrations on board, whether you're tying the knot or want to give a loved one an extra-special send-off.

Next, there's the business of staying healthy and avoiding that curse of the deep, *mal de mer* (seasickness). Plus, a few tips on keeping up-to-date with your business back home.

It's also time to set your feet back on shore in Port Canaveral. Nobody likes this part, but now is the perfect time to explore the mysteries of "customary gratuities" (tipping), the rules and regulations of U.S. Customs, and the rituals of debarkation. We've had a great time cruising with you! Alas, that it had to end so soon. Bon voyage!

Cruising With Kids

Disney cruises and kids go together like peanut butter and jelly! We've had the pleasure of cruising with kids several times, with Dave's daughter Allie (9), Dave's nieces Kayleigh (13), Melanie (11), and Nina (10), Dave's second cousins Bradley (2) and Andrea (1), and most recently with Jennifer's nieces Megan (3) and Natalie (2). So we've been "around the deck," so to speak. Here are our tips for happy cruising with kids, along with tips from Jennifer's sister Kim Larner, mother of Megan and Natalie.

Introduce kids to Disney cruising before you go. Order the free video/DVD, have a family showing, and encourage your child(ren) to watch it on their own. It builds excitement, and also breeds familiarity, which is important to kids.

Your stateroom choice depends on your budget, but spring for an **outside stateroom** if possible. Kim says, "The split-bathroom units were very convenient and the large porthole made the room feel very open." These are big pluses when cruising with kids.

Kids absolutely love **swimming**, and the pools onboard are lots of fun. They also tend to be very crowded, however, and "you'll need to keep an eagle eye on your kids in the pools," according to Kim. She also suggests you make time to go swimming in the ocean at Castaway Cay—"the kids loved the warm water, and found crabs and starfish."

The **Oceaneer Club and Lab** tend to be big hits with most kids, though there can be downfalls. Allie tells us she was disappointed when she was put in the age 8 to 9 group and her cousin Nina was in the 10 to 12 group. And while Megan fell in love with the Oceaneer Club, she had a "potty accident" due to the exciting and unfamiliar environment, and wasn't allowed back in to the Club for a while. Certainly let the kids know about the Oceaneer Club and Lab before you go, but don't build it up too much in the event there are disappointments. Kim also suggests you "put your kid(s) in the Club/Lab for at least one of your meals to allow you the chance to really enjoy the dinner."

Speaking of meals, **early seating** tends to work much better than late seating for kids, especially young kids. Kim says, "the kids enjoyed the start and end of the meal, but were impatient during the middle." Older kids like Allie, Nina, and Melanie also get impatient, and may beg to leave the table before the meal is over. Consider letting them go to the Oceaneer Club or Lab if it's appropriate.

The **stage shows** are popular with kids, though very young kids may find it hard to sit through one of these hour-long shows. On-stage characters can present difficulties, too. Kim says that "both Megan and Natalie wanted to go up to the stage and give the characters a hug, and Natalie cried about not being able to do it for some time."

Of all the **cruise activities**, it's most common for kids to love swimming and Castaway Cay the best. You may want to take at least two swimsuits so you always have a dry one.

Overall, we've observed that a Disney cruise is **better than a Walt Disney World vacation** when you're with young kids. There's less walking, less overstimulation, less exhaustion, and just as much magic. On every Disney vacation we've gone on with young kids (under 5), the kids (and their parents) were much happier on the ship than at the parks. Kim says, "The cruise was the best part of our vacation."

Childcare

Midship with Mickey

The Disney ships have a lot for adults to do during the days and in the evenings. Palo, Route 66/Beat Street, and the Quiet Cove pool are calling to you, and they don't allow children. As much as you love the little darlings, it's nice to get away from the kids for some nice, quiet, adult time. Parents rejoice! Disney has some of the **best childcare** on the high seas.

Kids at least three years of age and potty-trained can enjoy supervised play at the Oceaneer Club or Lab—see pages 123–124 for all the details. If your child is between twelve weeks old and three years old, or not yet toilet-trained, you can use the **Flounder's Reef Nursery**. Flounder's is the ships' full-service childcare center located on deck 5 aft, beside the Buena Vista Theatre. The nursery is equipped with a playroom filled with age-appropriate toys, Disney movies, baby bouncers, and rocking chairs, as well as a separate sleeping room with cribs for infants and mats for toddlers. A smaller third room holds changing tables.

Reservations are required for Flounder's, and it's one of those things that you need to do very soon after boarding, because it's a popular place. Only a limited number of spaces (about 20) are available, as Disney strives to maintain a child/counselor ratio of 4:1 (infants) and 6:1 (toddlers). Crew members take reservations in Flounder's on your departure day, typically from 1:30 pm to 3:30 pm and again from 4:00 pm to 5:00 pm. Disney may limit the number of spaces you can reserve in order to accommodate more guests. After the initial reservation period, reservations are offered on a space-available basis. If you are planning to dine at Palo, coordinating the two reservations can be tricky. Get your Palo reservation first, then visit Flounder's and indicate that you have a Palo reservation.

Unlike the Oceaneer Club and Lab, which are included in your fare, Flounder's Reef Nursery charges **$6/hour** for the first child and $5/hour for additional children. There is a two-hour minimum. Flounder's is open daily, typically from 1:00 pm to 4:00 pm and again from 6:00 pm to midnight, though times may vary for at-sea days and some port days may offer extended hours to accommodate guests going on shore excursions.

When you **check in** your young cruisers to the nursery, bring diapers, wipes, and anything else that may be needed, such as pre-made bottles, pacifiers, security items (such as a blanket), sippy cups, and/or jars of baby food. See page 106 for more infant feeding tips.

You will be given a pager when you drop off your child, in the event you need to be contacted for any reason during your child's stay. Please note that no medication can be dispensed to a child by a crew member, and children with obvious symptoms of illness will not be accepted.

Tip: Parents **traveling with infants** may be able to request a Diaper Genie for their stateroom. Ask your stateroom host/hostess. If a Diaper Genie isn't available (we've heard they may be phasing them out), just toss used diapers in the trash, as it is emptied frequently. Pack & play cribs are provided. Bring along extra-warm jammies as crib blankets are neither provided nor recommended.

Jennifer's niece Natalie gets into the spirit of things in the playroom

© MediaMarx, Inc.

Photographs

Say cheese! Whether you're taking your own photos or letting a ship's photographer snap the shot, a Disney cruise is the perfect photo op!

Bring your own camera and plenty of film and batteries. Should you forget this essential bit of cruising equipment, you can buy Pentax and Olympus cameras ($200+), Kodak single-use cameras, film, and batteries onboard. We use a digital camera, which allows us to take as many photos as we like and not bother with film—we recommend it! Camcorders are also very popular—if you bring yours, be aware that the high humidity in the Caribbean can be a problem for your camcorder. To keep moisture out of your camcorder, keep it in the shade whenever possible and allow at least 30 minutes to adjust to different environments (such as when you go from your air-conditioned stateroom to a steamy port).

Onboard photo processing is offered in **Shutters Photo Gallery** (deck 4 aft). Drop off your film before 11:00 am and it'll be ready the same day by 5:00 pm—otherwise your photos are ready the next day. For every roll of film you develop at Shutters, you get a free photo of the ship and a trading pin (as of press time). Developing costs are about $5 for 12 4x6 prints or $10 for 24 (double prints are 35 cents each). Shutters processes regular 35mm film and Advantix film, as well as prints from underwater, single-use, and digital cameras.

Ship's photographers are everywhere. In fact, the moment you board the ship, you'll be asked to pose for a portrait. Your embarkation photo will be available in Shutters between 5:00 pm and 11:00 pm that same evening. Candid and posed photos may be snapped throughout the cruise—just swing by Shutters to see the photos. Photos taken during the day are typically available in the evening, while photos taken after 5:00 pm or so are displayed the following day. Note that older photos are removed from the displays to make room for new ones. If you aren't sure which photos you want to buy, collect all your photos and stack them together on the display—they're more likely to stay available if you do this. Also, be sure to save your receipts, as you may get quantity discounts. And consider waiting until the end of the cruise to purchase photo packages. If you need photo reprints after your cruise, negatives may be archived for up to ten weeks after your cruise—call 800-772-3470 ext. 11.

Dave poses for a portrait in the atrium

The **professional photos** at Shutters come in two sizes: 6 x 8 and 8 x 10. The 6 x 8 prints are $10 each, or you can get a package (10 for $85, 15 for $120, or 20 for $150). The 8 x 10 prints are $20 each. If you go with a 6 x 8 package, be aware that the formal portraits, as well as some other shots, only come in 8 x 10. Purchased photos are placed in flexible cardboard folders, or you can buy padded folders or frames. Note that these photos are copyrighted and you can be fined up to $500 for unauthorized duplication at a photo lab—download a copyright release waiver at http://www.image.com/guest-postcruise.htm.

Shutters is **open** all day on at-sea days, and from about 5:00 pm to 11:00 pm on port days. Note that Shutters is also open debarkation morning from 6:45am to 8:30 am. We recommend you avoid the last night and morning, as they are incredibly busy.

Shopping Onboard

Both ships sport a 5,500-square-foot shopping area—combine that with extra shopping opportunities aboard and great shopping in port (see chapter 6), and you'll find it easy to shop 'til you drop anchor. As you might imagine, prices are a bit on the high side, but the quality is excellent.

Due to U.S. Customs regulations, the onboard shops **cannot be open while in port**. Check your *Personal Navigator* for shop operating hours, and keep in mind that the last night of your cruise is your last opportunity to shop. And before you splurge on that big-ticket item, see page 248 for details on customs allowances.

Mickey's Mates (deck 4 midship) is the Disney character and logo shop, filled with stuffed animals, souvenirs, logowear, trading pins, postcards, etc.

Treasure Ketch (deck 4 midship) is right across the hall from Mickey's Mates, and offers more upscale and practical merchandise, such as resortwear, jewelry (including loose gemstones and "gold by the inch"), collectibles, toiletries, film, batteries, books, and magazines. Tax-free gifts are also available here, such as watches and sunglasses. Collectors, check your *Personal Navigator* for Captain's signings—he'll sign posters, hats, T-shirts, pins, and ship models for free, increasing their value.

The shopping area onboard the ship

Preludes Snacks (deck 4 forward) is a small bar that sells packaged snacks such as candy bars, chips, and popcorn. Typically open from 6:00 pm–10:00 pm.

Up Beat/Radar Trap (deck 3 forward) offers duty-free liquor (over 45 brands), fragrances (over 60 brands), cigars (over 25 brands), and cigarettes, as well as snacks, candy bars, cameras, film, and batteries. Note that duty-free orders are delivered to your stateroom on the last night of your cruise—yes, that means you cannot consume that liquor you bought here while you're onboard. The shop is typically open evenings until midnight.

Shutters (deck 4 aft) sells compact cameras, frames, and photos. See previous page.

Silent Auction (deck 4 forward) features collectible Disney Cruise Line items auctioned to the highest bidder. See page 139 for all the details.

Pin Trading Station (deck 3 or 4 midship) opens nightly on the port side of the Atrium Lobby, typically from 7:30 pm–8:30 pm. This is a great place for limited edition pins.

A pool-side merchandise cart may be parked near the **Mickey Pool** on certain days.

Let's not forget the **onboard gift brochure** you receive with your cruise documentation before you embark—any items ordered from this brochure will be waiting for you in your stateroom when you board.

Check the **"On-Board Shopping" supplement** distributed with your *Personal Navigator* for daily specials, featured items, operating hours, and a list of where to find what onboard.

Shops are **busiest** from 7:00 pm–10:00 pm, so you may want to go earlier or later.

Formal and Semi-Formal Occasions

Perhaps we're suckers for tradition, but we simply love the elegance of formal nights at sea.

On the **3- and 4-night** Wonder cruises, there are no official formal nights. Instead, your semi-formal nights are determined by your dining rotation. On your Triton's night, you can wear semi-formal attire, such as a jacket for men and a dress or pantsuit for women, but it isn't required. Wear semi-formal attire for Palo. The other nights are casual or tropical.

On the **7-night** Disney Magic cruises, you have one semi-formal night—day 2 on Eastern Caribbean itineraries and day 3 on Western Caribbean itineraries—and one formal night on day 6 of both itineraries. Formal night is "black tie optional." Many men wear tuxedos and women typically wear long evening gowns, but semi-formalwear is fine, too. During the formal and semi-formal nights, the crew sets up backdrops and takes formal portraits of your family (see page 236). In addition, you are asked to wear semi-formal attire when your dining rotation moves to Lumière's restaurant.

Men's Formalwear: Fortunately, you don't have to rent a tuxedo and haul it across the country and back. Cruise Line Formalwear supplies formalwear on the Disney Cruise Line, and cruise-long rentals range from $85 to $120 (this price includes everything but the shoes), plus accessories ($5 to $20). Order at least two weeks before you cruise with the order form in your cruise documents, online at http://www.cruiselineformal.com or on the phone at 800-551-5091. You can also view the tuxedos and accessories on their web site. When you order a tuxedo from them, it'll arrive in your stateroom on your first day aboard (try it on right away to see if it needs any alterations). When the cruise ends, just leave it in your room. Note that Cruise Line Formal does keep extra inventory onboard for exchanges and last-minute rentals. Another option is to buy a tuxedo (try a local tux rental shop or http://www.ebay.com). Perhaps you'd like a Disney-themed vest and tie set to go with your own tux? If so, check on the Internet at http://www.tuxedosdirect.com.

Jennifer and Dave
decked out at Palo

Women's Formalwear: If you don't happen to have an evening gown or old bridesmaid's gown hanging in your closet, you can make do with a nice dress on both semi-formal and formal evenings. A "little black dress" is a popular choice. Feel free to wear your dress more than once on your cruise—accessorize to change the look. Consider adding a wrap for chilly dining rooms. Formal evenings see most women in long evening gowns—try shopping the department stores (such as J.C.Penney's) for good deals. You could also try Chadwick's (http://www.chadwicks.com) and Victoria's Secret (http://www.victoriassecret.com).

Kids' Formalwear: Obviously, many parents don't want to buy their kids nice suits or dresses for a cruise because they grow out of them so quickly. Dressing the boys in slacks and a button-down shirt is just fine. If your boy really wants to dress up like Dad in a tux, special order rentals are available through Cruise Line Formal. You can also look for a good deal at http://www.ebay.com or at http://www.tux4boys.com. The girls look great in sun dresses, and this is the perfect opportunity to wear Disney princess dresses (available beforehand at the Disney Store and onboard in Mickey's Mates). Of course, that's if they even dine with you. Some kids prefer the company of their peers and have dinner with the Club/Lab.

Special/Celebrity Cruises

Looking for something a bit special on your next cruise? Disney plans many special cruises each year—some are once-in-a-lifetime events, while others just feature celebrity guests. Here are some past and upcoming events to give you an idea of what to expect:

Inaugural Cruises—The first sailing of a new ship, or the first sailing of a ship on a new itinerary is a big deal. On the up side, you get the thrill of being "the first" to sail, and you may get a few extra treats—on the Western Caribbean Inaugural Cruise in May 2002, we were treated to a Mexican mariachi band before embarking, given special "fans" to wave as we set sail, and presented with complimentary champagne glasses. On the down side, an inaugural cruise often doesn't have all the glitches worked out yet (though we didn't notice anything wrong on our inaugural cruise). There are no dates set for the next inaugural cruise (new ship? new itinerary? who knows!), so watch our web site for details.

Celebrity Cruises—Many cruises have at least a minor celebrity or notable speaker, while others feature bigger names. For example, on the Disney Wonder in February, Roger Ebert and Richard Roeper do their annual Film Festival at Sea. A special package (for $175 extra) includes a sail-away cocktail reception with the famous film critics, screenings of four of their favorite films, open discussion sessions, and a book signing. Most celebrity guests have some connection with Disney, and include actors, artisans, and authors–recent guests have included Ernie Sabella (voice of "Pumbaa" in Disney's The Lion King—see photo below), Leslie Iwerks (granddaughter of Ub Iwerks), Raven, and former presidents George H.W. Bush and Jimmy Carter. Disney rarely announces their celebrities or speakers ahead of time, but you can call 888-DCL-2500 to inquire.

Holiday Cruises—If your cruise coincides with a major holiday, you can bet Disney has something special planned. Halloween cruises have costume contests, Thanksgiving cruises offer traditional dinners, December cruises feature magical holiday decorations and special holiday events, and so on. New Years Eve cruises are very, very popular—book early if you're interested in one. Note also that religious holidays (Ash Wednesday, Easter, Passover, Hanukkah, Christmas, etc.) have clergy onboard for observances.

Fan Cruises—Disney fans love to cruise together, and usually one group or another is organizing a group cruise. We're doing a 4-night PassPorter reader cruise as part of MouseFest 2004 on December 5-9, 2004—check http://www.passporter.com/gathering.htm for all the details (see page 241, too). And when your authors are cruising, we like to host a casual meet onboard—you can get details on these meets at the above address also.

© MediaMarx, Inc., used with permission of Ernie Sabella

Other Cruises—Keep an ear out for more special cruises, such as pin trading cruises, Disney Vacation Club and/or Annual Passholder cruises, and movie premieres. We expect that if the Disney Magic does move to the West Coast for a couple of months in summer 2005, there will be plenty of fanfare and special treatment for cruisers! Watch our web site for details!

Ernie Sabella and Dave
at Castaway Cay

Celebrating Special Occasions

We firmly believe there's always something to celebrate... even if it's just the fact that you're going on a cruise! And, of course, there are always birthdays, anniversaries, and holidays to remember. If you are celebrating a special occasion while you're onboard, be sure to let your travel agent or Disney reservation agent know when you book your cruise, or at least three weeks before you sail.

Bon Voyage Celebrations—Why not throw a party before you depart for your cruise? Invite your friends and family and make 'em jealous! Or if you happen to know someone going on a cruise, surprise them with a send-off party or a gift in their stateroom (see sidebar below). And don't forget about a celebratory drink when you board! Note: Only passengers are allowed on board or in the terminal, so parties with non-cruisers must take place before your arrival at the cruise terminal.

Birthdays—Let Disney know about your celebration in advance, and you'll be serenaded by your serving team and receive a small cake. You may also get a birthday pin! See the photo of Jennifer's Mom and her cake on page 97.

Honeymoons—The Disney Cruise Line is popular with honeymooning couples, and Disney offers some "romance" packages for the celebration (see page 41). Be sure to let Disney know about your honeymoon even if you aren't on a package. If you need help planning a honeymoon cruise, MouseEarVacations.com has agents who specialize in this—see page 265.

Anniversaries—We celebrated Dave's parents' 50th wedding anniversary aboard the Wonder in 2001—it was magical! Again, tell Disney about your celebration ahead of time and you may get a surprise.

Holidays—Disney does the holidays in grand style, particularly on Christmas and New Years Eve—look for Santa Goofy, a three-deck-tall tree, holiday feasts, a New Years Eve party, and a New Years Day tailgate party.

Tip: **Decorate your stateroom** and/or stateroom door in honor of your celebration! You can order basic stateroom decorations from Disney (see sidebar below) and they'll put them up before you arrive. Or bring your own decorations from home. Another fun idea is to buy (or make) magnets or banners with which to decorate your metal stateroom door (see photo).

Door decorations for Dave's "Who Wants To Be A Millionaire —Play It!" winning cruise

---

Stateroom Gifts

Disney Cruise Line offers a variety of gifts that you can order ahead of time and have waiting for you in your stateroom (or that of a friend or family member). Check the brochure that comes with your cruise documents, visit http://www.disneycruise.com and search on "gifts," or call 800-601-8455. If you're looking for something extra special, the Cape Canaveral-based company, The Perfect Gift, delivers delightful cruise baskets at good prices—you can even custom design your gift baskets. Call 800-950-4559 or visit http://www.theperfectgift.cc for more information.

Reunions and Group Cruises

A Disney cruise is ideal for a reunion or group event. Unlike a gathering on land, say at Walt Disney World, the Disney cruise allows groups to stay within close proximity of one another, offers a number of built-in activities and meals, and offers fun reunion packages. We've planned a number of reunions and group cruises over the years—here are our tips for a successful gathering:

Pick the best dates. Consult with the members of your group to find the dates that work best for their schedules and pocketbooks. While spring and summer breaks may be best for those with kids, those are also the priciest and may prevent some from joining you. Whenever possible, go for the less-expensive seasons, such as January, February, May, or early December.

If you're cruising as a family or small group, it may be possible to select staterooms in **close proximity** to one another, which facilitates communications and meetings. But if you cannot, don't fret—the ship isn't that big of a place.

Keep in **close communication** with your group both before and during your cruise. Simple notes or newsletters, via e-mail or on paper, can be very helpful to educating your group and notifying them of events and changes. Once you're onboard, you can leave one another voice mail and notes on stateroom doors.

When you book your cruise, let Disney know that you're traveling as a group and ask them to **link the reservations together** so you can dine in close proximity to one another. The dining room tables usually hold up to eight guests—on one of our family reunion cruises we had a family of 16, and we were seated at two tables of eight, end to end. We've found that having this time together at dinner is very important to the success of a group cruise. Keep in mind, however, that everyone in your party needs to be on the same dinner seating—discuss early vs. late seating with your group before making a unilateral decision.

If your group wants to **dine at Palo**, plan to get to the reservation session early! Large groups are hard to accommodate and space goes quickly. Tip: Only one member of your party needs to make the reservations for your group—just be sure to have everyone's names and staterooms handy.

Don't expect or try to do everything together. The beauty of a Disney cruise is that you don't have to hang together all the time to enjoy your group. You'll inevitably do some activities together during the day, bump into one another in the corridors, and then enjoy quality time together at dinner.

PassPorter Gathering and MouseFest Cruise

Interested in joining other PassPorter readers and Disney Internet fans on a fun cruise? Each year in early December we host a 4-night cruise—this year it is December 5-9, 2004. We plan all sorts of special activities and enjoy the company of like-minded individuals. And there are fabulous deals available through MouseEarVacations.com, too. If you're interested in joining us, visit http://www.passporter.com/gathering.htm for information and an RSVP form. Everyone is invited and welcome to join us!

Weddings and Vow Renewals

Ah, what is more romantic (or simple) than getting married or renewing your vows aboard a cruise ship? Disney Cruise Line makes it very easy to do both, and when compared to a land-based wedding, the prices are a good value, too!

First, if you're interested in either a wedding or vow renewal ceremony onboard a Disney ship, be aware that this isn't something you can arrange on your own. You'll need Disney's assistance, and you'll need to purchase their wedding or vow renewal package. To get started, visit http://www.disneycruise.com, click "Reservations," then choose either the "Weddings at Sea" package or the "Vow Renewal" package. This is where you'll find prices and package details. You can also call 321-939-4610 for information.

When you're **ready to book**, call a professional Disney wedding consultant at 321-939-4610 or contact your travel agent. You can book a wedding or vow renewal up to 12 months in advance, though it is not necessary to book it so early—you can plan a cruise wedding or vow renewal in as little as a month or two (based on availability).

Ceremony locations vary. Most wedding ceremonies are held outdoors at the Head's Up Bar at the far end of the family beach on Castaway Cay—the lagoon and ship provide a beautiful backdrop. You can also get married in either Sessions (Magic) or Cadillac Lounge (Wonder) on deck 3 forward. The lounges are also the typical spots for Vow Renewal ceremonies. Other locations may be possible under certain circumstances—inquire with your Disney wedding consultant.

Wedding ceremonies are **officiated** by an administrator of the Bahamas. Vow renewal ceremonies are usually performed by the Captain or a high-ranking officer.

Those getting married should note that you'll have a **private**, **legal ceremony** in the cruise terminal before your ship leaves Port Canaveral. This means you're technically married for your entire voyage, even though your public ceremony happens later in the cruise.

The **"Disney Weddings" e-book** by Andrea Rotondo Hospidor may be helpful, even though it concentrates on Walt Disney World weddings. Many of the tips on working with Disney's Fairy Tale Weddings department apply, as does much of the information on intimate weddings and vow renewals. For more details on this e-book, visit http://www.yourfairytale.com. The book is $19.95 and available for immediate download.

A Castaway Cay wedding

Preventing Seasickness

Sea sickness isn't life threatening, but once you have it, you might think it is. Nothing can make you wish that you could just curl up and die faster than this scourge of the seas. Thankfully, sea sickness is not a problem for most cruisers—Disney cruises in some of the calmest waters in the world and has excellent stabilizers. But if you do find yourself one of the unfortunate few, there are cures for sea sickness. Let's take a look at them:

✔ **Purely natural—**Go topside, take deep breaths, get some fresh air, and look at the horizon. The worst thing you can do is stay in your stateroom. Sea sickness is caused by the confusion between what your inner ear senses and what your eyes see. If you can look at something steady, it helps your brain synchronize these. Eventually your brain will get used to the motion and you get your "sea legs," but that can take a day or two. Drink lots of water and have some mild food, such as saltine crackers—avoid fatty and salty foods, and eat lightly.

✔ **Herbs—**Ginger is reported to help reduce sea sickness. It comes in pill and cookie form—even ginger ale can help. It's best to begin taking this in advance of feeling sick.

✔ **Bonine, or "Dramamine Less Drowsy Formula"—**These are brand names of Meclizine, which has far fewer side effects than its older cousin Dramamine (which we don't recommend). Try it at home before your cruise to check for side effects, then take it a few hours before departure for maximum effectiveness. Note that Bonine is only for those 12 years or older; use Dramamine (original formula) for kids ages 2 to 12. Tip: The onboard medical facility (discussed on the next page) provides free chewable Meclizine tablets (25 mg.) from a dispenser next to its door on deck 1 forward.

✔ **Sea bands—**These are elastic wrist bands that operate by applying pressure to the Nei Kuan acupressure point on each wrist by means of a plastic stud, thereby preventing sea sickness. Some people swear by them, some say that they don't work. Either way, they are inexpensive (unless you buy them on the ship) and have no medical side effects. They don't yet come in designer colors to match your formal evening gown, however.

✔ **Scopolamine Transdermal Patch—**Available by prescription only. It is the most effective preventative with the least drowsiness, but it also comes with the most side effects, such as dry mouth and dizziness. For more information about scopolamine, speak to your doctor and visit http://www.transdermscop.com.

✔ **Ship Location—**A low deck, midship stateroom is generally considered to be the location on a ship where you'll feel the least movement. If you know you're prone to seasickness, consider requesting a stateroom on decks 1-2, midship. But once you're onboard and you find yourself feeling seasick, the best thing to do is get out of your stateroom, go to deck 4 midship, and lie down in one of the padded deck chairs—then use the tips noted in "Purely Natural" above.

✔ **Choose Excursions Wisely—**Those prone to motion sickness may want to avoid shore excursions that rely heavily on smaller boats such as ferries and sailboats. Read the excursion descriptions in chapter 6 carefully for mentions of motion sickness or rough seas. If you don't want to miss out on anything, begin taking your preferred seasickness remedy well in advance of the excursion.

Introduction
Reservations
Staterooms
Dining
Activities
Ports of Call
Magic
Index

Staying Healthy

Staying healthy is easy with some preparation and knowledge. Folks who are already healthy may only have to worry about getting seasick (see the previous page) or picking up a virus. Here's what you can do to prevent illness:

Getting a virus is less likely than seasickness, but still possible—any time you get people together for more than two or three days at a time you're going to have some percentage become ill. Cruise ships are significantly less vulnerable than schools, hotels, nursing homes, and restaurants, contrary to the media attention the Norwalk-like virus received in November/December 2002—cruise ships account for 10% of the outbreaks, while restaurants, nursing homes, and schools account for over 70%. The Centers for Disease Control (CDC) report that normally 1-2% of a cruise population gets sick on a regular basis; during the Norwalk-like virus epidemics, this number may only rise to 2-4%. Nonetheless, Disney takes many precautions to avoid illness on its ships, including thoroughly disinfecting surfaces that are touched, encouraging hand washing, providing hand wipes in particular situations, and refusing passage to visibly ill passengers to reduce the risk of transmitting a virus to others.

To avoid catching a bug, get a full night's sleep before you embark, eat well, drink lots of water, and wash your hands thoroughly and frequently. Hand-washing cannot be emphasized enough. Wash your hands for at least 15 seconds after using the bathroom, after changing a diaper, and before handling, preparing, or consuming food. Regular soap and water does the trick—there's no need for antibacterial soaps (in fact, the Centers for Disease Control suggest that antibacterial soaps may contribute to the problem, and suggest you do not use them). Alcohol-based hand sanitizer can be used as a supplement in between times hands are washed, but it should not replace soap and water. There's no need to bring your own Lysol either—all surfaces are disinfected before you board as well as while you're underway (besides, Lysol does nothing to stop the Norwalk-like virus). Tip: To make sure both you and your kids wash your hands for long enough, try singing or humming the "Happy Birthday" song slowly while washing your hands—when the song ends, your hands are clean.

If you get sick, be aware that reporting illness to the cruise staff is taken seriously—the cruise line is required to report any onboard cases of gastrointestinal illness to the CDC. You may be required to visit the medical facility onboard (see below), and if you're found to have a gastrointestinal illness, you may be restricted to your stateroom to avoid passing the illness to others. And if you're sick when you check-in at the terminal, you may need to visit a medical professional before boarding—you may even be refused passage.

Viruses aside, there's one medical problem that far too many cruisers contract during their cruise—**sunburn**. Bring that sunscreen (SPF of 30 or higher) and use it. And wear hats and cover-ups whenever possible. Don't take your chances with a sunburn.

As much as we don't like to think about it, accidents happen and guests get sick. Knowing that this is unavoidable, Disney has put a well-equipped **medical facility** aboard—it's equipped with modern medical equipment such as cardiac life support equipment, ventilators, and an X-ray machine. Two doctors and three registered nurses are on staff. The care, we hear, is excellent and the fees are reasonable. Any medical care you receive is billed to your stateroom account and you bill your insurance company separately.

Doing Business Onboard

We know, we know... "work" is a four-letter word on a cruise. If you can avoid your work entirely on the cruise, we heartily recommend it! Alas, we know better than anyone that sometimes your business doesn't take a vacation just because you do. If you need to keep up with work while you're cruising, here are our tried-and-true tips:

Phone Calls—You have three options when making phone calls: use Disney's ship-to-shore phone system (the phone in your stateroom) for $6.95/minute, use your cellular phone when in port or sailing past islands with cell roaming service, or use a pay phone in port. Your stateroom phone system is detailed on page 85. If you opt to bring a cell phone, call your wireless provider to ensure that you have international roaming.

Laptop Computers—We always bring along our laptop, even though we cannot connect it to the Internet. Typically, we use the laptop to download photos from the digital camera, but on one cruise we had to manage our online bookstore. We viewed order information at the Internet Cafe, and typed the orders into our laptop. We printed the order information on our portable printer and had Guest Services fax it to our warehouse. We had no trouble using either the laptop or the printer onboard. Be sure to bring all necessary cables!

Internet Access—We've devoted two full pages to the Internet Cafe, on pages 132-133. If you're relying on Internet access to keep up with work, keep in mind that the Internet Cafe is the least busy earlier in the day and late at night. Note also that the Internet Cafe is not open on debarkation morning.

Faxes—You can send and receive faxes from the Guest Services desk (deck 3 midship). Cost is the same as ship-to-shore phone calls—$6.95/minute. We faxed several sheets during a 4-night cruise and found that each page takes about one minute to fax, though fax transmission time does depend on the density of the page.

Copies—The Guest Services desk is also the place to have copies made.

Meeting Space—Both Disney ships have small conference rooms available for rent. Additionally, public spaces may also be rented at certain times. You can also get audio-visual equipment. Call Disney for details.

Tip: If your work is portable, take it outside to one of the patio tables behind Topsider's/ Beach Blanket Buffet (deck 9 aft) or enjoy the solitude of the small area on deck 7 aft.

Joining the Ship's Crew

Ever thought of working on a Disney ship? If you are at least 21 years old, there are job opportunities. From what we understand it takes a huge time commitment (you typically sign a six-month contract and work about 70–80 hours a week) and it's difficult to be away from home for the long stretches required. On the flip side, Disney does offer several perks, such as crew-only areas (including a beach on Castaway Cay and an onboard pool), free theme park admission, and so on. If you'd like to learn more, call the job line at 407-566-SHIP or visit http://www.dcljobs.com.

Introduction
Reservations
Staterooms
Dining
Activities
Ports of Call
Magic
Index

Disney Characters

One of the benefits of a Disney cruise is the opportunity to meet your favorite Disney characters—you won't find them on any other cruise in the world. Typically, the Disney celebrities joining you on your cruise include Mickey, Minnie, Goofy, Pluto, Donald, Chip, and Dale (often in tropical attire) as well as appearances from special "face" characters like Cinderella, Snow White, and Alice. Here's where to meet your Disney friends onboard:

Character Appearances—The Lobby Atrium (both decks 3 and 4) is a popular gathering place for Disney friends, typically in the evenings for photo opportunities. If you forget your camera, there are often ship's photographers to snap a shot. You'll also find characters in the terminal before you board, at deck parties, the kids' clubs, and near the Mickey Pool. For schedules, check your *Personal Navigator*, the Lobby Atrium, or outside Shutters, or call 7-PALS on your stateroom phone.

Character Autographs: Bring a notebook or autograph book to the character meets— you can buy them in Mickey's Mates or just make one at home before you board (see photo on right). Take a photo of the Disney character autographing the book and you can later attach a copy of the picture to each autographed page—this makes a great keepsake! Another fun idea is to get a T-shirt or pillowcase autographed. Just bring a T-shirt, pillowcase, or other item that can be autographed (it can be from Disney or just blank), place it and a permanent marker in a bag labelled with your stateroom number, take it to Guest

© MediaMarx, Inc.

A home-made autograph book

Services (deck 3 midship) on your first day, and request that it be signed by characters. There is no charge for this service. Check back with Guest Services in a few days to pick up your autographed item! Note: This special service could be discontinued at any time.

Character Breakfasts—Guests on the seven-night cruises get the opportunity to mingle with Mickey, Minnie, Goofy, Pluto, Chip and Dale at a character breakfast in Parrot Cay. For more details, see page 100.

Tea With Wendy—This is a special character event on the seven-night cruise. Check your *Personal Navigator* for the day and time to pickup tickets (at no extra charge) and arrive early—this is a popular event and tickets go quickly. The half-hour "tea" is held in Studio Sea (deck 4 midship) on certain afternoons. As you might have guessed, the tea is hosted by Wendy Darling (from Disney's Peter Pan), who demonstrates the proper way to serve tea, and tells a story. Chocolate chip cookies and iced tea are served. The event is attended predominantly by young girls, but everyone is welcome—young or old, male or female. After tea, guests may greet Wendy personally and get a photograph with her. Tip: Crew members select two boys from the audience to play John and Michael, Wendy's brothers. Note: Some cruisers have reported this event may be available on shorter cruises (3- and 4-night cruises), but we have not yet been able to verify this.

Tipping and Feedback

Tipping is your way of thanking the crew members for their fine service. Here are the recommended gratuity guidelines for each guest:

Crew Member/Service	Per Night	3-Night	4-Night	7-Night
Dining Room Server	~$3.75	$11.00	$14.75	$25.75
Dining Room Asst. Server	~$2.75	$8.00	$10.75	$18.75
Dining Room Head Server	~$1.00	$2.75	$3.75	$6.50
Stateroom Host/Hostess	~$3.60	$10.75	$14.50	$25.25
Palo Server	Your discretion (on top of the $10/person service charge)			
Bartender/Lounge Server	If no tip was automatically added, 10% to 15%			
Room Service	Your discretion (usually $1 to $2/person)			
Kids' Counselors	Not necessary, but do reward good service			
Shore Excursion Tour Guide	$1 to $2/person			
Baggage Porters (at terminal)	$1 to $2/bag			

Feel free to **tip more** for crew members that provided exceptional service and less to any crew members whose performance was substandard. It's your chance to reward your favorite crew members. Don't forget to tip on your children's behalf also.

On your last day, **tip envelopes** will be left in your stateroom so you may give gratuities to the first four crew members noted in the chart above. Fill them with cash, or charge the tips to your stateroom account at Guest Services and they will give you receipts to put in the envelopes (avoid Guest Services on the last evening—it's very busy). Give the filled envelopes to each crew member—servers typically receive theirs at the last dinner.

Tipping is a form of feedback for services received, but you can give **additional feedback** on your experience. Neither we nor Disney Cruise Line would be where we are today without your feedback. For instance, did you know that those obstructed-view category 7 staterooms we mentioned on page 77 were reclassified (and lowered in price) based on cruiser feedback? And even with PassPorter, our depth of detail is a direct reader request.

The night before you disembark a **questionnaire** is placed in your stateroom. Take the time to fill it out and deposit it in the collection boxes at breakfast the next morning or on the gangway. If you had problems, there is a very small section to describe what happened—if you need to communicate more, read on.

To send **detailed comments** (complaints or compliments) to Disney once you return home, write a letter and mail it to: DCL Guest Communications, P.O. Box 10238, Lake Buena Vista, FL 32830. You can also send e-mail to dcl.guest.communications@disneycruise.com or visit http://disney.go.com/mail/disneycruiseline. Disney is typically very responsive to guest feedback, and you should hear back from them within six weeks.

Contacting us at **PassPorter Travel Press** is even easier. E-mail feedback@passporter.com or send a letter to P.O. Box 3880, Ann Arbor, MI 48106. You can fill out a survey about this guidebook at http://www.passporter.com/dcl/survey.htm. We also recommend you visit http://www.passporter.com/dcl/register.htm to register your copy, which is another perfect opportunity to tell us what you think. When you register, we'll send back coupons good for discounts on future PassPorters and accessories!

Customs Allowances

Ah, U.S. Customs. While we dreaded customs on our first cruise, we quickly found that the rules aren't hard to understand, and the process is smooth if you pay attention. If you feel unsure about customs and debarkation in general, attend the debarkation talk on the afternoon of your Castaway Cay day (or catch it on TV in your stateroom later that evening).

You are required to declare everything that you purchased or were given as a gift on the ship, in your ports of call, and on Castaway Cay. Fill out the **U.S. Customs Declaration Form** left in your stateroom on your last night (extra forms are available at Guest Services) Fill it in and sign and date the form—you will hand it to customs during debarkation.

Each guest is allowed a **total duty-free allowance** of $800 (3- and 4-night cruises and 7-night Western Caribbean cruises) or $1200 (7-night Eastern Caribbean cruises)—these allowances were last increased on 11/4/2002. Liquor and tobacco have special limits. One liter of liquor per person over 21 years of age is exempt from duties (Eastern Caribbean cruisers are allowed four more liters from the Virgin Islands). One carton of cigarettes and 100 cigars (other than Cuban cigars, which are not allowed at all) are exempt (Eastern Caribbean cruisers can add four more cartons of cigarettes if purchased in St. Thomas). If you exceed the customs allowances, you must report to the Customs Inspector before you debark the ship—check the debarkation sheet left in your stateroom. If you exceed your customs allowances, you will need to have cash on hand to pay your duties.

Read more about the **U.S. Customs Laws** online at http://www.cbp.gov/xp/cgov/travel (click "Know Before You Go!"). Keep in mind that anything that you don't declare is considered smuggled—don't forget any items you won onboard. The duties on declared items are low, but the penalties for smuggled items are high. And don't try to carry off items that aren't allowed, such as fresh fruit or flowers—you can face a stiff fine. You'd be surprised how many try to "smuggle" a banana unwittingly (see photo).

© MediaMarx, Inc,

Fruit taken off the ship

Immigration and International Guests

As we mentioned earlier in the guidebook, international guests yield their passports before boarding the ship. U.S. Immigration requires that all non-U.S. guests (and anyone who joined the ship enroute) present themselves at every U.S. port of entry. International guests on all itineraries must go through immigration in Port Canaveral. On the 7-night Eastern Caribbean cruise, immigration inspection is also held at St. Thomas for all passengers (U.S. and non-U.S.). In both cases, you will be directed to reclaim your passport—the details will be on a note placed in your stateroom the evening before. Alas, immigration happens pretty early in the morning—typically at 5:30 am to 6:00 am. Be sure to bring all members of your party and your passport receipt. All guests must clear immigration before any guests can debark in St. Thomas or Port Canaveral.

Debarkation

You've had a wonderful time, but all good things must come to an end. Thankfully, debarkation is smooth sailing with Disney. If you've been on a cruise where they make you wait to be called before debarking, you're in for a treat. Disney, the world leader in crowd control, has figured out how to debark 2600 people seamlessly. Here's how it works:

First, you need to **settle your onboard account**. If you put a credit card on your account at check-in, you're all set. Otherwise, visit Guest Services (deck 3 midship) to pay the total with credit card, traveler's checks, or cash. Do this the day before you debark.

On your **last night aboard**, pack your bags, remove old cruise tags, and attach the new tags provided (more tags are at Guest Services if you need them). Don't forget to fill out the tags and make a note of the tag color. When you're ready, place your tagged luggage in the passageway by 11:00 pm–you will not see it again until you're off the ship. Thus, it's crucial that you pack a small day bag to hold your toiletries, nightclothes, and valuables. And don't forget to keep out an outfit (and shoes) to wear the next morning! If you're hoping to get off the ship quickly the next morning, consider keeping your luggage with you and carrying it off the ship yourself—not as convenient, but a bit quicker. This is a good time to fill out the customs forms placed in your stateroom (see previous page). Also, if you have a pager for the kids clubs, return it to deck 5 midship this evening.

On **debarkation morning**, take your day bags and go to breakfast in the same restaurant in which you dined the previous evening (unless you ate at Palo, in which case you go to the restaurant you would have been in). Guests with early seating eat at 6:45 am, while late seating guests eat at 8:00 am. If you prefer, you can get "early bird" coffee and Danish pastries at 6:00 am to 6:30 am at the Beverage Station (deck 9 aft) or a continental breakfast from 6:30 am to 8:00 am at Topsider's/Beach Blanket Buffet (deck 9 aft). Be aware that guests must vacate their staterooms by 8:00 am. Shutters is open from 7:00 am to 8:30 am, but all other shops are closed. Drop off your questionnaire (see page 247) at breakfast or as you debark. Typically the first guest debarks at 7:45 am and the last guest debarks at 9:45 am.

Now it's time to **say goodbye** to all your "family." After breakfast, go to the gangway (deck 3 midship), stroll off the ship with your day bags, and head off to Customs. Keep your photo I.D., birth certificate, and/or passport handy. At the Customs area, claim your checked baggage in the color-coded area. Photography is not allowed in the Customs area—keep your camera down to avoid complications. Pass through Customs (usually you just present your customs forms and walk right through) and you're soon in your Disney motorcoach, car, or limousine. Porters are available to help you—don't forget to tip them. If you're flying out of Orlando Airport, several airlines (American Airlines, Delta, Northwest, US Air, and Continental) give you the option of checking your bags at the port, just outside of Customs.

Castaway Club

Once you've got a Disney cruise under your belt, you're an automatic member of Disney's Castaway Club. As a Castaway Club member, you get perks for future cruises, such as a special toll-free number, special check-in area, onboard reception with ship officers, and free gift in your stateroom. If you don't receive any information on the Castaway Club after your cruise, call Disney at 888-DCL-2500 to request it.

Magical and Wonderful Tips

Creating a "magical" and "wonderful" cruise takes a dash of planning, a pinch of knowledge, and a bit of pixie dust! Here are some more tips:

"After 9/11, Disney cancelled all **bridge tours** when they heightened security, but recently started offering them again! Check your *Personal Navigator* for information on getting the complimentary tickets—tour spaces fill up quickly. If you'd like to get a peek at the bridge without the tour, head up to the Vista Spa's fitness/exercise room. There in front of the treadmills are windows looking down into the forward part of the bridge as well as a wonderful view out the two-story bridge windows. The bridge is most interesting to watch when the ship is entering or departing a port and there is more bridge activity."
— *by contributing author Mickey Morgan*

Write to us and **share your experiences, memories, and tips**. If we use them in a future edition, we'll credit you by name and send you a free copy when it's published! Write us at P.O. Box 3880, Ann Arbor, MI 48106 or e-mail us at feedback @passporter.com.

Magical Memories

"We took a three-night cruise on the Disney Wonder as a party of 15 celebrating our parents' 50th anniversary. We used the PassPorter Field Guide extensively in preparing and on ship. We wanted to make Mom and Dad feel extra special for their anniversary so we did a couple of special things. First, I printed copies of wedding pictures, baby pictures, family pictures, etc. on magnetic sheets and decorated their stateroom door with pictures and a 'Happy Anniversary' garland. This got a lot of attention from people passing by. We also told our servers at dinner about our celebration—they brought Mom and Dad a little 'Congratulations' cake after dinner on our last night. All in all, my parents had a magical trip and felt like celebrities."

...*as told by Disney cruiser Kim Havick*

"To make the Magic last, we sat down a few days after the cruise and gathered all the photos we'd taken, including those with the underwater camera. We opened a special bottle of wine and "re-celebrated" our cruise by poring over the photos (while pouring the wine into our Disney Cruise logo glasses saved from the Sailaway deck party). We put some pictures in photo albums and separated others for use in our Disney Cruise scrapbook, purchased on the ship. During the cruise we saved clean cocktail napkins, extra copies of our Personal Navigators, and other colorful brochures and used them as scrapbook decorations. The Disney Cruise logo is pretty much on everything! Designating a couple of hours to relive our vacation was a nice way to ease back into the reality of everyday life. Plus, it is an event that can take place over and over again, every time we need a Disney (Cruise or other) fix!"

...*as told by Disney cruiser Denise Fillo*

Glossary of Terms

While this guide isn't exactly overflowing with salty terms, we thought a brief glossary could be useful, and a bit of fun.

Aft–Towards the rear. The *after* section of the ship. Also *abaft*.

All Ashore–The earliest time a passenger may disembark in a port.

All Aboard– The latest time a passenger may board in a port.

Amidships–The center of the ship, between fore and aft. Also *midship*.

Assistant Server–The crew member who assists your server, typically by looking after drinks, clearing the table, and carrying trays to and from the kitchen. On the Disney Cruise Line, a single assistant server attends your needs throughout your voyage.

Beam–The widest portion of a watercraft.

Berth–Any bed on a ship, but more commonly, the fold-down or fold-out beds in a stateroom.

Boat–A small watercraft, sometimes carried onboard a ship.

Bow–The forward-most section of the ship, pronounced *bough*.

Bridge–The location from which a ship is steered and speed is controlled.

Bulkhead–A vertical wall or partition.

Captain–Ship's officer responsible for the operation and safety of the vessel. See *Master*.

Cast Member–An employee at Disney's land-based theme parks and resorts.

Castaway Club–Disney's free club for past Disney cruisers.

Catamaran–A very stable, fast watercraft with two parallel, widely-spaced hulls joined by a broad deck.

Crew Member–A shipboard employee.

Cruise Director–Officer in charge of all passenger entertainment and recreational activities, including shore excursions. "Is everybody having a good time?"

DCL–Abbreviation for the Disney Cruise Line.

Deck–The covering over a vessel's hull, or any floor on a ship.

Diesel Electric–Propulsion system used by ships of the Disney Cruise Line. Diesel generators provide electricity to operate the ship's propulsion motors and other systems.

Displacement–Weight of the water displaced by a vessel, equivalent to the vessel's weight.

Dock–To come alongside a pier. See also *pier*.

Draft–The depth of the submerged portion of a watercraft.

Fathom–A measure of depth. One fathom is equivalent to 6 feet/1.8288 m.

Fender–A device for padding the side of a watercraft or pier to prevent damage.

Fore–Forward. Towards the front. Also, a golfer's warning call.

Gangway–A location on the side of a vessel where passengers and crew can board and disembark. Also, *a retractable walkway broader than a gangplank, connecting ship to shore.*

Guest Relations–Disney's term for a hotel's front desk operations. On the Disney Cruise Line, equivalent to the Purser's Office. Located on deck 3, adjacent to the Atrium Lobby.

Hawser–Long, thick mooring lines for fastening a ship to a pier.

Head Server–The crew member who supervises dining room servers and assistant servers. A single head server attends your needs throughout your voyage.

Hotel Manager–Ship's officer in charge of all passenger-related operations, including accommodations, housekeeping, food & beverages, and entertainment.

Hull–The main body of a watercraft. From Middle English for *husk*.

Keel–One of the main structural members of a vessel to which frames are fastened.

Key to the World card–Your personal room key, admission, identification, and charge account. Each member of your party has his/her own Key to the World card.

Glossary *(continued)*

Knot—A measure of speed equal to Nautical Miles Per Hour (6076 feet/1852 meters). Also, an undesired tangling of hair.

Latitude—Position north or south of the equator, expressed in degrees.

League—20,000 Leagues = 60,000 miles = 96,560 kilometers

Leeward—Away from, or sheltered from, the wind.

Line—Rope and cord used on a watercraft, or a tall tale told at a bar.

Longitude—Position east or west of Greenwich, England, expressed in degrees.

Mal de Mer—(French) Seasickness. Popular English language euphemism, akin to "green around the gills."

Master—The captain of a ship. *Master Mariner* is a government-issued license for merchant ship captains.

PFD—Personal Floatation Device. Life jacket. Sometimes known as a Mae West, for the pulchritude added to those who wear it.

Pier—A platform extending from shore for mooring and loading watercraft.

Pitch—The rising and falling of the bow and stern. See *Roll*. Also, black, tar-like substance used for waterproofing wooden vessels.

Port—The left side of the watercraft when facing Forward. Also, harbor. Also, a fortified wine named for the Portuguese port town of Oporto.

Porthole—An opening in the hull of a vessel. A round window.

Porthos—One of Alexandre Dumas' Three Musketeers.

Propeller—A rotary fan-like device connected to the ship's engines. When it turns, the ship moves. When stationary, the ship is at rest.

Purser—The ships officer responsible for banking, payroll, and passenger records. See Guest Relations.

Roll—Side-to-side, rocking motion of a vessel. In extremes, this can lead to capsizing.

Rudder—A flat, submerged surface at the stern, used to steer a vessel while underway.

Server—The crew member who attends your table in the dining room, takes food and beverage orders, and supervises the assistant server. Similar to a restaurant waiter. On the Disney Cruise Line, the same servers attend your needs throughout your voyage. Also, a networked computer providing services to network users.

Ship—A large watercraft, typically oceangoing, too dignified to be called a boat and big enough to carry boats of its own.

Shorex—Cruise industry abbreviation for Shore Excursion.

Stabilizer—Horizontal, mechanized, submerged flaps that can be extended from a vessel to reduce rolling motion.

Staff Captain—A ship's second-in-command, responsible for crew discipline and ship's maintenance. Also known as "Number One."

Starboard—The right-hand side of the vessel when facing Forward.

Stateroom Host/Hostess—The crew member responsible for your stateroom's housekeeping, baggage pickup/delivery, and your housekeeping-related requests. Sometimes known as a Stateroom Attendant or Steward.

Stem—The part of the bow that is farthest forward.

Stern—The rear-most section of the ship. Also, humorless.

Tender—A watercraft used to convey passengers and cargo from a ship to the shore. Also, easily chewed, as in Filet Mignon.

Thruster—A propeller positioned to move the ship laterally while docking and at other times when the ship has little or no forward motion.

Waterline—A line painted on the hull of a watercraft to indicate its typical draft when properly loaded.

Whorf—A character on "Star Trek the Next Generation." See *Pier*.

Windward—Travel into the wind.

Index

We feel that a comprehensive index is very important to a successful travel guide. Too many times we've tried to look something up in other books only to find there was no entry at all, forcing us to flip through pages and waste valuable time. When you're on the phone with a reservation agent and looking for that little detail, time is of the essence.

You'll find the PassPorter index is complete and detailed. Whenever we reference more than one page for a given topic, the major topic is in **bold** to help you home in on exactly what you need. For those times you want to find everything there is to be had, we include all the minor references. We have plenty of cross-references, too, just in case you don't look it up under the name we use.

P.S. This isn't the end of the book. The Web Site Index begins on page 258.

Introduction
Reservations
Staterooms
Dining
Activities
Ports of Call
Magic
Index

➤

Introduction

Reservations

Staterooms

Dining

Activities

Ports of Call

Magic

Index

Web Site Index

(continued on next page)

Site Name	Page	Address (URL)
Abanks Scuba Diving Center	211	http://caymanislandsdiscounts.com/AbanksDiveCenter.htm
About.com	28	http://cruises.about.com
Adults at Walt Disney World	11	http://www.adultsatwdw.com
Adventure Excursions (Antigua)	192	http://www.adventure-excursions.com/antigua.htm
All Ears Net	11, 28	http://www.allearsnet.com
Amazon.com	129	http://www.amazon.com
American Automobile Association	44	http://www.aaa.com
American Tours of Puerto Rico	186	http://www.puerto-rico-tourism.com/americantoursofpuertorico.htm
Amtrak	48	http://www.amtrak.com
Antigua Adventures	192	http://www.antiguaadventures.com
Antigua Official Travel Guide	190	http://www.antigua-barbuda.org
Antigua Paddles	192	http://www.antiguapaddles.com
AOL E-Mail	133	http://aolmail.aol.com
AOL Instant Messenger	133	http://www.aim.com
Aqua Mania (St. Maarten)	171	http://www.stmaarten-activities.com
AquaWorld	222	http://www.aquaworld.com.mx
Ardastra Gardens	158	http://www.ardastra.com
Art's Shuttle	58	http://www.artsshuttle.com
Atlantis Adventures	212, 222	http://www.atlantisadventures.net
Atlantis Resort (Nassau)	154–157	http://www.atlantis.com
AudioGuia	186	http://www.audioguiapr.com
AutoPilot	48	http://www.freetrip.com
AvidCruiser	28	http://www.avidcruiser.com
Badger's Disney Countdown	11	http://nhed.com/countdown
Bahamas Experience Tours	156	http://www.bahamasexperiencetours.com
Bahamas Official Site	154	http://www.bahamas.com
Bidding For Travel	58	http://www.biddingfortravel.com
Blue Lagoon Island (Nassau)	155, 158	http://www.dolphinswims.com
Bob Soto's Reef Divers	211	http://www.bobsotosreefdives.com
Bone Island Shuttle	206	http://www.boneislandshuttle.com
Brevard Medical Equipment	86	http://www.brevardmedicalequip.com
Butterfly Farm (St. Maarten)	170	http://www.thebutterflyfarm.com
Canada's Passport Office	61	http://www.ppt.gc.ca
Canaveral National Seashore	148	http://www.nps.gov/cana
Captain Bryan's Stingray Tours	214	http://www.cayman.org/captainbryan
Captain Marvin's Stingray Tours	214	http://www.captainmarvins.com
Captain Nautica's Snorkeling	180	http://home.att.net/~captainnautica
Cayman Islands Dept of Tourism	210	http://www.divecayman.ky
Centers for Disease Control	22	http://www2.cdc.gov/nceh/vsp/vspmain.asp
Chadwick's (womens formalwear)	238	http://www.chadwicks.com
Coastal Angler Magazine	150	http://www.camirl.com
Coki Beach Dive Club	179	http://www.cokidive.com
Comcast	133	http://www.comcast.net
Comfort Suites (Paradise Island)	154	http://www.vacationparadiseisland.com
Coral World (St. Thomas)	176	http://www.coralworldvi.com
Costco	44	http://www.costco.com
Cozumel Country Club	219	http://www.cozumelcountryclub.com.mx
Cozumel Mini-Golf	222	http://cozumelminigolf.com
Cozumel Dive Sites	218	http://www.travelnotes.cc/cozumel/links/scuba.html
Cruise Critic	28	http://www.cruisecritic.com

Introduction · Reservations · Staterooms · Dining · Activities · Ports of Call · Magic · Index

Web Site Index *(continued from previous page)*

Site Name	Page	Address (URL)
Key West Glassbottom Boats	206	http://www.seethereef.com
Key West Jungle Tour Mini-Boats	206	http://www.jungletour.com
Key West Sunrise/Sunset Times	202	http://www.usno.navy.mil
Key West Visitors Bureau	202	http://www.fla-keys.com
Kingdom Magic Travel	44	http://www.kingdommagictravel.com
Kings Casino	190	http://www.kingscasino.com
Kolb Family Disney Cruise Site	28	http://www.kolbfamily.com/2000cruise/disney_cruise
LaughingPlace.com	11	http://www.laughingplace.com
Legends of Puerto Rico	186	http://www.legendsofpr.com
Magical Disney Cruise Guide	10, 11, 28	http://www.allearsnet.com/cruise/Dcruise.shtml
Magical Journeys	44	http://www.yourmagicaljourneys.com
Magical Mouse, The	28	http://www.themagicalmouse.com/dcl
MagicTrips.com	11, 28	http://www.magictrips.com
Mahogany Run Golf Course	179	http://www.st-thomas.com/mahogany
Mail2Web.com	133	http://www.mail2web.com
Mallory Square (Key West)	202	http://www.mallorysquare.com
Mariners Guide	139	http://www.marinersguide.com
Maritime Telecom Network	85	http://www.mtnsat.com
Merritt Island National Refuge	148	http://merrittisland.fws.gov
Minnie's Disney Cruises	28	http://www.minniecruises.com
Motel 6	57	http://www.motel6.com
MouseEarVacations.com	44, 265	http://www.mouseearvacations.com
MouseForLess, The	11, 26	http://www.themouseforless.com
MousePlanet	11, 30	http://www.mouseplanet.com
MouseSavers.com	1, 11, 27	http://www.mousesavers.com
Mr. Sancho's Cozumel Beach Club	222	http://www.mrsanchos.com
Nassau Cruises	158	http://www.bahamasgo.com/nassaucruises.htm
Nassau Scuba Centre	157	http://www.divenassau.com
Native Way Water Sports	214	http://www.nativewaywatersports.com
Nautilus Undersea Tour	211, 212	http://www.nautilus.ky
Nelson's Dockyard (Antigua)	189	http://www.paterson.com/nelsonsdockyard
NetZero	133	http://www.netzero.com
Orbitz.com	44, 49	http://www.orbitz.com
Orlando International Airport	50	http://www.orlandoairports.net
Our Lucaya Resort	163	http://www.ourlucaya.com
Paradise Cove (Freeport)	161	http://www.bahamasvg.com/pcove.html
Paradise Island (Bahamas)	155	http://www.nassauparadiseisland.com
Paradise Point Tramway	180	http://paradisepointtramway.com
Perfect Gift, The	240	http://www.theperfectgift.cc
Pettit's Disney Cruise Site	28	http://www.richpettit.com/vacations/ourvacations.htm
Photo Copyright Release Waiver	236	http://www.image.com/guest-postcruise.htm
Platinum Castaway Club	28, 122	http://www.castawayclub.com
Port Canaveral Transportation	145	http://www.portcanaveral.org/about/transport2.htm
Port of Los Angeles	36	http://www.portoflosangeles.org
Priceline.com	49, 58, 66	http://www.priceline.com
Priority Seating Calculator	11	http://www.pscalculator.net
Radisson Resort at the Port	56	http://www.radisson.com/capecanaveralfl
Rico Sun Tours	186	http://www.ricosuntours.com
Quality Suites	57	http://www.qualitysuitescocoabeach-portcanaveral.com
Red Sail Sports	211	http://www.redsailcayman.com
Reef Tours (Freeport)	163	http://www.bahamasvg.com/reeftours
Resort on Cocoa Beach	57	http://www.vrivacations.com/Southeast/RCB
Ron Jon Cape Caribe Resort	58	http://www.ronjonresort.com
Rusty's Seafood (Port Canaveral)	150	http://www.rustysseafood.com
Safe Haven Golf Course	211	http://www.safehaven.ky/links.htm
Safe Sea	63	http://www.nidaria.com

Introduction

Reservations

Staterooms

Dining

Activities

Ports of Call

Magic

Index

PassPorter Gear

PassPorter was born out of the necessity for more planning, organization, and a way to preserve the memories of a great vacation! Along the way we've found other things that either help us use the PassPorter better, appreciate our vacation more, or just make our journey a little more comfortable. Others have asked us about them, so we thought we'd share them with you. Order online at http://www.passporter.com/store, call us toll-free 877-929-3273, or use the order form below.

PassPorter® PassHolder is a small, lightweight nylon pouch that holds your Key to the World card, I.D. cards, passports, money, and pens. Wear it wherever you go (see photo on page 239) for quick access to your essentials. The front features a clear compartment, a zippered pocket, and a velcro pocket; the back has a small pocket and two pen slots. Adjustable cord. Royal blue. $4 \frac{7}{8}$" x $6 \frac{1}{2}$"

Quantity:
_____ x $7.95

PassPorter® Name Badge personalized with your name! Go around the "World" in style with our oval name badge. Price includes personalization with your name shipping, and handling. Please indicate name(s) with your order.

Quantity:
_____ x $4.00

lemon yellow
Name(s): _____
_____

PassPorter® Pin is our new collectible, cloissone pin. Our 2004 version depicts our fun "hidden family" logo and reads "1999 • 2004 " around the top and "Five Years of Magic" around the bottom. More details and a coupon for a free pin is on page 264. Watch for new pins each year!

Quantity:
_____ x $6.00

Please ship my PassPorter Gear to:

Name ....

Address ....

City, State, Zip ....

Daytime Phone..

Payment: ❏check (to "MediaMarx") ❏charge card

❏ MasterCard ❏ Visa ❏ American Express ❏ Discover

Card number ....Exp. Date. ....

Signature ....

Sub-Total:

Tax*:

Shipping**:

Total:

Please include sales tax if you live in MI or NJ.
***Shipping costs are:**
$5 for totals up to $9
$6 for totals up to $19
$7 for totals up to $29
$8 for totals up to $39
Delivery takes 1-2 weeks.

Send your order form to P.O. Box 3880, Ann Arbor, MI 48106, call us toll-free at 877-WAYFARER (877-929-3273), or order online http://www.passporter.com/store.

More PassPorters

You've asked for more PassPorters—we've listened! At our readers' request, we developed the Deluxe Edition of same book you hold in your hands—it's proven phenomenally popular! And we also have a best-selling, award-winning guidebook to the Walt Disney World Resort. To learn about these and other PassPorters, visit http://www.passporter.com.

Deluxe Cruise Edition

Design first-class cruises with this loose-leaf ring-bound edition. Our popular Deluxe Edition features the same great content as this field guide, plus fourteen of our famous organizer "PassPockets" to plan and record your trip. Special features of the Deluxe Edition include ten interior storage slots in the binder to hold maps, I.D. cards, and a pen (included). The Deluxe binder makes it easy to add, remove, and rearrange pages... you can even download, print, and add-in updates and supplemental pages from our web site. Refills pages and pockets are available for purchase. Learn more about the Deluxe Edition and order a copy at http://www.passporter.com/deluxe.htm.

The Deluxe Edition is also available through bookstores by special order—just give your favorite bookstore the ISBN Code for the 2004 Deluxe Edition (158771017X).

PassPorter Walt Disney World Resort

It all started with Walt Disney World (and a mouse)! Our Walt Disney World guidebook covers everything you need to plan a practically perfect vacation, including fold-out park maps, resort room layout diagrams, KidTips, descriptions, reviews, and ratings for the resorts, parks, attractions, and restaurants, and much more! This edition also includes 14 organizer pockets you can use to plan your trip before you go, hold papers while you're there, and record your memories for when you return. Learn more and order at http://www.passporter.com/wdw or get a copy at your favorite bookstore. Our Walt Disney World guide is available in a spiral-bound edition (ISBN: 1587710129) and a Deluxe Edition (ISBN: 1587710137)—both have 14 PassPockets. You can order either on our Web site or through a bookstore.

Coming later in 2004—PassPorter Disneyland Resort and Southern California Attractions. ISBN: 1587710048 (spiral edition) and ISBN: 1587710056 (Deluxe Edition).

To order any of our guidebooks, visit http://www.passporter.com/store or call toll-free 877-929-3273. PassPorter guidebooks are also available in your local bookstore. If you don't see it on the shelf, just ask!

Note: The ISBN codes noted above apply to our 2004 annual editions. For later editions, just ask your bookstore to search their database for "PassPorter."

Money Saving Coupons

Ride in comfort with Tiffany Towncar

Save $15 on the following roundtrip fares...

✔ **From Orlando International Airport to/from Port Canaveral**

✔ **From Walt Disney World to/from Port Canaveral**

✔ **From Walt Disney World to Port Canaveral, and from Port Canaveral to Orlando Airport (or vice versa)**

To redeem this coupon, just bring along your PassPorter and show this page to the Tiffany driver at the Orlando International Airport. Void if copied or removed from the PassPorter.

Make reservations at 888-838-2161, or at Tiffany Towncar's web site at http://www.tiffanytowncar.com.

Offer expires 6/30/2005. May not be combined with other offers.

Tiffany Town Car Driver: Please leave this coupon in the PassPorter after redemption.

━━━ ADVERTISEMENT ━━━

Free PassPorter Pin with Online Purchase

Receive a free cloissone PassPorter Pin ($6 value) when you place an order of $17 or more in merchandise from our Online Store.

Show off your pride as as PassPorter planner with our popular cloissone pin. This is the second of a series of limited edition pins—great for pin collectors and gifts!

To redeem, visit our special offer page (before you place an order) at http://www.passporter.com/store/freepin.htm and have this PassPorter handy.

Valid for online purchases only. Limit one coupon per order, and one free pin per order. This limited edition pin may sell out—if it does, another PassPorter Pin will be offered with this coupon.

Money Saving Coupon

MouseEarVacations.com®
A Division of Cruising Co Etc.

Concierge-Style Service at No Extra Charge!

"I had always booked my own vacations and thought I got deals searching the internet for codes. My consultant was able to put a package together at a price that I could not match. She went above and beyond. I just can't say enough about her!" – B. Nevins

MouseEarVacations.com® will help create your magical vacation to: Walt Disney World® Resort, Disneyland® Resort, and onboard Disney Cruise Line®! We have representatives across the USA and we provide a unique level of service.

Book your trip with us and get additional FREE services, including:
✔ *A Personal Vacation Planner who will assist you with every detail.*
✔ *Toll-free number to connect you directly to your Vacation Planner.*
✔ *Complimentary Personalized Itinerary and Recreation Planning.*
✔ *Enjoy our exclusive offers & promotions.*
✔ *Complimentary expedited delivery of your documents.*
✔ *We can book most special discounts (i.e., Annual Pass, etc.)*
✔ *And... we watch for rate reductions and apply the savings for you!*

AUTHORIZED DISNEP
VACATION PLANNER
Not an agent of The Walt Disney Company or its affiliates
©Disney

MouseEarVacations.com® pre-reserves cruise space months in advance on select dates to provide you with the best savings!

For vacation quotes, client comments, or more info on our specialized services, visit us online at
http://www.MouseEarVacations.com
E-mail us at: info@cruisingco.com
Or call toll free: 800-866-8601

Mention you saw us in PassPorter and get a free gift with your cruise booking! *Offer expires 6/30/2005*

MouseEarVacations.com® a division of Cruising Co Etc Inc * http://www.cruisingco.com
est. 1987: for all your vacation needs. Member of CLIA, Signature Travel Network, and IATAN
licensed seller of travel WST 601729-148 / CST 2058090-40 - As to Disney artwork/properties: ©Disney

ADVERTISEMENT

Money-Saving Coupon

US BIRTH CERTIFICATE .net

Order Certified Birth Certificates and Passports
quickly and conveniently delivered to your door!

Save 10% off our basic birth certificate service fee.
To redeem this coupon, just fax a copy of this coupon with your birth certificate order (follow steps below or visit our web site to order).

Offer expires 4/15/2005
Offer good only on basic service fees for birth certificates; there is no discount on additional options.

We are a private, professional service that has years of experience dealing with expediting documents and can provide certified birth certificates for you, <u>in most cases</u>, in 2-3 business days. (Please visit our web site at http://www.usbirthcertificate.net/travel for exact process times.) The certified birth certificates that we obtain for you can be used for your cruise travel or anything else that requires a birth certificate. The certificates we obtain have raised, embossed seals or the equivalent and are sent directly from the state of your birth to your doorstep. We are also the only company on the Internet that offers 24-hour customer service.

Call now with any questions: toll-free 888-736-2693

You <u>cannot</u> order over the phone and <u>nothing is transmitted online</u> to prevent fraud and identity theft, so please use our web site at http://www.usbirthcertificate.net/travel or follow the steps below.

1. Go to http://www.usbirthcertificate.net/travel in your web browser.
2. Click on the "Order Birth Certificate" button on our web site.
3. Fill out the form that appears on your screen and print the completed page.
4. Make a copy of your driver's license or your state-issued identification
5. Sign <u>all</u> forms in all places.
6. Fax all pages of the order forms, this coupon, and your photo identification to us at 713-974-2221 or 713-974-6884. *(Note: California and Pennsylvania residents have additional forms and requirements—see order form for details.)*
7. Call our Fax Verification Department at 800-856-2526 about 5-10 minutes after you fax our information to verify that we have received all of your paperwork and everything is in order. (This number is not a fax number nor is it for general questions.)

We can also process your passport for you if needed. We give a $14 discount when we process your birth certificate and passport. Please indicate on your faxed information that you want us to process your passport also and you will be charged a $45 service fee for your birth certificate, $85 for your passport , and $17 for Federal Express shipment of your passport back to you when complete, for a total service fee of $147. Please read and follow the instructions for passports listed at http://www.usbirthcertificate.net/travel/site or follow the instructions listed on the bottom of the birth certificate order form.

ADVERTISEMENT

PassPorter Online

A wonderful way to get the most from your PassPorter is to visit our active web site at http://www.passporter.com/dcl. We serve-up valuable PassPorter updates, plus useful Disney Cruise information and advice we couldn't jam into our book. You can swap tales (that's t-a-l-e-s, Mickey!) with fellow Disney fans, enter contests, find links to other sites, get plenty of details, and ask us questions. You can also order PassPorters and shop for PassPorter accessories and travel gear! The latest information on new PassPorters to other destinations is available on our Web site as well. To go directly to our latest list of page-by-page of PassPorter updates, visit http://www.passporter.com/dcl/updates.htm.

Register this guidebook and get more discounts

We are **very** interested to learn how your vacation went and what you think of the PassPorter, how it worked (or didn't work) for you, and your opinion on how we could improve it! We encourage you to register your copy of PassPorter with us—in return for your feedback, we'll send you coupons good for discounts on PassPorters and gear when purchased directly from us. You can register your copy of PassPorter on the Internet at http://www.passporter.com/dcl/register.htm. Or you can write us a letter to tell share your thoughts and suggestions for the guidebook—mail it to P.O. Box 3880, Ann Arbor, Michigan 48106. Thanks!

Cruise with Jennifer & Dave in December 2004

We invite you to join us at the PassPorter Gathering/MouseFest 2004 aboard the Disney Wonder and at Walt Disney World. This is our annual gathering of PassPorter readers, fellow Disney fans, friends, and family... and the second year we take to the sea! This is a casual, family-friendly affair for the PassPorter and Disney fan community, during which we and our message board moderators host informal events—everyone is welcome! Most of our events are free (though you may need to be on the Disney Wonder or have park admission to participate), while a few events have a small registration fee (to cover supplies or prizes) or have prerequisites. To learn more about the PassPorter Gathering 2004 or send an RSVP, please visit http://www.passporter.com/gathering.htm. (Of course, if you check this site after December 2004, you'll learn about our next Gathering!) You can make travel arrangements on your own, through your favorite travel agent, or through MouseEarVacations.com (see page 265) who is offering excellent deals for this event. If you use MouseEarVacations.com, please tell them you heard about it in "PassPorter!" Hope to see you there!

Cruise At-A-Glance

Create an overview of your itinerary in the chart below for easy reference. You can then make copies of it and give one to everyone in your traveling party, as well as to friends and family members who stay behind.

Name(s):	
Departing on:	Time: #:
Arriving at:	
Resort/Hotel:	Cruise Ship:

Date:	Date:
Location/Port:	Location/Port:
Shore Excursion(s):	Shore Excursion(s):
Activit(ies):	Activit(ies):
Meal(s):	Meal(s):
Other:	Other:

Date:	Date:
Location/Port:	Location/Port:
Shore Excursion(s):	Shore Excursion(s):
Activit(ies):	Activit(ies):
Meal(s):	Meal(s):
Other:	Other:

Date:	Date:
Location/Port:	Location/Port:
Shore Excursion(s):	Shore Excursion(s):
Activit(ies):	Activit(ies):
Meal(s):	Meal(s):
Other:	Other:

Date:	Date:
Location/Port:	Location/Port:
Shore Excursion(s):	Shore Excursion(s):
Activit(ies):	Activit(ies):
Meal(s):	Meal(s):
Other:	Other:

Date:	Date:
Location/Port:	Location/Port:
Shore Excursion(s):	Shore Excursion(s):
Activit(ies):	Activit(ies):
Meal(s):	Meal(s):
Other:	Other:

Departing on:	Time: #:
Returning at:	

S0-AEH-797

Principles of Designing
& Releasing Web Products

product design for the web

Randy J. Hunt

Creative Director, Etsy

Product Design for the Web
Principles of Designing & Releasing Web Products
Randy J. Hunt

New Riders
www.newriders.com
To report errors, please send a note to errata@peachpit.com.

New Riders is an imprint of Peachpit, a division of Pearson Education.

Copyright ©2014 by Randy J. Hunt

Acquisitions Editor: Nikki Echler McDonald
Production Editor: Tracey Croom
Development Editors: Bob Lindstrom, Cathy Fishel-Lane
Copy Editor: Catherine Oliver
Proofer: Jan Seymour
Indexer: Jack Lewis
Interior and Cover Design: Randy J. Hunt
Composition: Kim Scott/Bumpy Design

Notice of Rights
All rights reserved. No part of this book may be reproduced or transmitted in any form
by any means, electronic, mechanical, photocopying, recording, or otherwise, without
the prior written permission of the publisher. For information on getting permission for
reprints and excerpts, contact permissions@peachpit.com.

Notice of Liability
The information in this book is distributed on an "As Is" basis without warranty. While
every precaution has been taken in the preparation of the book, neither the author nor
Peachpit shall have any liability to any person or entity with respect to any loss or damage
caused or alleged to be caused directly or indirectly by the instructions contained in this
book or by the computer software and hardware products described in it.

Trademarks
The word "Etsy" and other Etsy graphics, logos, designs, page headers, button icons, scripts,
and service names (together, the "Etsy Marks") are registered trademarks, trademarks or
trade dress of Etsy, Inc. in the U.S. and/or other countries. Many of the designations used by
manufacturers and sellers to distinguish their products are claimed as trademarks. Where
those designations appear in this book and Peachpit was aware of a trademark claim, the
designations appear as requested by the owner of the trademark. All other product names
and services identified throughout this book are used in editorial fashion only and for the
benefit of such companies with no intention of infringement of the trademark. No such
use, or use of any trade name, is intended to convey endorsement or other affiliation with
this book.

ISBN-13: 978-0-321-92903-7
ISBN-10:   0-321-92903-9

9 8 7 6 5 4 3 2 1

Printed and bound in the United States of America

For Mom and Dad.
You always trusted that I'd figure things out.

Acknowledgments

I owe a huge amount of thanks to my patient fiancée Kelsey Taylor Weireter. Her encouragement and enthusiasm for this book have been unparalleled. I couldn't have made it these many months without her support.

Thanks to New Riders/Peachpit Press and Nikki McDonald for the trust and faith in me for this first book. Bob Lindstrom and Cathy Fishel-Lane offered feedback, assistance, insight, and fresh perspective to help give ideas focus and direction. Catherine Oliver, Tracey Croom, Jan Seymour, Kim Scott, and Charlene Charles-Will helped keep me, my words, and my designs on track.

Thanks to leaders from Etsy for allowing me the opportunity to learn, explore, and apply these principles in an environment that also holds a deep purpose: to Rob Kalin for trusting and empowering me to do what I thought was best, with room to fail; and to Chad Dickerson and Marc Hedlund, both of whom have been incredible cheerleaders, confidantes, and sources of perspective and optimism.

A special thanks to all of the designers at Etsy who have trusted me to serve them well. They believe that the Etsy community is worth investing their hearts and souls; and they do incredible, incredible work with joy and warmth. Jay Carlson, thanks from the start for being an awesome companion in this adventure. A special nod to Kim Bost who introduced the idea of Problems, Solutions, and Tenets into our design process.

Many of the concepts, lessons, and approaches discussed in this book were directly based on experiences I had at Etsy between January of 2010 and June of 2013. A grateful thanks to the engineers and product managers who were willing to embrace an approach to design that looked different from what they'd seen in the past, and who made our Web product much stronger with their input and support: Kellan Elliot-McRae, Wil Stuckey, Dan McKinley, Erik Kastner, Frank Harris, Eric Stephens, Eric Fixler, and Nicholas Cook.

And a final thanks to Steven Heller for his encouragement and support.

Contents

Introduction

"People think that design is styling. Design is not style. It's not about giving shape to the shell and not giving a damn about the guts. Good design is a renaissance attitude that combines technology, cognitive science, human need, and beauty to produce something that the world didn't know it was missing."

—Paola Antonelli, MoMA's Senior Curator
of Architecture & Design + Director of R&D

In January of 2010, I stepped into a job I'd never had before, in a situation I'd never been in before. It had been years since I'd done anything other than work for myself and at businesses I'd started. The job was Interaction Designer for Etsy, the global marketplace for unique goods. The situation? Well, at the time, Etsy was a 50-person company.

Etsy was started in 2005. In 2009, it had sold $180 million worth of merchandise. Some people considered it a design-centric brand, but to say the design team was small would be an understatement. As a platform that enables artists and designers to sell

the physical products they've created, Etsy doesn't employ or need physical product designers. As a software product, it does need Web product designers. As the New Year began, there were zero Web designers on staff. My first week at Etsy was also the first week for the only other Web designer on the team. We had our work cut out for us. As time would pass, I'd learn just how my experience up to that point would help me figure out how to approach design at Etsy. For the time being, however, everything felt new.

There wasn't much of what you'd call "hallway conversation" because we didn't really have hallways. Still, I would pick up on conversations about this mysterious thing called the "product."

WHAT IS "PRODUCT"?

Our CEO at the time, Etsy's founder, was a "product guy." Designers, along with "product managers," were on the "product team." I honestly had no idea what "product" meant, and I was tasked with growing it! I'd been building another Web product for three years before joining Etsy, and had always called the process "building a website," or if I was talking to a savvy person, I'd say I was "building a Web application."

Over time, through lots of question-asking, frequent guessing (and getting it wrong), and absorbing, I arrived at an understanding of what "product" meant. The "product" was this thing we were building: the Web application, mobile apps, and the API (application programming interface). Many people hear "product" and think of a toothbrush or a toaster. At Etsy, the product was (and is) software.

Moving forward, I was able to understand the relationship between "design" and "product." I started referring to the team as the "product design team" because every other moniker seemed as ill-fitting as a cheap suit. Etsy is all about being one-of-a-kind, so we arrived at a bespoke answer for a unique situation. Or so we thought.

It turns out that our answer wasn't unique at all. Other software companies had been referring to "product design" as a discipline for quite some time. As many startups and other companies began developing software products, I realized that we needed a common language for our big, shared, and influential discipline. Web products have a fundamental impact on the day-to-day lives of billions of people.

Through trial and error, I came to an understanding of what product design is and how it works. I wrote this book because I wanted to define product design and share that understanding. More important, though, I wanted to share what I believe are fundamental principles of product design. What does it take to build and release a Web product?

After reading this book, you'll have a much more complete understanding of what's involved in designing digital products, how that design process works, and how to do it well.

Anyone working in the field of product design, Web design, online media, entrepreneurship, software development, or management and leadership will find value in what follows.

I hope you enjoy learning about the principles of product design as much as I enjoyed discovering them.

on product design

CHAPTER 1

What Product to Design?

What are all of those bookmarks in your browser? What are all of those apps on your phone? So many websites, mobile apps, services, and tools are already available on the Web—and yet, you have an idea for a new product. You imagine an experience that's yet to be designed. You have a problem that needs to be solved, along with a vision of the Web product that solves it. You identified unmet needs shared by a group of people, and you know how a product can help meet those needs.

How do you create an app that is noticed and a service that keeps people coming back again and again? Furthermore, how do you devise a way of working that allows you, your collaborators, and your product to keep up with changes in your audience, your marketplace, and the world at large?

This book will guide you in exploring the principles of designing and releasing Web products. You'll learn how to conceive and

implement design decisions that can support the full arc of a person's experience with a product. You'll learn what types of product can engage and serve the people you're building for. You'll also learn how the product can shape their responses and meet their goals (and yours) as they use it.

We'll make awesome designs and adopt a mindset for start-to-end(less) design—from product discovery, to user acquisition, to the use of the product, and beyond.

First, let's ask what *is* a Web product? What makes a product a product?

A Website Is Not a Product

Imagine a fabulous restaurant called Bella's. It's known for its delicious New York–style pizza pies. They're so good, in fact, that you end up ordering from Bella's once a week. Fantastico!

Bella's has a website, and you go there from time to time to get their phone number, see how late they'll deliver, find out about the daily special, or copy the address to send to a friend who's meeting you for dinner. For you, Bella's website works like a brochure.

But a "brochure site" isn't really a product. It's mostly static content—and your interaction is largely limited to browsing that content. Other than signing you up for an email newsletter, Bella's "brochure site" doesn't offer you much in the way of visitor input, content contribution, or interactive participation.

It's pretty easy to recognize two things about Bella's website:

- It's a good fit for Bella's business needs.
- It's a brochure, not a product.

So Bella's website is not a product—but it might be *using* a product.

Imagine you're the *owner* of Bella's. Each morning you arrive at the restaurant two hours before lunch. Some of your staff is already there, delivery trucks have been dropping off the day's orders, and you start your daily duties.

You learn that some extra mushrooms were delivered, and you haven't enough room to store them for the week. "Ah ha!" you think, "We'll run a funghi pizza special today so we can sell those mushrooms while they're still delicious." Wow, you're good at the restaurant business!

You sit down in your office, start your laptop, and open the admin dashboard of Bella's website. Here you can see all of the pages you have on the Bella's site: homepage, menu, reservations, history, and blog.

In the blog section, you click the "New Post" button and start a new entry to list the special: two-for-one funghi pizzas featuring four varieties of delicious mushrooms, available today only, delivery or dine-in. Before saving, you choose the "Daily Special" category for your post. When you click Save, the post appears on Bella's site.

Upon saving, the system also automatically posts an update to Twitter, creating a link to the blog post, so that all of Bella's Twitter followers are alerted to the news of the funghi special.

Just as we thought! Behind the scenes, Bella's "brochure website" *uses* a product. As the owner of Bella's, you've been using a Web product every day to manage how you present your business online, how you communicate specials, and how you build your business's reputation and relationship with customers.

The management, promotion, and communication of your business are facilitated by something that's much more than a website. The Web product you use may look like a website on the surface; but upon further inspection, you'll find that its features, functionality, intent, and design are very different. You might be using the same Web-browsing devices—computer, tablet, or cell phone—to access a website and a Web product, but there are profound and powerful differences that should influence how you design.

Attributes of a Product

Let's take a look and see what makes a product a product and how that differs from a website. Following are some general areas where we can start to distinguish a product from a website.

Frequency of Use

While users may visit a website occasionally (perhaps the most frequent use would be visiting a news site), a user may visit a Web product over and over again.

VISITS PER DAY

WEBSITE   WEB PRODUCT

Direction of Data and Content

Whereas a website typically passes content (text, photos, video, or audio) in only one direction—from site to visitor—a Web product will both deliver and receive content. In other words, a website is often a consumption-only experience, whereas a Web product is a creative or participative experience. A website may read from a database. A product reads from and writes to a database.

9

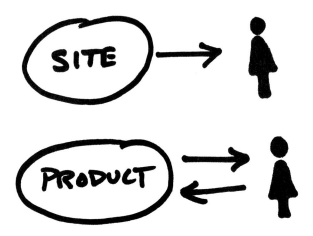

Navigation vs. Participation

A website interface is tailored for the consumption of content. A product interface includes more complex and multi-state interface elements that enable user input. Website navigation solicits user interaction only to browse media. Product navigation solicits browsing interaction, but also encourages users to add content, vote, enter ratings, connect to other users, group content, and use other products and services.

Presence of Accounts

In general, websites are accessible without logging into user accounts. Products often incorporate experiences and services that require unique user accounts. As a result, products can store information from and for an individual user, and create a unique experience with data that persists and evolves over time.

Pages or Flows

Website content may change over time, but the views and presentation are relatively static. It's common to refer to these views as "pages" because they're like the unchanging printed pages of a

book. A Web product is highly dynamic and includes many views. Each view often contains many states (such as a default state, a recently changed state, an error state, and an empty state), any one of which might be displayed to a user. Products often spread features and functionality over a sequence of views (typically called a "flow").

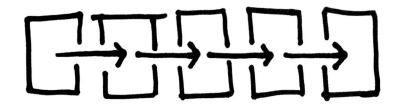

Beyond the Browser

While the website experience is limited to content browsing, a product may extend to other services, such as sending emails to your inbox, routing text messages to your phone, or communicating with an installed app on your computer or mobile device. As products grow, they may acquire features you never imagined initially, such as customer support and real-world interactions.

Web products are complex systems. That's where much of the challenge in design resides. They involve many devices, many people, and many features. They are certainly different from websites that feel simple by comparison; but you'll see later that your Web design skills are a great foundation for building Web products.

Some Products Are Loners; Some Products Need Friends

Thinking about the characteristics of a product, you've probably started to imagine many kinds of products with a staggering variety among them. While the possibilities are infinite, those possibilities can be grouped into a few categories to help you consider a product design strategy. Not all Web products are the same. Some products are fully experienced as stand-alone products. Other products are best experienced as part of a suite of products, and still other products are created as platforms upon which other products are built.

Stand-Alone Products

Stand-alone products are simply that: a product that provides its full intended experience and value when you use on its own. Each morning when I first look at my phone, I tap a raindrop icon, wait a few moments, and check out a pop-up weather forecast. Sunny, no chance of rain, seventy degrees. Perfect. (Yeah, right; I live in NYC!)

With this simple tap, I "passively" shared my location information with the weather app by allowing it to access the GPS data on my phone. I've also done a little active input, so I get unique data sent every time I open the app. Because this app works very well for my personal needs, it's a great example of a stand-alone product. But not all products are so simple or involve such straightforward use cases.

Ecosystem Products

Sometimes a product may provide some value and functionality by itself, but provides much more value when paired with other products, services, or people, like a suite of products. Ecosystem products are products that require more than one "connection point," a term I use to describe "stuff" that's more than me and my information at any one moment in time. Examples of these other connection points are other people, products or services, and third-party apps that allow me to use the product at many times, in many locations, or on various devices. Let's look at various connection points and how they relate to a Web product.

Other People

Ecosystem products often need friends. They import lists of people, connect to your other online accounts, allow you to search for people, and proactively suggest other people you might connect with.

By virtue of connecting to other people, the ecosystem product not only includes information that you input (or is generated for you by the software), but also includes information and experiences that come from other people within the ecosystem and are automatically pushed to you. This multiuser/multisource attribute of an ecosystem is often highly desirable for encouraging frequent usage. The more people you are connected to, the more likely it is that their actions will create reasons for you to increase your use of the product. And your interaction with the product will similarly increase those people's frequency of use.

A messaging service is a great example of an ecosystem product that relies on users' connecting to other people. As a communication tool, its core product concept requires at least two people, both connected, to communicate.

Other Products or Services

In addition to connecting to other people, an ecosystem product may initiate connections to other products or services. A great example of this is a product called IFTTT (If This Then That), which launched in 2010 to help people "put the Internet to work." This product creates an easy way to connect one product's API (application programming interface) to another product's API by using an instruction set that it calls "recipes."

An example IFTTT recipe might look like this: Whenever a user clicks the Favorite button on a Tumblr post, it publishes a link to that post on the user's Facebook wall. In this recipe, two products—Tumblr and Facebook—are connected via IFTTT, a third product.

Multiple Clients

Ecosystem products often have connection points that are Web products and native apps. Sometimes even third-party apps become important connection points because, for example, they provide native apps for a product that is primarily Web based and lacks a native app experience. This multitude of connection points allows you to interact with the product in many places and at

many times, fluidly and easily—effectively, these are "anytime, anywhere, any device" products.

Evernote is a note-taking product that allows you to create, edit, organize, and search text notes, along with embedded images and audio. A key feature of Evernote is that its notes are available from anywhere and on any device, so it's a Web-based product that also has iPhone, iPad, Android, Mac OS X, and Windows versions. In the background, the product has a syncing service that ties all of these clients together. It's a great example of a single product that is actually multiple products (Web app, mobile apps, desktop apps) that interoperate in a connected ecosystem.

Platform Products

Platform products support and enable features and functions for other products and are frequently invisible to the general user. However, most of the major Web services, social networks, and Internet brands have one or more platform products tucked inside their visible product offerings.

A great example is Amazon Payments, a product intended to simplify online purchases. By itself, checking out isn't much of a product experience. It becomes a product only when integrated with some other shopping experience. In this case, Amazon offers a platform product that works "inside" other product experiences.

Evolving Products

The lines between these different product types aren't always clear cut, and products may change over time. As they become more sophisticated and full featured, many products evolve from stand-alone products to ecosystem products to platform products. Many of the most mature products become all three product types. Sometimes they evolve because the people who use the products change or use them in new ways. At other times, the products change for business reasons.

Let's look at Facebook as an example of a product experience that touches all of these product types.

Although this scenario is uncommon, it is possible to use Facebook primarily as a stand-alone product. For instance, you can upload photos that you've taken throughout the year, and return to your Facebook Timeline to see a photographic history of your recent activities. If you keep your photos private, Facebook is functioning as a stand-alone product that serves you and only you via your Facebook account.

What's more common is to use Facebook as part of an ecosystem product that connects with other people and other services and products. For example, we may connect another product to our Facebook account and allow it to publish Facebook comments about what we're doing. I just listened to Red Hot Chili Peppers on Rdio. There, did you see that show up on my Facebook wall?

In addition, Facebook exists as a platform upon which tens of thousands of other products have been built. One of the best-known examples is Zynga's popular Farmville game, which built an entire business "on top of" the Facebook platform.

Native Apps as Web Products

"What about apps that run on iOS or Android?" you ask. That's a great question. Apps that you run directly on your device, rather than within a Web browser, are often referred to as "native apps." For example, Twitter for iPhone is specifically programmed for iOS, the operating system that powers iPhone and iPad devices. As such, Twitter for iPhone is said to be "native" to the iOS platform.

We've all used native apps for years on our desktops. "Desktop apps are old school," you say? Think again. Popular Web products such as Evernote have apps that run natively on every platform you can imagine, including Mac OS X and Windows. Because Evernote is available everywhere, you can use it easily and frequently. It's part of what makes the product useful and retains active users.

After using apps for a few years, I've come to believe that we should think about apps as we think about Web products. Sure, there are inherent differences (some of which make apps feel more like boxed software), but there are also similarities. Let's examine the differences and similarities, and consider how viewing apps through that Web-product lens can help you make better products and processes.

What Makes Apps Different from Browser-based Web Products?

Web products never have to be installed. Rather, they simply "exist" at a particular URL. Because of this, they are available to every browser everywhere (assuming that some reasonable attempt is made to address any cross-browser programming quirks).

Because the product code lives in one place, rather than being installed on every individual user's device, a browser-based product can be changed instantly and updated for every user in the world. That's pretty incredible. A Web product has a single point of distribution to every user, and users only have to visit the product online to experience the latest and greatest features that you've developed.

While Web products can be realized (for the most part) with a single body of code, app development requires knowledge of multiple programming languages, UI (user interface) assumptions and conventions, and other details. Furthermore, to create an app that is native to an operating system, you generally have to reprogram the app for each one of those operating systems—Android, iOS, Mac OS X, Windows, Linux, whatever. Even if you are developing a "clone" of a product for multiple platforms, a significant amount of unique design and engineering effort is often necessary.

If this is all sounding like reasons *not* to develop native apps, then you'll likely find good company among the school of product designers who believe that Web apps are the only way to go. So, why would you develop a native app?

One of the most obvious reasons native apps may be preferred is that a native app has deeper access to the hardware of mobile and native devices (resources such as memory chips, attached storage devices, cameras, microphones, GPS data, and so on).

Although this assertion is often contested, it's generally true that native apps perform faster and are more responsive to user input. In other words, they often "feel" better. Also, native apps can more easily be built so they don't require a data/Internet connection to work. This aspect can be important for users who commute underground, who live in areas with spotty data connections, or who control costs by limiting their data use.

Finally, in some cases your audience may prefer native apps to Web apps for any of the reasons above, or for less understandable reasons rooted in the perceptions of your target audience. They may prefer to buy software and have a sense of ownership, in which case a native app may be a great fit.

Why Think of Apps as Web Products?

Even though building and distributing Web apps is different from building and distributing native apps, and they don't have identical capabilities, your customers are likely using both. The type of app a person is using is ultimately secondary to the overall product experience that you provide. If your product serves them well on its own, they'll be satisfied. If they expect an experience that extends across many types of products, then you'll be challenged to meet or exceed their expectation.

Allowing Web products and native-app products to drift too far apart in your mind can compromise a well-considered product experience. This result would likely be bad for the continuity of your brand and image.

In many cases, some of the same people will be making Web and native products. The release, distribution, and installation constraints of native apps force a development process that is somewhat of a regression to less fluid working methods. You could accept this process and let it be, but I prefer reframing your thinking and treating native apps—as much as possible—as if they were Web products. This reframing can help you think about making your apps easy to change, fast to evolve, and iterating at a natural pace that coincides with how you build a Web product. We'll visit all of these ideas in more detail later in the book.

While apps may have some unique constraints, challenges, and opportunities, let's think of them as being the same as Web products. That's how we'll be approaching them throughout the rest of this book.

A Unique Opportunity

Web product design is a unique intersection of skills applied to a unique intersection of opportunities. Never before have so many people had access to tools and distribution that allow them to identify and solve problems, and then build such widely-available solutions.

While the proliferation of Web products can make it a challenge to cut through the noise, the opportunity is there for you. People need your perspective. You'll need to evolve your thinking to accommodate a world of design that is constantly changing and increasingly flexible.

You'll wear many hats as you learn to make quick design decisions and then test them with your collaborators and audience. You'll learn to let the output be seen as a means to an end—an ever-changing product experience in which your work is never done.

Therein lies the challenge. Let's tackle it.

CHAPTER 2

There's Work To Be Done

Product design is an intersection point of many principles. Part of its power is that it adds clarity and anchors many disciplines into something people can see, touch, and use. Part of its magic is that these intersection points—the overlapping, weaving, and blurring—are where great product design insights happen.

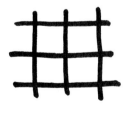

While most of this book takes a long, hard look at the places where various disciplines meet, it's helpful to look at each of these independently so that we can imagine the challenges and opportunities they create for product design. In this chapter, we look at the breadth of skills and range of work that can help you create Web products.

Usually when a product designer is working solo, she's doing most, if not all, of this work, herself. She might be wearing all of these hats and not even realize it.

Of course, there are other possible scenarios. For instance, some disciplines might not be related to the development of the product. In such cases, the overview that follows is useful as a checklist of areas to consider.

And if a product, business, or initiative grows, the designers will probably need to work with other professionals to solve even more complex problems, and they will likely be following many of the principles discussed next.

Create a Meaningful and Understandable Experience

UX, UI, IxD. It all sounds like BS! Let's look at these abbreviations, the work they represent, and the way they relate to product design.

UX stands for "user experience." In the world of product design I've come to know, "user experience" is about as misused and misunderstood as "brand." User experience design implies a design of a user's total experience. In that sense, product design *is* UX

design; however, the inverse is not true. UX design, as it's commonly understood, does not include the expertise of engineering or marketing. For me, product design is broad and blurry. Still, within its blurry borders are certainly core skills that are common to UX design.

The U is a user or, as I prefer, a person. The X is that person's experience. It's the sum of all of her interactions with and feelings about the situations created or enabled by what's been designed.

Product design tries to create an experience that is both understandable and meaningful. A thoughtful designer looks at the experience from beginning to end over a period of time. He might decide, for example, what is both displayed to and hidden from a person at any given point. He might decide what is asked for and how it is asked. For example, does a person choose from a menu of options or type text into a form input field? The designer might also determine if, how, and when one feature relates to another or connects to other parts of a product.

One piece of the product is the interface that people interact with directly. Even though I prefer "person" over "user," let's accept the established terminology of "user interface," or UI. People responsible for the interface are often referred to as "visual designers" or "UI designers." However, when the interface involves sound or movement that occurs without the user's touching a button or screen, the descriptive accuracy of "visual" breaks down.

Interaction design (IxD) is the design of the behaviors and events that compel a person to interact with the product and determine how the product responds. The interface design involves such

decisions as the placement of buttons and whether they even look like buttons. The interaction is the behavior of those buttons when pressed.

As our products become more advanced, the separation of these design roles from one another becomes questionable. To illustrate, imagine an audio-only interface that reveals itself only when you interact with it: "Hello, tablet." "Hi, Randy, what can I do for you?" "Can you turn on the air conditioner ten minutes before I arrive home?" "Of course." There's nothing visual about that interface, and the understandability of the interface is intertwined with the person's expectations of the interaction.

The responsibility to make an experience understandable requires that expectations are appropriately set: the interface elements must accurately reflect their intended purpose. When a person interacts with those elements, the result should fulfill the person's expectations. So, a superior product design includes behaviors that are either familiar to the person or appropriate to the content at hand—often both.

The understandable experience is one that:

- Sets the right expectations
- Lives up to those expectations

The meaningful experience is one that:

- Solves a problem or helps a person accomplish a goal
- And also delights (if we're lucky)

Organize Complex Information

IA, another of the initialisms I love to hate, stands for "information architecture."

The information architecture process involves observing and analyzing complex sets of information, and then designing a system in which they can be better organized, better programmed, and better understood.

Product design often deals with complex sets of information, so providing an organizing principle for that information can—for better or worse—affect the overall product experience. Imagine that you have a wide and varied body of editorial content, comprising both text and images that people submit as part of your product's use. The way you choose to organize that information—the architecture you build around it—can influence your product in a number of ways, including:

- The user's understanding of the intended experience
- The user's access to all parts of the product
- The user's focus on specific parts of the experience
- The way data is stored in a database
- Which parts of the product need to be optimized for speedy performance
- The perception of a product's ability to follow through on the promise of its value proposition

Some parts of the product experience are buckets or "containers" for content created by other people. Other parts of the product experience are explicitly designed and generated in full by the product creators. The terminology, grouping, and hierarchy of this information are important to the experience of the product. Creating a suitable taxonomy for this information is important for ensuring that the product is easy to use and evokes positive responses from first-time users.

Balance User, Technical, and Business Needs

Creating products can be a complex endeavor with many different influences to balance. Product management is the glue of the product development process. It tends to stick together all of the disciplines and relate them to each other. I remember once seeing a job ad from a company seeking a product manager who would not only ensure the trains ran on time, but also would help build the track. That's a perfect metaphor for summing up the role and scope of product management.

Product Management vs. Project Management

Don't confuse product management with *project* management, the latter being the process of coordinating tasks and meeting deadlines as part of the actual development workflow. At Etsy, we like to say that "Project management comes for free." That means that the best engineering managers or designers or product managers

are also very good project managers, so it becomes important not to confuse product management with project management.

You see, product managers balance at least three things, and in doing so can help guide the path the product takes. These three things are:

- The business needs of the product—What's the revenue model, or why is this product important for the strategic goals of the company?
- The technical constraints—These are the development realities that engineers communicate to the product manager or the team. These constraints might be database storage challenges, the time it takes to program, the running speed of the product, the complexity of integrating the code base with other systems, or simply the amount of work that is involved from a software engineering standpoint.
- The person's experience of using the product—The product manager needs to walk in the users' shoes, empathize with the users, and balance their many needs. It's in that role that the product manager is closest to product design, but the product manager is still acting as an overall advocate, whereas the product designer is often acting as the user's perspective.

There's some inherent tension between these concerns. The user rarely is aware of, or cares about, engineering constraints. Nor does the user prioritize the business needs of the product's creators. The product manager does, though, and for good reason. The product

needs to be engineered to be reliable and dependable. When it makes its way into the world, it must be compelling to use and able to satisfy the business objectives that will support its ongoing development and refinement.

Create Interfaces and Interactions that Shape Behavior

Next we come to the UI, the user interface, and the visual designer and/or interaction designer who creates it. Within this territory, we design interfaces and interaction patterns that suggest and shape the behavior of the user.

In my mind, UI is synonymous with visual design. It's what the product looks like. How are the buttons designed? What text is inside those buttons? Is the form input field a square-corner rectangle or a rounded-corner rectangle? Does the navigation bar at the top include a colored background that is brand appropriate, or does it include a neutral background that looks more like the operating system?

Interaction design is more concerned with the behavior of those interface elements. When I click *that* button, what happens? When I click a similar button, does it trigger a similar behavior? Can I encourage a specific user behavior by placing certain elements of the product interface in different places?

Write Code, and Make It Work

Engineer. Programmer. Developer. All of these terms kind of mean the same thing. This person's primary role is to write the code to make the product work.

⟨ MAKE IT WORK ⟩

GOOD IDEA

⟨ / MAKE IT WORK ⟩

In the same sense that one of the designer's nuts-and-bolts tasks is to choose the typeface used in the form fields' labels, the engineer chooses the code implementation strategy to make the product work, and her knowledge about how best to do that is essential in determining the ultimate form of the product. She has likely run into problems and challenges and has formed ideas about how the product can be better, faster, and smarter. In some cases, her comprehensive knowledge of available technology might lead to solutions that a designer or a product manager may never have considered.

Explain Ideas with Language

Writing is an extremely important and often highly underrated aspect of product design. As much as a "show, don't tell" mindset is the core of product design, some things still need explanation. And that need for explanation can extend throughout the design process to yourself, your collaborators, your bosses, your product testers, and your users.

Additionally, there is a lot—let me emphasize that: *A LOT*—of writing inside a product. Interface design often relies on text to communicate. For example:

- Navigation elements
- Button text
- Feature names
- Form input labels
- Error messages

Sometimes the best design change isn't a visual or interaction design change; it's the improvement of a button's text or a form input's label.

Be a Marketer

You have this cool new feature. It's well engineered and looks great. It elegantly balances business, technical, and user experience constraints. The text within the product makes sense. A person understands what the product is intended to do. The user interface is

consistent with your expectations, and it behaves in a way that is true to the product. So what? You need people to use the product or it simply sits there, untouched.

How do people find out about it? You've got to be a marketer. You need to make people aware that your product exists and help them understand why they should give it some of their precious time. Driving that awareness and understanding is what we call product marketing.

Product marketing assesses the features, attributes, and positioning of the product and delivers that message to its audience. That audience may be the direct user, media outlets, or other channels that help spread the message of your product. It all depends on the nature of your product.

Product marketing is about the thing itself, the actual software. Product marketing is related to but more specific than general marketing, where you might be talking about the overall promise a brand makes.

Product marketing is about what a specific feature—or set of features or flow or some other aspect of the product—can do, why it's valuable to people, why they should care, and why they should use it. It involves identifying and exploiting the mediums, channels, and formats that are best for getting that message out.

Do Your Research

Research, in one form or another, is always part of the product design process. At the most instinctual level, you're designing for

yourself, so get introspective and try to understand how you feel about what you're making. Even if you were designing a product just for yourself, you would still need to understand what your needs are and what problems you're trying to solve.

Most likely, you're not designing for yourself. In that case, you investigate, ask questions, and pore over information to acquire a better understanding of whom you're designing for, what you're designing, and how to do it. Let's acknowledge this research as a valuable part of the process. As part of designing, you choose when and how much research to do.

Let's also acknowledge that research can, and likely should, happen before, during, and after you've built a product. What you can learn at different stages of your product design is best served by different types of research. The range of possibilities here is quite wide. Your needs might lead you to:

- Market research
- User research
- Usability research
- Data analytics

The key here is to be asking questions...often. Chances are you're never going to get your product perfect. In fact, you're probably going to get it partially wrong. By asking questions and listening for answers, you'll stand a better chance of going from wrong to less wrong. And perhaps from less wrong to even-less-wrong. If you're lucky, you'll even get some things right.

Value research. Try it, learn from it, and apply it.

Forget Unicorns

I'd like to debunk the unfortunately persistent perception that you can't wear all of these hats. You can. In fact, in some cases, you must! What about that first product you're building at your kitchen table on nights and weekends? I assure you, you've taken on every one of these concepts. If you've already had that experience of launching a Web product, you know what I'm talking about. It's not easy, but it's not impossible, either. When you're able to wear many hats—even if you don't *need* to each day—you and your product design will be better for it.

There's also a persistent notion that designers with a particular combination of skill sets are impossible to find. Usually it's "designers who program" or "UX & UI design" or some silly bucketing of a subset of knowledge areas that are clearly related and integral to most successful Web products.

The people who think this multi-talent is impossible to find call these mysterious multi-talented designers "unicorns": the designer as mythical creature running in the enchanted forests, never to be found.

Please erase that limited view from your mind.

Designers with a combination of skill sets and experiences, with deep knowledge of many different disciplines, do exist in the world. I've seen them with my own eyes (and built teams of them). This school of design is growing rapidly. What may seem like a shortage will one day be the powerful engine of the design profession.

Why this insistence that such and such combinations of skills are impossible to find or, worse, inappropriate? I'd chock it up to fear ("Do I have to learn all these new skills?") and uncertainty ("I don't understand how this works, so I don't like it.").

As I see it, we all have many interests. While some fall further outside our professional responsibilities (say, cooks and bakes), others might be related (designs websites, draws typefaces, writes Python code to program OpenType font features). It's these clustered sets of skills and interests that are powerful in product design. It's not impossible (as the term unicorn would imply) to find a talented designer capable of sitting comfortably at an intersection point, ready to enthusiastically create digital products that are well planned, beautifully designed, soundly built, and smartly marketed.

think like a product designer

CHAPTER 3

Story First

Your product, your business, and you are all part of a larger story.

It's the story of a world in constant change—a story of increasing distraction, ease of communication, concerned citizens, powerful governments, political unrest, and the constant reinvention of the world around us. It's also a story of human beings and their desire to love, be loved, better themselves, and better the world around them. Somewhere between your audience/customers/users and your product is a story of problems solved, dreams fulfilled, life made easier, or moments made more enjoyable.

Lead with the narrative of your product and never stop telling it, whether you're talking to your audience, your team, yourself, your investors, or your friends and family (they're your investors, too). Your story is a clarifying and galvinizing force. Your biggest ideas require it, and even the smallest of design changes deserves it. Like you and me, a little line of code, a tweak to a UI, or an email to a user longs to be part of something larger than itself.

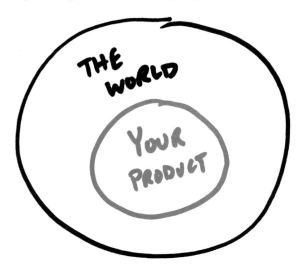

Crafting, telling, and sticking to a story can help you build your product with a sense of direction and purpose. By creating a narrative, you develop a context in which you must understand the end of the story, which can help you write the beginning. In other words, by defining the impact you want your product to have as you first begin working on it, you're more likely to understand the choices you can make. You can ask yourself, "Am I designing

to reach the end of our story?" By sticking to that story, you can maintain a consistency of vision and intent throughout the design process—and across your story arc.

In this chapter, we'll look at a technique for using stories when designing products. This technique is more than a template. It contains the following attributes that will help you build a product:

- A sense of direction
- Clearly described benefits
- A focus on people over technology

Write the Press Release First

One product development technique that has become quite popular is the exercise of writing the press release for a product as the initial expression of the product idea. The concept is that before you've made a sketch, written a line of code, or created specs, you go through this thinking and writing exercise to clarify your idea, step outside of the tiny details, and think about how your product could be described in a compelling way to a person who has never heard of it before.

I'm not suggesting that every good product or every project idea or every business idea is created to satisfy the press or conceived to be buzzworthy and headline friendly. Instead, the intention is that in the course of writing a press release, you will focus your thinking and distill the product concept down to its most important parts.

Why a Press Release?

A press release is a widely understood document. It's an ideal form for an exercise, even if you're never planning to have a traditional publicity plan as part of your product launch. To understand why this exercise is beneficial, let's start by considering what a press release does in normal use.

A press release is an official announcement that's sent to media outlets such as blogs and newspapers. It contains the basic news facts that allow a media outlet to share the news directly with its audience or motivate the outlet to further research the topic. It's not uncommon to see press coverage of software announcements that repeat a press release nearly verbatim. Even when this isn't the case, as with more in-depth coverage, the press release may still be the starting point for anyone who publicizes the news. These basic facts in the release are essentially the who, what, where, when, why, and how components of the product's story:

- *Who* is the product for, and *who* has designed it?
- *What* does the product do, and *what* is it called?
- *Where* will it be used, and *where* can someone get it to use it himself?
- *When* should it be used, and *when* will it be available?
- *Why* is it notable, and *why* does it matter to its intended audience?
- *How* does it fullfill a need, or *how* does it solve a problem?

Let's look at a short sample press release for a home automation product. Take note of the presence of the elements listed above.

Today (when), Robohome (who) released String (what) to the relief of forgetful homeowners. String is a state-of-the-art product/service suite that turns any lighting fixture in your home (where) into a programmable, Internet-connected device (what) simply by plugging a String node into a common electrical outlet. You can turn any light on or off from any location (where) — and not only when you're at home.

Using the String mobile app (how), you can program any light to turn on or off based on virtually any criteria you can dream up. You'll never again accidentally leave a light on, and you'll always know when a light is on, even when you can't see it yourself (why).

String node wall units are available for purchase, now with free next-day shipping, at the String website. The mobile app is available free for all major platforms.

Putting this exercise in the context of a press release makes it more accessible to its writer. Imagine saying to someone, "I want you to write a story." If the person doesn't consider himself much of a writer, that sounds like a seriously daunting creative challenge. Now, imagine saying to him, "You need to write a press release." That's a bit more tangible. While the result may or may not be brilliantly written, the value of this thinking and writing exercise cannot be underestimated.

The press release makes tangible the who, what, where, when, why, and how of your product. These are essential components to

articulate as you make trade-offs and choices that will realize an end result: Does the design serve the "who"? Is the audience prepared to understand the "why" and be familiar with the "what"?

Outcome-Oriented Thinking

The exercise of writing a press release channels your thinking into a form that is outcome oriented. In other words, it forces you to focus initially on the end result of what you're creating rather than getting mired in the details. Call it the development of a goal, call it creating a vision. I'll call it smart thinking.

A press release would never say, "We've released a new product description page. It has an orange button on the right-hand side that sits just below the name of the product." What the press release would say is, "We've made it easier than ever before to preview the contents of a product's package and made it faster for you to check out." There's no specific design detail described in the release because those details are behind-the-scenes design problems to be solved. To the user, those hidden solutions are framed by this more general, outcome-focused description. Every element of your design should be aimed at realizing that outcome.

Consistency of Vision

Now that we have our story, it functions as a structure on which our product can be built. We must make a product that fullfills the promise we said it would, that offers the value we knew it would. We can't do that only at the beginning of the product design process. We must do it throughout the design and development process.

Developing a clear narrative, as outlined in a press release, is a way to keep yourself and your team tuned into the idea that you initially wanted to realize. Consistency of vision is difficult to maintain, and simple tools such as a narrative can have a profound effect on the quality and focus of your product.

Describing Benefits and Value

When designers and developers are raring to leap into the process of creation and development, this preliminary step of writing may seem like unnecessary busy work. However, in addition to distilling your concept and simplifying it to its most important parts, creating that press release also forces the writer to think about the value proposition of the product, the *why*.

Who will care that this product exists, why is it important for them, what does it do for them, and how does it do it? When it comes time to explain your product idea to its potential users, this preliminary focusing of the concept will help you determine what to emphasize in your communications, your marketing, and the initial user experience of the product.

Explain It for the Uninitiated

Press releases are usually written with an uninitiated audience in mind—either the general public, or a press that will detail the story for a general public. This is precisely what we want to achieve with this press release exercise: simple language, concepts distilled into their basics, and verbal brevity. These attributes, too, will help your product along its way when you must explain it to customers, collaborators, investors, and colleagues.

The Elements of a Story

Every story needs a beginning, a middle, and an end. Your articulation of the narrative—in the previous example, a press release—is your beginning. The consistency of product vision is your middle—the meat of your story—which carries you throughout a journey of twists and turns. The outcome is your end product.

At that point, another story is told as your audience of users and potential users become the protagonists, and your product guides them through a new story arc based on the experience they have with your product.

Every aspect of your design should take your protagonists through the story arc that you've chosen for them. If you're delivering information, that arc is going from uninformed, to learning-motivated, to gaining a final answer. If you're selling a product, that arc goes from curiosity and browsing, to locating a desired item, to final purchase.

Design is storytelling: beginning, middle, and end.

CHAPTER 4

No Dead Ends

From the earliest days of the Internet, we saw everything presented there as a "page." Of course, that terminology springs from the printed page that everyone knew so well. The problem with applying this familiar concept to Web product design is that digital products aren't experienced in a single linear sequence, one static rectangle at a time.

Even today, without realizing it, we often accept an ill-fitting framework for Web products. If we pin our design to an out-of-date model, we're unlikely to create an experience that feels consistent with the medium for which we're designing.

Every experience that people have with digital products involves interactions over time, choices between multiple actions, user feedback, presentation of information, requirements for input, and demands on attention. It's important for us to consider exactly what we are creating when we design a digital product: how it is experienced, how it is constructed, how it works, and the connection between those three factors.

Go With the Flow

Let's accept a new model for our thinking: instead of a page, we design a *flow*, a word that implies a looseness of movement and, perhaps, an unpredictable pathway. Think of how water moves in a stream. It may run to the right or to the left of a rock. It may move faster in narrow areas or slower in wide areas. In some locations it may move so slowly that you can't perceive its movement. Eventually, it reaches a natural destination, its inevitable home, at the bottom of the hill.

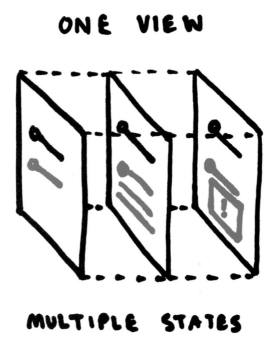

50

Flow as a model also implies the passage of time. Movement doesn't happen in a single moment. As we learned in our story framework in Chapter 3, an experience has a beginning, a middle, and an end. People don't experience a digital product in a single instant. People pass in and out of the flow, with each interaction leading to a new part of the experience. If the creator has done his job correctly, flow should ideally go on and on and on, offering more and different experiences over time.

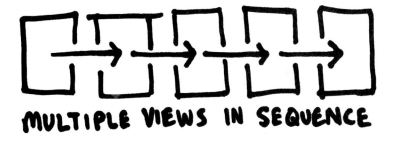

MULTIPLE VIEWS IN SEQUENCE

The elements that can appear or occur within a flow aren't limited to its presence on a specific medium, device, or screen. A person may interact with the flow through an app or online shopping site, but she is also interacting when she tells her friend about her experience or sees a printed ad in a favorite magazine. Each interaction helps that person understand what the product looks and feels like, how to use it, and whom it is for. Each of those moments is part of a larger flow that easily moves from online interaction to offline activity and back. A flow has the potential to go in a variety of directions, change its pacing, and be subject to manipulation

and multiple interpretations. Knowing this, a designer can thoughtfully and creatively craft an experience that never reaches a dead end. A dead end is a missed opportunity.

Create New Opportunities

Finding moments to extend flows demands broader thinking. In fact, it demands that you embrace uncertainty and accept that you will not really know where your flow should go next. Often, the next possible destination for a flow will reveal itself only as you're actually developing the product from your design.

Take a simple sign-up flow that has reached its natural resting place: a completed user sign-up. Where you take that user will depend on what part of the experience you want him to engage with immediately after signing up. You might offer multiple possibilities. You might prefer that he perform Action A if he arrived at the sign-up from Source A, or that he have a choice of Actions B or C if he arrived from Source B.

When you are refining a part of a product experience design, you must always be looking for opportunities to extend its flow. A user should never experience steps one, two, and three successfully, and then get to step four and discover that the flow ends with "Have a nice day; see you later."

For example, a customer at a shopping site has just placed an order. The natural product flow would seem to be complete and concluded. What was expected was fulfilled. Now what? Ideally, that flow should have the opportunity to continue. But how might

that work? Your product could present other items that this person might be interested in. It could display links to articles about the item the customer just purchased. It could direct the customer to a community of like-minded people. The possibilities are as wide as your mind is open.

When you're dealing with an unpredictable flow, the key to finding new opportunities is simply to open up to the entire world of possibilities. You could present information, ask for input, or prompt interaction. What kind of interaction? You could solicit feedback by asking a person to share her experience, or you could offer the customer a choice of several possible next steps. By presenting those possibilities, you can encourage the customer's next action in any number of ways.

Once you start to see the breadth of potential options, you can take the design of your product in almost any direction.

Connect One Experience to Another

We know that focus and continuity of outcome are important to the design of a strong product experience. But if you have limitless possibilities for the direction of any one flow, how do you generate focus by choosing a subset of those "limitless possibilities"? The previous checkout-to-recommendation scenario is a good example. If you're looking to turn a dead end into a not-dead notend, consider connecting it to other key flows—those essential flows that make up the core of your product and already exist in the experience.

Think about filling a glass to the very top with water. Just at the point when the glass will overflow, you put another glass below it to catch the water, then fill that glass, and then fill another and another. That's what your flow should be like. How can you continually extend the experience so that it remains beneficial for you and the customer?

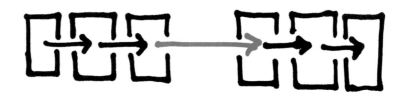

Some digital experiences do have logical ends. After you sign up for a new service by creating a personal account, that job is done. When you buy an item online and check out, that transaction is finished. Water has finished flowing into the glass. Its path has reached its natural conclusion.

However, you should start to look at these natural conclusions simply as touch points in the ongoing flow. Grab another glass, and start a new flow to pour into the next natural conclusion.

What if the glass has water in it but isn't completely filled? As mentioned above, you could direct someone who just made a purchase to other products or information. Ask what else you could offer at that point to fill and overflow the glass. How could connecting one experience to another enhance the experience, making it more valuable by combining experiences? You could offer to send a mobile update when the customer's order ships, or provide

a discount for a future purchase, or send tips on how to better use the purchased item.

All of these options extend the flow. The flow's timeline has been extended by connecting multiple experiences. In so doing, you keep that person in the flow even when she is not actively involved with your product. It adds value for the user and value to your product.

Flows Can Be Long

If we understand that a flow is a set of experiences that people have over time while interacting with your product, we should recognize that "over time" can mean a very long time, indeed. The length, breadth, and depth of an experience are also variables that we can design for. Typically, we tend to think of digital products enabling "fast" or "instant" results, and it is all too common to wrap things up quickly. But what if the experience was slow? What if you could not only design the "now" part of the experience, but also shape future experiences that the person will have while using your product?

If you are creating a shopping experience, for example, the flow may begin with a very quick checkout. But that person now has a relationship with your product, along with an opinion about it. You could come back to him after a week, a month, or a year to get additional feedback. Was the product he purchased durable? How is he using it? You can capture a lot of valuable information over time.

Also consider that you are working on a product that lets people start an experience now that might conclude in the future.

Those events could happen now or a decade from now. The user experience can become very long. You have to think differently about how you would create that flow so you don't accidently create a dead end later.

For instance, I might choose very different tools if I'm planning on accommodating an experience that can unfold over a long period of time. I might choose a very simple technology that seems to be stable and has been around for a long time, rather than take a risk with the newest, unproven technology. I might set up the product with a proven technology for its infrastructure, giving it a better chance of being serviceable and able to easily evolve many years from now.

The important thing is to open up your thinking for everything that might happen between now and the end of what could be a very long experience.

Connect the Dots

Sometimes as you work you will see the connection points between parts of the product experience, and sometimes they will not appear for a long time. The design process is always one of discovery. When we design a product for the Web, discovery is an important part of how we determine what the product actually is. When you reach the end of a flow—the edge of the product—imagine a dot, a connection point. Now it's time to discover another dot, and so on. There are no ends, only new opportunities to explore. Once you have connected a series of dots, you have a flow without an

end. You can design an experience to connect the end point of one key as to another.

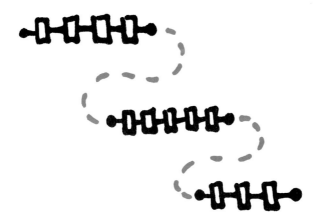

When you've identified which dots to connect, you need to guide the person across that connection point. It's up to the designer to help the user to understand, "What am I going to get out of this?" Why should the user continue on?

There has to be a reason for that person to continue with the experience. Whether it's informative, useful, or just plain fun, the ongoing path you create makes it more likely that the user will stay with you on the journey through your product.

CHAPTER 5

Remember the Invisible Features

When a user first experiences a product you've designed, that person can easily see the colors you've chosen, the letterforms of the typography, and the crop of a photograph. She sees a thoughtfully placed button that encourages action and suggests the benefit she will receive by interacting with the button. These elements are visible. They're obvious.

However, some other elements of a product design can't be seen. I call them invisible features. They aren't easily detected, but they are essential to the success of your product and the quality of its user experience. Invisible features are as important as those features you can see—sometimes more so—because of the emotional impact they have on users. As a result, these features *must* be considered as you design and plan your product.

When a user sees the colors, icons, and text that represent a set of features, she's experiencing more than the graphic style of the

text or the speed of a transitional animation. She is subconsciously forming perceptions and judgments about the quality and reliability of that product and ultimately the people behind it. Her sense of ease or unease, trust or mistrust, is developing. At this stage, her reactions are based on minimal experience, but those early impressions quickly start to cement her opinion of the product. Invisible factors can be steered by your design, thereby improving your chances for success.

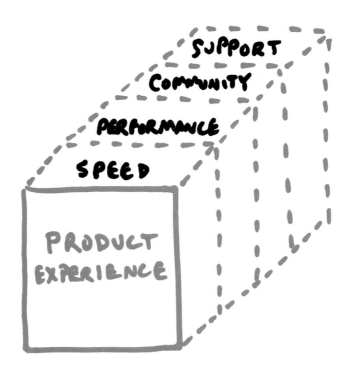

Consider a product experience from your own perspective. We all want feelings of safety and trust, excitement and enthusiasm.

We want to believe that our expectations will be met and nothing will go wrong. But those aren't desires that we consciously think about or voice. Imagine walking into a store and asking for a shirt that felt *trustworthy*. If you buy a shirt and you find out later that it was made in a sweatshop that mistreated its employees, that invisible factor could become very important to you. You might stop wearing that shirt, stop buying that brand, and tell your friends that they shouldn't buy that brand of shirt either. For another brand with invisible features that would be positive attributes, they'd be smart to make them known. If you were concerned about the manufacturing process behind a shirt, you might check the label inside the shirt for information. This would be a great place for the brand to make the invisible visible.

In this chapter, you'll learn how to build invisible features such as performance, community, support, and security into your design. Each of these ideas is discreet and distinct, but each is also interdependent and connected to the others. If you can improve performance, for instance, you will stand a good chance of increasing a user's sense of security. If you fail to achieve adequate performance, you risk losing trust.

Performance

Performance speaks to the product's quality.

Performance is measured by how people *expect* the product to work. Users usually come to your product with a set of expectations. Think of the situation like this: If you had the opportunity

to drive a high-performance car, you would expect it to spring into motion at the touch of the gas pedal and quickly respond to a touch of the steering wheel. You might not know anything about vehicles or engines, but you would expect this car to operate with a powerful ease and effortlessness, making the driving experience unique, fun, and even exhilarating. If the test drive did not meet every single one of those expectations, you'd probably be disappointed.

The same is true for Web products. A slow website or app doesn't feel "right." The user will assume that something is missing or broken or that the product isn't as good as other products she's already used. If your software must be downloaded, the speed at which it arrives might be your user's first experience of the product's performance. If that download is unbearably slow, that user may instantly form a negative opinion about it, even if your product is flawless in all other ways. Also, if the product is so large in file size or other needs that it causes a device to freeze or display a "no more space" message, the user will become unhappy before she even tries the product.

Speed

Speed is a major factor when customers gauge performance, and it can cut both ways. Speed represents the power behind the product. As you design, you need to consider hardware and software requirements. For instance, you need to be certain that the product publisher will have the server capabilities necessary to respond to requests from many people, and the people using the product

will have enough power and memory on their own computer or device to render the graphics, process data, and support the overall demands of the product. You need to be thinking about the range of devices that your product may appear on. Can each of them deliver the hardware performance you need? Then there is the matter of software performance: Is the software engineered to a degree of quality that it will perform well enough to meet user expectations?

Following are some issue to consider, as they can affect the speed of your product and the resulting user experience.

In your **design,** you can manipulate the elements that affect speed:

- Optimize image, video, and sound assets for size, file format, resolution, and so on.
- Implement animations and transitions in ways that use the fewest processor resources.
- Limit the number of unique elements in your product to improve speed.

In the product's **code,** you can find opportunities to increase speed. For example:

- Make conditionals and calculations more efficient.
- Remove redundant database calls.
- Reduce load and wait times by eliminating data requests and processing routines that were part of inactive or discarded features.

- Remember that requiring a client-side code library to fully load before displaying anything in a browser can make a product feel slower to respond because the user waits longer to see *something*. By displaying your product as it loads, you can improve the perceived speed even if the overall load time remains the same.
- Optimize the app's ability to recover from unpredictable circumstances, such as intermittent network connectivity problems or the sudden loss of battery power.

On the **device** a person is using to interact with your product, some local issues can affect speed:

- Storage capacity limitations can make a product feel sluggish. If your product pushes a local device to its storage limits, the slowness, or even bugginess, that can occur will be first experienced in your product and will be attributed to it, correctly or not.
- Insufficient processor power can compromise the app's ability to perform calculations or render computationally complex graphics.
- The choice of software used to display your product can also influence speed. Have you ever used a site that seemed sluggish in one browser, but much faster when you tried it in a different browser? The browser, not the site, was the culprit, but users almost always blame the site.

The **server** hardware can have limitations similar to those of the user's local device:

- Inadequate storage availability affects capacity, retrieval speed, and the database's ability to address search demands.
- Low memory compromises temporary storage and quick retrieval.
- Limited processing power slows response to the demands of multiple user requests.

Problems on the **network** connecting the user's device and the server can impose constraints on such factors as:

- The ability to handle incoming and outgoing requests.
- The availability of cellular data or high-speed data.
- The connection capacity to handle many users making requests at the same time.

Your product may have additional issues based on other product-specific concerns. For example, imagine that your product allows a user to scan a common UPC code with a phone or laptop camera. The quality of that camera and the way it handles lighting conditions might affect the recognition speed for that UPC code.

When you think about planning for speed, consider such questions as:

- Have you cached information that doesn't change frequently in your database, so you don't have to make repeated database calls to access that information?

- Should you be using a Content Delivery Network (CDN)? This system of servers in multiple data-center locations is specifically designed to efficiently deliver information to end-users. Because a CDN uses multiple computers in multiple locations—along with many other highly technical efficiency techniques—it is superior to a centrally located server for delivering content to locations around the globe.
- Did your team review images for appropriate optimization for various delivery formats? For example, are you confident that you're not trying to deliver high-definition assets to a device that has only a standard-resolution screen?
- How could you reduce the number of database requests on each load of heavily used views, while not negatively affecting the product experience?
- If you quickly hacked together an idea, and learned from your audience that it works, should you refactor the implementation to be more efficient?

All of these issues and questions have everything to do with fast, efficient delivery—you want that as much as your customers do. Yet it is very common to design without these factors in mind. In some ways, that's only natural because early in the design process you're probably more focused on just getting the product features to work. Or you may be testing the product only on your in-office Wi-Fi network and neglecting to try it on an overworked cellular network. But to guarantee a fast, positively perceived user

experience, you must test your creation in as many varied and difficult conditions as you can dream up. No matter how much you optimize, there are always more ways to accelerate your product.

I mentioned earlier that speed can cut two ways. A product that is too fast can generate as much user unease as a slow product. Imagine that you are making a big purchase online, and you click the button to confirm your purchase. If the purchase is completed instantly and there's not enough visual feedback, you might not have a lot of confidence that the transaction actually took place. The act of waiting in an experience like this helps create the impression that a more complex action took place than a lightweight product interaction.

In general, the heavier the importance of the exchange, the more carefully the pacing should be considered. When people are dealing with money, health, and other weighty issues, speed can be eased off a bit. I recommend a simple exercise. If the interaction is something you'd take a deep breath before completing, then take that breath! Use that breath as your measurement for a reasonably paced response time. Click. Deep breath. Response.

How can you make speedy performance visible? From time to time, you might tell your users how quickly your product works—any quantifiable value can work. You can gather endorsements from outside parties that speak well of your product's performance (such as with a quote about how quick it is). Or you can render speed metrics that are relevant to your audience, such as "this search took 1.872 seconds."

Reliability

Reliability is another important part of performance. It's characterized by a product that functions consistently, is free of bugs, doesn't crash, and fully loads every time. Its buttons respond each time you click them, and any gestures on a touch screen feel natural and appropriately responsive. That is, they accept your input but do not capture accidental actions.

Addressing these issues means fixing software bugs, and it's best if the fixes are made before the release. If bugginess is reported after release, you must be able to respond to it quickly. (Customer support is another component of reliability that we'll discuss shortly.)

Another aspect of performance and reliability is consistency over time. Your product must be able to accommodate change. However, understand how change feels to the user: a product that changes too often may convey unreliability. Users want to do tomorrow what they did today, and do it without fuss or confusion. Constant change can be upsetting. At the same time, the longer the product has been around and the longer the time between changes, the more upsetting a change can be.

Change may also make the user believe that something was previously amiss. Without an explanation, the user does not understand what you are doing—even if the change was a big improvement. We'll talk more about communicating the value of change in Chapter 11.

Community

Increasingly, there can be an unspoken assumption that when a lot of people are using a product, and/or the product has been around for some time, it is more reliable, efficient, and supported. It's like seeing a long line outside a restaurant: The food inside must be fantastic. This may or may not be true, but that's the perception.

An established, enthusiastic community gives new users a sense of security, assuring them that they are making the right choice. It also reinforces a sense of belonging for longtime customers. So you need to find a way to make the concept of "community" visible to your users.

Community actually has two parts. One part is your *internal* community. It can include customer service, industry and business partners, and the people who build the product (that's you!). Consider who and what you can assemble to demonstrate your collective powers, and then promote the benefits of those collective powers to the people that use or might use your product. Can you find authentic ways of calling attention to your internal community in the product experience? For example, you might send a reminder email for the user to try a feature but have the email signed by an actual member of the team that worked on creating the product feature.

The other part of community is the *external* community. This community develops over time and is probably the one "invisible"

feature that you have the least control over, as it tends to grow organically. The biggest source of this external community is your growing pool of customers. Find ways to show them getting involved with your product, such as by blogging about using it or talking about it on social media.

For example, if your product tracks footsteps and other physical activities for the user, in addition to providing personal reports, you could total all of the steps walked by everyone in the community: "We walked 142,000 steps today!" Sharing the positive reports with everyone encourages the group to walk even more, and the amount of success you can share tomorrow and the next day visibly grows and grows.

Another source of external community is the forums—created by people not connected with your company—in which your product is warmly reviewed. Direct people to view these complimentary forums. Also, make a lot of noise about events or articles where your product will be featured. Capture and promote what your community is saying about your product in social media, on blogs, and in conversation (if you can). The idea is to create the perception that a lot of people are already talking about and using your product.

Consider, too, that different people have different feelings about community. For instance, some people feel more secure having their money in a big bank. Some people get more security as a member of a small credit union. So remember that a big community is not what everyone is looking for. A solid, welcoming, trustworthy community will work for everyone, though.

Support

Support is the availability of resources, people, and/or information that can address a problem if it occurs. The support you offer needs to be solid and easily available. Think about how it feels when you get great customer service—when the clerk says, "It's OK if you don't have your receipt. We can offer you store credit or a refund; which would you prefer?" That moment feels great! How can your business create that same feeling for your customers?

Support is necessary in a host of situations. The product might be buggy, the customer may not have understood instructions, or she might want to order something different. Support can help resolve product misuse or abuse, inaccurate transactions, unwanted or unexpected messages, or a thousand other problems. It's tough to plan a support system that is comprehensive enough to address everything, but if a responsive system is not in place, customers will definitely feel it. Consider this: If a user is having a problem and then finds your support inadequate or unavailable, her unhappiness quotient didn't just double; it probably multiplied many times. And if you are having any other product problems— with performance, community, or security (which we'll talk about next)—bad support just amplifies your troubles.

Support can take conventional forms, such as a toll-free phone number, a website, or an online chat. But you can also provide video tutorials (or direct customers to third-party vendors who produce tutorials on using your product), participate in forums, or contribute to blogs. You can be available to answer support queries

on social media, or even actively monitor social media and offer support proactively. You might schedule real-time events and workshops to support your community in person.

It's not enough just to *have* great support, though; you also have to make it visible through your marketing and in your product. A simple way to do that is to offer it frequently. Perhaps your main screen includes a blurb that reads, "Need support? Just ask!" Even if users never take you up on the offer, just knowing that support exists builds their confidence in your product. Consistent support builds a good reputation over time.

Customer satisfaction reports provide a metric that is widely respected. Track these reports and share them with customers. Other metrics may be trackable and sharable. Wouldn't you be proud to say, "Ninety-nine percent of customer support inquiries are resolved within 15 minutes"?

Security

We want people to feel confident using our products. We want them to know that we have their best interests in mind and that we respect users and any access we have to their information.

But the invisible feature of security goes beyond that. It also means providing the confidence that we can prevent and police fraudulent behavior, such as hacking, theft, and so on, and that customers' credit card numbers and other personal information is stored safely. This factor is hugely important for any products that deal with financial or medical records—anything private, for

that matter. People also want to feel secure from bugginess, and when they do have a problem, they want to talk about it with a human being. They do not want to feel that product security is on auto-pilot.

Security relates directly to a sense of control. If a user feels that things are out of his control, he will not enter into a relationship with your product.

The absence of security can quickly lose current users and severely limit new users. Any gaffs in security, however small, can have significant ramifications. I may have a product that I really love, but if my information does not seem secure, I may quit using the product I prefer and switch to a lesser one that has better security.

Several visual cues can be used to imply security. You're surely familiar with seeing an icon of a lock or a safe on a checkout page. Although they are not required, don't underestimate the potential power of such cues. However, when misused, a cue like this (suggesting security for a product that is later revealed as insecure) can instantly destroy trust, which might never be regained.

Invisible No More

Because performance, community, support, and security are invisible, they are easily overlooked. But when they become visible by their absence, their importance becomes too clear, too late. Each of these invisible features should be designed as carefully as the visual elements of your product. If you fail to address even one of them, be

sure that you made a conscious choice to do so and that the omission was not made out of ignorance or disregard for the customer.

A side note: The more positive emotional connection between the user and your product, the more forgiving that user is prone to be. For instance, a leading social media outlet may suffer a security breach, and although users are momentarily alarmed and annoyed, they are unlikely to drop the service because the desire for that product doesn't go away. For a newer product, one that does not yet have that emotional connection, the relationship with users is much more fragile.

You build trust equity over time. If you do a very good job most of the time, customers will cut you some slack when you do make a mistake. But you can't do that very often, and when it happens, you have to rebuild. You can recover gracefully only so many times, especially if you have a competitor trying to lure away your users.

Certain unanticipated situations can cause you to miss the advantages provided by well-designed invisible features:

- Designers moving from website design to Web product design can tend to underestimate and under-design support and security features because they haven't previously had to deal with these features.
- Load can be underestimated, thereby making your product seem buggy.
- Customer support has to be timely. If it is not, the slow (or lack of) response multiplies the user's negative experience many times over.

Look at your product through the eyes of a person who is frustrated when things are slow, stops using an app that crashes, or doesn't trust a site with a publicized security breach; also look at your product as a customer who responds to a feeling of community with your product as well as feels like a responsible user of customer support. Make design decisions to create an exciting—and dependable—product experience for that person, so she can use your product without ever worrying about the invisible features. That's your job.

CHAPTER 6

Effective Over Clever

The key word for this chapter is *intent*. What is your intention for a product, and what is your user's intention for it? Every other consideration is secondary.

WHICH BUTTON LOOKS LIKE
IT WILL SAVE YOUR INPUT?

In every Web product you create, you should prioritize effective over clever. As you probably already know, sometimes the equation gets reversed. During the design process, you can easily want to

surprise and delight the user. So you create a design element—an interaction pattern, a naming scheme, a symbol, and so on—that is fresh and extremely inventive. However, the cleverness of your creation obscures the intent of the product. And the cleverness of that first impression doesn't hold up over time—and I don't mean over years; I mean over only the first few *moments* of use. After that first rush of newness, if the intended value of the product is not clear, or the functional intent isn't obvious, the novel idea means nothing.

Imagine this moment. A new app you've installed promises an elegant and easy way to capture simple notes as text. You're presented with a blank white screen and a keyboard, and you start typing. So far, so good. But when you finish typing, now what? How do you save your note? How do you create a new note?

In this example, suppose that the designer associated the Save action with an upward swipe from the bottom of the screen—the same gesture used to scroll through a list of items! It's a clever intention, but perhaps too clever. Clever solutions have their place—and we'll get to that—but they should always serve the effective use of the product.

This chapter will help you focus on intent and evaluate it as a prioritization filter. You will learn how to edit out the creative clutter that gets in the way of user understanding and product functionality. You will also discover that you can create products that are both effective *and* clever.

Recognizing Clever

What cleverness factors work against the intent of a design?

Unclear Naming

Typically, when you are introducing a new product or trying to attract new users to an existing product, clever language just puts more hurdles in the way of potential users. Every conceptual leap that you ask users to make reduces a product's potential for success. Understanding should be the result of one cognitive process, not several. That is, any language or naming scheme within the product should be descriptive rather than suggestive or metaphoric, especially when you are describing core features and elements.

Sometimes designers create new terminology for a product that isn't easily understood without explanation. For example, imagine a product that allows you to send a message to many people at the same time, and it's called Signal. That name does not convey the product's intent; better to call it Broadcast, which immediately makes the product's intent clear.

Over time, with any product, it is possible to apply a vocabulary that is based on the experiences people have with your product and allows them to acquire a deeper understanding of that product. A great example of new vocabulary that emerges from product use is *retweet*: the action of sharing a tweet that you've seen in your Twitter timeline. The term was started by the Twitter community

and later incorporated into the application itself. In this case, an invented word was integrated into the product, but it wasn't confusing. Its use had already been established by the product's users.

Does this mean that designers must produce dull, pedestrian work? Of course not. But the cleverness or "extras" that you add to a product should be like a little salt and pepper sprinkled on a well-prepared dish. They can add to and even improve the recipe, but the seasoning should not be a main ingredient.

Newness for Newness's Sake

Consider again the earlier example of using a swipe action to save a note. This kind of design excess is common in many programs and apps. What if a designer, in an effort to create something fresh, instead renames that Save action as *Done?* "Done" may describe a state of being, but it does not specifically describe what the user wants to do. When you're done, are you exiting, saving, saving and closing, or doing something else entirely?

It's natural when a creative person wants to invent something new. But what he can miss in that inventive moment is the opportunity to build on the knowledge that users already have. Part of a product design strategy is bringing the user farther down your current trail, not returning him all the way back to the trailhead to begin again.

For example, consider the concept of radio buttons in an app or program. Most users already understand that by pressing one button, they are making a single, exclusive choice. If you abandon that experiential knowledge and introduce a dial or some other

selection gizmo, your product must work even harder to help the user understand its intention. The clever design choice works against intent.

Pressure to Create a Marketable Product

The need to creatively market an updated product sometimes pushes designers toward overly clever choices. It is possible to wave around phrases like "new and improved" to cut through the noise of the marketplace, but once your product has the user's attention, its "new and improved" features must absolutely support the product's intent. Otherwise, they will simply challenge and frustrate the user by making a familiar product confusing and unnecessarily complicated. Your "improved" product will be seen as gimmicky, not valuable.

Personality Mismatches

Every design feature must consistently fit the personality of the product. Consider a first-of-its-kind app that helps you understand prescription drug interactions, a very serious topic. If the designer, in an effort to convey healthiness in her color and type choices, instead inadvertently creates a childlike feeling, the app's intent is derailed. A very straightforward, simple design would be a better choice, serving to convey the seriousness of the topic and the straightforward intention of the product.

Now consider a weather app. There are lots of them out there already. The weather reports presented via various media are very familiar to most people. It's a commodity product, so differentiation through style may be possible as well as strategically desirable.

It would be safer to add a new personality or twist to a familiar domain like weather, as long as the novel personality will resonate with the intended audience.

Correct Action, Wrong Application

The ability to make swipe gestures on touch screens is a good example of a novel or clever product feature. The idea of dragging a map from side to side or up and down with your finger is totally intuitive. You do it once and understand it completely. That sort of design feels like no design at all—it just feels inevitable. Those moments are when a design is most effective.

However, that swipe gesture does not translate to every application feature. It would be confusing to assume that a user would

intuit that she should swipe her finger to the left to stop a file from loading, for instance. In that context, the swipe doesn't match up with any previous user experience.

Problems arise when interface designs:

- Look like they should behave one way, but behave in another way.
- Are so new that they create more work than would a more standard interface.
- Become difficult to explain with language. (Imagine a friend trying to tell another friend how to use your product but being unable to describe it.)
- Solve for every single possible thing someone could want to do, at the expense of doing any simple action well.
- Rely on unclear symbols or text.

For example, some time ago at Etsy, we were building a feature that would allow members to connect with one another by following another user's interests and activities on the site. This relationship would enable users to view items that another user liked, along with all of her activity. The language and the conceptual framework for describing those features came down to two possible directions:

- We could name it for the action: Following. You would be a follower of other people whose taste interested you, and you would have a following of people interested in your taste.

- We could explain what you would see or create, and call the result Circles. (This idea predated Google's product with a similar name.) You could place someone in your circle, or other people could place you in their circles. The action was "to circle."

We ended up launching a product that we called Circles, and with that name, it turned out to be quite confusing. We should have focused on the core activity—following—with which people were already very familiar.

We tried, unsuccessfully, to change people's mental model. The distinctiveness that we were trying to create by using a unique feature name was already present in our product: that is, Etsy content is unique, and giving a feature a unique name may actually *prevent* a user from getting to that unique content. Software that allows you to connect with other people is important, but it is not unique. Following is what happens. We just needed to accept that. Eventually, we renamed the feature and the actions associated with it.

Turning On Your Filter

The designer's role is to reduce a product design solution to an idea that's as familiar and understandable as it can possibly be and still ensure that the product works as intended. Your goal should be to make sure that your design is usable and, therefore, is used by its intended audience. Products shouldn't be epically creative, or try to break perceptions, or ask a user to consider a whole world of new.

Your usability filter should be turned way up as you design. Every design choice you make should be viewed through that strict filter. Does this choice help the user? Does that choice improve her experience? Does it throw elements in her path that waste time and energy? (If so, the feature also wastes your time and energy.) Stay focused on your primary intent.

Sometimes the very best design answer is no design answer at all. Have you ever worked with a writer on a project and, when you were done, felt that the project had too much text? That's because writers tend to solve problems with words.

Designers are inclined to do the same. They tend to solve problems by over-designing features. It takes a selfless, critical eye to avoid over-designing your product. Just let it be what it wants to be.

Obviously, you shouldn't settle for bad typography or poor design. But if you are designing a screen that offers the user three choices and then expects them to click a Submit button, you needn't create a completely new design for this common activity. Start by designing what is already familiar to the user (a picture of that scenario probably popped into your mind as I described it), and before you try any other design solution, see if the standard solution will work for your product. In other words, un-design the experience before you design it.

Always remember that the cleverness should be in the product's concept, not in its execution.

Backward Satisfaction

But what about creative satisfaction and the joy of being innovative? When you're designing products for the Web, a lot of the pleasure you will receive will be in the form of the reverse satisfaction that comes when a product is successful and hordes of people use it. For me, it is exciting to see people successfully using a dashboard that I designed, for example, and I'm proud of how well it works. We become more satisfied with our design choices as the product matures and as everyone—users and designer alike—gets to know it better.

The creative joy isn't in the cleverness of the product; it's in the use of the product.

Such feedback doesn't occur in just one moment. It continues throughout the product's flow. Web products are never done, so nothing is precious and everything is subject to change. This constant need for change means that we are always getting new feedback, performing new testing, and getting opportunities to devise new, creative ideas.

There is a massive body of work that you and your collaborators build when designing and executing Web products. You make something and test it and throw it away and build it again. Part of your ongoing satisfaction will also come from your cumulative learning.

Is Clever Ever Good?

When all of the nuts and bolts that execute the design are in place, and when everything is operating properly, then you might consider adding an element that feels clever, or fun, or different, or whatever you would like to call it. For that feature to be effective, though, your user shouldn't even notice it. It has to support the intent of the product, not battle with it for attention.

Look back at the first illustration in this chapter.

"Let's do it!" was too clever for its own good in this case. So where might an interesting choice like that work?

When the context around the clever UI is made clear, it's better set up for the user's success and understanding. It is safer to apply it when voice and personality are least off-putting (in this example, as part of a marketing message and at the beginning of a flow). It is reasonable to expect that most people would not be confused by it there. In contrast, a similar solution in the context of a complex

view with many other interface elements would probably be inappropriate at best.

From time to time, a novel interaction (which also serves the product's intent) may inspire an entire class of other products. The initial learning curve may be overcome by many users because the ultimate utility of the interaction is sound.

CHAPTER 7

Carrots, Not Sticks

It may sound obvious, but it's essential that we, as designers, respect the people who use our products. If you're not solidly on their side, you're designing wrong and doing wrong by them. You might say that this shouldn't have to be said. But unless your design choices reward people for using your product in the way you intended—and in a way that benefits them—you are not their true advocate. In fact, you might be punishing them, which is unlikely to make them love your product.

As you've learned, designing products for the Web is very much about designing the *experience*. Our design decisions shape how users behave, how they go from inaction to action. Their perceptions, emotional responses, and decisions are guided by the information and structure we provide. We want to lead users down the desired path toward a good experience for them and a profitable experience for us. Our product will be at its best when everyone's goals are aligned and mutually beneficial.

The carrot-and-stick metaphor is old but apt. You can make a donkey move by hitting it with a stick, but that negative motivation does not make the donkey *want* to move. In fact, he might want to kick you! However, if you tie a carrot to that same stick and hold it in front of the animal, it will move forward of its own accord. Even if that carrot is always held just out of reach, the perception or anticipation of that reward is positively motivating.

Our designs need to provide goals that users can aspire to and understand how to attain; those are our carrots. Anything that gets in the way of a user's success is more punishing than encouraging.

Shaping Behavior

Training is all about shaping behavior. When you train a dog, he might get a treat for a desired behavior—say, stopping and sitting at an intersection. If he does not stop and sit, a common technique is to switch to another command that he consistently obeys, reward that success to get him back on track, and then repeat the stop-and-sit command. This technique switches the animal back into positive reinforcement mode.

People are not donkeys or dogs, of course! However, the point is that you are in charge of their experience with your product. If you want people to love your product and recommend it to others, you must always be offering positive reinforcement. Each of the following strategies will increase the chances of your success and the success of your customers. Test your product early and often, and

use your design discretion to determine what's best for your product and the people who use it.

Encourage the Intended

Remember to keep those carrots out in front. Lead people to the answers they want. At the start of their experience, show them examples of what you want them to do. Remember that at the beginning, the user hasn't yet had the opportunity to be rewarded, and she doesn't yet know her goal.

Imagine that I download an app for my tablet and get a brief overview of the product. It immediately tells me three things that I need to do to use the product successfully. Let's say that the app will organize my photo library by person. The overview might display a plus-sign button that allows me to select the people I want to identify. Then another button appears that, once pressed, will give the product access to my photo library. Finally, the product allows me to look at its suggestions to verify that it has correctly identified and organized my photos.

I don't need to know anything else about the product to achieve success. That's an important goal for the product designer: to reward the user with success from the earliest possible interactions. If the app had only shown written instructions on the screen, I might not have understood them or might have thought they were too time-consuming to read. Or maybe I just couldn't see where the experience was taking me. The designer would be inadvertently punishing me after I took the time to download his product. I would get no benefit, and he wouldn't get a customer.

Make Implicit What Is Intended

Instead of (or in addition to) explaining your product, your design choices can also imply what is intended. Maybe the button for adding people in my new photo app pulses. That draws my attention and encourages me to interact with that button first.

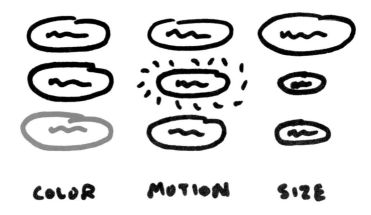

COLOR   MOTION   SIZE

Consider how you can carve out a clear path for your users. The cues you set out depend greatly on the sophistication of your audience, so you may need to be both implicit *and* explicit. Explicit cues might take the form of emphasizing through design and language what action is desired. Implicit cues might include removing all possible actions other than the desired action.

Make Explicit What Is Intended

Another option is to show explicit examples of the goal. Rather than staging the experience, you might start the user experience by showing how other users have achieved their goals. With the photo app, you could share the photo libraries of a few people so that the new user can experience the product through models of how it can be used. It's always good to offer a number of examples so that the new user can compare and contrast, as well as see how the technology can be used in different ways. Singular examples can be challenging, particularly if there is demographic diversity among the people who use your product. You don't want your examples to feel exclusionary.

Be Nurturing and Be Encouraging

All along the way, offer encouragement and feedback when the user does what you want him to do. With multi-step processes especially, we can reward success at each step. For example, maybe a status bar could show the user's progress through the setup process.

Or maybe simple messages appear: "You have now finished Step 1" or "Almost done!"

Or a feedback loop with positive reinforcement from a network of other people could encourage the next intended action.

Little rewards along the way orient the user in his progress.

Studies have shown that dopamine releases occur when our brains experience a reward. That chemical release gives us a feeling of satisfaction and elation. Though the feeling might be short-lived, you're likely to subconsciously remember its effect and

crave it again. Have you ever refreshed your email inbox or revis-
ited a social-media activity stream, hoping that a new message
would arrive? If so, you know the power of these small bursts of
satisfaction.

Discourage Unintended Behavior

Some people will intentionally try to misuse your product (see
"When Sticks Are Appropriate," in this chapter), but there will be
times when a user will unintentionally head down a wrong path.
The easiest way to prevent this is to remove the opportunity for
error in your design. If you want a user to select only A, then gray
out choices B and C, or better yet, don't make them visible at all.

You can also show examples of what is not intended (although
positive examples usually work better). For instance, you might
show what happens when someone tries to add a snapshot of his
pet to the photo library, when the software is designed to recognize
only human faces. Perhaps an error message or sad face appears.

You can also describe what the product will not do. Say the app can also identify photos by where they were shot. If the user is supposed to add the city and state or ZIP code, you could show an example—"New York City, NY" or "10010"—next to an example of what won't work—"NYC," for example.

Reward Intended Behavior

When a task is successfully completed, you want to use simple rewards to encourage people to repeat that behavior again and again. If your product's social network page wants users to share photos, and your user complies, he might be rewarded with a notification every time someone comments on his photos. The smart designer will send that notification but not include the comment's content. In that way curiosity is likely to drive the recipient back to the network site, where he might comment on that comment, which will in turn cause his friend to revisit, and so on. It's all about positive reinforcement.

Once rewarded, behavior becomes learned over time and repeated. So reward what you want repeated.

ACTION → REWARD
ACTION → REWARD
ACTION → REWARD

You can also reward good behavior through game mechanics, which basically use rules to encourage people to become engaged with gameplay. The airline industry has been using game mechanics for a long time, offering aspirational perks for customers who select their "game."

For instance, airlines may reward frequent flyers for their status or their amount of use—normal member, advanced member, or expert member—resulting in corresponding benefits (free drinks, additional checked baggage, free trips, and so on). Instinctually, a person at a lower level will want to move to a higher level and receive better benefits. The airline might offer interim and immediate rewards for people between stages to keep them moving up and using its products more often.

ACTION → REWARD
STATUS INFO
ACTION → REWARD
STATUS INFO
ACTION → REWARD
UPGRADE
STATUS INFO
ACTION → REWARD

Another way to reward users is to give them access to information that is inaccessible to others. With our photo app, I might be allowed to unlock additional features, such as sharing private photos with others, or be given a code that unlocks additional storage. Perhaps I'd gain the ability to edit my photos or fine-tune facial-recognition features. You can also offer customers priority treatment, processing their files faster or giving them 24-hour customer support. You might publish the names of top users—praising them in the public square, so to speak. As you can see, this is an area where you can get very creative by offering perks that are attractive to your specific customers.

THE NEXT LEVEL
SOMETHING YOU WANT

YOUR LEVEL

But it's not enough just to offer these pluses; you should also make these advantages publicly visible to other customers. Doing so introduces a social component to your product—as well as a subtly competitive element—so that others can see that you offer benefits to people who use features to the fullest.

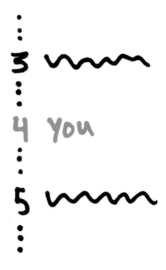

Revealing to a person her current status compared to the status of others—and then pairing that with an immediate action she can employ to change her status—makes for a powerful information-to-action design. Foursquare does a great job of delivering this kind of feedback in context. Check in at a location, and Foursquare will show you who is "mayor" of that location, how many times he's

checked in, and how many times you'll need to do so in order to become "mayor" yourself. They reveal a status that you don't yet have but make it clear what you would need to do to attain it.

When Sticks Are Appropriate

From time to time, you will have to contend with users who are intentionally misusing your product. Ideally, your product should be designed in such a way that misuse is impossible. But when misuse happens, aside from providing great feedback for improving the design of the product, it needs to be dealt with right away.

When people use your product incorrectly, it can create a less-than-ideal experience for other users. Let's say you've created a

product experience based on vintage portraits. Users can upload and share images of old photographs they've found—full images, details, restoration notes, and so on. Say a user starts to upload photos of vintage bicycles instead of portraits. What should you do?

Unintentional Misuse

Consider first what that person's motives might be. Perhaps he did not fully understand your rules for use. In that case, your instructions may need to be improved. Alternatively, you might just contact that person and ask him to take the photos down. Or you could just take down the photos yourself.

You might also consider developing a more agnostic view: Maybe users would enjoy seeing photos of other vintage objects. But that choice can become a slippery slope, and one that you will have to police almost constantly. Better perhaps to require users to stick to the rules, unless you are prepared to amend them.

Wrong Audience

In these cases, the misuser isn't trying to be malicious but has accidentally come to the wrong party. If you created an app for doctors to exchange information, and somehow, a non-doctor gained membership, thinking it was a health-information site, you simply need to remove that member. The app will not at all be what that layperson wants, and her presence might create a bad experience for your core users.

Bad Actors

These are people who are intentionally misusing your product, sometimes for illegal gain. Anticipate that this *will* happen, and have strong policies in place to foil such efforts. These people may interact with your legit members in unhealthy ways, harassing or even cheating them. This situation needs to be resolved right away, so have a plan in place.

It all goes back to your choices: How can you design out such break-ins? Fixes can be internal—the product code could be strengthened, for instance—or external—a feature could be added that allows users to flag inappropriate content or to report a bad user.

Specific Sticks

When a user simply refuses to comply with your rules of use, you can:

- Revoke membership or use privileges.
- Suppress features or limit access to features. This is a user time-out, so to speak. That person might not be able to post messages or send texts for a specific amount of time.
- Revoke features or the opportunity to receive premium features.
- Show all customers how bad users are handled. This is a powerful stick and should be used with caution. The idea is to create a sense of safety within your product, not fear.

As a preventive measure, perhaps you can periodically communicate to users some relevant points of your policies (which most people never read, anyway). Breaking the policies down into single points, or phrasing them in simpler ways, is a proactive way to prevent bad behavior, intentional or not.

Stay Positive

If you remember one thing from this chapter, it should be this: stay positive. Using direct and indirect means, explanation and exposition, and reward and incentives, encourage the kinds of actions that will make the product experience fun and productive for the people using it. They'll be inclined to use the product more and to tell other people about it, and they'll become valuable contributors to the experience you create as you build a successful Web product.

CHAPTER 8

Ship Early. Ship Often.

Creators traditionally spend as much time as necessary to create the best possible product. Then, only when it is completely finished, will they share it with others. As with a bust on a plinth, the intention is to unveil a flawless, fully realized artifact to the world. This attitude grew out of the non-malleability of the resources that produced tangible products.

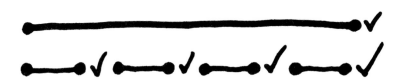

But with product design for the Web, we have almost complete malleability. Changes can be made, and they can be made frequently. We can adjust our ways of thinking to become more

flexible creators, and creators of flexible systems. We can build on the strength of the medium and embrace early, frequent, and repeated changes for the benefit of the people using the products we design.

The reason for building with frequent changes is simple: We create living products. The world that surrounds them is constantly changing, the people who use them live in that world, and our products need to change along with them.

One of the design books that most influenced me is *Practices of an Agile Developer* by Venkat Subramaniam and Andy Hunt (The Pragmatic Bookshelf). I suggest that you spend some time with it. Replace "developer" with "designer" and the book holds up like concrete.

In our malleable world of product creation, we're often encouraged to "ship early, ship often," a concept that is derived directly from so-called "agile development." This strategy has taken on a life—and developed into an industry—all its own. It is best expressed in the "Manifesto for Agile Software Development"—a document published in 2001 that is as relevant now as when it was written, perhaps more so. (See www.agilemanifesto.org for the full text.)

This manifesto urges us not to jump from the starting blocks directly to a completely designed product and then walk away without first getting user feedback. The time, resources, and energy expended to work like this are wasted, no matter how careful or skilled the designer is if human feedback is not at all part of the process.

Instead, we should create designs and share them with peers and customers, consider their feedback, adjust and redesign, and repeat the process over and over again on the way to developing a whole product. We should build quickly but responsively.

In other words, ship early and often. There's much to gain from doing so.

Manifesto for Agile Software Development

We are uncovering better ways of developing software by doing it and helping others do it. Through this work we have come to value:

- Individuals and interactions over processes and tools
- Working software over comprehensive documentation
- Customer collaboration over contract negotiation
- Responding to change over following a plan

That is, while there is value in the items on the right, we value the items on the left more.

http://agilemanifesto.org © 2001, The authors of this manifesto have stated that this declaration may be freely copied in any form, but only in its entirety through this notice.

Small Changes, Large Impact

A large quantity of lead bullets has a greater impact than one silver bullet—that is, many smaller gestures have a much greater cumulative effect than one grand gesture. Who knows if that one grand idea is any good? What if it fails? Then what do you do? Do you have other possibilities at hand and ready to launch?

Very early in the design and thinking process, we should be making things frequently, presenting our designs to peers and customers, and then tweaking and rethinking to create more designs. The creative process is not a static exercise in which we work alone. It is a living, breathing process that, over time, grows the best products because it directly benefits your ability to make creative decisions and collaborate.

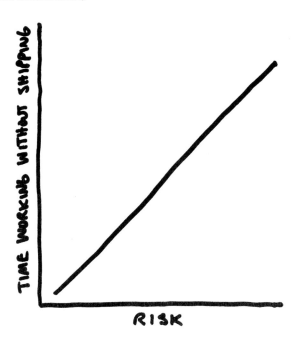

The Rewards of Frequent Collaboration

When you constantly collaborate with peers and customers, you receive gifts in the form of feedback. Don't treat ideas as precious commodities that you must save for the big reveal. Ideas are cheap

and easy; it's making them happen that's valuable and difficult. Input from other people makes those ideas even more valuable.

Sharing should happen often—as often as every few hours. Pursuing this mindset ultimately creates an environment in which you and the people you are working with are all in a state of continuous collaboration. The need for many interim deliverables is gone. You reduce the number of situations in which a large mass of work is created over a long period of time, and then needs to be approved all at once. For people who have never worked this way, it can be a challenge. When you practice a frequent-sharing way of working, the benefits of fewer disagreements, betting communication, and faster progress will outweigh the burden of altering your working patterns. It will, with practice, feel normal.

Everyone's efforts should be directed at making the product better. You want to ensure that design skills and creative energy are all going into the product, not into unnecessary—and unnecessarily fancy and polished—presentations.

Saving Time and Energy

Make the least possible investment in communicating an idea. Don't suffocate the process with Photoshop renderings or laboriously detailed sketches. Invest just enough time in your sketches or descriptions to communicate the essence of what you are trying to do. When you are trying to validate an idea, the simplest method is always best.

If you spend two weeks laboring over a pixel-perfect rendering of a new tablet, for example, and you show it to the engineer

and she tells you one minute later that such a design is impossible, you've just lost 14 days during which you could have been collaborating with her and improving your original idea or generating new concepts. A five-minute pencil sketch shared with the same engineer would have gotten you to the same place much sooner.

Remember that at this stage your goal is functionality, not polish. Share the idea, use it yourself, take it apart, and put it back together, over and over again—and do it quickly.

Getting Early Feedback

Getting early feedback on your designs validates your efforts. If a new app feature doesn't make sense or isn't wanted by your customers, early feedback stops you from wasting time and energy developing it. Also, asking sooner rather than later keeps you from getting off track, and it immediately brings other people into your process.

There's an interesting marketing technique called *false doors* that can help you test a product idea and gauge the interest of customers. You share your idea (in a semi-concrete way) with potential customers and collect their feedback. Say that you want to test

your idea for opening a pizza parlor in a certain location. Will there be enough traffic and interest? To find out, you create a simple sign that reads, "Pizza: $2.50 per slice," and for two weeks, post it in the window of the storefront where you would like to locate. If people enter the vestibule, they will see a "coming soon" notice and be able to leave their email address so that you can contact them when you do open.

You haven't made any pizza dough, employed anyone, or made any significant investment; all you have done is gather interest. If after two weeks, only 20 people entered, you know that this might not be the best location, at least for this type of business. If 200 people came in every day, you know that your idea is valid.

You can do the same thing with product design for the Web. Imagine that you have a new mobile application that allows people to keep track of their favorite pizzerias. You might want to introduce a new button that reads, "Publish to my profile." You can create a false door so that when someone clicks the button, he or she sees a "coming soon" or "notify me when available" pop-up notice. The feedback you can collect when people click this false door will help you determine how many people might be interested in your new idea.

With an actual pizza parlor, you could lower the price or offer different food to discover if that changes customers' interest levels. With the app, you could fine-tune how you share. Share only with friends? Let other people know your favorites? People will tell you what they want, and that information can guide your decisions.

Small Course Corrections

By getting feedback early and often, you can make regular (and much less painful) corrections to your plans rather than pushing out large and often demoralizing changes. Small changes mean less work for you and less adjustment for the customer. Plus, they set up a pattern in which you learn to learn regularly. You develop the ability to balance output and input in a constant and meaningful exchange.

These changes need to be very small, or your customers may start to feel that you are arbitrarily moving things around. Changes should be so small as to be almost undetectable. Users should never feel as though they are having one experience today and a completely different one tomorrow.

An example: Think of a Web-based email product. The primary means of navigating the site is a series of buttons across the top or down the side—Inboxes, Folders, Sent, Addresses, and Settings, in that order. Say the product's designer has a new concept that will surface the most important messages for the user. He would like to place that "most important" button above the regular inbox, as that is where most people click first, but that might disrupt his customers' experience too dramatically. So instead, he could put the new button in the second or third position. At that point, he has designed the code to make it work, but he has not yet asked the user to change her muscle memory.

Over time, if this addition does create a better experience for the user, the designer may decide to move the new button to the

top slot. This move prevents people from using the product as they did before, but the incremental change has (you hope) made them comfortable with the switch.

From a goodwill standpoint, it's crucial not to break the customer's trust. When you work this way—in tiny, tiny steps forward—you improve the customer's experience with a minimum of fuss. But, if after the slow introduction, your new feature proves confusing or not as useful as expected, it takes just another tiny step to resolve the problem or remove the feature.

Change as the New Normal

The spirit of working, sharing, and exchanging is fuel for the product design process. The pattern of constant change starts to feel so normal that peoples' hackles are much less likely to be raised. A constant state of change becomes the norm for the designer. Many users no longer expect a software product to be static or fixed. Consider what an enormous improvement this situation is over previous years and product cycles, when people bought boxed software at the mall and had to wait years for a future edition that would fix bugs.

Today, the status quo is typically a very long release cycle. But this new business model, with more frequent releases and updates, does raise an interesting question: If I buy an app for $5 and have learned to expect constant improvement, how does the maker support that strategy financially? He certainly isn't taking in any more money. It's something that definitely needs to be considered.

Uncalcifying Code

When changes are incorporated early and frequently, features and code can be added to or removed from the product with much less effort. The entire package needn't be redesigned; only very small pieces need to be, and these can be addressed one at a time.

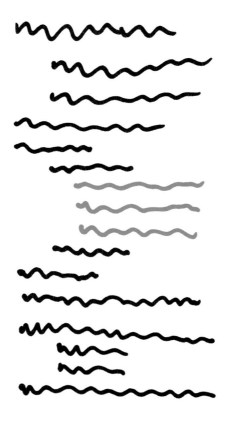

Nicholas Negroponte, founder and Chairman Emeritus of Massachusetts Institute of Technology's Media Lab, once said that we should pay developers for the number of lines of code they remove, rather than for the lines they write. Software products have a tendency to become very complex because we just add and add to them. Inside their DNA, entropy takes root, and eventually chaos grows because we are not constantly tending the garden. Every fix, every change, every removal, every test to improve flow—they are all tending the garden.

Isolating the Causes of Success and Failure

If something goes extremely well or poorly, you can pinpoint exactly which change caused the success or failure and likely even have parameters enough to measure the extent of the success or failure. This information is crucial for the success of not only the product at hand, but for the success of all future products, too, so you need to correlate changes with results. If you change lots of things at once, it's impossible to understand which of those changes prompted the positive or negative response.

Imagine this: I want to confirm my customers' email addresses. So I send each person a link that he or she can click to confirm, but only 50 percent of my customers actually follow through. I can move the link to the top of the message, turn it into a button, and change the wording, all in an effort to improve response. But now I've changed three things, and even if I do get a dramatically

improved response, I have learned nothing. Which change created the effect I wanted? What knowledge have I gained for future products?

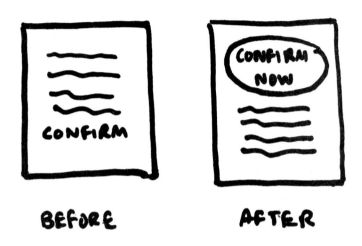

BEFORE   AFTER

If instead I make just one of these changes at a time, the positive or negative response will be evident. Then if more improvement is needed, I can make another change, and so on. It's all about identifying and isolating the successful changes.

Let's return to our email example. We look at our original design. We think that moving the button up will probably get more people to click it.

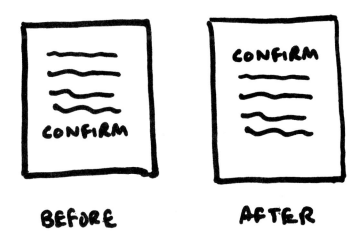

BEFORE   **AFTER**

We move the link up, but there's no change. Hmm, that's weird. It's a good thing that we first tried that out by itself.

So, we return the link to the bottom, but we change its size. Our click-through rate goes up. Very interesting. Maybe the problem wasn't sequencing (where the button appeared) but notice-ability (people didn't see it). Perhaps we've discovered a way to drive even more click-through with better messaging.

Now we're able to see that a different call to action had a slight improvement on our click-through rate. Had I made all of these design changes together, I'd not have learned about the positive (or negative) impact of each one.

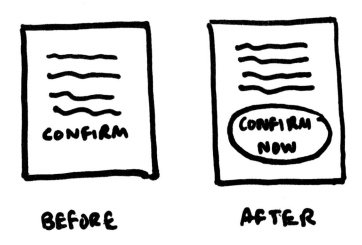

Risk Reduction

Making small changes is a form of damage control and a corollary to the previous point. If something goes wrong as a result of a small change, the result is likely to be similarly small, as will the fix. It's easier to fix glitches than to recover from catastrophes.

Dealing with Problems

So we changed our product and people are using it less. Ugh. Or maybe certain views hang and don't finish loading.

Problems will arise with any product, no matter how many times it is tested. The ship-early-and-often method of product development can also help us more easily solve these problems. Here's why:

- Problems are easy to detect when changes are made incrementally. We know exactly when a given problem emerged and we probably know what caused it.
- Problems are easy to attribute to a certain source. Instead of sifting through the work of everyone involved in the project, you can easily isolate the problem source.
- Problems are easier to fix if we know what or who the source is, what that source did, and why he/she did it. The solution is also likely to be small. Just go back to where you were previously. This solution requires less work as well.

Easier to Detect

Let's say our product is moving along swimmingly. Every day we get about 1000 new sign-ups, so our sign-up graph looks like this:

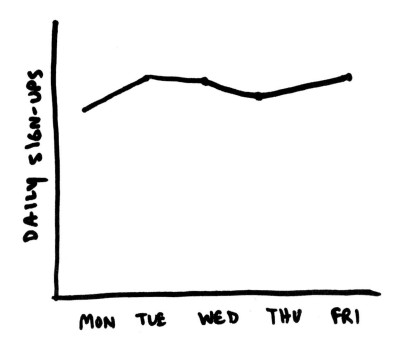

Then today, we see a change in the pattern:

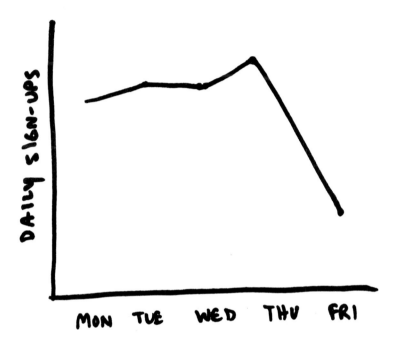

We've detected a problem; something is definitely wrong. Since we know we're making regular changes, we have confidence that we can identify the changes that occurred just before that problem began.

Easier to Identify

We shipped changes about ten times that day before the problem happened. And look—a few changes were made just before the problem began.

Now it's time to ask, what were those changes? Because everyone working on the product ships changes frequently and those changes are relatively small, it's easier to see when changes happened and who might know about the problematic ones.

Ah, ha! It looks like Steve released a change to the registration view about 15 minutes before the problem started. Now we know whom to talk to about the problem and what changes were likely to have caused it.

Easier to Fix

Because we've been able to easily identify the changes that appear to have caused the problem, we know where to investigate.

That negative change was relatively small—just a small interface change, a little bit of logic, and some language. All in all, it was a mere 15 lines of code across three files. Wow! This set of changes was so small that I could view them all on my laptop screen at the same time. If you've ever been hunting around, scanning code to look for problems, you'll understand what a luxurious situation we've created for ourselves.

And because we have our working process, tools, and methodologies optimized for making changes, we can release our fix to the

world right away. In fact, we can spend our time fixing the problem rather than first retreating to the old, previous design (though if we really needed to, we could do that, too).

How long does it take for you to detect a problem and fix it? Valuing small frequent changes sets you up to have a reduced time for both and to have a lower pain quotient for everyone involved.

Early. Often. Better.

Work fluidly, freely, and openly to generate ideas, make changes, and learn what might work. Ship those changes as early in the process as possible, and as frequently as possible.

Doing so will allow you to validate assumptions, identify opportunities, and try out new solutions. When problems happen, you'll be able to detect them and respond to them more quickly and with less effort.

That's better for you, that's better for your business, and that's better for the people using your product. That sounds like good design.

CHAPTER 9

Rinse and Repeat

This chapter is meant to challenge your way of thinking about what a "solution" is. In previous chapters, we've talked about making constant, small improvements to a product and about how that product—or solution—is really never completed. This chapter discusses something like that, but different.

Think about why you might go on an annual vacation: to relax, to see friends or family, to explore, to expose yourself to new experiences. Whatever the reasons might be, let's call them your goal. This year, you plan to go on a wonderful vacation and accomplish that goal. Great!

Now, does that mean you'll never go on a vacation again? Goal accomplished—done! Of course not! Next year you'll want to vacation again…and the year after that. Each year, you'll have similar goals—to relax, to explore—but it's unlikely that you'll repeat that same trip in exactly the same way. Your income may have changed, you may have to travel at a different time of year, or you might

want to travel with different people. The context for your planning is now different. You throw out your old route, budget, and plans, and you pull together completely new plans to reach your vacation goal in bigger, better, or deeper ways. In other words, you reach a goal, then rinse away all of the plans and ideas you made to accomplish that goal.

But instead, let's say you make a new plan to repeat the same goal, this time from a different direction. You don't have to throw out everything just for the sake of change. Instead, you pause, take a deep breath, reset, and then restart—rinse and repeat, over and over again.

You're never really "done" with the goal. It's a constant pursuit.

Apply this idea to product design. Your design may be released to customers who are happily using it. Now it's time to look at it again with fresh eyes.

Why would we want to "rinse clean" when we've been building up all of this product knowledge through testing, experimenting, and research? Because it's a thought exercise—sort of a brain-bender—that can force you to arrive at design solutions that aren't possible within another problem-solving process. It's about pursuing the same goals, but redefining the problem each time to force yourself into creative problem solving. Our brains are designed to follow patterns and to do things the same way over and over. If we want a different answer, we have to jog our thoughts out of deeply worn tracks.

Have you ever tried to fit too much copy onto one screen and found that it has ruined your design? You reduce the type size,

change the style, and mess with the line breaks without much success. Then someone walks up and asks why you couldn't split the copy into two screens. In one second, that person accomplished what you could not: She removed the constraint of one screen, thereby opening up new and better possibilities.

That is the sort of opportunity we're trying to set up for ourselves. The previous constraints are washed away, allowing us to start fresh.

Even if you changed a product only yesterday, you need to look at it through the lens of today. An example: Say you want to increase the number of people who register for a product. So you add a video tour that explains its benefits. If your new or returning visitors see the recently added video, the context for your product is now different than it was previously. Now you want to increase registrations for people who are viewing the video.

There are definitely benefits to learning from the past and building on your knowledge. It's just that for this part of the design process, the benefit is somewhere else, perhaps found in a different part of your brain. To renew our thought processes, we are hitting the reset button to learn more and different things.

Know the Goal

Before we delve too far into this technique, note this: It is clarifying to know from the start what your goal is and to maintain that goal throughout your design process. These goals might be numeric and quantitative, but they don't have to be. A goal could simply be

completing the addition of a new feature and making it available to your audience.

Some example goals might be:

- Increase registrations.
- Decrease bounce rates on a specific landing page.
- Have people add more content on their first use.
- Get more people to connect to their social networks.
- Create a first-use experience that explains the product in less than ten seconds.
- Create a mobile experience to complement a desktop browser product experience.

Let's revisit the registration scenario. Assume that you are getting 100,000 views on a product marketing page, but only 1 percent of those visitors are choosing to register—not a great number. You'd prefer that number to be 5 percent, which is slightly above the standard you set based on the performance of similar products. You should ask: Why are people not registering? Are they not interested in the product or the features it offers, or is it because the product hasn't captured their imaginations? Or maybe they don't care for the value proposition. Why are they not taking the intended action?

You shouldn't default to guessing to get answers (unless you know your audience very, very well, or you *are* your audience). Your first task should be to simply ask people about their decision by

delivering a simple questionnaire. Ask about both sides: those who register and those who do not.

Perhaps you discover that people understand the product's intent (what it's for), but they don't understand how easy it is to use. You can address that issue through demos and testimonials. You decide to add a video that plays automatically and shows the ease of use, and you redesign the landing experience to incorporate it. The new Web page is released for view, and registrations go up to 1.5 percent. That is an improvement, but not as much of an improvement as you wanted. Remember, we're aiming for 5 percent here.

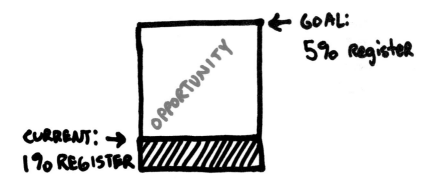

Now you can see that you're in a brand new situation. Your goal is the same (increase registrations to 5 percent of the people visiting the view), but the user's experience has changed. Whereas they used to see a static marketing image, now the 1.5 percent of the

people who register (and, more importantly for our problem, the 98.5 percent of the people who don't) are seeing a video demonstration of the product's ease of use.

It's time to take a deep breath and start again, asking more and different questions, exploring new designs, and looking for new insights that allow you to fine-tune the product yet again.

Say you find that 10 percent of the people are letting the demo video play through to the end. They could be motivated by the music or the content or the production values, but people are choosing to engage with it. They are allowing themselves to be exposed to the full content you have provided, even though they have the option of turning it off. That is an interesting bit of info, but you're not sure how to act on that.

Why else is the registration rate not as good as it could be? You just learned that people like *seeing* how easy the product is. What if you could design a solution with which they could *experience* how easy it is?

You could deliver the same information in the same order (what is essentially a linear tour in your video), but permit people to try the product for themselves. Once they've touched it and felt how easy it is, you might lead them to become invested in some way. If they enter information or use the tools you've provided, and actually experience first-hand how easy your product is to use, they may be more inclined to register and continue using the product.

Rinse ... Repeat ....

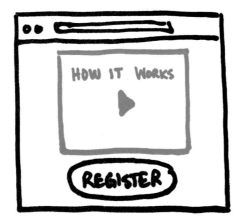

Rinse...Repeat....

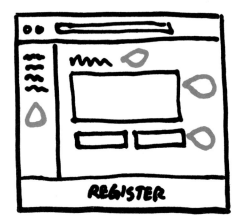

A caution: As you rethink and redesign, force your brain not to be limited by what you just did. The common response to working in small iterations—making many small changes over time—is to steer toward working in a very linear direction. The rinse-and-repeat way of thinking gives you freedom to be responsive in new directions.

Over and Over

Methodically repeating a process, with gradual improvements each time, is like using a whetstone to sharpen a blade. Patience and constant refinement sharpen the product into something more powerful and effective than it could have been in one singular design that was released and left in its initial state.

CHAPTER 10

People Matter Most

The desires and needs of the people who already use or who will use your product are the most important considerations in your creative process. It's very easy to forget, when you are constantly focused on the tasks at hand, that you must also keep in mind the larger context of your work.

A specific product may have quality, styling, and an excellent feature set, but unless it matches people's desires, their social nature, their intellectual levels, and their experiences, the product will not succeed. At the end of the day, people will be using your product. So you must put their needs first.

You might feel intimidated by the idea that design success requires you to be a sociologist and behavioral scientist, in addition to understanding software design, engineering, graphic design, marketing, and more. But actually, it's exciting that these aspects of product design can allow you to improve people's lives.

Consider this: When you are in line at the grocery store or waiting for a friend to meet you, you might pass the time by checking the feeds in your favorite social media products to see what friends have shared. Imagine if suddenly no friends were on the other end; your social media would become pretty worthless. Everything that is valuable to you about that product has to do with the people involved with it. Email and communication products are other clear examples of products that are essentially social; what good are they if there is no access to other people?

Other products are even more personal, and they, too, can have a great impact on people's lives. Imagine a product that tracks your progress as you bike or run or lose weight. The entire product is about your relationship with it. If you don't find the product useful or easy to use or relevant, it has no worth. But if the designer carefully considered your needs and interests as she worked, the product could become fundamental to your lifestyle, even shaping your behavior. In the best case, you might make healthier decisions or reach a goal that you've set for yourself. That's awesome!

The point here is that a product that maps your running isn't about maps or data; it's about people and what they do.

Another very personal product is a diary that encourages you to write every day. As the designer of that product, you could easily just start with the general concept of a daily writing diary and launch right into the design and engineering of something that captures and presents writing organized by days. Perhaps you'd

include some prompts for what to write, and you'd design an interface for looking back at what you've written previously.

But when you charge directly into building and don't ask who will be using a product and how they will use it, you miss half of the equation. What time of day are people most interested in writing: in the morning or in the evening? Why would people choose a daily interval instead of writing whenever they felt compelled? For what reasons do people write daily without the help of a product to encourage them? What do they do with their writing when they're done?

Some products, such as weather apps, provide a more passive user experience, and when you're designing one, it would be simple (and obvious) to just present information in an elegant and organized way.

But it's possible to give the product much more value by tying the information to the user's daily experience. What if a weather report was delivered just after a person woke up and started getting ready for work each morning?

What if it notified the person of weather warnings in other states where loved ones live?

What if it pinpointed low-humidity days in the next week that would be better for outdoor activity?

Could a weather product display reports on current conditions and forecasts in the context of a person's calendar of events?

You must imagine the needs of the user. What would be interesting to that person? Useful? Fun? Essential?

How to Discover What People Want

So how exactly do you find out what makes products valuable to people? You can just ask them (more on that in Chapter 13), but even before you get to that point, you need to answer some very basic questions:

- Who would use this product?
- What do they want to know?
- When would they want to know it?
- Where would they use it?
- Why would they use this product instead of any other similar products?
- How would they use the product?

Always start with the people part of your design. You will rarely know all of the answers to all of these questions. But there are ways to search out everything you need to know.

Talk to Your Customers

Working as a sociologist, you can gain a great deal of information from the people you are serving. Talk to them. Engage with them. They are a valuable resource that is right at your front door! Ask them what can make the product better, what works well for them, and if and how they talk about the product with others. If people are not using your product, ask them about their perceptions of the product, what they would like it to do, and what other products they are currently using.

Watch Carefully

Watch and observe people because what they say they do may be vastly different from what they actually do. It's not that they're deceitful or contrary. That's just how people are. See what is happening in their lives. Try to understand where the product can work in their lives and where it might not. What other products are they using at the same time? What other products could benefit them?

Always Be Listening

Listen to your customers and to your potential customers as well. You will be lucky if they come to you with unsolicited feedback, positive or negative. Listen to their stories about what they would like the product to be. What are people saying when they blog about your product? What does Customer Support note that people are saying? What are they saying about competing products and related problems?

Be Inspired by Customers

Look to your customers for inspiration. This is not just hearing that someone wished the product had a certain feature. Instead, it is observing how people use your product in ways you might never have anticipated. Those observations can be real gifts.

A classic example of this is the hashtag. Chris Messina, at the time a regular Twitter user, created the hashtag simply as an expedient way to enable searches among Tweets. This extended use

of the product was created on the fly and was quickly adopted by other users, and ultimately by Twitter itself. Twitter has since created other ways that hashtags can be used and made them an official part of the product.

The same thing has happened with Retweets: Users developed a behavior of preceding reposts with "RT," simply as a way to tell others that they are sharing someone else's info. Twitter has also built RT into the product by adding a share button.

These real-world examples underscore how people who are not engineers or software designers can lead you into new features and functionality. They can show you how to make the product better, but only if you are paying attention.

People Are Part of the Process

More than designing answers or engineering solutions or creating marketing plans, the one thing you have to remember in developing a new product is the people who will use it. Ultimately, everything goes back to them. The better you understand this and the more it remains top of mind, the better your products will be.

If you ask people for product ideas, their ideas may be limited by what they already know. But if you ask people for people ideas, they will tell you exactly what you need to know. What are you trying to do? What problems do you have?

People must be part of the design process; if they are not, the process is incomplete.

get it built

CHAPTER 11

Change and Happiness

Until this point in the book, we've been thinking about the product design challenges we face. Now we're going to get the work done; we're sitting at the keyboard, ready to get started. Now what?

If you have read all of the preceding chapters, you understand that it is important to share, test, and measure and to frequently change products in small ways. The objective is not only to improve the product but also to validate your assumptions, mitigate risk, and establish a pattern of evolution.

These patterns of ship-early-and-often, rinse-and-repeat, and share-constantly have a very marked influence on your happiness, as well as that of your entire team. Because the product is constantly improving, you also have the opportunity to make the people who use your product happier, too.

Everyone wants to feel that the work they are doing is valuable. They want to see that it is useful, that it helps people. No work models can guarantee this. Previous work models didn't even try to make it happen. For a long time, people worked behind closed

doors, hammering away on a single idea until it was time to make the big presentation to the client or the public. If, by some miracle, the product was perfect, the process moved ahead. If not, people retreated behind their closed doors and began again on a new idea and presentation. The freshness of the creative process was gone, replaced by a sense of menial repetition.

CHANGE ≠ FEAR

CHANGE = HAPPINESS

With the old model, the product couldn't easily or quickly be made better because the process was in the way. People weren't working on exciting ideas; they were working on PowerPoint presentations and slide shows and flow charts and all of the other trappings that make meetings dreadful. It's as if a chef had to spend all of her time creating the plates that her food was presented on rather than focusing on cooking. There's no joy in that. Let's spend our time on the delicious main course.

With a different work model, you maximize all of the essential, productive activities and minimize unproductive off-ramps. If you and your colleagues are enjoying the creative process, then your energy is maintained, even when things don't work out exactly as

planned. You feel fresh…and refreshed. When the working process is healthy and enjoyable, without tons of roadblocks, you and everyone else on your team will derive more satisfaction from the process and create more satisfying products.

Of course, not doing presentations will be a huge mind shift for some people. After all, that's how most formally trained designers were taught: Create dozens of sketches and then present them to the instructor. It's also how much of traditional graphic design works: Material is created in the designer's office and not presented to the client until the big reveal.

Adopting an alternative way of working may take some time. Try to inspire yourself and others to aim for the goal of arriving at a shared picture and traveling together all of the time. After a designer has been through this process a few times and seen the value of constant collaboration, he starts to appreciate how it cuts through the political process of getting approvals from those who probably weren't even involved in the creative process. Eventually, he'll want to abandon formalized presentations forever.

With the weight and burden of established ways of working cast aside, you're ready to get iterative. You're ready to accept that change is inherent in your process. You're ready to start designing, start *changing*, with purpose and certainty—particularly the certainty that you'll be designing and designing again.

You'll be doing similar work and processes in sequence. Through repetition, you'll be honing and refining. You're not toiling, but building and strengthening.

You Can Start Anywhere

If you have established an iterative process and are committed to designing, sharing, testing, measuring (as described in Chapter 13), and designing again, you truly can begin at any step in that process. Start wherever it makes sense to start today, and be aware that the starting point may change for each project.

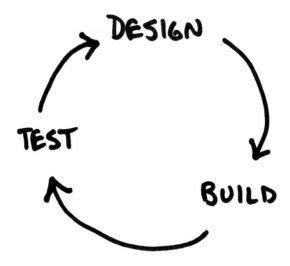

For example, if I start with measuring, by the time I am halfway through the process, I will begin testing. Yes, you may be working with an incomplete idea if you start with measuring, but not much time will have passed; and since you will go through your iterative process many times, the project will quickly gain shape and tighten up.

What happens when you have an idea and want to act on it? It might look like this:

1. Have the idea.
2. Test the idea informally by sharing it in a low-fidelity form.
3. Start to engineer it so that you have a functional thing to try to use.
4. Design a UI for the functional idea so that it's more approachable and understandable.

And then you proceed into a second iteration:

1. Start by sharing the idea again. How does that more "real," designed version feel?
2. Do some more design to improve and explore based on that quick assessment.
3. Engineer any changes in functionality and data.
4. Share the product.
5. Test it.

Then you start to get into a solid cycle, which might look more like this:

1. Design
2. Build
3. Test
4. Design
5. Build
6. Test

It's perfectly okay, and in fact it is encouraged, that your earliest steps in the process are incomplete, out of order, and otherwise rough. As you can see, completing a few cycles of iteration and exploration will get you into a groove: a pattern of designing, building, and testing your ideas in quick succession.

Identify Needs and Opportunities

Identify where the problems and opportunities are, and write them down. This is a statement of intent for the next phase of your design process. You start with the story: Imagine a product experience in which A-B-C happens and, most important, how people are affected for the better.

For example:

People are overwhelmed by the number of links and recommendations they get from friends and colleagues—watch this video, read this article, check out this photo. We're going to allow people to capture those in a queue so they can view them another time at their leisure, and then respond to the recommenders as they choose.

Then you state the current strengths and weaknesses in this scenario, and the principles you intend to uphold when addressing them. You might simply call this phase "weaknesses, strengths, and approach." At Etsy we have a similar scheme, introduced by one of our product designers, called PSTs—problems, strengths, and tenets. Identify each component, and you have the information in

hand to start a thoughtful design exploration, while keeping the following in mind:

- The **problem** or **weakness** can be big or small. For example, people don't know what to do at a certain screen, they are dropping out of the flow, or conversion rates are down.
- A **strength** could be a solution that solved an earlier problem and could be reapplied, a part of the existing product experience you could build upon, an enthusiastic user base, or another step in the process that is being redesigned and might help this situation.
- A **tenet** or **approach** is your statement of what you believe to be your intent as you start the design. You have only a limited amount of time in which to work. You know that any images you use will have to be small. Maybe you decide that you will present all of your plans in quick pencil sketches.

The way you organize this phase isn't particularly important. What's important is that you develop a sense of thoughtfulness and intent for yourself and your collaborators.

Validate

How do you know that your idea is going to work? The short answer is: you don't! But you can go through some quick and easy exercises to gain a little more information and confidence moving forward. This phase is more like validation with a lowercase "v."

Sometimes that validation may be conceptual. Is what I am trying to create actually going to solve the problem? You might be able to be simpler here. You are not trying to figure out how to solve the problem (via steps 1, 2, 3), but you're analyzing the validity of the idea—Will your idea solve the problem?

In our current example, you believe that people are overwhelmed by content suggestions and would benefit from time-shifting the consumption of that content. How can you find out if your product idea would resonate with them? Can you ask? Can you do some research? In this case, you're trying to quickly validate that there's a market for this idea. This is idea validation.

In other cases, you might be trying to validate certain behaviors or interactions. Let's say you had an idea to add a little book-marker to the browser bar that would allow people to save content to your product for later reading. You need to decide if your users would actually take advantage of this new feature. This is solution validation.

If your informal validation says that the idea doesn't have traction with your users, but you feel strongly about it, consider the simplest way to take it a little further with the lowest research investment. Maybe users need to see and feel it. Of course, you could also forget the idea and just move on to your next idea. Nothing is precious, nor should it be. Aim for forward momentum and don't hang on to any one answer too tightly.

It can be difficult to validate some ideas by only describing them or showing sketches or pictures. You may have to actually

build something to get it as close to real as possible. That's often called a prototype, and we value a certain kind of prototype most.

Prototype

One of my strongly held beliefs is that there should not be much difference between prototypes and the end product itself. You might sketch things out on paper very quickly, just to capture your idea, and show it to others for input. But the very next step should be prototyping, during which you try to use the exact same tools (software, platforms, code) that you would use to build the actual product. Don't get lost in choosing colors or typestyles too early. They may affect the experience of the end product, but they have little effect on the function of the product initially. Work quickly: Nothing has to be clean and perfect.

What you will create is definitely not releasable. It's still just a model on which you will base the real thing. But because you are using the same code and materials as you would for the real product, the switch from producing the prototype to producing the product will be relatively simple.

Build

Once the prototype has progressed through small and constant changes to the point where it can be released, the final building can take place. This is when you make the product work as you

intend it to, ensuring that it behaves as you want it to behave and looks as you intend it to look. And this phase is executed with the degree of quality that reflects the experience you want people to have with your product.

Because your product is already close to being "production ready" when it's in our prototype phase, the idea of a "build" phase that's been established in the past is now simply an access milestone; it puts your product in a form in which more people can productively use it and see it.

Communicate

We should prepare what we need to say when we're ready to share our changes with our customers. You can prepare just after the product change is completed or during the product change's development. You could create an announcement, press release, blog post, or email newsletter. Any and all channels are available—tweets, email messages, articles in the press—to tell people that a newly completed version of the product is available and to explain why they should use it. Choose the channel that is most relevant for your product and the people who use it (or whom you want to use it).

Communication planning should happen before you release the product because you need to determine when best to release. Perhaps you plan to send out a marketing email on Friday, then realize it's the Friday of a holiday weekend when many people won't be checking their email. This might be fine if you're planning

a quiet release of a minor update, but it might be disastrous if you want to motivate many people to use your all-new product at the same time.

Say you have created an app that helps people find bargains in brick-and-mortar stores. The best time to release this app, if you consider its use and when people would want it, would be just before a gift-giving holiday weekend, and not immediately after.

You also need to have preemptive communication in place before you release a product so that you are prepared to:

- Answer any questions that people may commonly ask.
- Inform customer service teams about changes and how to communicate and provide support for them.
- Provide information to the press.

This sort of information is especially important when you already know that some aspects of your product are incomplete or not completely perfected. For instance, your shopping app may support a limited number of stores when you first release it. You need to tell people that you will soon be including support for other stores.

Test

Next, let's consider testing your software product so you can be confident that it's free of bugs and technical problems. (Note that you're not testing your basic idea, which was vetted earlier in your validation phase. This time it's all about the software.)

There are two primary ways to test:

- *Manual testing* assigns a person or people to use the product, interact with all of its changed or new parts, and in effect, try to break it. A tester can also discover any bugginess, find out if it is difficult to understand, or see if it causes other bad things to happen (freezing or slowing down the device, for example). People who perform manual testing will try to use the product the wrong way as well as the right way. Their feedback will be invaluable in improving your design. In larger organizations, it is common for this role to be called Quality Assurance (QA).
- *Automated testing* uses software (that you can create yourself—it's just another product) to locate failure points. If any are discovered, you can create a log of bugs and issues to resolve before you release your product.

The process of manual testing is pretty self-explanatory, but if you haven't experienced automated testing, you might wonder what it's all about. How do you automate using a product? Let's say you created a test to make sure the address form in your checkout process functioned correctly. Your automated test might have sample information for 100 test users, with some information complete and some incomplete and with different lengths, address formats, and so on. When the automated test runs, it attempts to fill out the form with every one of those test users and logs whether or not it was successful with each one. That log would allow you to find errors and pinpoint where difficulties might arise.

Every time you release a new product or any revision to an existing product, it should be tested.

Release

This is perhaps the most obvious step: You make your product available to the general audience. There's a whole range of possibilities for launching your product.

In some cases, you might turn on your new product all at once. Ta da! We generally try to avoid *actually* doing that, but it might look or feel that way depending on how we communicate the release.

In many cases, we slowly release our product. If your tooling and infrastructure are sophisticated, you might even release to only a percentage of the people using your product. Or you might release a feature on one platform (say, mobile Web) and release it later on other platforms.

Once you're confident that your product is working as expected, and that it doesn't have any surprise problems, you can release it more widely. This approach is common for large and complex products.

As you first start product development, it may be premature to use approaches like partial releases, though you can start thinking about it early and be prepared to take advantage of it when the time is right.

If you're ready for some mind-bending perspective, consider this: At the point of release, *the build actually becomes a prototype*. It

becomes the canvas on which future changes are applied. You never revert to creating a completely new prototype. You always move forward.

Measure, Evaluate, and Learn

Once your product is in use, and people are interacting with your design, it's time to start observing again by collecting information, evaluating that information, and learning from it.

First, you want to make sure that everything works okay. (Is the product still working? Is the server up?)

Then you want to know about some basic health metrics. How many people are using the product each day? How many games were played? How many posts do people read in one sitting?

The degree to which you can collect information will probably vary based on the maturity of your product. What you can learn will certainly depend on how much tooling you've implemented to monitor your product. You might rely on an off-the-shelf monitoring tool in the early days of your product's use. As you learn to ask specific questions and assess certain needs unique to your product, you may ultimately build your own monitoring tools. We'll be talking about this in more detail in Chapter 13.

For qualitative information, you might conduct user research by using a variety of methods, both informal (interview over video chat) and formal (recruiting people for in-person interviews and observation in a testing facility).

Evaluating means carefully considering what you have learned and interpreting those findings. What worked and what didn't? What's happening that you didn't expect?

All of this helps inform your plan for the future. What should you do given the information you have received? Has it changed the dynamic of how people will use the product, and what is your response to that?

Iterate

Repeat all of these steps again and again and again, ad infinitum.

As most people know, change for change's sake is worthless and irritating. But change that brings clear benefits makes everyone happier. As the creator/designer, you gain a greater sense of self-worth. Your enthusiasm for further improving the product increases. And, of course, the product users are also satisfied and happy. Just by accepting the notion that the product can always be made better, everyone benefits.

But what about the assumption that if something isn't broke, don't fix it? For product designers, this is true only in a very narrow sense. Sure, the product may work just fine. But the context

for viewing it must necessarily be very wide. It can have more or different features that further improve the experience. Or perhaps the product could be rethought to reduce its resource strain. While it may not appear "broken" to the user, the product can always be refined.

Let me leave you with three key points that can help to maintain happiness:

- Always be listening to your customers. There will be compliments and complaints, and both can serve as valuable input.
- Most customers don't yet know what they want, or at least they can't verbalize it. It's your job to be looking out for them.
- People aren't comfortable with change, but the whole world is about constant change. As designers, we need to help people experience change as comfortably as possible.

CHAPTER 12

Use Whatever Works

In this chapter, we will be considering tools—ours, theirs, anybody's. In the world of product design, you can use existing design tools, create your own, or borrow what you need from other disciplines. It's a world where being tool-agnostic is crucial, if for no other reason than that new and potentially better tools are being developed all the time: You have to remain open and receptive to their emergence. All the while, some tools are timeless and continue to serve us well.

It's important to have a point of view regarding tools because they shape the way you work. You've probably had the experience of trying to draw something on a computer while fighting the software because it just isn't allowing you to do what you want. So you just revert to drawing on paper because of its simple expediency.

That's what it means to be tool-agnostic. You can stay focused on the product when you aren't worried about your choice of tool.

It stands to reason that solutions are also shaped by our choice of tools. If you have a hammer, you tend to solve problems with

nails. But tools should always be secondary. I would never rigidly commit to one or another tool. All tools should be considered equally. The best one for the job at hand is... well... the best one for the job at hand.

Tools in Every Step

Tools can either help or hurt your workflow. If you have a tree to cut up for firewood, a small hacksaw and a chainsaw could work, but a chainsaw might change your workflow. You'll need gas, safety equipment, and perhaps a helper and safety training.

Alternatively, you might choose a larger manual saw, or you may hire someone to do the job. The point is, choose the tool that allows you to follow the process you want. Don't let the tool dictate how you work.

Here's a simple example from product design: A graphics program asserts that as your first step you should use the program to create an image of the product. There's nothing inherently wrong with that; however, if you start there, then you're working in an environment that places appearance over structure. You can always overcome this—and the more experience you have, the more likely you'll be able to do that—but you'll always be working with an ill-fitting tool.

If you'd prefer to first decide how the content is structured in, say, an HTML document, then start there. Use an HTML (or plain text) editor to create the structure and organization of your

content in HTML before worrying about what it looks like. Once you have that structure defined in a simple document, you may find that it's easier, faster, and more flexible to "style" that structure with CSS and view it in a browser than it is to use a graphics editor to decide what it should look like.

Be One with the Product

When possible, use tools that are as close as possible to your product. This goes back to the idea of not making mock-ups or anything else that keeps you from efficiently reaching a functioning product.

Suppose you are trying to sketch out a concept quickly and easily, but the tool you've selected uses a JavaScript library different from the one that you will use in the actual product. That is not a good choice: It starts you down a path that diverges from the ultimate goal.

Another common (bad) example is designing a print piece using software meant to provide RGB output. It's a fundamental mismatch. Find tools close to your product whenever possible. When you do, less will be lost in translation as you fill in the gaps between what the tool is intended for and how your product is actually built.

The Tools You Build with Are the Tools You Use

Pulitzer Prize–winning photojournalist Barry Staver gave a wonderful answer to the question, "What is the best camera?" "It's the one you have with you," he said.

The actual tools don't matter that much as long as you use them regularly and become skillful with them. If you have chosen a tool and found it frustrating to work with, then it is probably the wrong tool. Ditch it. Try another. Bored of this one? Ditch it. Try another. The tool that allows you to work quickly, confidently, and comfortably is the best tool *for you*.

An example: When programmers edit code, it's often a very personal thing. Each programmer may use a different application to edit code, according to his or her preference. If you were to ask twelve people about their favorite text editor, you'd get twelve distinct opinions. Whichever one you like is the right one to use—the cool one, the new one, the old standby, or whatever. Just don't waste energy fretting about which is the "right" one.

Duct-Tape It Together

Hack it together. The tools you use do not have to be fancy. Any infrastructure will work. One tool may not solve all of your problems, so you may find yourself using hacky ways to pull things together—that's perfectly OK. If a single tool will do all jobs, but you aren't comfortable with it, it really isn't worth your time. With relatively little effort, you can build new tools or assemble a kit of existing tools that get the job done just as well as a jack-of-all-trades tool.

However, if you're uncertain, do try using a tool designed for the job you're trying to complete. For editing code, use a code editor. If you want to see what a product looks like in a certain browser, use that browser whenever possible. Don't simulate it if you don't have to. If you want to test how something works on a particular device, try to get it on that device and use it.

Beg, Borrow, and Steal

As I mentioned at the start of this chapter, use tools from many places. Some of my favorite design tools, namely text editors, were never created to be design tools. They were created for software engineers. So be it!

If another person is using a process that looks like it will work for you, just use it. There is no shame in modeling your tool setup or your process after a solution that is already working for someone else. (Don't copy product ideas, of course.) Someone else likely has solved the same tool problem or a very similar one. What you're trying to figure out may be unique to your situation, but it's probably not unique to the world of product design. Stand proudly on the shoulders of other designers. It's your product that demands uniqueness, not the tools that you use to create it.

Good answers and examples can be found in many places—on forums, at in-person meetups, on Q&A sites, and on personal and company blogs. People like to talk about their own good ideas, so sharing is common. Open-source software products and their creators can also be fertile sources of solutions.

Invent Your Own Tools

One of the great things about being a product designer is that you can design tools customized for your exact needs. Don't be afraid to create your own solutions. As part of the product deployment process, moving from initial designs through testing and into production, lots of things have to happen in the background. You can write software, or create a different interface, or do whatever you need. You can create an automated test that examines your design and returns a performance report with the simple touch of a button. Just think about what would make your work easier, and then create it. If you're not sure how to make it, share your thinking with your team, colleagues, and friends. They just might be willing to help.

Designing your own tools goes back to the very first point in this chapter: that tools support the work. The tool and the process are intimately connected, so tools also shape the way you work. Don't choose tools that force you to work in ways you don't like.

The Product Designer's Toolkit

The following tools are common to most product designers. You may not use some of them now (or ever), but it's important to be aware of their usefulness and your ability to add them to your kit if they can help you work better and more efficiently.

Some of these tools are simple; some are very complex. Use as few as you possibly can, and only when they are really needed.

Every project is different, and you may need to use different tools for different projects.

Text Editors

These are an essential, core tool for product designers. You will use text editors to write and edit code, whether it's HTML, CSS, Java-Script, C++, or any number of other possibilities.

Text editors come in a whole range of sophistication levels, from a very plain text editor that comes with your operating system, such as TextEdit on your Mac, to more specialized tools whose primary job is still text editing.

Vim is a popular editor that's distributed with most UNIX systems. It is highly configurable and very powerful, though its

learning curve for designers may be higher than average. Vim and its siblings don't have the GUI that a designer would expect to see in desktop software. In some cases, as when you need to access files remotely on a server or in specific technical environments, you may have to learn how to use these products. They are powerful tools, so it's to your advantage to know them.

In many cases, text editors fall between these two areas. Current examples that are easier to learn include Sublime Text, TextMate, and Coda, with other examples coming into popular use all the time. These editors aren't full of steep learning curves but do have features that are specialized for code editing. Most will offer common features such as auto-completion of standard code tags, syntax highlighting, color coding of specific portions of code, and auto-formatting. These visually oriented features can be convenient for designers who aren't fully adept at reading code. You can use them for editing any kind of text file, and you will commonly use them for HTML, CSS, and JavaScript editing.

Less common are language-specific text editors. Their application is obviously more limited since they can edit only one kind of text file, but they can still be helpful tools. I recall using a specialized CSS editor, aptly named CSSEdit, when I was first learning CSS. Because its GUI was designed specifically around CSS, I found that CSSEdit helped me learn how to write the actual CSS syntax. Later, when I'd more fully mastered CSS syntax, I took the step of using a simpler and more direct tool without a GUI.

The most advanced and complex text editors are called Integrated Development Environments (IDEs). These are not simply text editors. IDEs also understand the logic and relationships within code, have features to check for bugs in your logic, and can suggest ways of refactoring code. IDEs tend to be specific to a particular programming language. Xcode, the primary tool for authoring iOS and Mac OS X software, is an IDE.

In general, people tend toward the simpler tools, unless special needs demand otherwise.

Graphics Editors

These include photo-editing, vector illustration, and motion graphics tools. They can be used for producing screens and mock-ups, although, as stated earlier in this book, it's best not to be producing mock-ups. But from time to time, you will find that you do need one.

Sometimes you need these tools to produce media—such as motion graphics, video, edited photos, and illustrations—for the product you are creating. In addition to knowing how to produce such media, you must understand the proper output formats to use. Output formats have enormous implications for your product and its performance in terms of quality, size, and color space. For example, the right graphics editor can help you discover the format sweet spot for saving a photo file that provides adequate visual quality and still allows your product to load quickly.

Previewers

These tools allow you to see or use your product while you're designing it. They are very helpful when you have to design for multiple screen sizes, browsers, and other variables. And as I've mentioned previously, it's always preferable to look at the product in the real world, and sometimes it may be faster to do that using a previewer.

These Web-based tools simulate different environments. Some tools let you see the product on your own desktop, while others send results to multiple mobile devices so you can see your work there.

Some previewers are even more specialized. A great example of specialized previewers are those that show how email messages will render in a variety of environments. Email design is difficult because there are so many tools, platforms, and devices used to read email, each with its unique quirks and capabilities. An email previewer will allow you to see how your email renders with far more variety than you could ever expect to see without the tool's help.

Mock-up Tools

These are different from the graphics editors described earlier. They include specialized tools for creating wireframes, simulating interface behaviors, or mocking-up transitions in animations. As with any side street that takes you away from the main development

path, you should prefer not to use them, but from time to time, they may be necessary. Consider them an *ad hoc* member of your kit.

Code Management and Version Control Tools

These identification tools structure some of your work methods and store what you are creating as you proceed. Git, Subversion, and Mercurial are common examples. While you work, your code changes along with other assets that needn't be stored on your local computer. In fact, for the sake of redundancy and backups, it's often a best practice to store your code and assets remotely. When you're working with many people on the same project, these tools become essential. They allow many people to collaborate on a single set of code, without the risk of harming or overwriting each other's work.

Code management tools record who is doing what to which part of the code. They track every change that was made since the start of a project, which makes it relatively easy to back up and evaluate previous versions and make changes. These tools are fundamental to the precept of shipping products early and often, as well as being tremendous aids to making small and frequent changes. There's plenty to learn about code management and version control, but completing some basic tutorials online will get you started from a design standpoint. Once you learn how powerful and helpful code management is, you'll find yourself using it on every project, large and small.

Tracking and Monitoring Tools

These help you see how your product is performing, providing quantitative feedback on how people are using your product. You can search results, make queries, produce graphs and charts, and more, so that you can always be aware of status changes or anomalies.

The most common and readily accessible of these tools is Google Analytics, but there are many other competing products, simpler tools, and more specialized tools available. Depending on your needs, you may choose one over another.

Communication Tools

These allow people creating a product to exchange information. They can be as simple as email or a sticky note, or they can be as complex as a large-scale project management tool. Some tools are structured around collecting feedback, including monitoring online conversations about your product.

A Means to an End

The tools you choose to use can make your work easier... or more difficult. Start with simple tools and prefer simple tools. Don't get too clever about them, or opt for complexity in anticipation of what you might need in the future. Use what works for you right now.

Add new tools when your current tools aren't sufficient for addressing new problems. Replace your tools if they aren't working, you don't enjoy them, or you discover something better.

The tools you choose are a means to an end, so stay focused on that end and let the tools take on the supporting role they're meant to have.

CHAPTER 13

Listen and Learn

Whenever we design a product, we want to know if it had its intended effect. We also want to understand all aspects of what happens to it once it leaves the nest. Learning what happens requires feedback. When we learn how people feel about their experiences, it can be motivating or inspiring or educational or even humbling. We can also find out that our creation is being used in ways we never imagined.

Feedback—positive or negative—is very valuable. With Web product design, we can create scenarios in which getting feedback is not a one-way or one-time event. Instead, through *feedback loops*, we can receive more and more reactions over time and through repeated contacts, all along the way, and all of that input can be used to improve the product, identify problems, and take advantage of new opportunities. It's not enough to sit back and watch what happens. Acquiring useful, pertinent feedback requires proactive

information gathering. In addition, there are ways to build the tools and infrastructure for feedback into the product itself.

In this chapter, let's discover what kinds of things you can learn from regular observation and user inquisitive engagement. It's worth your time.

Quantitative and Qualitative

The forms of collecting feedback—research—can be categorized into one of two buckets: quantitative research and qualitative research.

Quantitative Research

Quantitative research is research that you can measure with numbers. For example:

- How many people registered?
- How many people downloaded the app?
- How far did people scroll down the page?
- On average, of the people who searched, how many search results matched their queries?
- What percentage of people check out immediately after adding an item to their cart? What percentage of people come back and check out another time? What percentage add an item to their cart, but never check out?
- How many people visit your product every day because of links sent via email?

Because quantitative research is inherently numeric, it also means that the results can be presented in graphs and charts. Images of data can be pretty, but that's not our concern.

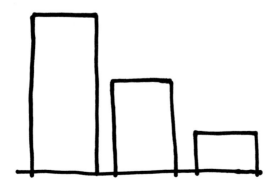

Quantitative data made visual allows you to see patterns and anomolies. You can use your visual skills to identify elements that aren't working well. If you see a pie chart showing that many people leave immediately after visiting your product's marketing page, that chart probably makes you want to address that problem and improve that page.

Qualitative Research

Qualitative research gathers feedback on the kinds of things that you can't easily count and put into numerical form—feelings, tastes, unstructured observations, and responses to open-ended questions.

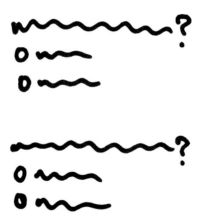

For example:

- What's your favorite part of the product?
- How did you feel after seeing that the blog post was written by a college student?
- Why did you decide to use the product?
- How would you describe this experience to a friend?
- Why didn't you buy the item after you added it to your cart?

Qualitative research ususally requires subject area experts to help craft questions and interpret results. Without some expertise in market research, it can be easy to ask leading questions or misinterpret information. It's great to ask and research; just be sure to not inadvertently over- or undervalue the information you gather.

Sources of Feedback in Early Development

You can collect each kind of feedback in many ways, and each method provides a different learning opportunity. It is important to understand that you don't need to gather every kind of feedback for every iteration of every project. Some kinds of research will be more valuable than others for specific projects, and likely, you will form a hybrid approach, applying different levels of research to the same project. As you explore various information-gathering techniques, you'll assemble a useful kit of tools, and you should strive to

understand how and when to use each one. Let's look at how to get feedback while you're creating your product and how to get it after that product is out in the world.

Feedback from You

As stated in previous chapters, the sooner you can get to an operable product, the better. Then you and your team can actually use it and gather perceptions about it. That is your first feedback loop—from yourself and your team. It's a readily available source of information, which you can gather quickly and inexpensively, it's constantly incoming, and it will be very useful in the development stage.

But you will be getting feedback from only a limited group of people who may be biased toward seeing only positives. Also, you are not dealing with cold users; your team members already know what the intended outcome should be, and that knowledge inevitably colors their opinions. Another shortfall of this source of feedback is that it doesn't open your mind to possibilities you may not have anticipated. You get information only on what is already there, not on what could be there.

Dogfooding

The phrase "eat your own dog food" is usually used in business to refer to a company that publicly uses its own products to demonstrate confidence and transparency to customers. In product design, it has a slightly different meaning: Get the product operable

as soon as possible and start using it so as to develop immediate feedback loops.

A good example would be a communication product. If the developer immediately begins to use it, the team is forced to work out annoying features, refine speeds, and evaluate its appearance. The team enters the flow right away and begins to understand (and act on) the product's benefits and challenges.

Some products may not be constant-use creations. If that's the case with your product, you need to find ways to use it as frequently as possible. High-volume use yields the most fruitful feedback loops.

Casual Feedback

To acquire casual feedback, you might ask co-workers and other people who are not directly related to the project—friends, family, and acquaintances—to review early trials. You can directly observe and question these people, ideally through regularly scheduled interactions (perhaps once per week) with your product. This loop is frequent but not constant.

The value of this sort of collection is that it is within reach, it's generally accessible, it doesn't take a lot of time, and it's inexpensive. You will gain broader perspectives than you would if you queried only the project team, especially because these other people come to the project without preconceived notions.

But you can improve the quality of information you gather by targeting people who can give you specifically informed feedback.

I'm a sushi aficionado, so let's say I want to create an app that helps people find the nearest sushi restaurant and look at its menu. I'll gather the most useful feedback about my app by asking other people who know and appreciate sushi to try using it.

The narrower the product's appeal is—just sushi fans, in this case—and the closer it is to your own experience, the more likely it is that this sort of casual feedback can work well. But you may be able to improve the value of the feedback even more.

Assume that you are a designer who has created a project management product for designers. You might just ask other designers to test your product. But if you bring in other creative professionals—writers, videographers, photographers, and the like—then you will receive more and more varied feedback that you can use to broaden your product's use and appeal.

Formalized Feedback

At the most formalized end of the feedback-gathering spectrum is user testing, conducted by professionals. This is the sort of testing in which two-way mirrors are used to observe customers being asked questions written by trained researchers to eliminate bias and inadvertent steering.

This feedback returns the most objective information—bias is neutralized—so it's usually very actionable information. Also, the selection of people providing the feedback is more targeted, so you should be able to find people reflecting the demographics you want for your product. Finally, the people who conduct the research can also help interpret the data.

The expense of this level of research often puts it out of reach for bootstrapped operations. Even for projects with healthy budgets, the price tag of this type of research may make it an infrequent option.

Sources of Feedback Following Release

You've released your product into the world. Now, the feedback will follow. User feedback arrives in a variety of forms. It's good to be able to anticipate all of the possible forms, some being more obvious than others, so that you're prepared to look for (or motivate) them.

Incoming Comments

If your product is already out in the world and has a following, the avenues are open for a constant feedback loop, but you need to plan for ways to receive that feedback. You may have inbound support or commenting through email, and it's probable (as people are much more likely to complain than to compliment) that you will get input on those aspects of your product that people find buggy, confusing, or inadequate. This sort of information, although sometimes discouraging, is essential, especially if received in any volume. Find a way to formalize its receipt, perhaps through a dedicated staff or an email address that is checked constantly. You'll often get a sense of how serious a given issue is through the repetition of similar comments. Conversely, if, out of a lot of feedback, you receive only one comment on an issue, it might not be a major issue.

Community Feedback

Informal communities such as forums may make your product a topic of discussion. Perhaps there are Q&A sites or even actual events where customers—current and prospective—are gathering. None of these were created with the express purpose of gathering feedback for you, but they can allow you to see what people think about your product, sometimes compared to other competitive products.

Data Collection

This is a constant and very powerful feedback loop. Every connection with a customer is another opportunity to mine feedback, not in what he says, but in how the product performs for him. How long does new content take to load? What screens or instructions are ignored? Where does flow slow down?

You can also collect behavioral data. How does the customer interact with the product? What does he look at first? How much time does he spend with the product each day? How often does he load his own content? The possibilities here are endless.

As with incoming comments, the best learning usually comes via a large volume of information. Contact with 100 users over 100 days is more valuable than contact with 10 users over 10 days. You can string together these behavioral metrics, aggregate them, and come to definite conclusions. Perhaps people who scroll all the way to the bottom of a page are shown to make more purchases than

those who tap out of the opening screen immediately. What can you do to encourage those who tap out to scroll instead?

Furthermore, you can compare similar customers. If you have two people who both created a new account on the same day, you can compare their behaviors, or *onboarding flow*, over time. How long does it take each person to find the material that interests her most, and how does she find it? Does she use the "most popular content" button, or search on her own? By studying comparative behaviors over time, you may find ways to give the product more value for everyone.

Steps of the feedback collection process

1. Decide what to ask. What do you want to learn?
2. Through verbal inquiry, observation, or data collection, collect the information.
3. Listen to and carefully consider all information. Don't cherry-pick just what you want to hear.
4. Interpret what you have learned and derive conclusions from it. The answers may not be immediately actionable, so you need to translate the information into a future plan.
5. Decide what to do with the answers.

Everything you learn in this process is strong input into another iteration of feedback collection. The more frequently these loops happen, the more iterations you can achieve. Small, frequent iterations hold real value.

Don't Forget to Listen

The worlds of research, user studies, data visualization, and feed-back interpretation are deep, complex, and nuanced. They're also extremely powerful. Hopefully, if you're not already a hungry feed-back feeder, your appetite has been whetted.

Our approach of shipping early and frequently is only half of the product design equation. The other half is finding out what happened. Were all assumptions true? Did the design help or hurt? Are there any new or previously unrevealed dynamics you should be aware of? Feedback and research are the only ways you'll know.

CHAPTER 14

Design Together

No matter where you are located, and no matter what the nature of your product is, you are unlikely to be a team of one individual. Even if you conceptualize, design, and produce a product by yourself, it's likely that you'll have designers, engineers, marketers, business advisors, and even more people as part of an extended team. The number of people will vary over time, and folks will come and go, but the fact is, you have to plan for the involvement of others.

Working with teams creates circumstances that can make the product design process easier, or if you aren't prepared for them, more complicated.

First, accept that you will benefit from being inclusive rather than exclusive. Open yourself and your process to the ideas, experience, and intuition of others. You stand to benefit from a collaborative effort in many things you do, particularly in those parts of the design process you haven't previously experienced. Collaboration,

however, doesn't happen by default. It happens by choice. Plan for it, and encourage it.

Let's look at three team sizes: a team of one, a small team, and a large team. The lines between them are arbitrarily chosen (a small team doesn't need to be fewer than five people), but I've organized them this way to provide general buckets that will help frame your understanding. The intention is that you will learn about the similarities and differences between teams of various sizes. Understanding the strengths and weaknesses of each team size will help you choose an initial team for your product and chart the trajectory for team involvement as your product grows.

You can apply large-group principles to smaller groups and vice versa. It's all about design teamwork, even when you're a team of one.

A Team of One

Working by yourself is, in some ways, the designer's condition. Designers picture a grumpy Paul Rand (designer of numerous influential twentieth-century corporate logos) or a focused Dieter Rams (famed designer of many Braun products) alone in their studios, burning the midnight oil, seeing through a singular design vision. If you're an art-school-trained designer, you might have a similar image of the designer-as-artist.

Working alone can be great for focus. We know that constraints can create benefits for creative problem-solving that would be otherwise unavailable. We also know that it can be easy to get

caught in one's common ruts without the jolt offered by other people to challenge our conventional thinking.

Characteristics of Working Alone

- What you say goes. You have full agency to make all of the decisions.
- You are the representative of all of the information and points of view.
- You have no one else to answer to.

Strengths of Riding Solo

- You needn't communicate with others, so you can spend a maximum amount of time designing.
- You don't need to balance or compromise your thoughts with other perspectives or opinions, so you can work faster and more smoothly.
- You are wholly responsible. When things go well, you can take full credit.

Challenges of Riding Solo

- You have no other perspectives or experiences to add to your product.
- You are wholly responsible for what goes wrong.
- You are not forced to examine your ideas and processes carefully.
- It's less likely that you will have serendipitous discoveries or surprises.

Working by Yourself

The hardest part about working by yourself is you! You're going to be stuck with that voice in your head, both encouraging and nagging, so you'd best learn how to work productively with it. Even if you do, you may want a surrogate team to help you have new insights and different perspectives. Find a community of people, in the real world and online, whom you can connect with, and lean on them. Identify a mentor, someone who has been there before, and query him or her frequently.

The Small Team

Many products are designed and built by small teams of people. Small in this example is what I might also call optimal: four to seven people. Why is that size optimal? With fewer members,

you don't have much more than several solo contributors. It's less a team, and more a gang. With more members, you'll spend a significant amount of your time coordinating, communicating, and...gasp...managing. (I can say it like that because I'm a manager.) Within small teams, especially well-composed ones, you're going to have many minds, diverse perspectives, and the potential magic that occurs when they intersect. Ever heard the phrase "productive tension"?

Characteristics of a Small Team

- Various perspectives are present.
- It's likely that many and varied skills will be available.
- Every conversation will have multiple voices, as well as multiple communication paths among members.

Strengths of a Small Team

- You benefit from diverse points of view and skill sets.
- Other team members will have interests and expertise different from your own.
- The group's combined mental and emotional capacity means that you are more resilient. Others can take the lead when necessary, and responsibilities can shift to make the group more adaptable and responsive.
- Team members can work in parallel so that the group can work on many different things at the same time.

Challenges of a Small Team

- The small team requires a framework so that everyone understands his or her position. Who is leading? Who has the final say? Does the group need to reach consensus? Is it a democracy?

- Coordinating the process to completion can be difficult when even a few more people are involved.
- The more people who are involved, the more overhead you have. Personnel will likely be your largest single cost, so you have to either have more money at the ready or make your operation more efficient to support the team.

Working in a Small Team

The sooner the group agrees that the most important goal is to repeat, as often as possible, the make-release-make-it-again process, the better. This agreement underlines the fact that nothing is precious and incontrovertible, which in turn removes the dynamic of having to be "right." Actually, being "wrong" creates more learning and progress.

Committing to an iterative design process also means that collaboration points and compromises are temporary, not calcified. The group will spend more time learning and making, and less time selling, politicking, and pontificating. Of course, it's impossible to completely remove that tendency from a human equation, but in general, this approach produces a more positive team.

Another thought: When you develop a small team, it's best to have a business plan in place from day one. Developing a product can take a long time (really, it never ends when you are making small and frequent changes), so it's best to map out a safe path in advance to reduce risk.

The Team of Teams

If you're working in a big team or are growing into one, know this: Big teams don't work. There, I said it! So, how do you work in a big team if big teams don't work? You need to break big teams into smaller teams, and subdivide big projects into smaller ones. Turn your team of twenty into smaller, more focused teams, working in groups of four to seven members, ten at the most. Work hard to lessen the overhead of communication and coordination that can obscure the value that the group offers. Accomplishing this requires a coordinator of the small teams who is trusted and respected. This may be the single most difficult challenge in a large team: finding and maintaining the right kind of team leadership.

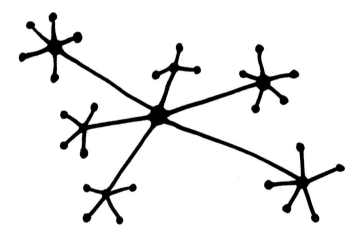

Characteristics of a Team of Teams

Large teams are large. They tend to astound or confound with the number of people. Some people work well in these environments, and some people don't. Management, leadership, and communication become even more important within large teams. This is precisely why breaking a large group into smaller and more nimble, manageable, and communicative teams is a recommended approach.

Strengths of Large Teams

- You can more easily relate to a large set of needs.
- You can do many things in parallel and handle more complex processes. As a result, you can often get more done in less time.
- You can serve more people.
- You can break down problems into separate parts and assign different people to all of those parts.

Challenges of Large Teams

- The bigger the team of teams is, the more complex it is.
- The more complex the team gets, the greater a struggle it is to keep things human and focus on putting people first.
- It's more difficult to keep project values in view.

- You can't be overly committed to the continued relevance of any one person's efforts.
- A team of teams requires careful and constant management. An unmanaged team tends to work too much on justifying its existence and less on getting the hard work done.

Working with a Team of Teams

Look back to the ways of working with a small team. Now, how can you make those dynamics happen with a team of teams? It may require a torch-bearer—a believer in the process, mindset, and methodologies—who will help make the product design principles visible and mutually valued. It might seem like a thankless role, but it will be empowering for everyone involved.

When you have a team of teams, focus subteams on meaningful parts of the product. Because we know that people using the product will define the success of the product, it may be beneficial to organize your subteams around the demographics or activities of those people. That might mean a different team for different audiences (core users, advertisers), different use-cases (shopping, selling), or different products entirely (your commerce product, your content product).

Product Design Principles as Product Team Principles

The same principles we use to guide our thinking and designing when creating products are excellent principles to remember when thinking about your product design team and how it works.

If you're looking to build a team, think of simple, small changes. The same goes for evolving from a small team into a larger team. Drastic changes can shock the system. Unless that's your intent, work hard to make sure that doesn't happen. If you develop a team, test your ideas to see if they work. Look for data that indicates whether or not your team is working at its best. Ask for feedback from team members.

As we discussed in Chapter 10, people matter most. The team you design will impact the product you design.

the product is never done

CHAPTER **15**

Nothing Is Precious

I came into the profession of creating Web products even before
understanding what Web products were—at least, not in the sense
that their design, process, tooling, and most importantly, the
mindset they require, is different from standard software. It wasn't
until I looked back on my work that I realized just how different
my thinking and my output had become.

Designing Web products, particularly your own product, is
drastically different from designing on demand for clients. When
I was designing for clients, a known end was always in sight. At
some point the project would conclude, final payments would be
made, and the design would be out of your hands. If you were lucky
(or unlucky, depending on the client), the contract might include
some ongoing maintenance or a chance to revisit the product later,
but most likely, it wouldn't.

I'm not sure about you, but the first version of a design I send out in the world is rarely the best version of it. As soon as it reaches its audience, I realize there are things I could and should have done better. More importantly, I begin to hear reactions, see how it's working, and determine if and how it was successful. When you're working with a client, you usually don't have the opportunity to do anything about those discoveries because the product is no longer yours. The most you can do is internalize those lessons for the next project and the next client.

Designing Web products is also quite different from creating physical products. Because Web products are software-based *digital* products, they are fluid and changeable; it's *easier* to evolve digital products. But a physical product, once reproduced, is economically and logistically difficult to incrementally evolve, particularly small, frequent changes delivered to someone that already has your product. That's not to say that iterating digital products is simple or painless. It requires the same personal, intellectual, and creative struggles as any design. However, the digital form is adaptable, and the environment is supportive of change.

Perhaps the most important of my realizations was that Web products are never finished. The product can, should, and will change. The choices that were made initially and the design decisions that were implemented are not precious. They must be seen through a critical lens and never stay the same simply because the design team isn't willing to improve them with new knowledge.

The world is changing all around us, so our products and processes also have to change or be left behind. Thankfully, this obligation is also an opportunity: the medium and the culture surrounding the use of digital products is one of the most direct and powerful ways we can affect lives.

I had to learn to avoid a static point of view and to treat any product that I create as a living organism. It's a different way of thinking, but one that actually translates across design disciplines. Constant change can mean constant improvement, a benefit no matter what world of design you are working in. Today you're starting to see the ethos and spirit of iterative software development and Web product design appear in increasingly wider and varied applications.

While I was working on large, multifaceted products that serve wide audiences in an ever-changing world, the principles in this book slowly revealed themselves to me. I did not discover them. These revelations happened over time, and in truth, they continue to evolve, much like the products we are creating. The development of any product is not a destination but a journey, in which improvement is made in small, constant steps. Along the way, we balance forward movement and critical evaluation. This also happens to be an ideal analogy for my development as a product designer.

Product design is inherently a question-asking process. Each answer introduces a new question. We learn from our last answer, look around for opportunities to create a better answer, then get to work again, designing better each time.

Take It Away

I hope you have learned what a product designer actually is, and which Web design skills best complement your current skills, in addition to those skills that you need to develop. And hopefully you've learned how to think like a product designer and how to get your product out to the public. I also hope you know:

- The principles outlined in this book are designed to serve you well for a long time. It's important to recognize that they aren't married to the present. Don't just learn them, try them once, check them off, and move on. Revisit them often, especially when you are not sure how to handle a particular situation. They can help you make better decisions. Also, as user expectations and technology evolve, so will these principles. You will certainly discover some of your own.
- The product you create is characterized most of all by the expectations of the people who use it. People are the most important consideration in the design process. Users understand the product through the narrative you create. This narrative isn't necessarily a story, but it certainly has a clear beginning, and an end through which users gain greater understanding.
- Dead ends hurt your product experience. Avoid them. A user should never feel that an experience ended before she wanted it to or that she was pushed out of an experience.

And when that person decides for herself that she is done with the experience, you have to design in such a way that she is compelled to come back time after time after time for new experiences.

- It is crucial to be reductive, straightforward, and simple in your design, and waiver from that approach only when a digression is a central part of a high-quality experience. Everything else is a distraction. A product should be usable first, and magical second. Spirit without utility doesn't last. Utility without spirit isn't memorable or compelling.

- Any well-designed product has many underlying features that may not be apparent on the surface. Speed, reliability, and user support—these and many other factors may not be evident even after you have thousands of users, but their absence can spell disaster for a product.

- It is possible, through design, to shape people's behavior, to motivate them to take the actions that you want, and to prevent them from doing what you don't want. Be explicit in defining what you hope users will do with your product. Articulate those changes as goals, and research and measure results to determine if your designs are successful at effecting behavioral change.

- Large problems and challenges should be broken down into smaller ones. When we reach solutions, it's important to test and validate our assumptions to see if we truly understand the results. If we don't, then because we are dealing with

smaller solutions rather than a single large one, any risk of failure is reduced and the steps toward a better solution are more quickly and easily implemented.

- We learn from small changes. Small repetitive cycles grow the product and constantly improve it (and as designers, we grow and improve as well).
- The tools we choose to design with dramatically affect our processes, so select them wisely. Change tools when needed. Use tools in ways they were intended, or in ways that suit you. Choose the simplest tools, or invent your own.
- There are myriad ways to evaluate iterative design decisions, validate those decisions, and discover things we would not have otherwise known about the product and its users.
- It is possible to seek out data that can be quantified in addition to data that cannot. Both kinds of data contribute to a more complete understanding of your design's impact.
- Greater team and customer satisfaction is improved by constant design-test-release-evaluate-learn-and-repeat cycles.
- Product design can be done by an individual as well as by small and large teams. Each strategy has its strengths and challenges.

Make It Happen

Build Web products with these principles in mind and you'll produce great work that you're proud of. You'll gain satisfaction, not just from a job well done but from a job that can be well done again and again and again.

Products designed for the Web are immensely influential. It's a space with a ton of momentum and no sign of slowing. That opportunity for a design professional or entrepreneur is increasing, and will continue to increase, with the volume of available digital products. Even physical products blur with your services now: Because digital products are so integrated into our lives, physical products that already are (or would like to be) integrated with our lives need to acknowledge and integrate with Web products and services.

This is where the future is. It can happen to you, or you can make it happen.

More at: randyjhunt.com/product-design

Index